SHE HATH BEEN READING

The Neville Shakespeare Club of Green Bay, Wisconsin, 1902. Photo courtesy of the Neville Public Museum of Brown County.

SHE HATH BEEN READING

Women and Shakespeare Clubs in America

KATHERINE WEST SCHEIL

CORNELL UNIVERSITY PRESS
Ithaca and London

First published 2012 by Cornell University Press

Printed in the United States of America

Library of Congress Cataloging-in-Publication Data

Scheil, Katherine West, 1966–
   She hath been reading : women and Shakespeare clubs in America / Katherine West Scheil.
      p. cm.
   Includes bibliographical references and index.
   ISBN 978-0-8014-5042-6 (cloth : alk. paper)
   1. Shakespeare, William, 1564–1616—Appreciation—United States—History.   2. Shakespeare, William, 1564–1616—Societies, etc.   3. Book clubs (Discussion groups)—United States—History.   4. Women—United States—Societies and clubs—History.   5. Women—Books and reading—United States—History.   6. Women—United States—Intellectual life.   I. Title.
   PR2971.U6S34   2012
   822.3'3—dc23   2011051560

Cornell University Press strives to use environmentally responsible suppliers and materials to the fullest extent possible in the publishing of its books. Such materials include vegetable-based, low-VOC inks and acid-free papers that are recycled, totally chlorine-free, or partly composed of nonwood fibers. For further information, visit our website at www.cornellpress.cornell.edu.

Cloth printing   10 9 8 7 6 5 4 3 2 1

For my family
And for the many women in
this book who paved the way

❦ Contents

✎ PREFACE

In September 1894, Elizabeth Armstrong organized a group of thirty women in the village of Avon, Illinois, to gather weekly and read Shakespeare in her home. Inspired by reading *The Merchant of Venice*, the group called itself the "Portia Club" and chose as its goals "mutual improvement and self-reinforcement" of members and "promotion of social and civic welfare of Avon and community." At the time, Avon had a population of just under 700 citizens, who would certainly have noticed the impact of this club, which existed for a century. Over the course of hundreds of meetings, club members "studied, memorized and acted in Shakespeare's plays, learned about the continents of the world . . . cooked dinners, held bake sales, sold fruitcakes, pushed for better education, helped with food for school children, supported [General] Federation [of Women's Clubs] charities, proved women were smart enough to vote . . . attended meetings regardless of weather, believed that an educated mother was a better mother, were devoted to their community, wanted to bring new ideas from all over the world, wrote essays by hand and by lamplight."[1] The activities of this representative club—studying, memorizing, and performing Shakespeare; promoting education and suffrage in their communities; advocating for local charities and schoolchildren; supporting educated women—were not confined to an isolated group in rural Illinois. Such pursuits occupied thousands of American women, from the late nineteenth century through the twentieth, in more than five hundred Shakespeare clubs across America.[2] In Concord, New Hampshire, for example, at least ten Shakespeare clubs were active at the end of the nineteenth century.[3] What motivated women in particular to read and perform Shakespeare in a club and to engage in public and community action? And what influence did the hundreds of Shakespeare clubs have on Shakespeare's place in American cultural life? This book offers answers to these questions, focusing on two major issues: First, what possibilities did reading Shakespeare open up for women's clubs? And second, how did these clubs help shape Shakespeare's place in America over the last two centuries?

In an 1876 letter, amateur Shakespearean Joseph Crosby observed, "There are more Shakespearians in the country than I had ever 'dreamt of.'"[4] Taking

Crosby's statement as a cue, this book illuminates the substantial number of "Shakespearians" in late nineteenth- and twentieth-century America in order to give women readers a place in that narrative. Based on material from public and private archives, I map the widespread influence of Shakespeare clubs across America, track how these groups affected Shakespeare's position in American culture, and explore how reading and studying Shakespeare shaped women's lives and influenced their local communities.[5]

Beginning in the late nineteenth century, more than five hundred Shakespeare clubs formed across the United States, from Peoria, Illinois, to Pomona, California; many of these clubs continued into the late twentieth century, and some still meet regularly. A broad cross-section of women (in terms of class, education, and occupation) were involved, and most clubs participated in public and civic activities that extended the association of Shakespeare and civic improvement beyond the boundaries of the club.[6] Through a variety of national and local activities, women engaged in plans of study and civic involvement that kept Shakespeare accessible, available, and relevant. For some women, the study of Shakespeare also provided a venue for social and political action, and through their engagement with Shakespeare, women could discuss such topics as marital relations, political issues, women's rights, and women's place in society and in the home.

The majority of Shakespeare clubs were formed by women, from roughly the 1880s to the 1940s, a period marked by major historical events affecting women: the right to vote, two world wars, the Depression, and the increasing entry of women into higher education and the workforce. While it is impossible to specify exactly when the phenomenon of Shakespeare clubs began, it is safe to say that numerous women fulfilled their intellectual and social needs by reading and studying Shakespeare, largely in the period leading up to women's suffrage and to greater women's participation in higher education.

The geographical distribution of these grassroots organizations reveals a hidden layer of intellectual activity and social activism not only in metropolitan areas such as New York, Philadelphia, and Boston but also in smaller towns across the country. The appendix to this book lists clubs in areas such as Mobile, Alabama; Flagstaff, Arizona; Tampa, Florida; Marietta, Georgia; Mishawaka, Indiana; Manhattan, Kansas; Manchester, New Hampshire; Cuba, New York; Bowling Green, Ohio; Enid, Oklahoma; Eugene, Oregon; Elkland, Pennsylvania; and Waxahachie, Texas, among many other places. Americans across the country, particularly women, were reading Shakespeare, meeting with other women and men to share their literary interpretations and demonstrate their intellectual prowess, and frequently channeling their efforts into more public action, not just in Boston and New York but in areas often not considered part of late nineteenth-century America's cultural life at all.

Historians of the women's club movement have already outlined the importance of women's clubs from a variety of angles. By focusing on the role of Shakespeare in women's reading groups, I combine work in women's intellectual history with the body of material on Shakespeare in America and on the reception history of Shakespeare.[7] In telling the stories of these women readers—both in clubs that read only Shakespeare and in groups that had a substantial focus on Shakespeare—I illuminate how the reading practices of both individuals and groups can influence private and public life and, in turn, how these reading practices were shaped by Shakespeare as the object of study. The combination of the club movement, with its push for self-education, and the widespread availability of Shakespeare's plays, democratized Shakespeare as reading material for women across America, no matter the locale. In addition, Shakespeare's works provided the perfect study material for clubs. His inclusion in rhetorical manuals and in the widely circulated McGuffey readers made him safe and authorized material for female readers, and he had already been "vetted and approved" by women critics such as Anna Jameson and Mary Cowden Clarke.[8]

Many Shakespeare clubs participated in civic activities, which helped solidify the reputation of Shakespeare in communities across the country: permanent memorials, newly founded libraries, and social and civic work all contributed to the idea that reading Shakespeare was connected with public and personal improvement. The efforts of club women to enrich their communities also embedded Shakespeare as one of the many local foundations of American culture: as a marker for learning, self-improvement, civilization, and entertainment for a broad array of social groups, from New York City literati to midwestern housewives. The history of reading involves not just educational institutions and famous men but also women from small towns who actively contributed to improving their lot in life and making their society a better place. Concurrent with their interest in Shakespeare, these female groups often took action on larger social issues such as women's suffrage, philanthropy, and civil rights.[9]

For many women, Shakespeare signified a larger intellectual world to which they wanted access but were denied the opportunity through official channels. Although I discuss the influence of academic settings on these groups, this book traces the more informal yet crucial history of Shakespeare and the common reader in the lives of those who scrubbed floors, gave elocution lessons, or taught school during the day and met to read and discuss Shakespeare in their leisure time.[10] Shakespeare clubs gave women opportunities outside the academy (and outside any formal institutional structures) to do intellectual work: they engaged in literary analysis but were also quizzed on material, undertook research and wrote essays, established libraries, read plays out loud, performed plays for their communities, and even published their work.[11]

Shakespeare's place in American culture was influenced by a large but largely overlooked segment of the population who read, studied, memorized, recited, performed, and memorialized Shakespeare in their parlors and in their communities, and who clearly felt that they were doing important work.[12] In many clubs, members served as historians, compiled scrapbooks, and printed annual programs; numerous clubs left their papers, minutes, and ephemera to local archives and to major research libraries—in effect, creating and claiming their own place in American literary history and preserving a vibrant legacy of women's contributions to Shakespeare studies.[13]

★★★

The first two chapters of the book lay the groundwork for the origins of Shakespeare clubs and their reading practices. The last three chapters cover more specific topics pertaining to the effects of these clubs on women and their society: in the home, in the outpost, and in the community of black club women. The introductory chapter, "Origins," explores the social and cultural institutions that made the phenomenon of more than five hundred Shakespeare clubs possible: the development and growth of the women's club movement in America, including the founding of the General Federation of Women's Clubs; the influence of publishers in promoting editions of Shakespeare for club use; and the development of periodicals aimed at amateur Shakespeare readers. The elocutionary movement was also a central factor in familiarizing a large population with Shakespeare and solidifying his position as a model for study and imitation. Clubs provided an organized format for study, often with an ideology of social activism and productive work, as well as group pressure to learn and to educate. The exclusive nature of many clubs accorded Shakespeare privileged status as worthy reading material for competitive organizations. Shakespeare was the object of a lifelong privilege, the prize for the woman fortunate enough to be voted in. This form of "wholesome hero worship," to use the phrase of one club, was often passed down from mother to daughter and helped create a grassroots cult of Shakespeare as material for women's heritage and at times for establishing various social divisions. This introductory chapter contextualizes the women's clubs amid mixed-gender and male groups in order to identify what is distinctive about the women's clubs; for many women, reading Shakespeare offered an alternative, non-establishment form of advanced education outside the male-dominated world of academia.

In the first chapter ("Reading"), I discuss the range of literary practices for women readers of Shakespeare—what they read and how they read it—collectively and individually, and how their reading and study practices enticed them to channel their enthusiasm for literacy into various public programs (especially libraries), often with Shakespeare as the foundation. National publicity aimed at clubs encouraged women to read and study Shakespeare, and their collective experiences reflect their participation in the emerging field of Shakespeare scholarship and public literacy. These clubs offer a complex picture of the ways women read Shakespeare, both as solitary readers and as communal readers: club members read Shakespeare on their own and then attended meetings where the plays were often read aloud and discussed. This process complicates the boundaries between public and private reading, and the dynamics of a reading group shaped the interpretive practices of its members by encouraging discussion, debate, and argument. Inherent in Shakespeare's plays and in women's literate practices was the potential freedom for women to branch out beyond narrowly confined roles and to explore alternatives for female behavior under the guise of "studying Shakespeare." Building on recent work on literacy and reading practices in America, I look at how women's private reading practices shaped the public sphere—through charitable activities, political activism, and public lectures, all brought about through the practice of reading Shakespeare in a club of women.[14]

Chapter 2, "The Home," looks at how Shakespeare clubs affected the domestic life of club members and how study of Shakespeare could help establish the home as an intellectual domain. Women appropriated a number of domestic practices for their Shakespeare work and in the process merged reading and studying Shakespeare with their household duties. Women participated in various commemorative acts—creating and preserving programs of study and club histories, in effect creating their own archives of carefully preserved printed programs, member lists, meeting dates, study materials, scrapbooks, and other materials—and felt they were doing something worth preserving. Through a variety of means, including civic activities, group reading agendas, and personal reading of club members, Shakespeare clubs set up an infrastructure that commemorated Shakespeare as part of American literary culture, both in public and in private. In the home, "Shakespeare" signaled material that was safe and culturally valorizing for women to read and study, allowing them to take time away from their domestic duties and devote their energies to self-education. For individual club members, the generational effects on families were often significant: many clubs had legacies of mother-daughter members, passing down the conviction that knowledge of Shakespeare was important and desirable for women.

In the third chapter ("The Outpost"), I explore the farthest outreaches of Shakespeare clubs, tracking the vast readership across America, not just on the East Coast but also in rural communities in nearly every state. This chapter widens the scope of women's intellectual history beyond eastern urban centers such as New York, Boston, and Philadelphia to consider how reading Shakespeare shaped women's intellectual lives across the country. Without resources to attend the theater or other cultural events, regularly gathering to read and discuss Shakespeare's plays often served as one of the only intellectual outlets for women in numerous geographical areas where even performances of Shakespeare were scarce. The Shakespeare club provided a rare source of intellectual independence for women in remote areas of the country, a respite from physical labor, and an avenue for establishing culture and sponsoring local community reforms. The repercussions of a literate culture grounded in Shakespeare are still evident, in public libraries, gardens, and other community projects sponsored by club women, and such activities positioned Shakespeare at the fore of a developing American literary culture.[15]

The penultimate chapter looks at the role of Shakespeare for black club women in the context of the black women's club movement and in connection with issues of class, upward mobility, and "racial uplift." I draw on material from clubs in areas of black urban development in the early twentieth century, such as Chicago, Cleveland, Dallas, Denver, Detroit, Durham, Topeka, and Washington, D.C. Few black clubs read only Shakespeare, for a variety of reasons connected with more imperative social and community needs, as well as the desire to read works by African American authors. Shakespeare was thus often part of a program of black upward mobility through access to culture and education, but the context in which these groups read Shakespeare was different from that of white clubs. This chapter takes up the call by historians of the black women's club movement to provide further depth about reading, study, and literary practices and to locate the place of Shakespeare in African American literary culture.

The conclusion offers an arc of development for the history of Shakespeare clubs and for the Shakespeare clubs that still meet today. Returning to the example of the Portia Club of Avon, Illinois, which opened this book, I track how the study of Shakespeare has evolved along with changes in women's rights, roles, and education. This final chapter underlines the importance of restoring the lost history of women readers and uncovering the significance of Shakespeare in the intellectual life of American women.

★★★

The archival materials related to American Shakespeare clubs are daunting and relatively untouched. From the lovingly handwritten minutes of the Brooklyn Shakespeare Club to the formally printed programs of the Colby, Kansas, Shakespeare Club, the overflowing boxes in my study hold dozens of examples like the ones I relate in this book. I have by no means attempted to be exhaustive (nor would readers appreciate the repetitiveness of such a method); rather, I offer representative examples of the ways women's Shakespeare clubs functioned and of their importance to individual members, to their communities, and to Shakespeare's place in American culture in general. I attempt to avoid the pitfall of generalizing on the basis of an isolated instance, and where possible I supply multiple examples to support my conclusions. The appendix provides a fuller sense of the breadth of evidence on which I base this book, and it illustrates the extensive readership of Shakespeare across America.

Although reading Shakespeare in a club setting preoccupied both men and women in the period, this activity was particularly important for women, who formed the majority of Shakespeare clubs and who also found opportunities for leadership within co-ed clubs. In addition, many of the longer-running clubs for men have received more serious study, while little has been documented about the role of these groups in women's lives. I have thus tried to maintain a focus on the importance of these groups for women, in single-sex and co-ed clubs alike.

The nature of this evidence is uneven: some Shakespeare clubs kept extensive minutes, meticulously documented scrapbooks, and copious records, and some members even wrote diaries or club histories with personal accounts of their experiences with Shakespeare. Some clubs reported their activities in local newspapers, in Shakespeare journals such as *Shakespeariana*, and even in the academic journal *Shakespeare Quarterly*. Other clubs kept a bare outline of their reading lists and membership rosters, and many clubs left no public evidence of their existence at all aside from their club name. Nevertheless, enough evidence survives to make a clear argument for the importance of this array of readers and to suggest their significance for American history from a number of angles—in domestic life, in their communities, and for women in general.

By taking on the name of a "Shakespeare Club," these groups deliberately invoked particular connotations of Bardolatry and connections with national and international scholarly networks.[16] Some Shakespeare clubs focused entirely on Shakespeare's works, reading through the entire canon multiple times.[17] Others used the name "Shakespeare" as an umbrella for a variety of activities, some connected to Shakespeare and others not at all. Study of Shakespeare meant different things in different clubs, from reading the plays in depth as well as contemporary criticism, to hosting annual birthday parties in April and cooking meals. Some clubs were interested in studying Shakespeare as a form of history, others in examining Shakespeare's characters as a way to discuss female behavior. Nevertheless, such clubs signaled their awareness of what "Shakespeare" signified in their communities, by their choice of the name in their club title. Throughout the book, I explore what "Shakespeare" meant to these clubs— sometimes the plays and poems, sometimes the writer himself, sometimes the cultural resonances of Shakespeare—and how those meanings translated into actions. And, of course, since the material covered in this book spans more than a century, studying Shakespeare meant something different in the 1890s in Iowa than it did in the 1930s in New York, and I have tried to attend to these historical variations wherever possible. I hope this will reveal the wide variety of ways Shakespeare was used by late nineteenth- and twentieth-century women as a flexible body of material and connotations which could be adapted for personal and public use and which shifted according to cultural and historical changes for women related to education, roles in society, and intellectual and social opportunities.

Many women looked to Shakespeare as a guide for their intellectual achievements, and they often discovered that knowledge of Shakespeare could generate influence and authority in many arenas—for example, they could transfer their energies and enthusiasm about Shakespeare to developing public libraries. They could justify taking time out of their domestic work to read and engage in literary study because they were reading Shakespeare. For black club women in particular, these cultural associations of Shakespeare were especially important in a larger scheme of educational goals for "racial uplift."[18]

★★★

The inspiration for this project began with a group of women who read Shakespeare on the other side of the Atlantic, over a hundred years earlier than the women I write about here. While discussing my work on the Shakespeare Ladies' Club of 1730s London, early modern scholar Mary Ellen Lamb mentioned that her mother had been a member of a Shakespeare club in Grove City, Pennsylvania. This was the beginning of my discovery of more than five hundred Shakespeare clubs in America, composed mainly of women, in nearly every state. The journey to recover their records and to reclaim their place in history involved attending a meeting of the Anne Hudgins Shakespeare Class in Georgia followed by a special trip to see the "Shakespeare Closet" in one member's home; and copious correspondence with archivists, librarians, and club members eager to see their local history given its due place in the history of Shakespeare in America. For me, the path from knowledge of one women's Shakespeare club in 1730s London to the discovery of hundreds of clubs across America, and the subsequent realization of their neglect in the historical record, has been both humbling and energizing.

In her handwritten reminiscences about the work of the Detroit Study Club, a black women's club that read Shakespeare (and celebrated its 100th anniversary in 1999), member Lillian Bateman wrote, "I cannot begin to tell you all the good and benefit this little club has been to each one of us personally, brightening our minds and developing latent qualities."[19] The following chapters tell the story of Shakespeare and American women readers like Lillian Bateman.

❧ ACKNOWLEDGMENTS

Many people and institutions made this project possible. Funding for research was provided by the Folger Shakespeare Library, the Bibliographical Society of America, and the Historical Society of Southern California. At the University of Minnesota, a sabbatical and sabbatical supplement, a McKnight Research Award, and a Grant-in-Aid have all allowed me to complete the book in a timely fashion. My two research assistants, Sara Cohen and Elissa Hansen, have heroically read countless reels of microfilm, contacted dozens of archives, and tracked down innumerable esoteric references. Thanks also to Ellen Messer-Davidow, my department chair, for her support.

I owe a great deal of gratitude especially to the many librarians, archivists, and local historians who provided materials on these women readers and answered my questions. I thank the following in particular: Ann Barton, Texas Women's University Blagg-Huey Library; Mary Beth Brown, Western Historical Manuscript Collection, University of Missouri–Columbia; Linda Carroll, Cary Memorial Library, Lexington, Massachusetts; Steve Charter, Bowling Green State University Archives; Elaine Davis, Daughters of the Republic of Texas Library; Teresa Dearing, Danville, New York, Public Library; Aurora Deshauteurs, Free Library of Philadelphia; Shanna English, Old Jail Museum and Archives, Barnesville, Georgia; Dawn Eurich, Detroit Public Library; Andrea Faling, Nebraska State Historical Society; Michael Flanagan, Onandaga Historical Association, New York; Michele Hansford, Powers Museum, Carthage, Missouri; David M. Hays, University of Colorado–Boulder Library; Rachel Howell, Dallas Public Library; Sarah Hull, Plainfield Public Library, New Jersey; Karen Jania, Bentley Historical Library, University of Michigan; Christine Jochem, Morristown and Morris Township Library, New Jersey; Norwood Kerr, Alabama Department of Archives and History; Bob Knecht and the staff at the Kansas State Historical Society; Karen Kukil, William Allan Neilson Library, Smith College; Keith Longiotti, University of North Carolina–Chapel Hill Library; Chandler Lyons, Peoria Historical Society, Illinois; Karen M. Mason, University of Iowa Library; Tom Mooney, Nebraska State Historical Society; Alison Moore, California Historical Society; Louise Pfotenhauer, Neville Public Museum of Brown County,

Wisconsin; Jean Putch, Ilion, New York, Public Library; Kate Reeve, Arizona Historical Society; Susan Richards, Dallas Historical Society; Victoria D. Schneiderman, Medford Public Library, Massachusetts; Kayin Shabazz, Robert W. Woodruff Library, Atlanta University; Nancy Shawcross, University of Pennsylvania Rare Book and Manuscript Library; Geraldine Strey, Wisconsin Historical Society; Bruce Tabb, University of Oregon Library; Paula Taylor, Arkansas History Commission; June Underwood; Anthony Vaver, Natick Shakespeare Club, Massachusetts; Harrison Wick, Indiana University of Pennsylvania Library; Georgianna Ziegler, Folger Shakespeare Library; and the Interlibrary Loan staff at the University of Minnesota.

I am especially grateful to the members of the Anne Hudgins Shakespeare Class of Marietta, Georgia, especially President Candice Azermendi, who welcomed me to one of their meetings and shared their private archives. Scott Rubel generously provided the photograph of his great-grandmother's club, the Wednesday Morning Club of Pueblo, Colorado. DeAnn Ruggles of the Peoria, Illinois, Women's Club met me on a holiday so that I could get a copy of the photograph of the Peoria Shakespeare Class for the cover of this book, and gave me a tour of the charming theater where the women performed Shakespeare. Mary Ellen Lamb encouraged this project from the start and also kindly put me in touch with the women of her mother's Shakespeare club in Grove City, Pennsylvania. The late Sasha Roberts shared her enthusiasm for women readers early on; I miss her kind spirit and optimism.

Many colleagues and friends generously read parts of the book and offered helpful comments: Tanya Caldwell, Clara Calvo, Michael Dobson, Andy Elfenbein, Susanne Greenhalgh, Michael Hancher, Ton Hoenselaars, Becky Krug, Nabil Matar, Andy Murphy, Heather Murray, Robert Sawyer, Monika Smialkowski, Anne Thompson, Ginger Vaughan, and John Watkins. I was lucky to have Ed Griffin read the whole manuscript diligently and thoroughly. The two anonymous readers for the Press were encouraging and their comments invaluable. Peter Potter, my editor at Cornell, inspired and encouraged me and kept the project on track, as did Ange Romeo-Hall and Katherine Liu. Shirley Nelson Garner suggested the title of this book, which comes from *Cymbeline*. She pointed out the appropriateness of using words from Shakespeare's villain Iachimo to frame a book on women's (sometimes subversive) acts of educating themselves.

Earlier versions of some material have been published as "Commemorating Shakespeare and Domestic Practices," *Critical Survey* 22.2 (2010): 62–75; "Women Reading Shakespeare in the Outpost: Rural Reading Groups, Literary Culture, and Civic Life in America," in *Reading in History: New Methodologies from the Anglo-American Tradition* (Pickering & Chatto, 2010), 91–99; "Shakespeare's Comedies and American Club Women," in *Shakespeare's Comedies of*

Love: Essays in Honour of Alexander Leggatt (University of Toronto Press, 2008), 55–64; and "Public and Private Reading: Shakespeare and American Women's Reading Groups," *Reader: Issues in Reader-Oriented Theory, Criticism, and Pedagogy* 55 (Fall 2006): 36–55.

My greatest debt is to my family: first, to my parents, who saw to it that I never experienced the obstacles to education that plagued many of the women I write about. And an equal debt to my wonderfully generous and thoughtful husband, Andy, who not only read the whole manuscript but also at times single-handedly provided my sole source of intellectual stimulation amid the challenges of domestic life. Finally, to my children, William and David, whose young lives have progressed alongside this book and who make it all worthwhile. As Shakespeare's Kate says, "Too little payment for so great a debt."

❧ INTRODUCTION

Origins

> To read Shakespeare's works even superficially, is enter-
> tainment; to linger over them lovingly and admiringly, is
> enjoyment; to study them profoundly, is wisdom moral
> and intellectual.
>
> Mary Cowden Clarke, 1864

In the late nineteenth century, more than five hun-
dred Shakespeare clubs, composed mainly of women, formed across America to
read Shakespeare. From Pasadena, California, to the seaside town of Camden,
Maine; from the isolated farm town of Ottumwa, Iowa, to the mining village
of Cripple Creek, Colorado; from Swanton, Vermont, on the Canadian border,
to Mobile, Alabama, on the Gulf Coast, women were reading Shakespeare in
astonishing numbers and in surprising places. The figures are impressive: thirty-
seven clubs in California, fifty-one clubs in Texas, fifty-four clubs in New
York, and thirty-four clubs in Kansas; most of these clubs were formed between
1880 and 1900. How might we explain this explosion of women readers of
Shakespeare? What factors made such a remarkable number of groups possible?

First, club life was certainly familiar to many women; roughly two million
women belonged to clubs at the turn of the century.[1] As Anne Firor Scott
puts it, "Women's associations were literally everywhere: known or unknown,
famous or obscure; young or ancient; auxiliary or freestanding; reactionary, conservative, liberal, radical, or a mix of all four; old women, young women, black
women, white women, women from every ethnic group, every religious group
had their societies." Women's associations "lay at the very heart of American
social and political development" and permeated the infrastructure of American
society.[2] Shakespeare often held a prominent place in these associations that
were so closely linked to the American social and political climate. If we accept
Anne Ruggles Gere's assertion that women's clubs "wove themselves into the

fabric of nearly every American city, town and village," what were the repercussions of those clubs that focused on Shakespeare, for women individually and collectively, and for their communities?[3] What needs—personal, cultural, social, and intellectual—did Shakespeare clubs fulfill for women?

As I argue, the intersection of the women's club movement, the growing availability of Shakespeare's plays, and the national and international networks of Shakespeare studies encouraged the formation of hundreds of grassroots organizations whose members met to read and study Shakespeare, an author whose significance they could carry into their communities and their home life.[4] The remainder of this book shows that Shakespeare clubs were crucial for women's intellectual development because they provided a consistent intellectual content that more general women's clubs did not necessarily offer, and because women discovered a world of possibilities, both public and private, in the works of Shakespeare. The *Michigan State Library Bulletin* for 1896, for example, explained the value of clubs that focused on a single subject like Shakespeare: "The provision of continued study on one subject prevents the waste of thought and energy common in clubs which take up a topic one week only to drive out of mind the next by one totally different."[5] Shakespeare clubs could concentrate primarily on the development of women's scholarly, analytical, and argumentative skills as individuals and as a group; as one typical club member attested, her Shakespeare club was devoted "solely to making ourselves wiser and better."[6] Such initiatives had consequences in the home, across the country, and across racial lines (the topics of Chapters 2, 3, and 4). Shakespeare clubs had other advantages over more general women's clubs; through publications that encouraged study and circulated news of clubs, members could participate in national and international networks of scholarship.[7] For many women, reading Shakespeare involved regular contact with a larger scholarly community along with the personal benefits of being among supportive women.

The relationship between women and Shakespeare was mutually beneficial: the majority of these women readers were not just passive "hero worshippers" (to use the phrase of one club) but rather engaged in civic activities under the banner of their Shakespeare club. Many of their projects resulted in permanent testimonials to Shakespeare in hundreds of American communities, in connection with the founding of community libraries, public gardens, wartime efforts, scholarships, kindergartens, and other educational and civic programs, and even the devotion of physical space to Shakespeare study (such as the Shakespeare Room in the Fowler Public Library in Concord, N.H., discussed in Chapter 1). Through reading and study of Shakespeare, women could carry out legitimate intellectual work without receiving the type of critique often directed against general women's clubs.[8] Their work could be circulated and publicized nationwide through such journals as *Shakespeariana* (in the 1890s), and some clubs even developed their own "degrees" in Shakespeare study. Members of the Kate Tupper Galpin Shakespeare Club of Los Angeles (c. 1901), for example, received "certificates" when they had completed study of twenty plays, and each spring the club (like numerous others) printed commemorative programs in honor of Shakespeare's birthday, for women to keep as souvenirs of their annual accomplishments.[9] Club women in turn often extended the legacy of their Shakespeare study to daughters and granddaughters through club membership, to future readers through libraries, to students through scholarships, and to local citizens through sponsorship of public parks, gardens, and other social improvements.[10] As Chapter 3 discusses in greater detail, club women also modeled intellectual work to their children, showing them that reading and studying Shakespeare were valuable intellectual activities for women.

Even clubs not devoted solely to Shakespeare frequently included Shakespeare as part of their study program. The Traverse City, Michigan, Woman's Club, for example, had as its mandate "the advancement of its members in the knowledge of literature and current events, the discussion of social problems and the promotion of good will toward each other and all the world." Averaging eighty-five members in the late 1890s, the group included Shakespeare as part of its program of study.[11] Likewise, around the same time, the Muskegon, Michigan, Woman's Club studied such topics as "Tendencies of Club Life," "Labor and Capital," "Primitive Life of the Britons," "Woman as a Ruler," and "Shakespeare, the King of the Drama."[12] The Every Saturday Night Club of Waterville, New York (which began in 1886), similarly combined readings of Shakespeare plays with meetings on the history of ancient Greece, the Persian Wars, and Greek drama.[13] Thus, to the more than five hundred clubs listed in the appendix, we might add an additional layer of clubs in which women occasionally read Shakespeare as part of a more general curriculum of literature, history, and current events.[14]

The Origins of American Shakespeare Clubs

Of course, women were not the only ones reading Shakespeare; they were part of a larger phenomenon of literary activity in America related to Shakespeare. By 1926, one writer could boast, "It is inspiring to think of the many thousands of men and women, particularly of the women (who predominate in numbers), meeting regularly in every part of the land to participate in cooperative appreciation" of Shakespeare.[15]

Several exclusive men's Shakespeare clubs offer evidence for the place of Shakespeare in established literary circles in urban centers. The main contender for the first Shakespeare club in America is the Shakspere Society of

Philadelphia, an exclusive male club begun in 1851 (and still meeting), which included members such as editor Horace Howard Furness, who joined in 1860.[16] According to one member, for a hundred years the society's "fortnightly meetings have gathered a group of men foremost in Philadelphia. One has read Shakspere there with a cabinet-minister, a chancellor of the bar association, a Judge of the first rank, a great physician as well known in the art of letters as in the letters of his art, and a novelist, whose best seller has not had its total exceeded." Open only to "scholars and men of affairs," the club remains a reminder of Shakespeare's complex position in America, and its extensive membership shows the range of Shakespeare's influence in the upper echelons of society.[17]

In other East Coast literary centers such as New York, men could study Shakespeare at the Shakespeare Society of New York City, an all-male organization incorporated in April 1885. Its mandate was to "promote the knowledge and study of Shakespeare's dramatic works" and "collect and maintain a library of books, papers and pamphlets" related to Shakespeare and Elizabethan drama.[18] Society publications included a twenty-volume Bankside Edition of Shakespeare, edited by members and read by many clubs across the nation.[19] Meetings entailed the reading of a paper for the evening, followed by discussion. The society also engaged in occasional social projects, such as a campaign to save Poe Cottage.[20] The club took no interest in female members, and membership was open only to male residents of the United States, though the men deemed English author and Shakespeare scholar Mary Cowden Clarke appropriate as an honorary member.[21] Although the club had less impact on American cultural life than women's clubs because of its restricted membership, its journal, *Shakespeariana* (discussed later in this chapter), had a wide national influence, disseminating news of Shakespeare clubs and providing guidelines for study. Aside from these two exclusive clubs, there were relatively few all-male Shakespeare clubs across the country. The all-male Shakespeare Club in Wheeling, West Virginia, for example, lasted only a few years, suggesting that it wasn't only reading Shakespeare that gave a group longevity.[22]

American Shakespeare clubs were important particularly for women, and women belonged to both single-sex and co-ed clubs; each type had its advantages. In single-sex clubs, women could gain argumentative and public speaking skills in a supportive environment of fellow women. Many women's Shakespeare clubs belonged to the General Federation of Women's Clubs (formed in 1890), linking them to a national network with an active commitment to women's issues such as suffrage.[23] In women-only clubs, members could focus on topics of special concern to women, often in connection with Shakespeare, as we see in Chapter 2. The members of the Peoria Women's Club, for example, who performed Shakespeare every year on his birthday, in 1902 emphasized the

FIGURE 1.   The Shakespeare Club of Tarboro, North Carolina, 1880. Co-ed Shakespeare clubs, which were not uncommon in the nineteenth century, provided a place where women could share their opinions and thoughts equally with men. Photo courtesy of the North Carolina Collection, University of North Carolina at Chapel Hill Library

importance of their female community in their goals of "mutual sympathy and counsel" in addition to their educational pursuits.[24] Even after women gained the right to vote in 1920, club women still valued the female companionship provided by clubs. In the words of a member of the Hathaway Shakespeare Club of Philadelphia (founded 1923), the women were united by "the strong bond of fellowship due to our common literary interest and singleness of purpose."[25] Similarly, the president of the Dallas Shakespeare Club (founded 1886) remarked on the dual importance of the women's club and the focus on Shakespeare: "how conjunctive to my very life and soul it has become, and with it the love and worship of Shakespeare."[26] For a broad cross-section of women, study of Shakespeare was a link to a supportive female intellectual (and sometimes political) community, one that shifted its emphasis according to the needs of women.

The groups where women and men gathered to read Shakespeare together were equally important but for other reasons—here women could voice their opinions and articulate their thoughts on equal footing with men. Unlike the popular rhetoric movement of postbellum America, which "defined relatively separate and distinctly unequal rhetorical spheres for women and men," co-ed Shakespeare clubs had no restrictions for female members' participation.[27] Women were both founders and leaders of many co-ed clubs in the late nineteenth and twentieth centuries, and according to numerous club records, they were equal participants with men. The Fortnightly Shakespeare Club of New York City, for example, was founded by Anna Randall-Diehl in 1875, who continued as club president (her husband was also a member). Women formed the majority of contributors to the Fortnightly's journal, the *American Shakespeare Magazine*, and held most offices in the club.

Elsewhere across the country, men and women gathered to read and study Shakespeare, with no indications of gender inequality in club activities, even in pre-suffrage America. Women often held leadership roles, read parts equal to men, and shared opinions about Shakespeare that were respected and valued on equal terms with those of men. Notes from a meeting of the co-ed Rochester, New York, Shakespeare Society in 1883, for example, praised member and former actress Mrs. O. W. Moore as "one of the conspicuous members of the Club, and her dramatic education and intellectual gifts render her readings most valuable and enjoyable."[28] In 1888, the Natick, Massachusetts, Shakespeare Club included papers, presentations, and discussions by an equal number of men and women.[29] Women in the Brooklyn Shakespeare Club also participated on a par with men, even taking on male parts; in the club minutes for March 1901, the secretary commended Miss Ayers for her reading of Prince Henry in *Henry IV, Part 1*, "which could scarcely have been better."[30] Even the Old Cambridge Shakespeare Association of Massachusetts, run by scholar/editor William J. Rolfe, had a female treasurer (Miss A. M. Jones) in 1898 and was later run for sixty years by Walter Deane and his niece Mary Deane Dexter.[31] In Woodland, California, in the late 1880s, many women reaped the benefits of both co-ed and women-only Shakespeare clubs by belonging to the Woodland Shakespeare Club, where they read Shakespeare with women only, and to the Mutual Club of Woodland, where they read Shakespeare with their husbands.[32]

One noteworthy example of the unusual opportunities that reading Shakespeare provided for women comes from the N. T. Lupton Conversation Club, a co-ed reading group in 1890s rural Auburn, Alabama, composed of women and men, including Robert Wilton Burton, a Confederate veteran and bookseller in Auburn. Member Kate Lupton read a paper before the group titled "Woman in Shakespeare," in which she praised Shakespeare for his "fidelity to the many sidedness of feminine nature," arguing that women must pursue their aims "by more or less indirect methods" but nevertheless are "all powerful." One wonders how the co-ed audience reacted to Lupton's declaration that there is "a steady current of feminine purpose" ruling "the lives of individual men," and the wife is "the true propelling force" of "many a proud man." Lupton relied on a number of examples from Shakespeare of "men who are, more or less openly, led on to the determining acts of their lives by the influence of women." Lupton ended by extolling Shakespeare's power of observation: "The more one studies Shakespeare's women, the more the conviction grows that there is nothing in feminine nature so subtle or elusive as to have escaped his discerning eye." Like Mary Cowden Clarke's "Shakespeare as the Girl's Friend" (1887), Lupton's depiction of Shakespeare as a poet in tune with women would have circulated to the men and women in her club in the 1890s. Her use of Shakespeare to illustrate female agency was apparently received without critique and was subsequently made available outside the club to an even wider audience when it was published in 1895 in the collection *Alabama Women in Literature*.[33] Kate Lupton was no stranger to controversy; she was the first woman to graduate from Vanderbilt but was not allowed to accept her diploma publicly, receiving it instead in the privacy of her home. She later taught physics and chemistry in Farmville, Virginia, and published articles in scientific journals.[34] The fact that she found a kindred spirit in Shakespeare's treatment of women, and felt free to share this in a co-ed club, testifies to his resonance for women who sought models for what Lupton called "feminine purpose" and "influence."

An enterprising and strong-willed woman in Zanesville, Ohio, also used Shakespeare as her modus operandi. Agnes Fillmore (a relative of Millard Fillmore) initiated a Shakespeare club in the late 1870s and persuaded amateur Shakespearean Joseph Crosby to be the leader, in part as a way to set up a courtship with him. In his letters, Crosby gave a humorous account of the genesis of the club in 1877:

> We walked much farther than there was really any need for, our talk was so thoroughly & mutually agreeable. As I was parting from her, she told me she had something on her mind to say to me. She wanted my help with a 'Shakespeare Reading Club'; but as she knew I had so positively declined, & refused some two or three other ladies, she feared it was hopeless to ask me. Something in her manner, &, besides, something in my own heart, so attracted me, I gave a sort of hesitating consent. In less than a week, she had organized the club—to meet at her house—where they elected me President . . . and her, Secretary. This threw us together a good deal, and so this whole matter started.[35]

It is worth pointing out the success of Fillmore's plan—she married Crosby a year later, and the club disbanded not long after it had fulfilled Fillmore's agenda.[36] Fillmore saw in Shakespeare an opportunity to take the initiative and organize a club of local men and women at her own home, where intellectual exchanges based on Shakespeare could form the basis for her relationship with Crosby. One wonders about the dynamics of their marriage, given the fact that both held leadership roles in the club.

Despite women's struggles for suffrage and other equalities in the early twentieth century, the previous examples suggest that when women studied Shakespeare with men, they were allowed to lead, organize, and even dominate. Perhaps most important, I have found no evidence that women's opinions were valued less than those of men or that they were given inferior positions or treatment in clubs. Shakespeare study thus offered a space where both men and women could contribute equally, and where women's opinions and thoughts were given equal weight to those of men.[37] As this chapter shows, women were *not* encouraged to remain silent or confined to their homes for their Shakespeare studies; they were urged to read, study, write, speak, argue, and spread their enthusiasm for Shakespeare, publicly in their communities and through national Shakespeare publications and networks, such as the journal *Shakespeariana* (sponsored, as noted above, by the all-male Shakespeare Society of New York).[38]

Unlike the popular rhetoric movement, in which women "found themselves stranded in the parlor with little hope of securing a voice in public affairs,"[39] reading Shakespeare provided women with opportunities to move beyond the parlor, both physically and metaphorically, and to participate in vigorous programs of public service and civic life.[40] One account of the Pasadena, California, Shakespeare Club in 1917, for example, noted that these women "have met together and started movements where mere man has not been invited or considered," and that "the Shakespeare Club, though composed of women only, is not afraid to undertake any problem, no matter how intricate or how difficult." Indeed, according to this history, the Pasadena Shakespeare Club is part of a larger movement in which "women individually and collectively, have forwarded many affairs of civic and social betterment in their own way," and often these efforts involved a connection with Shakespeare.[41]

The Women's Club Movement and Shakespeare

Of the more than five hundred American Shakespeare clubs for which I found records, the majority were composed of women only, no doubt owing to the expansion of the women's club movement around the turn of the century, which helped create a mass audience (largely female) ripe for the study of Shakespeare.[42] The General Federation of Women's Clubs (GFWC), formed in 1890, organized groups across the country into more focused social reforms and civil projects.[43] For black women, the National Association of Colored Women, begun six years later, offered a similar organizational structure (as discussed in Chapter 4).

The national unification of women's clubs also involved Shakespeare clubs; numerous Shakespeare clubs belonged to the GFWC, which circulated and promoted their Shakespeare activities. In 1927, for example, a newspaper article from Lewiston, New York, announced, "New and numerous are the ways devised by women's clubs to honor the great Shakespeare. No longer are they satisfied to merely study his plays, but, as April 23, the anniversary of his birth approaches, thousands of the member clubs of the General Federation of Women's Clubs, announce plans for special observance."[44] This type of public proclamation would have encouraged other clubs to follow suit, whether or not they focused primarily on Shakespeare. The Zetetic Club of Weeping Water, Nebraska, was one of the numerous clubs that devoted their annual April meetings to Shakespeare study in honor of the poet's birthday, while turning to other topics for the remainder of their yearly programs. A 1926 article in the *Shakespeare Association Bulletin* lamented the geographical separation of clubs but noted that the GFWC "has proved a stimulating and directing influence past reckoning. All who have at heart the cause of Shakespearean study in America must be forever grateful for such notable and signal service."[45] The vogue for studying Shakespeare combined with the burgeoning women's club movement encouraged the growth of clubs for women, promoted women's need for intellectual development, and inspired clubs to take on activities for public betterment, frequently organized around the study of Shakespeare.

State and local club federations also helped promote Shakespeare, and Shakespeare clubs were often active in these organizations. In Texas, the Dallas Shakespeare Club organized a meeting of delegates from clubs around the state in order to form the Dallas Federation of Women's Clubs in 1898.[46] Likewise, in New York, club women met in 1894 to discuss founding a state federation. Among the 118 delegates were women from the Portia Reading Club of Brooklyn and from the Seneca Falls, New York, Shakespeare Club.[47] In California, the Woodland Shakespeare Club was a charter member of the California State Federation of Women's Clubs (formed in 1900) and was also involved in District and County Federated Club meetings; the club history recounts that "minutes of the Shakespeare Club abound with reports of Federated Club meetings and activities."[48]

In turn, club federations brought Shakespeare clubs in contact with important social issues such as suffrage. In South Dakota, for example, fifty-two clubs belonged to the state federation in 1910, including Shakespeare clubs in Aberdeen and Hot Springs and seven other clubs with a concentration on Shakespeare. In 1911, at the annual meeting of the state federation, suffrage was a key topic, covered in the addresses "Why South Dakota Woman Should Have the Ballot" and "Woman Suffrage."[49] In the Midwest, members of the Peoria, Illinois, Women's Club (who performed Shakespeare annually) were supporters of suffrage as early as 1907.[50] Suffrage was a topic of discussion for the men and women in the Plainfield, New Jersey, Shakespeare Club in 1909, but their minutes do not reflect the details of that discussion. The GFWC did not endorse suffrage until 1914, and the variety of responses to suffrage may reflect geographical variation in women's involvement in social issues.[51] Nevertheless, study of Shakespeare often became a platform for women to engage with current social and political issues.

In fact, many clubs had mottoes similar to that of the Twelfth Night Club of Concord, New Hampshire (founded 1895), whose members described their Shakespeare study as "active, progressive, and keep[ing] pace with the onward movement of the times."[52] The typical Shakespeare club woman was involved in a broad range of civic and political causes, in addition to work on Shakespeare. In the early years of the twentieth century, many of the women in the Woodland, California, Shakespeare Club read plays but also "wished to work actively for women's suffrage, for the improvement of the lot of women and children, for town beautification, and for many other civic matters."[53] Likewise, in Georgia, Annie Cochrane, the organizer of the Barnesville, Georgia, Woman's Shakespearean Club (founded 1895), was also the first treasurer of the Georgia State Federation, which promoted traveling libraries, scholarships for women, free kindergartens, and child labor laws; as early as 1896, Cochrane was involved in lobbying the University of Georgia to admit women (which it did not do until 1918).[54]

In the Midwest, the Grand Haven, Michigan, Woman's Club, which had a weekly Shakespeare study class, was known in 1896 for its "earnest work and a progressive spirit."[55] On the West Coast, the Pasadena, California, Shakespeare Club "became a forum and launching-point for numerous 'progressive' ideas of the new century. Public kindergarten, public restrooms, Juvenile Court and the Pasadena Humane Society are but a few of the projects initiated by Shakespeare Club volunteers" since founding their club in 1888.[56] Alice Armstrong, one of the founders of the Woodland, California, Shakespeare Club in the 1880s, also worked for women's suffrage, campaigned against saloons, and helped start the local public library.[57]

Women in Placerville, California, discovered that starting a Shakespeare club was a clever and safe way to carry out their progressive social agenda. According to one member in 1897, "The men said no to a woman's club. . . . So, the women decided to start a club to study Shakespeare. The men couldn't say no to that. The first thing [we] did was close the brothels."[58] Although club women were often criticized for selfishly developing their own intellects and had to be "careful about how they portrayed their own literacy practices," Shakespeare clubs seemed immune to such criticism, and for many women (like those in Placerville), Shakespeare provided a safe way to facilitate their larger agendas of social activism.[59]

Shakespeare and Women's Education

In the commemorative program to celebrate its 100th anniversary in 1982, the Ladies Shakespeare Club of Decatur, Indiana, included an undated poem titled "A Tribe Called Shakespeare," written by member Anita Kalver. The poem opens with the following stanzas:

> In the land of Hoosier natives,
> By the River Kekionga
> Lived nine squaws so young and eager,
> Eager to acquire knowledge.

> So the squaws all got together,
> Formed a tribe and called it Shakespeare;
> Met in Council in each tepee,
> There to smoke the pipe of culture.[60]

It is not surprising that Shakespeare was the subject of choice (the "pipe of culture") for women seeking intellectual improvement, or "eager to acquire knowledge," throughout the early twentieth century. Shakespeare's works had been excerpted in rhetorical textbooks as early as 1782,[61] and Nan Johnson points out that Shakespeare was prominent in post–Civil War rhetorical texts designed for the general public. Shakespeare became a popular subject for public recitations as part of the curriculum in rhetorical schools in the late nineteenth century, and many women would have been familiar with Shakespeare through this tradition.[62] For example, Anna Randall-Diehl, president of the Fortnightly Shakespeare Club of New York, wrote several rhetorical handbooks from 1869 to 1888, and numerous members of that club participated in various forms of rhetorical education in the late 1890s.[63] Emma Dunning Banks was "famous for her skill in originating recitations of all varieties," and two other members (Mary Haviland Sutton and Mme Mercedes Leigh) were known for their readings and monologues. Lucia C. Balcam even served as the resident "orator and raconteur of the Fortnightly" and could "condense a story into a few words."[64]

Women in the late nineteenth and early twentieth centuries would likely have encountered Shakespeare through the most popular nineteenth-century educational reader, *McGuffey's New Fifth Eclectic Reader*, which featured passages from Shakespeare as a form of moral education. The McGuffey readers, first published in 1836 and 1837, were "one of the chief instruments for weaving [culture and morality] into the fabric of American life."[65] According to one estimate, the McGuffey readers, "combining lessons in elocution with moral instruction, contributed more than any other written source to establishing Shakespeare throughout the Mid-western frontier as first among English-language poets."[66] Given William Holmes McGuffey's belief that students should "read the Bible first, Shakespeare second," it is no surprise that Shakespeare was the most widely used author in the collection.[67]

Many women also began to read Shakespeare in the late nineteenth century through the Chautauqua educational program, a form of community education made up primarily of lectures, self-study, and traveling programs, described by one scholar as "a place where American culture was made and remade."[68] Shakespeare held a prominent place in this grassroots system of American education; the Shakespeare course in the Chautauqua University was described as "as extensive as that of our best colleges." The Chautauqua Literary and Scientific Circle (C.L.S.C.) granted a seal for completing a Shakespeare course, and the Chautauqua School of Languages included a substantial section on Shakespeare. One writer in 1883 remarked on the implications of Chautauqua for Shakespeare study: "The Chautauqua movement for popular education being so large and successful, it may easily be seen that the attention given to Shakespeare will be productive of the highest good."[69]

Many women's clubs were inspired by their Chautauqua work to begin or continue their study of Shakespeare. The Shakespeare Club of Santa Clara, California, was started in 1893 by women who had completed the Chautauqua Circle, and the Romeo, Michigan, Monday Club spent two years studying Shakespeare under the Chautauqua study plan in 1887–89.[70] Some groups even alternated between independent study of Shakespeare and Chautauqua programs. Throughout the 1890s, the Hart, Michigan, Ladies' Literary Club did four years of C.L.S.C. work, followed by three years of Shakespeare study, followed by more Chautauqua work.[71] It is noteworthy that Shakespeare was a significant part of the Chautauqua program, famously described by Teddy Roosevelt as "the most American thing in America," which (like the McGuffey readers) located Shakespeare as a part of American culture. For many women, studying Shakespeare was a seamless part of American culture, delivered via the Chautauqua system in an easily accessible and inspiring format, particularly through circuit Chautauqua programs that toured around the United States.[72]

At the same time that women across America were forming clubs and study groups centered on Shakespeare, Shakespeare was becoming part of the curriculum in U.S. high schools and universities.[73] In 1872, Harvard inaugurated its "English" Department with a course on Shakespeare in 1876 by Francis James Child, later to be taken over by George Lyman Kittredge in 1896.[74] With the founding of Vassar, Smith, Wellesley, and Radcliffe colleges between 1860 and 1890, the possibilities increased for women in higher education.[75] Even so, the number of women who went to college was relatively small. According to one estimate, as late as 1920 only 7.6 percent of women between eighteen and twenty-one went to college.[76] For the majority of American women who did not attend college, Shakespeare could serve as a curriculum of self-education that they could carry out on their own through an alternative club-based system.

Although scholars such as Anne Ruggles Gere have noted an opposition between the establishment of English studies in the academy and the intellectual activities of club women, such tensions seem relatively nonexistent for Shakespeare clubs.[77] In fact, several of the founding members of English departments in American universities (Francis James Child at Harvard, for example) and prominent editors of Shakespeare (William J. Rolfe) actually encouraged women's study of Shakespeare through editions, works of criticism, and even sometimes club lectures. The Woman's Shakespearean Club of Barnesville, Georgia, for example, boasted that its programs "have been considered worthy of an introduction by the Shakespearean scholar and critic, Professor W. J. Rolfe."[78]

The women in the Barnesville club also stated their goal in 1896 to "seek broader culture for ourselves."[79] Women readers of Shakespeare seemed to engage in their reading and study practices not to emulate male-dominated academia but rather to fulfill their own intellectual needs through alternative means, which they carried out in a wide variety of formats and literate practices (discussed further in Chapter 1).[80] Even so, the rigor and seriousness of many Shakespeare clubs approached the level of college study; according to one member of the Woodland, California, Shakespeare Club, who in 1913 "was fresh from college courses in literature," the club's study of Shakespeare was "equal in quality to that at Stanford University."[81]

Women's Shakespeare clubs were a way to obtain an alternative education, apart from any formal credentialing or desire to attain a professional specialization, for women "in danger of mental starvation," as one club member put it. A rich variety of club histories around the fin de siècle recounts women's passionate (and at times desperate) desire for knowledge.[82] The women in the Thursday Literary Circle of Selma, Alabama, for example, noted that they began their reading and study group in the 1890s to "save many from literary stagnation." Likewise, in 1892, Kate Tupper Galpin began her women's Shakespeare club in Los Angeles as "an unfailing remedy for breaking the crust of the mind in rust, and releasing latent powers of which the possessor had never dreamed." Such phrases are characteristic of how women voiced their intellectual needs.[83] Copious examples of women readers of Shakespeare make obvious their desire to stimulate their minds as their primary goal, achieved through reading Shakespeare. This impetus suggests a possible reason for the decline of Shakespeare clubs as the twentieth century progressed: the increasing numbers of women in higher education. According to one estimate, the number of women enrolled in higher education more than doubled between 1940 and 1960, an increase that parallels the decrease in club activity.[84]

A few samples of typical club practices might serve as a preamble to a lengthier discussion of exactly how women carried out their study agendas. When the women in the Locke Richardson Shakespeare Class of Oakland, California, had completed their study of a Shakespeare play in the late 1880s, they were tested on material for "reinforcing and strengthening the individual hold upon all the points developed during the study of the play." Likewise, members of the Woodland, California, Shakespeare Club read each play twice, focusing on pronunciation; scriptural, classical, and mythological allusions; history; character study; and discussion of passages. The Shakespeare Club of West Philadelphia assessed members' grasp of Shakespeare's plays during each meeting, in which an appointed "Critic" paused at the end of each scene, "requiring of each lady explanation of any obscure passages, mythological or historical allusions occurring in her part, and in the event of her failure to do so, [the Critic] must be prepared with such explanation herself."[85] Numerous Shakespeare clubs read the entire canon of plays and poems; in 1887, the members of the Stratford Club of Concord, New Hampshire, reported that by the end of the year they would have read them twice.[86] Even though they were not necessarily part of a formal academic institution, many women nevertheless found in Shakespeare the material to create their own systems of personal and intellectual achievements.[87]

Shakespeare Journals and the National Promotion of Shakespeare Study

In addition to national and state women's club organizations, several journals and publications promoted the study of Shakespeare by devoting space to news of Shakespeare clubs, printing study suggestions, and even publishing club members' essays. In the early decades of the twentieth century, the *American Shakespeare Magazine*, *Shakespeariana*, the *Shakespeare Association Bulletin*, and its later incarnation, *Shakespeare Quarterly*, all printed news of Shakespeare clubs and encouraged clubs to contribute details about their activities.[88] These national publications used the common ground of Shakespeare to enable women to forge intellectual connections beyond the boundaries of their local communities and to join a scholarly network of fellow readers. The publication of several prominent works of Shakespeare criticism by and for women in these journals also linked readers to larger traditions and networks of female intellectuals such as authors Mary Cowden Clarke and

Anna Jameson, whose work numerous clubs consulted.[89] Such opportunities offered further reinforcement for this alternative form of Shakespeare-centered education.

The journal *Shakespeariana*, sponsored by the Shakespeare Society of New York, provided a space for Shakespeare clubs across the country to connect, printing their news and providing models for study methods. President Appleton Morgan reported in 1895 that "more than thirty local Shakespeare societies have opened communication with us, sought our advice, invited our co-operation, and exchanged compliments with us on our fraternal occasions."[90] From 1883 to 1887, *Shakespeariana* was edited by Charlotte Endymion Porter, whose presence further underlined the acceptability of women's study of Shakespeare.[91] By printing (and legitimizing) essays by women, *Shakespeariana* "opened up opportunities to write and act in the public sphere."[92] The journal even sponsored prizes for the best essay on selected topics, often written by women; winners in 1885, for example, included Mrs. J. F. B. Mitchell of Flushing, New York, for an essay on Shylock and Mrs. S. A. Wetmore of Seneca Falls, New York, for one on Prospero.[93]

In 1886, the journal began a study program called "A School of Shakespeare," which provided study guides and materials for the "large and ever-growing class of students in towns, villages, and home-circles" and for "the serious attention of men and women who have not given up growing." The response was enthusiastic; one year later, the members of the Norwich, Connecticut, Shakespeare Club reported that they "were encouraged to renewed efforts by the announcement that *Shakespeariana* would offer us suggestions as to study" and they became "determined to follow the *Shakespeariana* course as closely as possible." The Norwich club recounted that same year, "We are bound together by a common feeling of wholesome hero-worship . . . with the aid of *Shakespeariana*'s plans, new revelations are continually opening before us, in the works of the world's greatest dramatist." A year later, the 1888 issue of *Shakespeariana* noted that the journal had received further "news of its encouraging effect upon many old clubs, and of its direct influence in the formation of a number of new ones, in different parts of the country." The Shakespeariana Class of Grand Rapids, Michigan, for example, relied on the reports of Shakespeare societies and Shakespeare news in the journal, which they read at their meetings, illustrating "how Shakespearian matter here collected may be brought to bear on club programmes," thus linking them to a larger community of Shakespeare study. Other clubs sent in responses of gratitude for the journal's creation of a national network of Shakespeare study: the men and women in the Natick, Massachusetts, Shakespeare Club wrote in 1888 that they "wishe[d] to be included in the fellowship of the Shakespeare Societies made public through *Shakespeariana*." Likewise, a letter in 1889 from the president of the Clearfield, Pennsylvania,

Shakespeare Society (which comprised both men and women) credited *Shake-speariana* for the club's "renewed interest in Shakespeare's writings."[94]

Following the success of *Shakespeariana*, a second journal began in 1895 called the *American Shakespeare Magazine,* "published monthly in the interest of Shakespeare Clubs and Societies, and for the benefit of Teachers and Students in general." The journal was edited by Anna Randall-Diehl, the president of the Fortnightly Shakespeare Club of New York City, who overtly encouraged readers to develop clubs nationwide: "If there is not a Shakespeare club in your town, form one." To aid in such pursuits, she included a "Study Department" in each issue, with questions and suggested themes for discussion geared to "clubs, school classes, and private students."[95] Randall-Diehl even reached out to general women's clubs through the New York State Federation; in a speech titled "The Study of Shakespeare" read at the New York State Confederation of Clubs at Syracuse in 1897, she urged her audience, "Form a Shakespeare club if you do not already belong to one. When you have studied Shakespeare, your taste for all higher literature will be immeasurably increased. You will find a new interest in nature, and much to remind you of Shakespearean characters in the men and women about you."[96]

By 1897, the *American Shakespeare Magazine* announced its increase in sub-scriptions and its coverage of "every State and Territory, to Canada, the West Indies, England, France," and the magazine disseminated the idea that women across the world should read and analyze Shakespeare. The Maria Mitchell Club of Mason City, Iowa, was one of many clubs inspired by Randall-Diehl's enthusiasm, and in 1898 it reported that its weekly meetings relied on the questions in the *American Shakespeare Magazine*.[97] The influence of the magazine even extended to the stage; the November 1887 issue included a promotion for Shakespeare clubs from theater impresario Augustin Daly, who claimed that clubs are "the greatest of all factors for keeping the Shakespearean drama on the stage. Those who have studied *Hamlet*, *Macbeth*, or *Much Ado*, are not willing to let the opportunity go by of seeing them acted. If the interest in reading Shake-speare increases during the next ten years as it has the last ten, the Shakespearean stage will hold itself against all other departments of the drama."[98]

The desire to establish a national Shakespeare club network continued with the *Shakespeare Association Bulletin* (the precursor to *Shakespeare Quarterly*), which started a column in 1925 called "The Club Forum," designed to "make us all conscious of the thousands of 'confederates' united in our common enthusiasm and love for Shakespeare; to offer the opportunity of becoming acquainted with each other; to exchange our ideas and suggestions about programs and Shake-speare study in general; and to catch the inspiration that comes from the news of each other's activities and methods." The growth of Shakespeare clubs since the end of the nineteenth century is clear in the journal's call for a more formal national union of clubs; the editor notes that "we are separated geographically by immense distances and only in exceptional instances can we meet face to face, but this is the place where we can talk to each other.... Here Shakespeare will introduce us, each to all." The response to its initiative was enthusiastic; the journal boasted of receiving annual club programs "from Maine straight across the country to California."[99]

In 1929, editor Mrs. Robert Carlton Morris (of the Toledo, Ohio, Shakespeare Club) urged "Shakespeare clubs, large or small, new or old" to "tell us what you have done and are doing. Tell us what you are *going to do*—are there gifts to public libraries in your plans for the future? Do you expect to celebrate Shakespeare's birthday next April? Is there a Shakespeare tree on the campus of your High School? Will there be a beautiful and significant Shakespeare Garden in your town some day?"[100] Later issues became even more direct in their suggestions for Shakespeare-based community intervention; in one 1929 issue, Morris urged clubs to extend their celebration of Shakespeare's birthday into their local schools, public spaces, libraries, and amateur drama groups:

> Offer prizes throughout the schools for poems or essays on some subject related to Shakespeare. Also offer prizes for best posters of well-known scenes from the plays. Plant a memorial tree on an appropriate site and outline a suitable dedication ceremony of songs, poem, addresses. Produce a pageant of characters, assigning to certain schools or clubs the representation of the historical plays, the Roman plays, the comedies and the tragedies. Consult with the manager of your public library. Is the Shakespeare shelf lacking in books of reference, or newest publications? If so, make a gift to your library on Shakespeare's birthday of books, perhaps a bust of the poet. . . . Produce a play, or scenes from several of the plays. Seek the cooperation of local dramatic clubs. In whatever way you decide to observe the day, remember that Shakespeare is for all of us—to remember, to enjoy, to applaud.[101]

For clubs still at a loss for how to celebrate Shakespeare's birthday, Morris even offered to mail poems for recitation.

In the 1930s and 1940s, some Shakespeare clubs pursued worldwide connections to other readers of Shakespeare. In 1930, Kate Friend was both the leader of the Waco, Texas, Shakespeare Club and a member of the Shakespeare Society of Stratford-upon-Avon.[102] Likewise, the Friday Shakespeare Club of Santa Cruz, California, corresponded with the Stratford Society in the 1940s and was invited to affiliate with it; the club secretary proudly wrote, "We voted to be the first club to enroll in the international group."[103] No such extensive scholarly organizations existed for other types of literature—Robert Browning, for example, was the second-most popular literary focus for clubs, but Browning studies did not entail the national and international networks available for the study of Shakespeare.[104]

Later in the twentieth century (starting in 1950), *Shakespeare Quarterly* (previously the *Shakespeare Association Bulletin*) included a section titled "Notes and Comments," which contained "notices of significant Shakespeare meetings, reading groups, stage presentations, and other activities." Some clubs apparently found *Shakespeare Quarterly* useful; the Modesto, California, Shakespeare Club listed "Gleanings from *Shakespeare Quarterly*" as a topic for one of its meetings in 1951–52. By the early 1970s, the "Notes and Comments" section rarely mentioned Shakespeare clubs, suggesting a shift in focus from common readers of Shakespeare to academics (the readership of the journal today).[105]

Publishers and Editions of Shakespeare

Another factor that contributed to a growth in readers of Shakespeare was the increasing availability of Shakespeare's plays in nineteenth-century America. Louis B. Wright notes that as early as 1834, a bookseller in St. Louis advertised seven different editions of Shakespeare "when St. Louis was still a rough staging area for emigrants pushing westward."[106] In the latter part of the nineteenth century, a number of editions of Shakespeare designed for the general reader were published in the United States. Andrew Murphy points out that the popularity of editions such as Henry Hudson's and the availability of cheap reprints demonstrate "the extent to which Shakespeare's works had finally gained a solid foothold in American culture by the middle decades of the nineteenth century." William J. Rolfe's editions, for example, were "immensely popular," including "Shakespeare for the School and Family" and the "Friendly Edition of Shakespeare," and were "found in the homes of thousands who have never seen any other edition."[107]

Shakespeare clubs took advantage of this variety of available editions of Shakespeare. The Stratford Club of Concord, New Hampshire, seemed to take great pleasure in the plethora of editions, reporting in 1887 that "all kinds of editions are used in our club, though I think there is rather a leaning in favor of Rolfe. Still, Hudson has many friends, Grant White is admired, Knight is highly valued, and the handy-volume edition is not despised. I have never counted, but I should think that there might be twenty-five different kinds of Shakespeare editions in the possession of the members, ranging all the way from expensive English books down to the humble five-cent volume."[108] In fact, in an 1886 letter to the Monday Club of Des Moines, Iowa, Horace Howard Furness recommended just such a method: "If you can afford it, it would add variety to your meetings if each one had a different edition, such as White's, Singer's, Knight's, and the Cowden-Clarke's, and Staunton's."[109]

Publishers realized the potential profit in this growing readership of Shakespeare, and they offered incentives to encourage individual and group study. In the 1898 pamphlet *How to Organize a Shakespeare Club*, distributed by Doubleday and McClure, the publisher offered editions of Shakespeare on a layaway payment plan of only one dollar a month, free lesson papers, plus a free set of Shakespeare books for every six sets purchased: "To any person who will organize a Shakespeare Club to take up these studies, or to any club that will use the Morley Shakespearean Library, the Publishers give, absolutely free, one complete library additional for every six ordered." Doubleday and McClure had its own "Shakespeare Department," which offered to "gladly aid and encourage, by additional suggestions, any organizations studying these lessons. All who would enjoy this expert instruction in the study of the Shakespearean Drama and the delightful associations that would result from the formation of a club should write immediately."[110] They also provided a list of standard Shakespeare reference books designed for club purchase. Such amenities made it relatively easy nationwide to obtain resources for the study of Shakespeare, even in some of the more rural locales discussed further in Chapter 3.

Women as Shakespeare Critics

Supplementing these journals and editions of Shakespeare, the publication and reprinting of several nineteenth-century works of Shakespeare criticism by women, specifically Anna Jameson's *Characteristics of Women: Moral, Poetical, and Historical* (1832; reprinted through the century), Mary Cowden Clarke's *The Girlhood of Shakespeare's Heroines* (1850–52), and Helena Faucit Martin's *On Some of Shakespeare's Female Characters* (1885), established Shakespeare as acceptable subject matter for women's scholarly pursuits, as Chapter 1 shows in greater depth.[111]

In 1887, the journal *Shakespeariana* reprinted Mary Cowden Clarke's essay "Shakespeare as the Girl's Friend" for this growing American readership. Cowden Clarke praised Shakespeare for his "feminine portraits," and the circulation of her essay helped spread her reputation as a woman reader and critic of Shakespeare:

Our great poet-teacher, who has given us 126 clearly-drawn and thoroughly individual female characters, who has depicted women with full appreciation of their highest qualities, yet with accurate perception of their defects and foibles, who has championed them with potential light by his chivalrous maintenance of their innate purity and devotion, while showing the points wherein their natural moral strength may be warped and weakened by circumstance, who has vindicated their truest rights and celebrated their best virtues—himself possessing keener insight than any other man-writer into womanly nature—Shakespeare may well be esteemed a valuable friend of woman-kind.

Cowden Clarke encouraged readers to turn to Shakespeare "for moral introspection and self-culture," a path followed by many women readers of *Shakespeariana*.[112]

Other works by women, such as Elizabeth Wormeley Latimer's *Familiar Talks on Some of Shakespeare's Comedies*, were geared to the Shakespeare club audience. Already a novelist, translator, and historian, Latimer initially began her volume as a series of "Parlor Lectures" to a women's group in Baltimore, Maryland, but soon realized its use for a growing audience of women readers. Latimer sketched out a particular agenda for acceptable feminine discourse on the comedies, leaving "all points of what is called Shakespearian Criticism" to the "erudite who write for University men." She reportedly examined "great masses of Shakespearian criticism" in preparing her book, including Jameson's *Characteristics of Women*. Her goal was to make Shakespearean analysis more accessible for readers without resources—in her words, to open the "'mighty book' for those who have not time or facilities for searching out what I have done from various sources." The review of Latimer's book in *Shakespeariana* described it as "a personal, feminine, light and quite modern touch," making it ideally suited to the educational needs and desires of a wider social class of women readers who were eager for more Shakespeare criticism.[113]

Other reference books designed for the general reader also persuaded both men and women to join Shakespeare clubs. John Phin's *Shakespeare Cyclopaedia and New Glossary* (1902) included a section titled "Shakespeare Clubs and Societies," in which Phin cited F. J. Furnivall's call for citizens to organize in their study of Shakespeare: "Get one or two likely friends to join you in your Shakspere work, if you can, and fight out all your and their difficulties in common; worry every line; eschew the vice of wholesale emendation. Get up a party of ten or twelve men and four or six women to read the plays in succession, at one another's houses, or elsewhere, once a fortnight, and discuss each for half an hour after reading. Do all you can to further the study of Shakspere, chronologically and as a whole."[114] The communal language in Furnivall's decree sets up Shakespeare as suitable for community building, in which men and women "join" together, study "in common," and read as "a party." Such prescriptions promote a community engaged in discussion and debate about Shakespeare—to "fight out," "worry," and "discuss," not accept wholesale—for both men and women.[115]

Phin built on Furnivall's group study plan, pointing out that "when several minds are thus brought together to work on a common object, the stimulus of association enables them to attain results which none of them could reach singly." Significantly, Phin included women in his vision of collective work on Shakespeare, bringing "several minds" together "on a common object," further reinforcing Shakespeare study as a space where men and women could contribute equally. Phin contended that even those who "join such a club merely for the name of the thing or for the sociability which it offers" and "would like to have the reputation of being literary, and especially of being supposed to be admirers and students of Shakespeare without doing the hard work," will benefit from the curative powers of Shakespeare: "It will be impossible to bring a dozen people together and get them to read a play or even part of a play by Shakespeare without imparting new ideas to most of them, and thus improving the minds of all."[116] Phin's assertion that reading even a little bit of Shakespeare would impart "new ideas" and improve the minds of the community puts Shakespeare at the center of communal intellectual development, the cornerstone for social advancement for both sexes.

Even women unable to join a club or society had Shakespeare study resources available through Anna E. Ticknor's Boston-based "Society to Encourage Studies at Home," which included a substantial Shakespeare department taught by women volunteers and lent out books to individuals and study groups across the country for the cost of postage.[117] By 1882, the society had enrolled nearly a thousand "students," with more than seven thousand students and dozens of clubs in its twenty-four-year history.[118] One student's 1897 testimony illustrates the importance of Shakespeare particularly for lower-class women: "A poor, illiterate woman, working hard all day in her husband's lumber camp in Maine, was lifted out of the 'slough' by the daily efforts to get a little time for S.[tudies at] H.[ome]. She was led through one branch after another (even the spelling corrected) until she obtained the proud distinction of having her essay on Shakespeare one of those chosen to be read at the June meeting."[119] For this unnamed "poor illiterate" woman, the journey to literacy (and "out of the 'slough'") culminated with the achievement of writing an essay on Shakespeare. Countless other American women at the turn of the century saw Shakespeare as an attainable goal for self-study and for group scholarship, as well as a way to lift them to a higher intellectual level, a charge taken up particularly by the black women's club movement, discussed in Chapter 4.

From Socialites to Housewives: The Great Variety of Club Members

Women at a variety of social and economic levels read and studied Shakespeare; as Frances M. Abbott of the Stratford Club of Concord, New Hampshire, put it, women of all classes and occupations should take on the edifying task of

Shakespeare study, because "no one should feel too poor or too busy to form one of an assemblage under the influence of the master."[120] A few examples illustrate the variety and diversity of Shakespeare club women at the end of the nineteenth century.[121] Far removed from the "poor, illiterate woman" who read Shakespeare in Anna Ticknor's home study is socialite Mrs. Bernard Peters, a prominent member of the upper echelon of New York society in the late 1890s whose membership in a Shakespeare club was part of a larger civic agenda. The wife of the proprietor of the *Brooklyn Times*, Peters was "senior Portia" and president of the Portia Reading Group, in addition to her role in other charitable organizations: she was involved in the Brooklyn Bureau of Charities and was Patroness of the Brooklyn Free Kindergarten Association, president of the Caecilia Ladies' Vocal Society, an honorary member of the Brooklyn Diet Dispensary, and one of the founding members of the Chiropean Club.

For more typical club women, domestic responsibilities left little time for such an assortment of civic commitments aside from Shakespeare study, which often served as a rare intellectual venue for women such as midwestern housewife Mary L. Freeman, who wrote in her lengthy diary about her experiences in a Shakespeare club in 1885. Plainswoman Martha Farnsworth similarly recounted a daily routine of physical labor, followed by reading Shakespeare in the Topeka Coterie Club in Topeka, Kansas, in 1906; and high school teacher Verlie Robinson Thomas divided her time among teaching, working in the library, and attending the Milton, Florida, Shakespeare Club in the early decades of the twentieth century. Socialites, housewives, and working women alike participated in the nationwide trend of studying Shakespeare; for members like Mrs. Bernard Peters, Shakespeare study was part of an extensive cosmopolitan social life, but for other women, the Shakespeare club was a treasured mental activity.[122] A report from the Thursday Literary Circle of Selma, Alabama (population c. 8,000), in the 1890s attests to the community-building nature of such groups, which involved young and old women alike: "It was interesting to see the older ladies of our number book in hand turning their steps each Thursday afternoon in the direction of the weekly meeting-place. Many an hour was thus agreeably spent, and much concord and harmony of spirit prevailed."[123] Shakespeare clubs flourished in both small rural towns and large urban centers and attracted members from a range of social strata.

Shakespeare clubs were formed by a variety of women as well, including actresses, mothers and daughters, and love-struck bachelorettes; Shakespeare became the conduit for an array of beneficial situations for women. The reasons women formed Shakespeare clubs range from intellectual camaraderie to community building. A mother and daughter in Lebanon, Missouri, spread their enthusiasm for reading Shakespeare by forming a club in 1882, which soon grew to eighteen members between the ages of

15 and 60. In Pasadena, California, two women who met for the first time at a church social discovered their mutual desire for a literary club. Shortly afterward, they formed a Shakespeare club that was so successful that in 1927 the Shakespeare League was established for daughters and nieces of the Shakespeare Club.[124] Women across the country discovered a mutual interest in Shakespeare that was conducive to club formation under a variety of circumstances, and during various historical and social conditions, from the 1880s through the 1930s.

For some women, reading Shakespeare was a way to establish an intellectual outlet in their community. Former New York City actress Josephine Heard Cutter started the Worcester, Massachusetts, Shakespeare Club in 1887 in an effort to re-create the theater and literary life she had left behind in New York City.[125] Similarly, when Mrs. George Washburn, wife of a Presbyterian minister, moved to Washington, Missouri, she suggested that local women might be "interested in the intellectual entertainment such as [a] reading group to meet at members' homes" on Tuesdays, "alternating with the Embroidery Club." By 1894, her Shakespeare club included married women, single women, and relatives.[126] In Raleigh, North Carolina, a group of neighborhood women with a "yen to study Shakespeare" started the Tuesday Afternoon Book Club in 1903.[127]

Even so, many of the founders of Shakespeare clubs could not put their fingers on an exact genesis for their group. In 1896, Mrs. A. M. Lambdin, of the Woman's Shakespearean Club of Barnesville, Georgia, offered several reasons for its start the previous year, both internal and external: "what caused the organization of the Shakespearean club is yet an unsettled question. It may be that the impetus given to club life and work among southern women by the Atlanta Exposition touched a responsive chord in the minds of Barnesville's daughters, or that there was among them independent of this influence a simultaneous desire for broader culture and mutual improvement."[128] Lambdin identified external influences of regional club work but also suggested a more general desire for an intellectual environment.[129] Whether building an intellectual community or extending their enthusiasm for Shakespeare, members, as the Norwich, Connecticut, Shakespeare Club expressed it, were "bound together by a common feeling of wholesome hero-worship."[130]

The story of one emblematic club further illustrates the wide variety of women and motivations for initiating Shakespeare clubs. The two women who founded the Woodland, California, Shakespeare Club in the 1880s had strikingly different backgrounds. Alice Armstrong was an enterprising teacher from Michigan "who would have formed a reading circle, whether home had been by the Atlantic or Pacific, on the ice dunes of the North or the snowy prairies of the South." She had the support of her husband, who was "a man of means and most liberal and also a lover of literature," which enabled her to "command the time and the money to gratify her taste along that line." In contrast, cofounder Anne Blake Ryder traced her interest in Shakespeare to a rooming house in San Francisco in 1882, when she found herself without anything to read. Ryder recalled, "I asked the lady in whose house I was rooming if she had any books she would let me read. She brought me a dilapidated copy of Shakespeare, which I read with delight for several weeks." Unlike her cofounder, Ryder did not come from a background of privilege; her parents were textile mill workers from Manchester, England, and she immigrated to the United States at age sixteen and began work as a maid. Yet she "always had books around her for reading in her leisure time" and was "self made as far as her intellectual attainments went." When she returned to Woodland, she sought out women who had a common interest in Shakespeare, which led her to Armstrong. Together they invited other women "to bring their volumes of Shakespeare and read," and soon after formed the Woodland Shakespeare Club.[131]

Elsewhere in America, women in search of intellectual development gravitated to Shakespeare as ideal material. In Concord, New Hampshire, Ellen R. Morrill gathered a few women to read English history in 1881 but soon turned to Shakespeare's history plays, which "proved so interesting that it was decided to read only Shakespeare," and thus the Stratford Club of Concord was born.[132] Other groups met intellectual and social needs by combining study of Shakespeare with other interests; the Shakespeare Club of Medford, Massachusetts, for example, began with twenty young women in 1867 who gathered to read Shakespeare aloud at each other's houses followed by a dance.[133] The Shakespeare Club of Zanesville, Ohio, as we saw above, was started by Agnes Fillmore as a way to woo amateur Shakespeare scholar Joseph Crosby. Shakespeare clubs did not involve only upper-class literati; they also included housewives and neighbors in search of community-building activities, generations of women establishing common ground for study, and even women seeking romance through the study of Shakespeare.

Membership—Supply and Demand

The longevity of many Shakespeare clubs and the demand for membership among their communities suggest a consistent and widespread audience for reading and studying Shakespeare throughout the late nineteenth and early twentieth centuries. Often the constraints of meeting space necessitated competitive admission to clubs and required methods for selecting new members. The Woodland, California, Shakespeare Club limited its membership to twenty-five "to avoid crowded rooms," but by 1932 there were so many women on the waiting list that the club increased its size to fifty and began meeting in a local hotel and later in a women's clubhouse.[134] The Shakespeare Club of Pasadena,

California (founded 1888), even had its own clubhouse, with a limit of seven hundred members, but as of 1917 it reported no vacancies.[135]

The history of the Stratford Club, one of ten Shakespeare clubs in Concord, New Hampshire, puts the demand for studying Shakespeare in perspective. Founded in 1888, it was limited to sixteen members because of parlor space. Its membership procedures provide insight into the prestige often attached to studying Shakespeare: "When a vacancy occurs, different members send in the names of one or more candidates to the president. A list of these is read, and the members ballot. The name which receives the most votes is then announced, and the members ballot again, voting yes or no as they choose. If the result is not unanimous the candidate is rejected, another name is chosen, and the balloting is carried on as before. It is thus seen that no one can be admitted to the club who is not perfectly agreeable to every member." Membership in the Stratford Club was basically for life, and the club reported that "nothing less than death or removal to another part of the world would induce any of the members to resign their places"; fines of five cents for tardiness or absence "for any cause whatever" kept members attentive to their commitment.[136] Such demands on members are especially impressive given the fact that there were at least nine other Shakespeare clubs meeting in Concord at the time.

In some communities, membership in a Shakespeare club was passed down from mother to daughter, a process further entrenching local Shakespeare study.[137] The Shakespeare Club of Smithfield, Virginia, begun in 1905, recorded that "membership, which is limited to twenty, is much coveted, especially by the daughters of the charter members."[138] Similarly, the Belleville, Kansas, Shakespeare Club reported that as late as the 1980s, there were two grandmother-mother-daughter sets of members and five mother-daughter sets.[139] The Shakespeare Club of Morristown, New Jersey, founded 1886, involved both men and women, including "several third- and fourth-generation families," but limited membership to fifteen families, "to correspond with the maximum number of characters in the Bard's plays."[140] Numerous women's Shakespeare clubs had similar well-established roots in their communities; they helped inaugurate the study of Shakespeare as an accessible, desirable, often competitive, and long-term ambition for generations of women.

The competitive nature of some Shakespeare clubs suggests that these organizations may have served other social functions in some communities. Many clubs began almost simultaneously with the establishment of their towns (discussed further in Chapter 3), which situated Shakespeare as part of the infrastructure of frontier life, as a foundation of local culture. Some clubs required spotless social records for membership (indicated by the requirement of a unanimous vote), and thus membership was indicative of social status. In most cases, membership in Shakespeare clubs could be earned, but in the Dallas Shakespeare Club, for example, according to one history, "social lines were tightly drawn and requirements for eligibility were rigid . . . membership was so eagerly sought that in time it came to be said, 'One is not elected to the Shakespeare Club but has to be born in it.'"[141] Though I have found no evidence that particular women were excluded or expelled from clubs, such events are unlikely to be recorded in club minutes.[142] We might impart to these clubs a role in the establishment of class and social boundaries in some communities, and it is of no small significance that such structures were organized around knowledge and mastery of Shakespeare. While not all clubs were exclusive, it is worth pointing out that the ability to commit to a reading and study program of Shakespeare could affect one's social status in various communities across the country.

Writing Their History

The significance of Shakespeare clubs is supported by the fact that many groups saw fit to preserve their activities and create their own archives. Numerous clubs reported their scholarly activities to journals such as *Shakespeariana* and the *Shakespeare Association Bulletin*.[143] Most groups compiled minutes of their meetings; the Shakespeare Club of Montgomery, Alabama, for example, began their meetings with quotations from the Shakespeare play under consideration, which the secretary preserved in the minutes, and the Dallas Shakespeare Club secretaries had to keep minutes in verse.[144] Scores of groups donated their study materials to local archives and public libraries, further demonstrating their sense that their intellectual work should be documented and preserved. The Shakespeare Society of Plainfield, New Jersey, for example, began depositing its materials in the Plainfield Public Library in the late 1880s for safekeeping, and more than a hundred years later it donated its records from 1887 to 1998, consisting of six leather-bound volumes of club minutes, photographs, correspondence, newspaper clippings, and other artifacts, including an undated "Shakespeare Society rubber stamp."[145] Likewise, Susan M. Brooks, president of the Medford, Massachusetts, Shakespeare Club, wrote in 1967, "For some time I have cherished the idea that the Annals of the Medford Shakespeare Club be put into some abbreviated form for posterity"; members had kept "irreplaceable papers, pictures, and other memorabilia . . . in attics and closets here and there in the homes of officers and members for a hundred years," materials that were then put in a special repository at the Medford Public Library.[146] The group began thinking about its work as worthy of preserving as early as 1869, at a meeting in honor of Shakespeare's birthday, when members met for "an aesthetic Shakespeare Kettledrum," at which they read papers on Shakespeare, "uniformly copied out and very beautifully bound through the kindness of Mr. John C. Rand, making our first Archives."[147] For most groups, preservation came at a later stage; the scrapbook of the Shakespeariana Class of Grand Rapids, Michigan, contains a 1987 letter from member Lorna A. Wilson to Elizabeth Niemyer at the Folger Shakespeare Library. Wilson writes, "At a recent meeting of the group, it was overwhelmingly voted to place the book, together with some interesting memorabilia, in your hands, as an inspiration to other organizations devoted to the study of Shakespeare."[148] Their materials now reside in the Folger. Through these activities, women readers forged their own place in the history of Shakespeare studies.

The Influence of Shakespeare Clubs

Given the widespread number of women reading and studying Shakespeare from the late nineteenth century through the twentieth, what were the effects of this grassroots study movement, beyond the personal fulfillment of members? A brief glance at some of the surviving contributions to American civic life illustrates the long-term significance of these women readers. Many women's Shakespeare clubs were involved in projects of social outreach, thus linking Shakespeare's cultural value with intellectual development and civic responsibility; one 1880 account even described women's clubs as "the popular custodians of literature in America."[149] Numerous clubs combined their goals of improving their minds and enhancing their communities, at the same time commemorating Shakespeare as a symbol of progress, improvement, and community betterment.

Most Shakespeare clubs were involved in a combination of local and international causes. Wartime efforts in the twentieth century occupied many women; the Shakespeare Round Table Club of Bowling Green, Ohio, knitted for soldiers in World War I and supported a French orphan, as did the Pleiades Club, a Shakespeare club in Idaho, which sent food and clothing to a French family after World War II.[150] Locally, numerous public spaces across America owe their existence to Shakespeare clubs. Gardens dedicated to Shakespeare were particularly popular and typically included plants mentioned in Shakespeare's works or transplanted from England. One Shakespeare garden in a local park in New Rochelle, New York, maintained by the Avon Bard Club, included "a sun dial inscribed with a quotation from *The Merchant of Venice* and a luxuriant bed of English ivy, grown from cuttings brought directly from Stratford-upon-Avon." In Plainfield, New Jersey, the Shakespeare club began a Shakespeare garden in 1928 with flowers and shrubs labeled from the plays, making it "educational, and on many days ladies and teachers with children are found in the garden."[151] A 1927 newspaper article on Shakespeare celebratory gardens in New York, Cleveland, and Toronto attests to their importance in communities, calling them a "worthy enterprise that has proved effective in increasing affection for the great plays, bringing them close to the young folk and reawakening interest of mature readers."[152]

Residents of Cleveland, Ohio, could enjoy a stroll in an authentically "Shakespearian" garden, including "trees from the original Birnam Wood." One observer remarked in awe, "That Birnam forest should come to Dunsinane seemed to Macbeth impossible, but that saplings from the famous grove should be growing near Lake Erie seems incredible." Additional wonders in Cleveland included "a luxuriant growth of ivy transplanted from the alleged tomb of Juliet."[153] On the West Coast, residents of Woodland, California, might encounter the trees and stone bench donated by the Shakespeare Club to a city park, though they might have to look a bit harder to discover the copy of the Woodland Shakespeare Club yearbook placed in one of the cornerstones of the Woodland City Hall in 1936 to commemorate "the continuing influence of the Club in the community."[154] In nearly every part of the country, it is likely that one could find a public space with a link to a Shakespeare club.

One of the most ambitious Shakespeare community projects was undertaken by Kate Tupper Galpin, the leader of her own Shakespeare club in Los Angeles. In 1901, Galpin was responsible for planning the Shakespeare House, a replica of Shakespeare's Stratford birthplace, to serve as a meeting place for local study clubs, including Galpin's Shakespeare group. The interior, replete with reproduction "heavy beams, the old oak wainscoting, the quaint fireplace, the rough plastering," was designed to contain "Shakespeareana in the shape of books and pictures, together with busts of Shakespeare, of Julius Caesar, Cleopatra, and other characters of Shakespeare's creating." The building also included a reception hall, an audience room with a stage, a gym, a banquet room, and four club rooms, as well as an English garden with flowers from Shakespeare's works.[155]

The work of Shakespeare clubs in other communities similarly permeated multiple aspects of local society. The women of the Dallas Shakespeare Club were particularly industrious; in the 1920s, they helped organize the Dallas Public Library, purchased bronze lamps ("the first to be brought to Texas") for the building, and promoted the Dallas Art Association, the Dallas Symphony, and the Little Theatre. They sponsored public lecturers and readings, established scholarships, and performed plays, including Clement Dane's *Will Shakespeare*. In honor of the Shakespeare Tercentenary in 1916, they put on "a very impressive pageant" in conjunction with "the private schools of Dallas." They also organized the Dallas Woman's Club, of over eight hundred members, and sponsored a Woman's Club building, which "serves as a centre for the social, cultural and literary activities of the women of Dallas."[156] Even in a city as large as Dallas, one would have been hard-pressed to avoid encountering the effects of this group in the early decades of the twentieth century.

As well as setting up Shakespeare-centered civic activities, many clubs promoted the study of Shakespeare in schools and helped establish Shakespeare as a part of the curriculum; vestiges of these activities still survive in the American educational system. In Oklahoma, the Enid Shakespeare Club encouraged the local study of Shakespeare by giving two awards a year for the best papers in the Shakespeare class at Phillips University, and the Shakespeare Club of Lawton endows a scholarship at Cameron University in Lawton for students who plan to teach English in high school.[157] The Waxahachie, Texas, Shakespeare Club sponsored a $1,000 scholarship at Trinity University for girls (the Howell T. Livingston Scholarship) and presented dictionaries to students every year at the local high school and elementary school, gifts sponsored by the husband of a past president in memory of his wife.[158] In New York, philanthropist Esther Hermann, a member of the Fortnightly Shakespeare Club of New York City, carried out her enthusiasm for Shakespeare by donating "handsome copies of Shakespeare's work as prizes to schools and scholars, or as presents to club libraries."[159] For clubs that had not yet publicly expressed their enthusiasm for reading Shakespeare, Mrs. Robert Carlton Morris, writing in the *Shakespeare Association Bulletin*, encouraged them to commemorate Shakespeare's birthday: "plan a community celebration,—public and private schools, libraries, book shops, dramatic organizations, art clubs, musical societies should all have a part."[160] Through such activities, clubs extended their influence and spread their passion for Shakespeare.

The town of Payette, Idaho, might serve as a case study for the substantial effects Shakespeare clubs could have on individual communities. In this town of roughly 500 citizens, the Portia Club was formed in 1895, four years after the town was incorporated.[161] In addition to starting the town library from books gathered from their homes, club members addressed village sanitation through waste boxes; insisted the village authorities "tend to the 'chicken nuisance' and to the 'fly question'"; promoted fire escapes, fire drills, and drinking fountains in the local high school; held annual art and poetry contests; formed a "Look Out Committee," which provided food, clothing, medicine, and Christmas toys to needy families; donated linens to the nearby veterans hospital; and began a long-running May Day celebration that garnered them a lasting reputation for civic and cultural improvement. One citizen of Payette recalled the group's founding in 1895: "By the time I was in second grade, a group of ladies in Payette had formed the Portia Club, an organization whose mission was to bring culture to the town and area." She later credited the club with making Payette "the cultural capital of the Northwest."[162] In addition to civic work, the group was known for sponsoring "lectures on laws that affected women and children," holding "debates on women's issues," and spreading "the virtues of art and literature throughout Payette."[163] In a town of well under 1,000 people around the fin de siècle, the Portia Club must have assumed a large responsibility for local cultural and civic activities, from the time the club was founded in 1895 through most of the twentieth century.[164]

Conclusion

Women readers in large cities and small towns across America helped spread the idea that Shakespeare was for everyone, not just cultural elites in metropolitan areas.[165] The efforts of club women to improve their communities also established Shakespeare as a local foundation of American culture and as a marker for learning, self-improvement, civilization, and entertainment for a broad array of populations, from New York City literati to midwestern housewives. Though these readers have been left out of the history of Shakespeare in America, the women themselves clearly felt that they were doing important work. Many clubs appointed historians, compiled scrapbooks, and printed annual programs; numerous clubs have left their papers and ephemera to local archives. The range of women, in terms of class and occupation as well as geography, suggests a widespread knowledge, appreciation, and even desire for Shakespeare. The remainder of this book continues my argument for Shakespeare's importance for American women—for readers both collectively and individually in Chapter 1, as they negotiated their intellectual and domestic spaces in the American home in Chapter 2, across the country in Chapter 3, and for black club women in Chapter 4—all of whom were engaged in variations of Mary Cowden Clarke's description of lingering over, studying, and reading Shakespeare.

At the end of the nineteenth century, the position that Shakespeare would have in American literary culture was by no means clear. Many Americans were uneasy about according Shakespeare a prime place in the American literary canon; among many American literati, there was a push to find an American equivalent of Shakespeare. Writers such as Herman Melville argued that it was only a matter of time before an American Shakespeare was discovered, claiming that "Shakespeares are this day being born on the banks of the Ohio . . . he is sure to be surpassed by an American born now or yet to be born." Mark Twain famously doubted Shakespeare's authorship, and for Walt Whitman, "the great poems, Shakespeare included, are poisonous to the idea of pride and dignity of the common people, the life-blood of democracy."[166] However, in areas not normally considered the usual suspects in the formation of nineteenth-century literary culture (in geographically remote areas and in the home, for instance), women were already at work reading and studying Shakespeare to make sure he maintained his position in American literary culture as an author who, in one club's description, "has influenced the intellectual life of our day more than any other man mortal born."[167]

 CHAPTER 1

Reading

At its heart, this is a book about women reading—
white women and black women; mothers and daughters; with men and with
other women; in urban and rural locales; amid housework, child care, jobs, and
other time commitments. And it is about women reading something specific:
Shakespeare. A remarkable cache of material survives about these women readers of Shakespeare, from the late nineteenth century through the twentieth. In
many instances, we know exactly what texts they read and how often they met,
how quickly or slowly they read each text, what criticism they read, what material supplemented their study of Shakespeare, how they chose members, what
papers they wrote, what topics they discussed and debated, how they carried
their enthusiasm for Shakespeare into civic work, and in some cases, if diaries
or other private writings survive, what their personal reflections were about
reading Shakespeare.[1]

Based on this largely untouched material, this book argues that reading Shakespeare was a potentially transformative activity for many American women and
for their communities, beginning in the 1880s and lasting well into the twentieth
century.[2] But how exactly did women read Shakespeare? And what was it about
reading Shakespeare specifically that was so appealing to women? This chapter
focuses on the various literate practices of women readers and how each of those
practices helped empower them through the public speaking skills and analytical
strategies promoted by clubs and through the confidence gained from mastering
(and sometimes performing and adapting) Shakespeare, by and large in the period

before women could even vote.[3] Women engaged in elaborate and intellectually demanding work on Shakespeare: they read plays closely; researched unfamiliar words or phrases; contextualized the plays in history, contemporary literature, and art; memorized passages; wrote essays; read aloud and sometimes performed plays; often kept up with the latest Shakespeare criticism; and frequently expressed their enthusiasm for Shakespeare publicly, by sponsoring libraries, educational scholarships, public gardens, and parks: all lasting memorials to these grassroots readers and to their passion for Shakespeare.[4] As such, they make a case for Kate Flint's description of reading as an act that "provides liberation through the imagination" and facilitates "inward, social, and political exploration."[5]

Unlike the popular rhetoric movement of the late nineteenth century, which "persistently directed the American woman to the domestic sphere as her proper rhetorical space," Shakespeare clubs allowed women to forge their own intellectual lives during this period, mostly with other women but also at times with men.[6] The repercussions of reading Shakespeare extended beyond the confines of individuals and clubs and had an impact on society. Under the banner of the Shakespeare club, many women spread their enthusiasm for reading by spearheading public efforts to promote reading in their own communities, thus linking the name of Shakespeare with literacy and education.[7] Publishers targeted Shakespeare clubs for Shakespeare editions; clubs purchased works of criticism for libraries, and they often accumulated substantial collections of Shakespeare's works and criticism as the base for public libraries and served as librarians. Many early twentieth-century libraries enshrined Shakespeare's works as the foundation of their collection, sometimes devoting shelves, cases, and rooms to Shakespeare resources, all of which reveal the roots of women readers in local communities and institutions.[8]

Recent studies in book history have suggested the need to reevaluate the role of readers in influencing cultural life, and women readers of Shakespeare offer us an important opportunity to assess some of the central questions related to reading and public life.[9] In this chapter (and elsewhere in the book) I explore the transformative possibilities of reading Shakespeare for women, both collectively and individually, combining work on women's clubs with recent work on the role of reading for individual and collective agency. I focus on the variety of ways Shakespeare was read by American club women in order to suggest some of the repercussions of their literate practices for individual women, for groups, and for their communities in the decades around the fin de siècle.

While women of course read in the late nineteenth and early twentieth centuries, many women have attested that membership in a Shakespeare club encouraged them to read more regularly and in more sustained and focused ways, but also with a wider frame of reference, providing what Elizabeth Long calls "the social *infrastructure*" necessary for sustained reading.[10] The Norwich,

Connecticut, Shakespeare Club, for example, began in 1887 as a general reading club focusing on elocution. As one member put it, when the club began to
study Shakespeare, "we naturally found new fields opening before us, and were
thus led to band ourselves together in a very informal way, for the pursuit of
these more 'desperate studies.'"[11] Likewise, in 1894 the three women who began
the Benton Harbor, Michigan, Ossoli Club, which focused on Shakespeare,
American history, art, and music, sought to remedy the "lack of intellectual
culture" with the "benefit and stimulus accruing from organized effort and
systematic study."[12] Caroline Louise Hooper, a member of the Thursday Literary Circle of Selma, Alabama, also noted the sense of satisfaction her group felt
when completing its collective study of Shakespeare: "each of us, I think, closed
our books with the sensation that one more good book had been accomplished,
and something like critical study given to it."[13] Not all women read Shakespeare
in the same way, but most seem to have derived a similar sense of accomplishment and pride in their achievements, and an appreciation of group dynamics.

Even though they were communities of readers, it is worth underlining the
fact that Shakespeare clubs were eclectic in their reading and study methods.
Some clubs worked toward the goal of reading the whole canon and then
started over again, while others studied history through Shakespeare or combined Shakespeare's plays with other topics (as discussed in the next chapter).
The literate practices of some groups resembled those of a modern graduate
program in English, and others covered Shakespeare as part of a wider literary
or cultural agenda—yet the overall goal of each club was determined by the
members themselves, according to their intellectual, social, and cultural needs
and desires, mediated through reading Shakespeare.[14]

Although various frameworks existed to suggest ways of reading and study
(the Shakespeare journals mentioned in the previous chapter, for example), not
every club followed the same protocol. Of course, it is impossible to track
exactly how each individual woman read Shakespeare, but we can distill some of
the most common reading practices and extrapolate their possible significance
for women. Most club women took part in a number of literary activities:
solitary reading, communal reading, reading aloud, performance, memorization,
literary analysis, research, writing essays, and conversation (or "booktalk").[15]
Women's Shakespeare clubs complicate the boundaries between public and private reading since they involved both the solitary reading practices of members
as they prepared their assignments and the communal reading of groups as
members read Shakespeare together and discussed individual interpretations; as
such, they bridge the gap "between solitary reading and collectivity" and offer
a "site for investigating the relationship between the public and private aspects
of social life."[16] For American women in the late nineteenth and early twentieth centuries, reading Shakespeare was also a way to connect in geographically

isolated locales, amid home duties, and in a shifting political climate for women's rights.[17]

By offering women opportunities for intellectual growth and independence through private reading, public speaking, and often more significant leadership positions, Shakespeare clubs were crucial in preparing women for more public tasks.[18] The women in the Kettledrum of Tuscaloosa, Alabama (founded 1889), who read Shakespeare, noted these benefits for members: "The meetings of the club have been the means of developing the latent executive talent of its members. Many ladies, too timid at one time to speak in any gathering, can now conduct the exercises according to parliamentary rules, with the greatest ease and dignity."[19]

Homework: Solitary Reading and Memorization

Although club work entailed solitary reading in preparation for club meetings, such reading was carried out within the context of preparing for a group discussion.[20] Several examples illustrate the variety of "homework," the term I use for those literate practices carried out at home in preparation for communal reading.[21] Many groups circulated homework in advance for women to complete on their own. In 1896, the leader of the Lansing, Michigan, Shakespeare Club distributed "a type-written set of questions prepared for each member and given out the week previous for study and preparation."[22] For easy access, the Waxahachie, Texas, Shakespeare Club even printed its study questions in the local newspaper.[23] In order to carry out their intensive discussion of Shakespeare in 1886—meeting two hours a week, one hour for each act—members of the San Francisco Shakespeare Class were given weekly study questions to complete and had to recite their answers in front of the group.[24] Similarly, the Plainfield, New Jersey, Shakespeare Club distributed parts to be read; they were "given out by card a week or more in advance, so it does not become onerous to anyone."[25] Kate Tupper Galpin distributed written questions for her Los Angeles club women to answer "to instill confidence and elicit every shade of meaning," but she acknowledged the need for women to develop confidence through this process: "an experienced leader knows the support of the system of a slip of paper."[26] These various methods extended reading practices into the home life of members and helped secure Shakespeare's place in American cultural life.

In 1886, the journal *Shakespeariana* published several recommendations for completing homework. Readers were advised to "set apart some spare quarter or half hour each day for reading the play your club will take up, and don't wait till you meet to get perfectly familiar with it." To aid in preparation for communal reading, the journal suggested to club members, "Treasure [Shakespeare] up in your mind and learn it by heart. Read it, and having read it, read it again . . . tell yourself the story and the thoughts you have gathered. Write them out patiently, the better to get hold of them. . . . And then, reading over the play again you may find yourself in a fit frame of mind to be an appreciative, and useful member of a club-meeting to read the play in assigned parts."[27] For women who read Shakespeare intensely and closely and memorized passages, this allocation of time to study had significant ramifications, as we see in Chapter 2.[28]

In line with the recommendations of *Shakespeariana*, the men and women in the Mutual Club of Woodland, California, were advised by their leader in 1888 that their study of Shakespeare was serious business: "Reading should be made a means of study and not merely a source of entertainment. Each member should have a system of study, and that system should be his own. If possible, each member should own the books he reads. They become the most valuable and the most unselfish companions."[29] Women (and often men) were not just meeting for tea and casually reading through plays; they were engaged in extensive behind-the-scenes preparation and were encouraged to develop their own system of self-study.[30]

Homework: Research and Writing Essays

As well as reading Shakespeare at home, most women engaged in study practices that involved extensive self-education; as one writer put it in 1883, "as an incentive to *self-education* there is nothing better than Shakespeare."[31] Usually this took the form of researching and writing essays on preassigned topics, presenting them at club meetings, and at times even publishing them. This type of literary work functioned as an alternative form of education, tailored to the needs and interests of women readers, but often was as rigorous as a college-level course and frequently relied on the latest Shakespeare scholarship. The previous chapter outlined the possibilities for women in higher education. A few examples of club methods illustrate how Shakespeare was configured to fit various curricula.

The members of the Mutual Club of Woodland, California, developed their own research and study system for Shakespeare, giving each member a guide that listed sources to read for each topic. In the club's 1887–88 season, Mrs. Chamberlain shared her research on Elizabethan education in "Parallel Reading from the Nine English Bibles," and Miss Callie Vivian presented "Shakespeare in Criticism."[32] The women in the Shakespeare Club of West Philadelphia (c. 1886) had their own "Books of Reference" under the care of a club librarian for women to consult when preparing their material.[33] The Locke Richardson Shakespeare Class of Oakland, California, was also determined to develop its Shakespeare library for readers to use in their research; the group reported to *Shakespeariana* in 1887 that to the "original nucleus of a library—the Furness

Variorum Tragedies, and other volumes, presented by Mr. Locke Richardson—it has been gradually adding the more essential portions of crucial apparatus, the Concordances, Lexicons, Facsimiles, Grammars, and Manuals."[34] Miss L. B Easton, the leader of the San Francisco Shakespeare Class, was comprehensive in the resources she provided for members, reporting in 1886 that she used "Rolfe, Hudson, Thom, Cl. Press, Dowden's *Mind and Art*, and everything else I can lay my hands on" when preparing for her club meetings.[35] The women involved in more formal institutions of higher education would not have noticed much difference in the methods of studying Shakespeare.

Even though many readers perused Shakespeare criticism, much evidence suggests that women were not necessarily constrained by those interpretations. In 1886, *Shakespeariana* recommended that readers not value "the opinions of others about Shakespeare for your own reading and understanding of him" and reminded them to "be sure that you are exercising your power to make your own product."[36] The members of the Friends in Council Shakespeare Class of Topeka, Kansas, followed this principle of valuing their own opinions before being influenced by the views of critics. According to their 1887 program, members had to complete a study of the play's text, bibliography, history, and "ethical and character studies" before they were "allowed the privilege of walking in company with grown-up critics, dramatic and literary," but they noted that those scholars "seldom escaped minor criticism from us, our senses having been sharpened under such healthful regimen."[37] Other women readers did not necessarily adopt interpretations from Shakespeare criticism wholesale; the women in the Lebanon, Missouri, Shakespeare Club noted in 1885 that they "do not consult any notes until we have first interpreted the text for ourselves." These methods gave women readers confidence based on their own interpretive abilities, leading the Lebanon women to boast that "we can pass as creditable an examination" on Shakespeare "as any Club in America."[38]

Numerous club records note that women frequently turned to Shakespeare criticism written by women, specifically Anna Jameson's *Characteristics of Women* (1832 and reprinted through the century), Mary Cowden Clarke's *The Girlhood of Shakespeare's Heroines* (1850–52), and Helena Faucit Martin's *On Some of Shakespeare's Female Characters* (1885).[39] As early as 1883, an essay in *Shakespeariana* praised "the brilliant and solid work of women in recent years on Shakespeare—both as writers and as interpreters of his gracious heroines," citing Cowden Clarke, Martin, Mrs. Siddons, and Jameson, all of whom "can be most worthily cited and compared with the best workers among the men."[40] Club women also used Elizabeth Wormeley Latimer's *Familiar Talks on Some of Shakespeare's Comedies* (1886), designed for the nonspecialist reader, and resources from other female editors such as Charlotte Porter and Helen A. Clarke, who issued study guides to Shakespeare as part of the magazine *Poet Lore* as well as the "Pembroke Shakespeare" in 1903.[41] The female readership of these early texts by women suggests an informal but influential network of women readers and critics.

Another common form of club homework was memorization of Shakespeare, which often involved reciting a passage from Shakespeare at roll call. A typical example comes from the Shakespeariana Club of Grand Rapids, Michigan, whose sixty-four members were encouraged to "commit to memory the most note-worthy thoughts contained in the play" as part of their reading; they began their celebration of Shakespeare's birthday in 1888 with all members reciting "Shakespearian mottoes suitable to the occasion."[42] Two other clubs in different parts of the country had similar practices that same year. The Round Table Club of Quincy, Illinois, began each meeting with "Class quotations," and members of the Avon Club of Concord, New Hampshire, "exercised" their memories by reciting quotations, which they collected in a colloquy for Shakespeare's birthday, "deemed worthy of being loaned to a club in another city, to be used at a similar gathering."[43] Many clubs likely experienced scenarios related to memorization like the one in the Woodland, California, Shakespeare Club, where "discussion went on freely. Often a member might be reminded of a similar passage in another play and would quote from memory."[44]

The process of memorizing lines from Shakespeare is perhaps more important than it might seem at first. In *Metaphors of Memory: A History of Ideas about the Mind*, Douwe Draaisma remarks, "Remembering is precisely reliving something, *plus* the consciousness that the experience can be located in one's personal past."[45] The process by which women readers memorialized Shakespeare was extensive, as I suggest in a number of places throughout this book—in public libraries, monuments, gardens, scholarships, and other civic projects that kept Shakespeare alive in popular memory.[46] For the individual readers who memorized Shakespeare, this process had additional personal significance. As Louis B. Wright comments, "Memorizing and reciting the jewels of Shakespeare became an evidence of culture [in America]. This manifestation was not academically inspired but developed directly from folk interest."[47] Memorizing Shakespeare was a subtle but pervasive way of keeping Shakespeare a vibrant part of cultural knowledge and, importantly, claiming Shakespeare as part of American culture.

Communal Reading

One of the most influential features of Shakespeare clubs is the fact that they brought together women (and often men) to form a community where reading, discussion, and other social interactions took place around the nexus of Shakespeare. Evidence of communal reading practices suggests that they varied from informal group readings of scenes with ad hoc casting on the spot to roles assigned and prepared in advance, with members responsible for every word in their assigned parts.[48] Reading aloud often shifted or merged into performance—sometimes just among club members, sometimes as a public charity event or part of an annual celebration (often for Shakespeare's birthday in April). Because many Shakespeare clubs were involved in civic activities, the repercussions of their reading practices extended the ideologies associated with Shakespeare into public life.

Although Shakespeare clubs involved communities of readers, this involvement did not mean that particular interpretations were necessarily imposed on club members, and I have found no evidence of members being chastised for dissenting opinions.[49] In fact, most clubs documented the communal structure as one that encouraged debate, dissent, and often argument, terms that frequently recur in club records, such as those of the Hathaway Shakespeare Club of Philadelphia, which in 1929 described a typical format in which "members interpret scenes from the plays, or offer papers, discussions, debates."[50] A similar example of club debate comes from the twenty women in the Zetetic Club of rural Weeping Water, Nebraska, who recorded in their minutes an "animated and interesting discussion" of *Othello* at their 1898 meeting on Shakespeare's birthday.[51] Potential for discussion also led to the choice of Shakespeare as reading material for the women in the Woodland, California, Shakespeare Club, who attested that "from the outset, Shakespeare, as something dynamic, inexhaustible, and 'worth while' was chosen for work. . . . The reading was interspersed with comments and excited discussions. There was no limit as to the time spent on any suggestive point or passage; often six or seven weeks would be occupied in the study of one play." The club historian noted that "each member had studied the work under consideration, and so was prepared for the very lively discussion which followed."[52] Numerous club records indicate that readers expected Shakespeare to engender debate and discussion rather than passive reading.

The terms "fierce debate," "argument," and even "heated discussion" recur throughout various club descriptions of their communal reading practices.[53] Many of the topics women prepared for their meetings were posed as questions or debates for them to address. This format was conducive to members developing their own interpretations, expressing their viewpoints, and practicing their rhetorical and argumentative skills. The journal *Shakespeariana* also encouraged readers to read actively and voice their opinions frequently: "agreement and opposition both will have their use in giving you new light and fresh suggestions. Discuss it as freely with others as you can. Let not the tongue-tied spirit of man hamper you, and never decline your turn in the conversation. Never think you have not facts enough to the purpose, others have no better than you have and your book furnishes. Dare to speak as you feel and you will find not only that you have unlocked hidden stores of your own but of your author's and of other peoples, and the inspiration of conversation may begin for you in your club."[54] Thus reading Shakespeare was not the only goal; conversation, discussion, and debate were equally as important. The Quincy, Illinois, Shakespeare Class printed its study outline for *Julius Caesar* in the 1885 volume of *Shakespeariana* as a sample for other clubs to follow. It listed nearly thirty questions, such as "Does Shakespeare's Brutus agree wholly with the Brutus of history?" "Are such differences due to ideal truthfulness and unity of dramatic effect?" and "Why does the poet introduce Portia and Lucius?"; and it included a suggested paper, "Portia and the Condition of Woman in Rome."[55] Additional evidence from the journal shows that many clubs were following suit.

The meeting format of debate and discussion often extended to topics other than Shakespeare. The Kettledrum of Tuscaloosa, Alabama (founded 1889), composed of thirty married women, studied Shakespeare as well as a progressive agenda of women's issues. In addition to Shakespeare, they included an evening "reversing the commonly accepted order of classification, woman, and then man"; "on the latter subject Mrs. Belle R. Harrison read a spicy article," which unfortunately is not described in any further detail. Mrs. Harrison's article was provocative, and the club's report notes that in subsequent meetings, "debates, occasioned perhaps by the discussion of these subjects, next amused and enlivened the club." Some of the questions debated were "Should Women Vote?" "Elizabeth Justifiable in Signing the Death Warrant of Mary Queen of Scots?" "Is Deception Necessary in Society?" "Would the Emigration of the Negro be Beneficial to the South?" "Are There as Good Fish in the Sea as Have Been Caught Out?" and "Is Marriage a Failure?"[56] Of course, the Kettledrum records do not contain details about members' reactions to such debates, but they nevertheless brought Alabama women into contact with the latest issues of their day.

Group reading took a number of forms, including emphasis on rhetorical skills, on dramatic ability, and even on the sheer enjoyment of reading Shakespeare. The Rufus Adams Shakespeare Class of Philadelphia had a clever way of maintaining its focus on rhetorical reading and recitation; men and women were provisionally admitted "on a two weeks' test of their ability as readers," and the group assigned two critics per meeting in the 1880s, one for orthoepy (pronunciation) and one for "gestures."[57] In contrast, women in the Lebanon, Missouri, Shakespeare Club noted in 1865 that in their meetings, "pronunciation is closely criticised, but we devote no time to elocution."[58] The men and women of the Plainfield, New Jersey, Shakespeare Club also protested against ostentatiously proficient readers, decreeing that they were "not a learned society or literary club; they simply liked to read Shakespeare aloud." Their handwritten rules from 1909 playfully observed that "accomplished and experienced readers are debarred from membership. They would create a discord in the placid harmony of the club." Club rules also prohibited any overly dramatic reading, warning that "anyone attempting to change the usual tone of his voice while reading or to put any expression with the part shall be warned at the first offense, and when repetition of the same he shall be expelled from membership. If artistic readings were allowed, the club would soon degenerate to the low level of professional actors."[59]

One of the most common club formats was a combination of reading and on-the-spot literary analysis and explication, which allowed for club members to further demonstrate their expertise. The Locke Richardson Shakespeare Class of Oakland, California, followed a typical format; they read only one scene per evening in the 1880s, with two goals: "a firm basis of knowledge of the play itself in all the features of its embodiment—historical, textual, and linguistic" and "a knowledge of its art, its purpose, and its power." The group paused mid-scene for "a general interchange of question and answer, comment, criticism, and suggestion, the discussion thus started, often widening in its scope till it touches the deeper questions of soul and of art."[60] For this club, communal reading practices reinforced an emphasis on understanding the language and the period history. By allocating meeting time for discussion, it induced readers to approach Shakespeare not passively but rather with a spirit of inquiry involving "question and answer, comment, criticism, and suggestion." Members were also encouraged to use Shakespeare as inspiration for reflection on larger philosophical questions—"deeper questions of soul and of art." While the records do not offer details about these discussions, it is clear that the club's meeting structure encouraged interpretive and analytical discussion as well as venturing beyond the Shakespeare·play itself to whatever "deeper questions" might arise.[61]

Literary Analysis and Personal Accomplishment

Like the Locke Richardson group, most clubs engaged in some form of literary analysis in their meetings. Often clubs appointed a "Critic" who was responsible for leading the analysis. The twenty-three ladies in the Shakespeare Club of West Philadelphia, for example, met each week in the late 1880s for two hours. Every play had an appointed "Critic" who asked each woman at the end of a scene to explain any obscure passages or allusions.[62] The women in the Lebanon, Missouri, Shakespeare Club reported to *Shakespeariana* in 1885 that they also used a "Critic," a member who focused on "language and sentiment," making sure that "every reference to mythology, science, botany, and historical events is carefully investigated, not neglecting the geography of all places mentioned."[63]

In order to carry out such a thorough analysis, many clubs provided substantial guidelines for members to use in preparing their Shakespeare studies. An

1888 program from the Shakespeariana Club of Grand Rapids, Michigan, listed an elaborate "Method of Study":

> Reading of the Drama. Study the questions upon the play. Note carefully the year in which the action is laid; among what people, their manners, customs, dress and their temperment [sic]. Group the several characters, and find out his or her prominent virtue, vice, or passion. Review for mythological, classical and scriptural allusions. Commit to memory the most note-worthy thoughts contained in the play. Study the speeches of the characters grouped around the prominent character. Look to the filling in of detail the niceties of inflection and gesture.

In addition to prescribing how to read Shakespeare, the program listed reference books to use, including the journal *Shakespeariana*.[64] The list of tasks in the "Method of Study" entails a significant engagement with Shakespeare's texts, not just a casual reading.

Other clubs kept track of members' analytical skills through quizzes or other evaluations. When they had completed a play, members of the Locke Richardson Shakespeare Class took a quiz for "reinforcing and strengthening the individual hold upon all the points developed during the study of the play."[65] A sample quiz on *The Tempest* submitted in 1888 by the club president to *Shakespeariana* included more than fifty questions on the text, grammar, and diction; the date; the relationship to other plays; the characters; the machinery and action of the play; and literary criticism, ending with the question, "Sum up the deep and abiding effect of *The Tempest*."[66] Likewise, the women in the Shakespeare Society of Seneca Falls, New York, did not just read; they were required to answer in 1887 what they described as "an exhaustive list of questions" after finishing each play.[67] The San Francisco Shakespeare Class had an equally rigorous method; when members completed a play, they had to identify three quotations and provide an analysis of a character, "either from memory or from written notes," an assignment given at the start of their study so that each reader could be "on the look-out" for her designated character while reading. The leader, Miss Easton, reported in 1886 that these in-depth reading practices produced "animated discussions" about each play and prompted women to articulate their opinions and defend their views.[68]

This type of intensive study had a deep impact on numerous women, many of whom attested to the personal value of Shakespeare studies in their lives. In her presidential address in 1892, Loraine Immen Pratt, of the Shakespeariana Club of Grand Rapids, Michigan, reflected on the benefit of Shakespeare to club women: "aside from the intellectual pleasure that we have received," she pondered, "what lasting benefit has the five years of study of some of Shakespeare's dramas been to us? Are we better prepared to cope with life in all its various moral struggles, to choose the good, the true from the bad, the false? Have we broader love, more charity for humanity?" In answer to her questions, Immen commented on how Shakespeare's plays had a direct relation to the lives of her fellow club members: "How many pleasant hours were spent with the comedy of the 'Merchant of Venice,' discussing the relation of man to property; Portia's belief that 'mercy should season justice;' Antonio's friendship for Bassanio." After reading *King Lear*, she noted that "whenever our eyes fall upon an aged person whether kith or kin, we shall recall Cordelia's filial love and well-performed duty." Immen found that her reading and analysis of Shakespeare with a female community had a life-changing effect on her: "For five long years we have studied together these wonderful creations of Shakespeare and consciously or unconsciously have also been studying each other and I trust that a pure and abiding friendship has been formed thereby. . . . The remembrance of the precious words of friendship have brightened my pathway and banished many a cloud of sorrow that has for the moment appeared upon the horizon of my life."[69] Other women left similar testimonies. In 1885, the women in the Lebanon, Missouri, Shakespeare Club attested to the value of their Shakespeare study: "We think we have been greatly benefited in many ways. A multitude of thoughts and subjects have been opened out before us, and our memories strengthened, so that we may not go down to the grave forgetting everything but our past youth."[70] Reading, studying, and analyzing Shakespeare had significance for women beyond the intellectual work itself—these literate practices forged connections between women and gave them a sense of lifelong personal accomplishment.

Booktalk

Recent work on readers has underlined the significance of "booktalk" as a literate practice: the idea that "meanings emerge in conversations about books and about literature in different contexts."[71] The records of numerous Shakespeare clubs show that significant time was spent on (and allotted to) booktalk and more extended sociability, and that these oral dimensions made an important contribution to members and to their social connections.

In setting up their club in the 1880s, the women of the Stratford Club of Concord, New Hampshire, made sure that "plenty of time is given for discussion, not only of the text itself, but of those matters of history, ethics, the stage—in short, those thousand and one things which the page of Shakespeare cannot fail to suggest to the open mind."[72] Many other clubs used Shakespeare as a springboard for discussing such topics as politics and current events. The two dozen or so husbands and wives in the Plainfield, New Jersey, Shakespeare Club noted that their object was both to read Shakespeare and "to afford a convenient excuse . . . for a free discussion of the affairs of the universe, and especially of our own neighbors."[73] The women of the Barnesville, Georgia, Woman's Shakespearean Club emphasized the benefits of study and community in their club in 1896: "There is a temptation to tell of the many social features attached to these sessions and of the charming hospitality that we have enjoyed. But pleasure has not been the sole end attained. There has been solid work and earnest study."[74] The minutes of the Shakespeare Club of Clinton, Missouri, note that this midwestern group kept up with current events in Shakespeare studies; in 1892, after studying *King John*, Mrs. Collins gave "a short account of the purchase of Anne Hathaway's cottage" and "several of the members gave some interesting current events."[75]

Co-ed groups in particular saw the value of including social activities as a way to extend their literary discussions, and in the process they helped secure Shakespeare's place as a form of educational entertainment. Through reading and study of Shakespeare, club members helped solidify their personal connections in their communities. The men and women in the Des Moines Shakespeare Society, for example, had a formal dinner before their evening study program, and they noted in 1929 that "with truly Shakespearean friendliness the meetings are open to non-members who are interested."[76] The co-ed Shakespeare Club of Kearney, Nebraska, engaged in extensive socializing in connection with Shakespeare; club meetings were often hosted by Judge Hostetler and his wife, who served elaborate dinners with unusual delicacies, followed by cigars for the men. Afterward they met in the living room to read Shakespeare: "All present, including guests, participated, with the judge directing the reading."[77] The 21 May 1892 handwritten minutes of the Shakespeare Club of Clinton, Missouri, noted that after the members had finished their Shakespeare study, "Miss [Kate] McLane then invited the ladies into another room, and seated them at invitingly spread tables. Refreshments, such as would almost have made Falstaff turn over in his grave were served. The capon would have delighted his soul," though the secretary made sure to note that the women were "not such gluttons as he."[78]

Likewise, the Shakespeare Club of Brooklyn, New York, involved both men and women in reading Shakespeare and extensive socializing. Bimonthly meetings on Friday evenings entailed reading Shakespeare and discussion of issues related to the play as well as current events, such as the personal conduct of General Grant and the charge of drunkenness, causes of the Civil War, democracy, medicine, and elocution, all recorded in extensive minutes.[79] Often this co-ed club partook of elaborate dinners following their reading. For instance, in November 1901, the secretary recorded that after reading two acts of *Antony and Cleopatra,* "we feasted upon scalloped oysters and various other good things. The only thing we are sorry about . . . is that we cannot eat the *china,* too, it is so pretty."[80] Lest we dismiss such groups as simply supper clubs, it is important to point out Shakespeare's place in the scheme of leisure activities and the process by which combining study of Shakespeare with sociability made him a commonplace of civic life for club members and created a sense of social cohesion. This type of community building and cultural formation was particularly important in rural areas of the country, as we see in Chapter 3.

The men and women in the Plainfield, New Jersey, Shakespeare Club even tried to separate their study of Shakespeare from their social components; they humorously noted in their rules for 1909, "Anyone guilty of discussing a play of Shakespeare after the reading is finished shall be fined five dollars—the fines to go toward the annual picnic." The club had meetings in members' houses, ending with a candlelight dessert reception, and the gastronomic details of each meeting are dutifully chronicled in the club minutes: "If only one type of cake was offered or ice cream was not, it was noted in the meeting minutes without fail." The appeal of Shakespeare and sociability was undeniable, and according to the club history, members often lingered at meetings until after midnight: "Meetings ran from 8pm to 11pm; sometimes ending closer to the proverbial witching hour if conversation was more lively than usual (or the hostess included brownies on the menu)."[81]

Despite the pleasures of such sociability, the author of "Shakespeare Societies of America: Their Methods and Work," published in *Shakespeariana* in 1885, warned about the dangers of too much socializing and too little Shakespeare, contending that Shakespeare societies flourished better in small towns because clubs in large cities "have a fashion of gradually drifting into dining societies, while in the country, the absence of a first-class caterer prevents all such deviation from the path of duty."[82] Many clubs seemed to heed this warning; the Locke Richardson Class of Oakland, California, was among the most stringent. According to its 1887 account, there were "no refreshments, no stated dues, almost no running expenses" except a dime fine for tardiness to help finance its small library. The Shakespeare Club of Union, South Carolina, also prohibited any kind of refreshment and maintained its focus on Shakespeare and "united love of study—not so much as a cup of tea or any social feature" was permitted.[83] For its seventy-three years, the Woodland, California, Shakespeare Club "followed the Spartan custom of not serving refreshments, on the traditional concept that the meetings should be devoted entirely to study," but in 1959 it capitulated by allowing "a simple cup of tea" at the end of each program "to encourage sociability and discussion."[84] The Worcester, Massachusetts, Shakespeare Club also gradually grew to appreciate the combination of study and pleasure, and it gravitated toward more amenities for meetings. Beginning with only water, the club later voted to offer lemonade and wafers. At the final meeting of their third year (in 1890), members agreed to provide "a more festive air by serving ice cream, the prospect of which attracted some of the gilded youth for whom Shakespeare had proven an insufficient lure."[85]

In her 1908 retrospective, Lorraine Immen, of the Shakespeariana Club of Grand Rapids, Michigan, captured the importance of booktalk and sociability in addition to reading Shakespeare. She wrote that now that she had read nearly all the plays and poems of Shakespeare with her club over twenty-one years, "the thought comes, Did we choose our subject wisely? Including all the social life, the loving friendships formed, the self-development that comes from united study of any subject, and the many passages fraught with treasures of knowledge, that we have made our own, I say unqualifiedly—Yes!"[86] It was not just reading Shakespeare that led to the liberating opportunities of these groups. Rather, it was the combination of social life, friendship, self-development, and study inspired by a common connection to Shakespeare.

Talking Back to Shakespeare: Challenges, Revisions, and Appropriations

Most Shakespeare clubs followed some version of the reading and study practices I outlined above: assigning a Shakespeare play to be read at home before the meeting, memorizing passages, reading aloud during the meeting, engaging in literary analysis and discussion about the text at hand, and venturing into related topics for discussion and extended sociability. We can gain further insight into the complex relationship between women and reading Shakespeare by examining the many ways that women readers could "talk back to" Shakespeare and thus participate in the history of women adapting Shakespeare according to their needs.[87] As a number of examples show, women participated in what Julie Sanders describes as "a parallel process of textual takeover and adaptation" in which "Shakespeare is not invoked simply as an authenticating male canonical presence . . . but, rather, as a topos to be explored, dissected and reconfigured."[88] Women did not necessarily read Shakespeare as a reinforcement of traditional patriarchal values (though some women certainly did); instead, reading Shakespeare could facilitate collective and individual engagement with issues of gender, marriage, sexuality, social structure, and the place of women in society and in the family.[89]

One opportunity afforded by Shakespeare as opposed to most other reading or study material is the opportunity for performance, which according to one description "at once encouraged community and individuality" and demanded "a more creative kind of collective activity."[90] Through performance, adaptation, parody, and related modes of interaction, women did more than read Shakespeare passively; rather, they often responded proactively to Shakespeare as material for discussion, debate, and refiguring to suit their own needs and interests. Performative elements in clubs ranged from actual performances (as in the Peoria Shakespeare Class and the Fortnightly Shakespeare Club of New York) to readings of plays, sometimes with men and women (as in the Brooklyn Shakespeare Club) and sometimes just women (as in the Boston Saturday Morning Club).[91] Most often, Shakespeare was "performed" through a group reading in a private home, sans costumes or choreography. The degree to which women engaged in performance depended on the circumstances of the club, but just by virtue of reading a dramatic text, even in private, women could participate in the potentially liberating aspects of performance.[92]

A few examples illustrate the extent of the often innovative performance practices available to women. In 1888, the Nashville, Tennessee, Query Club engaged in a "Shakespeare masking" performance in which women chose a character to impersonate, and others had to guess the character; on the other side of the country, as late as 1954, the Shakespeare Club of Pomona, California, established an annual Character Day, for which each member dressed in "a Shakespearean costume and quoted a few lines from the plays."[93] The Shakespeare Study Club of Lima, Ohio (c. 1907), prided itself on amateur performances in which members not only performed and directed but also made their own costumes, sets, and armor.[94] Although the Woodland, California, Shakespeare Club did not initially set out to perform Shakespeare, the addition of a new member in the 1930s, Mrs. Helena Richardson Fitz, who had graduated from the Emerson School of Oratory, inspired women to perform Shakespeare. For Shakespeare's birthday luncheon one year, two members went so far as to present a skit of *Romeo and Juliet* "in Dutch dialect, which 'brought down the house.'"[95] Likewise, in 1930 the Shakespeare Study Club of Detroit put on "an original sketch" written by member Helen Chaffee Workman, "in which Shakespeare's famous women characters appeared" and performed it in honor of a Shakespeare Birthday lunch with the Toledo Shakespeare Club.[96]

One group clearly felt that performing Shakespeare was a gendered and private activity, suitable only for women to view. The Saturday Morning Club, "composed of leading society women" in the Boston area, performed Shakespeare in Copley Hall but restricted its performance to women only; when members put on an all-female production of *The Winter's Tale* in 1895, they were adamant that "no men need apply" even in the audience, and "any presumptuous male who had the temerity to ask for admission was promptly denied."[97]

The substantial effects that performance could have on women are captured by an account of the Shakespeare division of the Peoria Women's Club, which performed a Shakespeare play annually on his birthday throughout the early years of the twentieth century.[98] In her handwritten account of the club, Frances A. Wittick recalled the effect of performing a cross-dressed role: "My mother and I each owned a pair of long black tights and these appeared in practically every play as a part of some actor's costume. They didn't always fit very well which added to the pleasure of the audience. . . . We felt very bold and daring when we appeared in tights, although of course there were never any men in the audience."[99]

The "bold" and "daring" response of Frances Wittick in Peoria is echoed by a 1902 account of a Montana club woman. Mrs. Charles Heisey was "a busy housewife" but was so determined to memorize Hermia's lines from *A Midsummer Night's Dream* that she pinned the lines to her sleeves to read while scrubbing her floor. When she demonstrated her part to the club's committee, she "got down on her knees and went at it, scrub brush keeping pace with her voice as it arose quoting Shakespeare: 'Never so weary, never so in woe, Bedabbled with dew and torn by briars, I can no further crawl, no further go. My legs can keep no pace with my desires.'" One fellow club member recalls Mrs. Heisey's motivation in getting the part of Hermia: "She just *had* to have that part, she said. Didn't Hermia have two lovers? How exciting for an over-worked housewife!"[100] The transformative potential of becoming Hermia for a brief period indicates what performance could signify to women readers around the fin de siècle: an activity that was "bold," "daring," and "exciting."[101]

As well as performing scenes from Shakespeare, many women wrote and performed adaptations. Anna Randall-Diehl, the president of the co-ed Fortnightly Shakespeare Club of New York, crafted her own "Shakespearean Comedy" in 1895, entitled *The Marriage of Falstaff*. In this imaginative amalgamation, set in "Castle Montague" in Hoboken, New Jersey, Falstaff "becomes a happy Benedict," accompanied by fellow characters Romeo ("the gracious host of Castle Montague"), a tamed Petruchio and a Kate who did not go to the "taming school," and a Juliet who "entertains Will Shakespeare's friends" and "flirts without a balcony." Although Randall-Diehl wrote a fairly conventional story by maintaining the marriage plots from Shakespeare, she nevertheless engaged in an important process of revision by imagining an untamed Kate and a more aggressive Juliet than she found in the original plays.[102]

Elsewhere in the United States, club women adapted Shakespeare's work and took ownership of his material. According to one member of the Eugene, Oregon, Shakespeare Club (founded 1909), the women "would read parts from different plays, and sometimes do parodies that one of us had written."[103] In the 1920s, Grace T. Stimpson, of the Germantown, Pennsylvania, Shakespeare Club, wrote a one-act comedy based on *Othello* for her group to present, titled "Drop the Handkerchief."[104] In Texas, the women in the Shakespeare Club of San Antonio regularly offered comical versions of Shakespeare at their annual Shakespeare dinner, often with topical political and social allusions. For the 1936 dinner, at the height of Roosevelt's New Deal "alphabet" agencies, one member wrote a spoof involving Portia:

To this august assemblage of my peers
From ancient courts of law and equity
To be Chief Justice for a single day
In cap and gown comes Portia, L.L.D.
It grieves me much that '36 A.D.
Should find the B.C. methods followed yet
And that the mighty court of U.S.A.
Deals not with law but with the alphabet.
The A.A.A. and N.R.A. are out
And other projects dear to F.D.R.
The H.O.L.C. and the F.H.A.
May join the limbo where the others are.

At a later Shakespeare dinner, the San Antonio club composed "The Shakespeare Times" with an editorial titled "Much Ado About Nothing" and Cleopatra as society editor.[105] For the combined 401st anniversary of Shakespeare's birth and the 75th anniversary of the club in 1965, the club continued its playful adaptation of Shakespeare by requiring members either to write something original about Shakespeare or to find a tribute to present.[106]

Sometimes women found ready-made skits parodying Shakespeare to suit their interests. In 1927, the women in the Plainfield, New Jersey, Shakespeare Club acted Mary Porter's farce *The Ladies Speak at Last*, a conversation among Juliet, Portia, Lady Macbeth, and Ophelia, all of whom complain about their husbands.[107] Juliet has to hide her reading from Romeo because "it makes him so angry to see me read a novel. He says that a woman's first duty in life should be to make her husband comfortable."[108] Lady Macbeth, in a Scottish accent, even condemns Shakespeare for using women as subjects in his plays, calling him "a pettifogging young scamp wha just gaes about poking his nose into people's most private affairs, finds out about them fra servants and sic-like, and writes all the dreadful stories he hears into juggles or plays."[109] When they discover that Shakespeare is observing them for dramatic material, the women band together to stop him from writing their stories:

PORTIA: Oh, the dreadful creature!
OPHELIA: O cursed spite!
JULIET: The designing villain!
PORTIA: What will he say about me?
OPHELIA: And me?
JULIET: And me?
ALL: What shall we do?
JULIET: Bribe him.

OPHELIA: Drown him.
PORTIA: Prosecute him.

Remaining true to their literary inclinations, they decide to write a letter to
Shakespeare, protesting that women are "far from being the defenceless and
helpless creatures that you appear to consider them, [and] are quite capable of
defending themselves to the last gasp. Nemo repente fuit turpissimus—you
will repent your temerity."[110] Using Shakespeare's heroines to defend women
appealed to more than one club; this skit was popular with several other groups
across the country, including the Woodland Shakespeare Club in California,
which performed it in 1913.

Other club women were inspired to use Shakespeare's material for adaptation.
In each issue of its journal *The American Shakespeare Magazine*, the Fortnightly
Shakespeare Club of New York, founded by Anna Randall-Diehl, printed
numerous parodies, spin-offs, and inspirations from Shakespeare written mainly
by women. For example, in 1895 "The Seven Ages of Woman: Shakespeare Up
to Date" was offered as a companion piece to the original speech in *As You Like
It* for "effective recitation":

All the world's a wardrobe,
And all the girls and women merely wearers.
They have their fashions and their fantasies,
And one she in her time wears many garments
Throughout her seven stages.

Last scene of all,
That ends the sex's Mode-swayed history,
Is second childishness and sheer oblivion
Of youth, taste, passion—all save love of dress.[111]

One could certainly wish for a more progressive depiction of women as having interests beyond fashion, yet the mostly female readership of the *American
Shakespeare Magazine* suggests that the 1895 author of this parody was poking
fun at a stereotype of women through her playful adaptation of a well-known
speech, which readers would have had to know in order to understand the
humor.

One of the most intriguing adaptations of Shakespeare is a one-act play
called "Shakespeare's Heroines in Club Life," written by Mrs. Will Madders
around 1902.[112] In this skit, Portia calls together eight of Shakespeare's
women to form a club. She begins by reading the proceedings of the General Federation of Women's Clubs meeting in 1901, remarking on "the
books and papers written by these brainy club women of the 20th century.
They write of learning, law, religion and the conduct of life. Ah, me! I fear

we Shakespeare women are all too simple to form a club." After the women gain enough confidence to form their club, they conclude their plan with a statement of gender equality taken from Tennyson's poem "The Princess": "The woman's cause is man's: ? They rise or sink / Together" and "Sit side by side."[113] Through these many creative endeavors of performance and adaptation, women readers across the country participated in what Marianne Novy describes as a "history in which many women have used Shakespeare to empower themselves."[114]

Shakespeare's Bawdy

Just as Shakespeare's texts offered opportunities for women to "talk back" to Shakespeare through performance and adaptation, the content of the poetry provided fodder for discussion of otherwise taboo topics. Numerous clubs followed comprehensive reading practices in which members were intent on knowing the meaning of every word and phrase. Given these in-depth reading practices and the notorious bawdy content of Shakespeare's texts, it is no surprise that Shakespeare's coarse humor could offer unusual opportunities for women readers.[115] Though such discussions are rarely recorded in club minutes or histories, a few examples survive to suggest the possibility for additional instances that were not formally documented. Bawdy humor allowed women to broach matters of sexuality and to venture into otherwise unacceptable topics of conversation, particularly in a co-ed environment.[116] Amateur Shakespearean scholar Joseph Crosby related two such incidents from meetings of the co-ed Shakespeare Club of Zanesville, Ohio, in 1878:

> Sometimes a funny circumstance occurs. Not long ago, while reading *Rich. II* (II, 1, 237), an unmarried lady, of some 30 or 32 summers, and one of the keenest, *knowingest*, sharpest, of the "club," was reading the line "Bereft and *gelded* of his patrimony." She read it, & then looking me right in the eye, asked, "Mr Crosby, what is 'gelded'?" Fortunately I never smiled or showed any embarrassment, but I just quietly said "O, it is an old Saxon word, meaning *deprived*." Now, I am well convinced that *she*, of all others (her name is Miss Emma Allen) *knew* just as well as I did what *gelded* meant; for she prides herself on her fine education, and powers of sarcasm & satire in conversation.

The ladies of Zanesville found an unexpected freedom when discussing Shakespeare and apparently enjoyed broaching risqué subjects couched as genuine interpretive questions. Crosby recounted a second such incident:

> Last night a married lady was reading the line in *Much Ado* (III, iii, 146), "like the shaven Hercules in the smirched, worm-eaten tapestry, where his

codpiece seems as massy as his club." She read it, & looked up with—"Mr Crosby, what is 'his codpiece'? is it his *head*?" But I was so busy explaining by a drawing I was trying to make of the watchman's *bills* of old times, that I did not hear her, i.e. she thought I did not, and I went on with my picture of the "bill," talking fast of the poet's quibbles on these *bills* and the *promissory notes* that "commodities" were "taken up" on; & she sensibly *forgot to repeat* her question.

It is especially important to note that Crosby had previously given his club explicit instructions to avoid such indelicate topics; he wrote, "I told the members at the beginning, that I had not enough of expurgated editions to go round; & if I had, they were not expurgated alike; so we use the regular full, best editions; and whenever a reader comes across a word or passage that she or he thinks too broad to be read out loud, they just quietly pass over it. I would not allow any *substitution* of more modern or presentable words to be read at all. *Aut Shakespeare, aut nullus.*"[117] The women in this club were clearly violating club protocol by raising taboo subjects under the guise of "interpreting Shakespeare." Such incidents would have allowed women to reach beyond the bounds of acceptable conversation while remaining within the safety net of studying Shakespeare.

Many clubs required members to be familiar with all the words, phrases, and meanings in their study of Shakespeare, so explications of bawdy passages were bound to have occurred more often than they are formally documented. Like the Shakespeare Club of West Philadelphia, which had a "Critic" assigned to explicate any obscurities, each member of the Shakespeare Club of Clinton, Missouri, founded in 1886, had to "explain all difficult passages which occur in the character about which she read."[118] Likewise, the women in the Woodland, California, Shakespeare Club often spent six or seven weeks on a play, covering "parallelisms, classical allusions, slang, fine passages for rhetoric, description or sentiment, obsolete words, the plot, history and climax of the drama."[119] Because they were explicating passages from Shakespeare, these clubs could safely venture into discussion of a "codpiece" or similarly risqué topics in their analysis of "slang" and "obscure words." Understandably, few of these discussions have survived in official club records, but any group that subjected Shakespeare's plays to such intense linguistic scrutiny must have either entertained discussions like the ones Crosby recorded in his private letters or deliberately noted the presence of such forbidden material, inadvertently calling attention to it by excluding it (as in Bowdler's edition). Some clubs even took pride in rejecting expurgated editions. Frances M. Abbott, a member of the Stratford Club of Concord, New Hampshire, remarked in 1887, "We put no trust in an expurgated edition. We read every word just as it is."[120]

The men and women of the Plainfield, New Jersey, Shakespeare Club poked fun at the lewd potential in Shakespeare, playfully joking in 1909 that club members were to read "selected and strictly expurgated works" and that "only safe plays should be read. The safest of all is *Julius Caesar* which should come before the club at least once a year." Further teasing members to engage with Shakespeare's bawdy language, they noted, "Anyone failing to [speak] in reading such words as hell, damn, strumpet, vile, or such lewd phrases and sentences as so often occur in Shakespeare, as well as in Holy Writ, shall be guilty of a misdemeanor."[121]

Shakespeare's Heroines and Women Readers

Just as the bawdy passages in the plays offered material for women to study and explicate, Shakespeare's heroines served as both role models and objects of critique for late nineteenth- and early twentieth-century American club women.[122] The women of the Barnesville, Georgia, Woman's Shakespearean Club recorded just such a range of reactions to Shakespeare's women in their first year of study (1896): "We have pitied poor Ophelia, felt a profound admiration for the true, womanly spirit of Portia, and dropped a sympathetic tear over the fate of the gentle Desdemona. Nor has the proud Lady McBeth [sic] been left alone. While not condoning the great crime which stained her 'little hands' with the blood of her king we have cast the mantle of charity over her and decided that she is not altogether as black as history and tradition have painted. Then we have indeed 'picked characters to pieces' but not as vultures to find only decay but rather to learn from them to better our own."[123] Learning from Shakespeare's characters was clearly a goal of self-betterment for this group. It is natural to suppose that many club discussions resembled that of the Woodland, California, Shakespeare Club, where characters were treated "as if they were real personages whose virtues were to be emulated, or their weaknesses decried."[124]

Perhaps the most progressive reaction to Shakespeare's heroines appears in an 1884 essay in the *Manhattan* magazine. Josephine Heard Cutter, the founder of the Worcester, Massachusetts, Shakespeare Club, argued that "women in Shakespeare's plays were the noteworthy characters; they provided the evidence that Shakespeare saw and admired the searching and subtle mental powers of women. These were the characters who could inspire women in the United States to cope with masculine minds, to dare to seek the vote, and even to aspire to the presidency itself."[125] While no evidence exists that Shakespeare prompted women to seek the presidency, other instances substantiate the important role Shakespeare's characters played for women readers.

Women club members such as Cutter were often motivated to express their support for Shakespeare's women or in turn to voice their dissatisfaction with their plight; such discussions led to debates about the status of contemporary women and their proper place in society.[126] A member of the Shakespeariana Club of Grand Rapids, Michigan, made just such a connection. She humorously remarked, "In the study of Portia's character we are expected to emulate, so far as possible, her mental qualities, but as there is nothing on record describing her state of mind when suffering with the toothache, they would not have that immediate and personal application to me I could wish this afternoon."[127] Shakespeare's material provoked a spectrum of responses, from adoration to vilification.

The Taming of the Shrew: A Test Case in Interpretation

Perhaps no character or situation in the canon rivals that of Katharine in *The Taming of the Shrew* for stirring emotions and eliciting responses from women.[128] An 1895 issue of the *Fortnightly Shakespeare* addresses this very subject, and the variety of reactions from club women gives us a cross-section of possible ripostes, which were circulated to readers of the magazine across the country. Petruchio was extolled by readers such as Mrs. C. B. Bishop, who submitted a poem in his honor, praising his "love" and "wisdom" in taming Katharine and recommending that his tactics "Might be happily copied / By husbands to-day." Other women added their support to Petruchio; Mary C. Morford viewed the play as "the old, old story of the redeeming influence of love." In the course of the play, Kate "learned what love means, notwithstanding all of Petruchio's mad-cap tricks and ways, and gradually she yielded to the divine passion. She was his wife, the magnetism of his personal presence began to work its charms, she began to think of some one else and their will instead of her own." For readers such as Morford, Kate was a selfish woman redeemed by the love of her husband.

In contrast, in the same issue of the journal, other women readers resisted this interpretation in favor of defending Kate. Nettie Arthur Brown described her as "a Shakespearian prophecy of the 'new woman,' irresistible, irrepressible, and not too easily tamed." After Kate is tamed, she becomes "so uninteresting that if the twentieth century girl should become so insipid, there would be many a Petruchio investing his substance in horsewhips, for the purpose of making her more spirited." Charlotte J. Bell's essay "Shakespeare's Women" proclaimed a similar dissatisfaction with Kate: "Did the woman ever live who would have yielded to her husband thus, unless he was a madman and she was obliged to humor him?" Bell even claimed to have "heard ladies say that they considered it an insult to be invited to see the performance of this play."[129] For some women readers, Shakespeare's Kate provided an acceptable outlet for voicing concerns about women's place in marriage and the relationship between husband and wife; these reactions were then circulated nationally, further extending the association between Shakespeare's material and women's issues.

The Taming of the Shrew was a touchpoint for women's expression in other contemporary publications as well. An 1895 issue of the conservative magazine *New York Truth* published a spoof of Kate titled "The Fin de Siècle Duel," in which "the New Woman is a Shakespearean shrew who needs taming."[130] The speaker criticizes women who "fight for a place in business," "fight for a chance to speak," "fight for the right to study / With men their Latin and Greek." The poem concludes:

> We laugh at your pert presumption,
> You dear, divine, little shrew!
> Yet every man among us
> Would like the taming of you.

The speaker boasts, "You may scold, and sneer, and scoff us, / You may play your Katherine's part," but claims "Petruchio is victor / If he but aim at your heart." Though presented through a male persona, the piece was signed by Ruth Hall.[131]

Perhaps due to the provocative reactions of the readers of its journal, the Fortnightly Shakespeare Club chose this play for one of its annual performances. An 1895 account in the journal reported, "'The Taming of the Shrew' was recently acted by members of the Fortnightly Shakespeare Club, at Maspeth, Long Island, for the benefit of the Home for Blind Women."[132] The husband of club president Anna Randall-Diehl played Petruchio in the production; one wonders what sort of exchange occurred between the aggressive and independent-minded Diehl (president of her club, editor of her journal, public speaker, and advocate for women's rights) and her husband (playing a shrew-taming character), but the club records provide no details.

Portia: The Ideal

Like Kate in *The Taming of the Shrew*, Portia from *The Merchant of Venice* elicited both praise and condemnation. Shakespeare's famous heroine was often lauded as an example for progressive nineteenth-century women, and several clubs were named after her.[133] The women in Payette, Idaho, a rural town on the Oregon border, chose "Portia" as the name for the club they founded in 1895, aiming "to improve themselves culturally by reading good books and plays."[134] The fifteen women in the Portia Reading Group of Brooklyn, founded in 1879, clearly voiced their support for this character; Portia clubs also existed in San Diego; Topeka, Kansas; and Avon, Illinois.[135] Not surprisingly, no club took on the name of Lady Macbeth, though several adopted Anne Hathaway and Mary Arden for club names.[136]

Portia also served as the inspiration for a paper read in 1890 at the board meeting of the State Federation of Literary Clubs by Mrs. Lauch Maclaurin, a member of the Shakespeare Club of Dallas.[137] Maclaurin titled her talk "The Woman Whom Shakespeare Did Not Contemplate," and she used Portia as

FIGURE 2. A number of Shakespeare clubs were named after Anne Hathaway, Shakespeare's wife. Here the Anne Hathaway and West Philadelphia Shakespeare Clubs commemorate the 314th anniversary of Shakespeare's death, April 24, 1930. Photo courtesy of the Free Library of Philadelphia, Print and Picture Collection.

an example of Shakespeare's neglect of businesswomen in his plays. Maclaurin criticized Portia for not earning the money that attracted her suitors, for inheriting Belmont from her father and not purchasing it herself, and for not being independent in her choice of a husband. Criticism of Shakespeare's female character thus led to Maclaurin's discussion of the virtues of a businesswoman: practicality, thoroughness, common sense, and sagacity. Maclaurin lamented the position of Shakespeare's comic heroines: "Alas, poor girls! There was no business for them but love-making, and no bargain but the 'world without end' bargain."[138] For Maclaurin and her audience, Portia was admirable because she is "a beautiful, clever, kind lady of quality," but she lacks the progressive qualities of the businesswoman. Here Shakespeare's comic heroine provided a way to convey an alternative opportunity for women outside the domestic sphere, couched within the confines of "Shakespeare criticism" and identified with a progressive agenda.

Shakespeare's heroines could also serve more underhanded agendas. In a lecture given before the Twentieth-Century Woman's Club in 1897, Priscilla Leonard seemed to challenge the adulation of Shakespeare's women in her talk, "The Mistaken Vocation of Shakespeare's Heroines." She introduced her subject as "one which women alone can fully appreciate" and announced her position as a "loud and convincing protest from the progressive Womanhood of this new era against Shakespeare's attitude with respect to his heroines." Leonard then accused Shakespeare of "criminal injustice in placing his heroines in every play at a disadvantage." She aimed to prove that "the whole structure of Shakespeare's dramas rests upon the disfranchisement of those heroines whom he is falsely supposed to idealize." After describing the unfavorable situations for Shakespeare's heroines, Leonard urged her audience to see Shakespeare as "well-meaning, but inadequate—blind to the true powers of Woman and the illimitable wideness of her sphere." Leonard recounted that "here the lecture concluded amid continued feminine applause, and cries of 'Down with Shakespeare!'"[139]

Leonard's use of Shakespeare becomes more complex when we consider that Priscilla Leonard was a pseudonym for Emily Bissell, a prominent Delaware anti-suffragette who started the practice of Christmas Seals in America. Her anti-Shakespearean rhetoric was actually a pose for her anti-suffragette views; Bissell constructed a fake denouncement of Shakespeare to encourage her audience to defend Shakespeare and to endorse a more conservative view of women.[140] Bissell was not the only one who took a conservative approach to Shakespeare; the women in the Saturday Shakespeare Club of Greensboro, Alabama, took great pains to note in 1895 that "there are none of us 'new women' in the accepted meaning of that term," using Patroclus's lines from *Troilus and Cressida* as support: "We have learned from our Master that, 'A woman impudent and mannish grown / Is not more loathed than an effeminate man / In time of action.'"[141]

Records from other Shakespeare clubs would no doubt further underline the complex reactions women readers had to Shakespeare's texts. Whether they saw in Shakespeare matter to emulate or to critique, Shakespeare offered abundant opportunities for women to "talk back," individually and collectively. Through the solitary reading in preparation for club meetings, women could establish intellectual space in their homes (as the next chapter discusses in greater detail). At club meetings, communal reading allowed women to practice speaking in front of others and to express their ideas and interpretations through debates and discussions. Researching and writing essays brought women into contact with a developing scholarly world of Shakespeare studies and inspired them to react to issues in the plays and in the scholarship. Booktalk was crucial for developing speaking skills but also for community building and for intellectual and social discussion. Performance provided some club women the chance to step out of their domestic roles and experiment with gender and identity in daring ways. Adapting and parodying Shakespeare offered them further opportunities to craft personal responses and reactions around the nexus of Shakespeare and women's issues.

Coda: Shakespeare and Reading Initiatives

In addition to the numerous individual and collective benefits discussed so far in this chapter, reading Shakespeare inspired women to publicly promote literacy in their communities. The work of women readers of Shakespeare in founding public libraries is one of their most enduring contributions: numerous libraries across America were founded by Shakespeare clubs, constituting a more permanent statement of their investment in learning, social progress, and Shakespeare. Their determination to establish community libraries embodied their values of "remembering the past and embracing the future," channeled through Shakespeare.[142]

Paula D. Watson has recently rewritten the history of public libraries to include the significant role women's clubs played in their development.[143] What has not been uncovered, however, is the fact that many of these clubs were Shakespeare clubs: Shakespeare reading groups were influential at almost every level of public library development. Many Shakespeare clubs used their own collections to secure Shakespeare's works and criticism as the bedrock of community libraries. Club members raised money for library buildings, helped acquire Carnegie funding for libraries, and often served as librarians. In a 1904 essay, a trustee of the Owatonna, Minnesota, Public Library underlined the communal importance of libraries: "a library is not merely a storehouse for books; it may be a live force and power in the community."[144] According to one author in 1907, libraries were also public spaces where ideas were circulated: "The end and aim of a public library has been said to be the dissemination of ideas among men; but judging from the clubs which gather under our roof, this library will cause a dissemination of ideas among women."[145] Many Shakespeare clubs were involved in this process of disseminating ideas, thereby placing Shakespeare at the developing fore of community education, culture, and ideas.

A summary of representative Shakespeare clubs across the country involved in libraries illustrates the degree to which these groups permeated the development of libraries.[146] In the Northeast, the Shakespeare Club of Lyndon, Vermont, joined three other clubs in the late 1890s to contribute money to the town library, which was housed in a store, with 3,835 books available three afternoons and two evenings a week.[147] In Concord, New Hampshire, the work of the numerous Shakespeare clubs was commemorated by a Shakespeare Room in the Fowler Public Library for use by any club that read Shakespeare.[148] Citizens of Concord took full advantage of the Shakespeare resources; the librarian remarked in 1901, "We try to stretch the Shakespeare material to go around among the ten clubs which bear his name."[149]

In the Midwest, the Shakespeare Club of St. Marys, Ohio, began its public library in 1921 "for the purpose of supplying correct reading matter to our boys and girls," and members served as the first librarians.[150] The Shakespeare Club of Celina, Ohio, held a public lecture series to raise money for a "Shakespeare Public Library" run entirely by club members, who donated reference books and acted as librarians.[151] The Shakespeare Round Table Club of Bowling Green, Ohio, worked to establish a public library in its town through bake sales, socials, teas, and other events. In 1914, the club led the effort to rent two rooms in the Exchange Bank building as the first subscription library, which eventually grew into the Bowling Green Public Library.[152] The club also established a school district library based on its own collection.[153] In Illinois, the women of the Mt. Vernon Shakespeare Club opened a circulating library in a local department store in 1895, and in 1899 they offered to the city "our books, our bookcases and the use of our club room as a library, free of rent, provided we may select the majority of the directors of the Public Library."[154]

On the western frontier, Shakespeare club women were equally industrious in their library initiatives.[155] The women of the Shakespeare Club in rural Hot Springs, South Dakota, organized the city library in 1898.[156] In Payette, Idaho, the Shakespeare Club began a library with books from the homes of members, followed by a mailing of "five hundred hand-written postcards . . . sent out by members requesting donations of books."[157] The Shakespeare Club of Eugene, Oregon, began in 1922 to buy books for a Shakespeare shelf in the city library.[158]

In the South, numerous Shakespeare clubs helped establish public libraries, including those in Conway, Arkansas; West Palm Beach, Florida; and Lebanon, Missouri.[159] The Barnesville, Georgia, Woman's Shakespearean Club had a particularly industrious library plan; members gave a series of lectures and entertainments to help establish a Shakespeare reference library for "students of all ages and both sexes." The club history relates, "Who of you in this assembly of professional men and women who like to look deep into all things has not felt the need of books of reference that your individual collection does not contain? How often when any special theme is under consideration upon which all the light of history and research is needed are we compelled to send away for books or be deprived of the needed information. Realizing this necessity the Shakespearean club proposes to establish a grand reference library to which all students can have access." Shakespeare, of course, was the bedrock of this collection; the club added that "as a nucleus for this we have twenty volumes of notes on Shakespeare." The club's goal was twofold, to meet the present needs of its community but also to serve posterity: "Mindful of the lack of this great advantage in our own youth we desire to prepare better opportunities for our children."[160]

In Texas, a member of the Lancaster Shakespeare Club served for twenty-six years as the librarian for the Lancaster Public Library, which operated for seventeen years on Tuesday afternoons from a room in a bank building.[161] In Denton, the Junior Shakespeare Club lobbied for a public library and went door-to-door to collect more than four thousand books for the library collection.[162] The DeLeon, Texas, Public Library was started in the home of a member of the DeLeon Shakespeare Club with a few donated books. According to the club history, "the heart of the Club has always been the Library," and women were remarkably creative in raising money for books: "the projects were book reviews, Halloween carnivals, white elephant sales, Jr.-Sr. banquets and each year a booth at the Fair selling watermelon slices."[163]

One of the most compelling examples of club women's efforts to both preserve Shakespeare and secure his future cultural value comes from the Dallas Shakespeare Club. Member Bobbie Cullum purchased a Shakespeare First Folio to donate to the Dallas Public Library in honor of the club's 100th anniversary in 1986. Cullum had the Folio restored by the Folger Shakespeare Library staff, and then she paid for a Brinks truck to transport it to Dallas, where it now resides in a special case in the Dallas Public Library, appropriately placed near the broadside copy of the *Declaration of Independence* for all visitors to view.[164]

Conclusion

The participation of Shakespeare clubs at almost every level of the development of public libraries across America had a significant influence on countless communities and created lasting associations among Shakespeare, literacy, public education, and civic improvement. The ramifications of these women's public literacy activities were significant. As Anne Firor Scott points out, "It was not a very big jump from founding small local libraries to lobbying in the legislature for library commissions and supporting taxes for public libraries."[165] The women of the Flatonia, Texas, Shakespeare Club, for example, began by donating books to form a library, but they soon became involved in other civic issues; they "influenced the city council to pass a law prohibiting expectorating on sidewalks and in public buildings; bought garbage cans for the city, and had the school children sign a pledge promising to throw all scraps and fruit peelings in the garbage cans."[166]

At the end of her article on women's clubs and the formation of public libraries, Watson discusses the possible motivations behind club women's support of libraries, ranging from "the triumph of conventional values" to "truly improving the quality of life of others less fortunate than themselves."[167] For the Shakespeare clubs involved in public libraries, I would add that some of the reading strategies discussed in this chapter may have persuaded them to encourage other readers of Shakespeare, and that a correlation existed between their personal and collective reading experiences and their desire to share those experiences beyond the bounds of their homes. The next two chapters consider the influence of these women readers, first in domestic life and then beyond to nearly every corner of nearly every state.

 CHAPTER 2

The Home

A late nineteenth-century account of the Shake-
speare Class of Peoria, Illinois, includes the following anecdote about an amateur performance of *The Merry Wives of Windsor*: "Mrs. C. E. Nixon was
playing the part of the 'fat knight' and had her own interpretation of the scene.
She cut out the bottom of her laundry basket and when the proper time arrived
she draped herself in a sheet, stepped into the basket, took hold of the handles
and walked off the stage followed by the two servants. The director [a fellow
club member] was a little upset but the audience enjoyed it hugely."[1] The transformation of a typical domestic item, Maud Nixon's laundry basket, into a stage
prop for a transvestite role is emblematic of the transformative possibilities that
Shakespeare entailed for women in late nineteenth- and early twentieth-century
America. Rather than confine herself to her home to attend to domestic duties
(such as laundry), Maud Nixon was spending her time reading, studying, and
performing Shakespeare with a group of women.[2]

Many of the literate practices discussed in the previous chapter took place in
the home (e.g., the "homework").[3] In the late nineteenth and early twentieth
centuries, women's domestic life was undergoing a variety of challenges and
changes, and debates covered topics from women's suffrage to their domestic
responsibilities and moral and intellectual life.[4] As we shall see, Shakespeare
clubs affected home life by bringing women out of their homes, as numerous club women attest, but also by refashioning the home as an intellectual
space where women could carry out their household duties and engage in

intellectual development. In addition to reading, studying, and performing Shakespeare, many women co-opted a number of domestic practices, including cooking, sewing, and scrapbooking, as ways to domesticate Shakespeare and incorporate him into the labor of the household.[5]

Catharine Beecher's influential *Treatise on Domestic Economy,* first printed in 1841 and frequently reprinted for the next fifteen years, made a case for the domestic sphere as "central to the national life" because women were "agents in accomplishing the greatest work that ever was committed to human responsibility . . . the building of a glorious temple." Beecher made a claim for the importance of the home by arguing that "the American domestic experience could promote the national good"; women thus had an "obligation to spend every hour for some useful end," although in addition to household tasks, some time could be spent on what she called "intellectual improvement."[6]

The scientific homemaking movement of the early twentieth century also coincided with the growth of women's study of Shakespeare and often necessitated a delicate balance of housework and leisure. Scientific homemaking urged women to use their labor productively and efficiently and "treated the home as a factory and the homemaker as a worker and/or administrator."[7] One 1913 proponent of the "scientific management" of housekeeping even advocated that women's duties "be formulated and professionalized."[8] Likewise, C. W. Taber argued in 1918 that homemaking "is as much a business enterprise as is the running of a store or office, or as is the operation of a factory."[9] In fact, in the 1920s, the Bureau of Home Economics, of the Department of Agriculture, collected data on the time spent by women on various homemaking activities. Anna E. Richardson, a supporter of the movement, maintained that "not only is it worth while to know the total amount of time spent in home activities, but from the standpoint of administration it is desirable to learn how it is distributed."[10] Thus, much was at stake ideologically in the devotion of household time and labor to Shakespeare in a period when women's domestic roles were in flux.

But what were the practical realities involved for women to carry out intellectual work around the fin de siècle? If we think of the household as a "workplace," to use Wendy Wall's term, what did it mean that some of the "work" for women now included reading Shakespeare, memorizing lines, preparing parts to read, cooking food in honor of Shakespeare's birthday, compiling scrapbooks, and the like? What did it mean that for women, some of the household labor was now devoted to Shakespeare rather than to the family?[11]

Shakespeare often played a key role in establishing space in the household for women's intellectual life and in creating opportunities for women to develop skills beyond household tasks, such as writing, debating, public speaking, and performing, in the context of "an increasingly politicized domesticity."[12] Through such practices, Shakespeare played an important part in forms of "domestic feminism."[13] As one description of clubs in the Black Hills of South Dakota put it, "The old traditions, which commanded woman to keep silence and limited her activities to domestic life, have been banished long since by the spirit of self-culture and advancement."[14]

We have already seen in the previous two chapters how Shakespeare functioned as a form of alternative education for women. An address by lecturer (and later World War I reporter) Jessie Lozier Payne at a national women's club meeting in 1894 highlighted the importance of clubs as a form of education for women, specifically in a domestic context: "Through the club education is more widely diffused . . . and women in the homes are reached. Through the woman's club housekeepers have been brought into the current of affairs—women whose accomplishments have been buried under an avalanche of shirts and puddings. They have passed through a time of physical weakness, care, and bondage, and an infinite number of petty details, and been in danger of mental starvation. At the club they gain individuality."[15] Lozier identified the club as a crucial way to move women from the domestic realm into the public sphere, from domestic-centered "mental starvation" to a more public and civic-minded way of life. The women in the Silver Creek, New York, Shakespeare Club (founded 1889) noted just such a shift in their history: "The world was moving on, new agencies springing up on all sides, social service finding its place in the county and the Shakespeare Club was allied with these progressive movements. . . . It was no longer just a little local study club; it was a factor in the rapidly developing progress of the outside world."[16]

This chapter maps out the ways Shakespeare became part of American home life in the late nineteenth and early twentieth centuries through women's Shakespeare clubs. How did these clubs domesticate Shakespeare—how was he woven into the fabric of domestic life—and what were the results and repercussions? How did women incorporate reading and studying Shakespeare into their domestic routines, and how did Shakespeare become part of domestic life for these women? Lastly, how did reading, studying, and performing Shakespeare in turn bring women out of the home, through civic engagement, philanthropic work, and public activism?

Shakespeare in the American Home

Shakespeare became part of American home life in a variety of ways: through individual club members' reading and preparation and also through club meetings, which usually took place in members' homes, often once a week for several hours.[17] The 1898 pamphlet "How to Organize a Shakespeare Club" advocated using the home as a meeting space conducive to sociability: "A Shakespeare Club may meet regularly in the same place, in rooms especially provided for its use, or from week to week, at the houses of different members. . . . For new clubs, the plan of meeting from house to house is excellent and encourages a sociability and hospitality which should be a feature of the meetings. After the reading and study it may be found a pleasant custom to serve light refreshments."[18] Most clubs embraced this home-centered study system, which combined intellectual study of Shakespeare with a nontraditional academic setting (a home). In fact, many clubs seemed to take pride in transforming their homes into intellectual spaces, noting these details in their permanent records. The Thursday Literary Circle of Selma, Alabama, for example, recorded that it began in 1894 when "a dozen or more ladies met, by invitation, one pleasant winter afternoon in the parlors of a private residence."[19] The Shakespeare Club of Washington, Missouri, met that same year "with Mrs. Tibbe in the old family home with the windmill watertower."[20] Likewise, the Shakespeare Club of Pomona, California, organized in 1904, reported that fifty years later, "Meetings are still held in the charming homes of the members, and tea is served after the program."[21] Despite the pride that women took in opening their homes to academic work, however, domestic space had its limitations. The Stratford Club of Concord, New Hampshire, was restricted to sixteen members, "as that is about as many people as one parlor will comfortably accommodate when all want good light on their books."[22] Nevertheless, most clubs seemed to welcome Shakespeare's invasion into this contested domestic arena.

Shakespeare also occupied women in terms of their time and labor; club women were expected to keep up with a rigorous reading schedule and had to memorize passages, research and write papers, and often chronicle their club's activities in minutes, a printed program, or a scrapbook. These obligations allowed Shakespeare to further infiltrate the home life of club members, as women had to carry out club responsibilities alongside their other domestic tasks and to integrate reading and study of Shakespeare with their domestic responsibilities; one club actually used the term "home reading" for such activities.[23] The women in the Portia Club of Avon, Illinois, founded 1894, noted the effect of Shakespeare study on their home life: "each week was packed with assigned at home reading and study, and members were appointed to lead discussions on authors, locations, art and music of the time."[24] Members of the Shakespeariana Club of Grand Rapids, Michigan, codified their study practices by specifying a certain amount of time for members to spend on Shakespeare each day: "Every member must agree to take part and to give 15 minutes every day to the study of the play under consideration." Several accounts note the challenges for women in particular; one member of the Stratford Club of Concord, New Hampshire, pointed out that although the goals of her club were "making ourselves wiser and better," such objectives were a challenge when "twelve of the sixteen members are married and have household cares."[25] Miss L. B. Easton, who ran the San Francisco Shakespeare Class, pushed members to find time for intellectual work in spite of their domestic responsibilities. This class of a dozen women met once a week for two hours. After completing a play, each woman had to identify three quotations and provide an analysis of a character. In 1886, Miss Easton remarked on the difficulty for some members of adhering to this demanding schedule: "Married ladies have so many claims upon their time, material, domestic, and social, that one has to handle them very gingerly, in order to obtain any results whatever."[26] Not all clubs allowed women to default on their study commitments. Women in the Fenton, Michigan, Monday Evening Club were warned in 1896 that they would have to forfeit their membership for "failure to prepare a paper without notifying the committee."[27]

Finding a balance between home duties and intellectual work also preoccupied black activist Mary Church Terrell. In an 1894 issue of the black women's magazine *Woman's Era*, she recounted the reaction of one woman when hearing that her friend was studying literature: "What becomes of your house, your children and your sewing? I've neither chick nor child, and I haven't one minute to spare after the monotonous household affairs have been dispatched. From morning till night I am equipped with a kitchen utensil, a broom or a dust-cloth . . . by the time the little things have been attended to I am either too tired or too worried to study." The friend's response echoes the dictums of regulated time characteristic of scientific housekeeping, only with intellectual work added to her duties: "How I manage to save a few minutes for mental improvement is not difficult to explain . . . I systematize my work . . . it may [seem] a little like self-imposed servitude and self-tyranny at first, but the good results soon justify its adoption. . . . I simply arrange my work so as to leave a certain amount of time for study, and whether I feel like it or not I go at it religiously, unless I am positively ill." Terrell's example points to the challenge for women of including intellectual work in their domestic duties, as well as the benefits of such "mental improvement" for women's lives.[28]

The impact of Shakespeare study on home life of course depended to some degree on issues of social class. Some women had household staff, whose services were often shifted to Shakespeare club tasks. Sarah Gibler, of the Shakespeare Club of Huntington, Indiana (founded 1895), had her maid bake cakes for the club; the club history notes that "Mrs. Gibler's maid had to bake 9 sponge cakes before she succeeded in getting one perfect enough to serve her guests."[29] Other club women, such as Mary Freeman of Illinois and Martha Farnsworth of Kansas, did their own housework. Whether the household labor was actually carried out by the club women themselves or by their servants, it is significant that Shakespeare rather than the family was the recipient.

As late as 1952, the women in the Manchester, New Hampshire, Shakespeare Club found the balancing of intellectual and domestic work to be increasingly difficult, given the demands on their time. One member remarked, "Now, the Serpent is more subtle than any beast of the field. And he has taken many leisure hours away from woman. . . . But woman is almost as subtle as the Serpent. . . . And now twenty-seven of them . . . steal time to delight their souls in at least two plays a year and write several papers."[30] The phrase "stealing time" emphasizes the fact that time spent reading and studying Shakespeare meant less time spent on domestic responsibilities and was in conflict with the rigors of scientific homemaking; "reading" was not one of the approved tasks measured by the Bureau of Home Economics in its survey of women's homemaking activities.[31]

Studying Shakespeare required a serious commitment from women who juggled family responsibilities, and the efforts of club women to read and study Shakespeare must have had an impact on their home life. The organization of the Shakespeare Round Table of Bowling Green, Ohio, founded 1904–5, provides a typical example of how Shakespeare study was interspersed with domestic life. Each member was expected to host the club in her home once a year. Members were also required to attend every meeting, and each member was given two program books, "one for your purse and one to be kept by the telephone so we can check before we promise, if the activity interferes with Shakespeare."[32] In many similar households, commitment to Shakespeare study was accorded a high priority in terms of family activities.

In a 1907 essay "What the Club Does for the Club-Woman," in *Colored American Magazine*, Josephine T. Washington remarked that literary clubs were essential for motivating and encouraging women to do intellectual work: "the most palpable gain is found in the club with a literary feature. Here the members study standard authors, read the latest books, discuss current events, and compare opinions on questions of interest." She contended that "some of these women would read at home; others would not," and that clubs "cause many an active house-wife to find the time for study that she thought she did not have." Clubs were also crucial for allowing women to break out of their domestic routine: "Sometimes the husband has little faith in the ability of his wife to do anything outside of the domestic sphere," she commented, but women's desires extend beyond the home: "We feel that we owe something to those outside of the home-nest."[33]

Shakespeare and Home Life

For those within the "home-nest," the presence of over a dozen women reading and analyzing Shakespeare, taking part in the literate practices described in the previous chapter, would have had an effect on the household, particularly on the children. Women were responsible for providing a home environment conducive to the moral development of the family; according to one 1929 description, "as the home is the environment responsible for shaping the early years of our children, it is imperative that we recognize the importance of the influences of the everyday experiences in developing their physical, social and emotional life," including the stimulation of "intellectual and aesthetic tastes, through pleasure in good literature, in the arts and in creative work and play."[34] This type of "influence" certainly happened in the households of Portia Club members in Avon, Illinois. The club had a circulating library, which grew to three hundred volumes but was disbanded, and according to the club history, "the books were divided among those who had sponsored it. Many homes therefore contained these volumes, and it is almost certain, that the younger generation then grow-ing up, was more or less influenced by the atmosphere of culture which they inspired."[35] In quite the opposite way, members of the Portia Club of Payette, Idaho, took books from their home libraries to start the town library; in 1917, women were invited "to gather up all the books that could be spared from their home libraries and bring them to a club meeting, which they did. And were they ever proud to be seen taking the books up the street in a baby carriage!"[36] Families of club members would have certainly noticed this traffic of books, whether they were added to the home library or donated from it.

A few surviving accounts give us a personal window into the effects of Shakespeare clubs on home life. Barbara Janes's mother became a member of the Portia Club of Avon, Illinois, in 1906. Janes recalls that "Portia members were her close friends and so we knew them all at our house. During her two year term [as president] Portia dominated our lives. Tuesday night suppers were early and hurried, to give Mother time to be off to the Library Portia Room well before meeting time. My father usually drove her there on his way to the office. Then, at last, she had time to compose herself and be ready to conduct the meeting." Although the meeting did not take place in Janes's home, her mother's participation in the club disrupted the family's domestic routine, and her children remarked on their mother's intellectual and leadership roles. The situation described in this rare account was doubtless the same for numerous families with women involved in Shakespeare clubs, women's whose intellectual "work" was allocated a place in the household.[37]

Likewise, Elizabeth Greenfield, the daughter of Anna Nelson, a member of the Great Falls, Montana, Shakespeare Club in 1902, described how as a young girl she observed meetings from her hiding place under the dining room table while her mother "studied over a little red leather copy of *A Midsummer Night's Dream* with a pencil and sheet of paper before her." Greenfield related the story of the club's amateur reading of the play and the domestic preparation that was involved for club women. One club member, Mrs. Charles Heisey, was "a busy housewife" but made time to memorize Hermia's lines from the play while doing her housework. With two lovers, Hermia was "exciting for an over-worked housewife!"[38] In Chapter 2, we saw how Mrs. Heisey's experience as Hermia gave her a liberating performance opportunity. Here it illustrates the effect of Shakespeare on her home life. The transformative potential in becoming Hermia, albeit briefly, provided an inspiring respite from her daily chores.

In addition to preoccupying Mrs. Heisey as she scrubbed her floors, the amateur production of *A Midsummer Night's Dream* took over the Nelson household, even affecting the household staff; the family cook "was glad to concoct the refreshments, even adding many tidbits after glancing through the pages of *A Midsummer Night's Dream*." The ranch foreman, however, remained uninspired by Shakespeare and was not as supportive of Mrs. Nelson's "cultural frolic," but he realized "he couldn't talk back to the boss' wife," and thus he supplied a hay wagon to transport the club women and townspeople to a meadow on the ranch, where they held their performance.[39]

Another example of the ways Shakespeare clubs influenced home life comes from the Shakespeariana Club of Grand Rapids, Michigan. The club's scrapbook, now held by the Folger Shakespeare Library, contains a photo of the house of club founder Lorraine Immen, with the following handwritten note: "The place where Mrs. Immen conceived the idea of a Shakespearian Society for Grand Rapids. . . . Perhaps the ball room on the 3rd floor contributed to a feeling for the theater for Elizabeth Wilson who grew up there with her family. She has since been in many theatre roles, both on the stage and movies."[40] Other club children were similarly influenced by their mothers' literary activities. The daughter of a member of the Shakespeare club in rural Waxahachie, Texas, recollected that "frequently on late summer afternoons our porch and lawn became the class room for the study groups" that her mother belonged to, and she recalled that her mother was a "gifted conversationalist, a great reader and exceptionally well informed on all public questions."[41] Some clubs even involved entire families in Shakespeare study; the Cambridge, Massachusetts, Shakespeare Club (c. 1882) was made up of "merchants, army men, lawyers, city officials, their wives and children."[42] From a housewife inspired to memorize Hermia's lines while scrubbing her floors to a budding actress soaking up drama, the infiltration of Shakespeare into American home life had lasting effects, not only on women's intellectual activities but also on their household space, families, and allocation of time. Mary Ellen Lamb recalls how her mother's participation in the Grove City, Pennsylvania, club affected her as a child: "I remember seeing her as Juliet in a small 'bits from Shakespeare' that the club performed, and (as a small child, about 5 or 6), I was blown away by how beautiful she was. And she took me to a little performance of [*As You Like It*] when I was in 4th grade because she was supposed to be there—and it really was the beginning of my love affair with Shakespeare. . . . I still remember that the young woman who brought in the signs—i.e. Act I—did a somersault. I was enthralled."[43] Lamb has since gone on to an impressive career as an early modern scholar, inspired in part by her mother's participation in the Grove City Shakespeare Club.

In many communities, generations of family members were involved in Shakespeare clubs, a continuity that would have had an impact on the smaller towns in particular. The Shakespeare club in Lebanon, Missouri (with a population just over 2,000 in 1900), originated in the home of one family when Mrs. J. C. Wallace began reading Shakespeare with her daughter in their home and subsequently decided to invite other women to "enjoy the benefit with them."[44] Similarly, the San Antonio, Texas, Shakespeare Club was started by Mrs. John Baskin, who "was afraid her sons were becoming better students of the Bard than her daughters," and thus organized a Shakespeare club "to teach her daughters Shakespeare." As part of her daughters' Shakespeare education, "Shakespeare quotations accompanied the girls' homemaking duties," and the club grew to include other community women, who met every Thursday after school in the Baskin home. Daughter Lida remarked that "her earliest memory is of waving her arms about and intoning, 'Friends, Romans, countrymen . . .'" Such an influence must have occurred in households of other club members as well.[45]

The trajectory of the three Baskin daughters provides further evidence of the Shakespeare Club's long-term effects on their families; Mrs. Baskin was "an early Women's Libber" and "encouraged her girls to high accomplishments"; daughter Janet graduated from the University of California–Berkeley, taught college, wrote a dissertation on Shakespeare, "was a vital force in shaping the cultural concepts and ideals of the community," and had a library named after her at a local college. Daughter Lida was later a president of the Shakespeare Club and was known for her "vast knowledge of Shakespeare" and for her extensive memorabilia, including "many Shakespeare mementoes: the engraving of Shakespeare and his friends; the bas-relief, the bust, the tiny porcelain head, the engraving of the poet; the picture of Stratford-on-Avon." Daughter Mildred became an elementary school teacher and principal (with a school named after her), served as one of the first board members of the San Antonio Little Theatre, and took over from her mother as a leader of the Shakespeare Club. The club apparently influenced other women as well; many remained members for more than sixty years, and the club still maintains the progressive slant of its founder. A report from the club in 1976 stated that "Woman's Lib is still worked into today's programs."[46]

This snapshot of the Baskin family legacy of commitment to Shakespeare and education no doubt occurred in other families. Betty May Exall Stewart relates a similar influence from her grandmother, May Dickson Exall, who began the Shakespeare Club of Dallas in 1886 and served as president for fifty years. Stewart remembers listening to her grandmother read Shakespeare until she was old enough to read herself and could "read Shakespeare to her in Latin. If I mispronounced a word or quoted incorrectly, she always knew it. . . . She knew all of Shakespeare and could quote most of it from memory." Stewart remarks, "I was 12 years old before I knew that her dear friend Shakespeare, was dead. It made me very sad."[47]

For many American families like the Stewarts and the Baskins, study of Shakespeare became part of their history, a domestic legacy passed down from generations, much like a family Bible or other treasured item. Numerous clubs had legacy membership procedures that formally secured places for several generations of women.[48] In some cases, extended family members were involved in Shakespeare clubs; Lydia Scott, president of the Manchester, New Hampshire, Shakespeare Club, had a four-year-old grandson who was an honorary member of the club, and the Shakespeare Club of Huntington, Indiana, even tried to stake a claim on members' newborn children.[49] The latter club, founded 1895, was "so devoted to the study of Shakespeare that when charter member, Mrs. U.S. [Minnie] Lesh, gave birth to a son, some members thought she should name him William. However, she named him John, a family name, as well as the name of Shakespeare's father."[50]

On a more personal level, a few club women left diaries that can help us trace how women integrated reading and study of Shakespeare into their domestic lives. Illinois club woman Mary Freeman wrote a diary that relates what must have been a typical schedule of combining domestic duties with Shakespeare study. On Saturday, 11 April 1885, she recorded that she had to attend to her mending, baths, and housecleaning before she could go to her Shakespeare club meeting in the evening. Freeman did not find it easy to balance domestic duties and club demands; in one entry she lamented the lack of reading time, amid varnishing the dining room floor and cleaning her house.[51] Illness did not interfere with her determination to complete her household tasks *and* read Shakespeare; even when sick to her stomach, she was able to get herself to the meeting of the Shakespeare club.[52] The challenges of finding time for study were so common that the 1896 rules for the Lincoln, Nebraska, Woman's Club listed one of the categories of members as follows: "The tired woman, full of domestic responsibilities, who wants to be a sponge, fold her hands, take in what the bright, free woman, who needs an audience, has learned, and then go home refreshed to her treadmill."[53] Martha Farnsworth, a member of the Coterie Club in Topeka, Kansas, wrote a similar personal account of domestic duties and club work in 1906; she completed her housework despite a broken arm so that she would have time to read Shakespeare in her club: "Swept the stairs and hall and scrubbed my kitchen this morning all with my one arm, also churned. Mrs. F. Washburn came after dinner and took me to Coterie Club at Mrs. Seiler's."[54]

We might ask why women such as Mary Freeman and Martha Farnsworth bothered to spend time reading Shakespeare after scrubbing floors, sewing, baking cakes, and attending to other domestic duties. Despite the often exhausting experience of integrating intellectual work with home life, Anne Firor Scott observes that "for some women, working toward collective goals tapped wellsprings of creativity that had been quiescent in the narrow round of domesticity," and they were "exposed to a wider range of social experience than would have been common in family life."[55] For actress Fanny Davenport, Shakespeare's Beatrice offered her exactly this type of escape from domestic life; in her 1887 essay published in *Shakespeariana*, she wrote, "I can never picture [Beatrice] with knitting nor darning-needle in hand" because she is instead "brave, passionate, impulsive and thoroughly womanly."[56] Other accounts suggest that Shakespeare study fulfilled a need for women to be "brave" and "passionate" and to escape from their daily routines. Jessie Lee Rembert Willis, a member of the Dallas Shakespeare Club, put it this way: "Through the changing world of carriages and coachmen on quiet streets to

Figure 3. The Dallas Shakespeare Club, 1911. Meetings were held in members' homes, providing a welcome respite from daily routines. Courtesy of the Dallas Historical Society. Used by permission.

that of the modern city with its crowded thoroughfares, automobile parking problems, throngs of women absorbing stereotyped lectures and consuming stereotyped food, the Dallas Shakespeare Club meetings, in the homes of its members, with the challenge of writing-it-yourself papers, and the ever fresh appeal of Shakespeare, is a refuge, indeed, from the chaotic world of today."[57] For many women, Shakespeare provided this type of a "refuge," a sacred space where they could develop their intellectual interests while carrying out meaningful "work," even after a long day of physical labor.[58]

Shakespeare and Home Improvement

One of the intriguing aspects of many Shakespeare clubs is their use of domestic practices such as cooking and scrapbooking as a way to express their commitment to Shakespeare and as a form of commemoration. For many clubs, reading Shakespeare was often combined with programs on domestic improvement, an emphasis reflected in their plans of study and their philanthropic aims. The history of the Portia Club of Avon, Illinois (described in the Preface), illustrates this mélange of domestic duties, intellectual tasks, and civic activities. The history (which ranges from 1894 to 1994) describes a group of women who studied, memorized, and performed Shakespeare's works, but who also cooked, held bake sales, improved their neighborhood schools, engaged in community service, and advocated for female education and for suffrage.[59] Like numerous other club women, the Portia Club members were not just reading Shakespeare; they were carrying out a serious program of civic engagement and self-education under a veneer of domestic improvement.[60]

Such activities did not come without criticism, however. A 1905 attack on club women by former president Grover Cleveland reflected anxiety about women's domestic responsibilities being overshadowed by club life. Cleveland warned that if a woman engages in club work, "cheerlessness will invade her home, and that if children are there they will be irredeemably deprived of the mysterious wholesomeness and delight of an atmosphere which can only be created by a mother's loving presence and absorbing care." He cautioned that club women "must bear her share of liability for the injury they may inflict upon the domestic life of our land." Cleveland identified the home as the greatest site of danger from women's clubs, contending that they are "not only harmful, but harmful in a way that directly menaces the integrity of our homes and the benign disposition and character of our wifehood and motherhood." Specifically, he pointed to "waste of time and perversion of effort" as the problems for women who abdicated their domestic duties in favor of club work. The solution, therefore, was to keep women in the home and shelter them from the dangers of the outside world: "the best and safest club for a woman to patronize is her home."[61] Although club women strongly objected to Cleveland's attack, it serves as a reminder of the anxieties and tensions that surfaced when women "stole time" for intellectual work at the expense of their household duties.[62]

Even though I found virtually no criticism of women's participation in Shakespeare clubs, some women apparently took precautions against such criticism by combining their literary study of Shakespeare with an emphasis on domestic improvement. In addition to Shakespeare and other literature, many of the topics covered in clubs had to do with improving domestic life in some way, such as modernized processes or new products.[63] As a component of these programs, study of Shakespeare became part of the process of improving domestic life. Reading Shakespeare thus allowed women to hone their interpretive skills and develop their rhetorical prowess while adhering to their home duties. By writing papers on issues that addressed home life, such as "Dust and Its Dangers," women could then carry out study of *Macbeth*, though the juxtaposition of topics is often quite incongruous.[64]

For example, in 1911–12, the Library Club of Clay Center, Kansas, did intensive reading and study of Shakespeare and *Hamlet*, along with papers on various domestic topics such as "Economical Uses of Soup," "The Dangerous Fly," and "Cellars and Refrigerators." When they could depart from their usual domestic-centered agenda and turn to Shakespeare, the topics of their discussions reveal an important process of questioning Shakespeare, interpreting his texts, and offering opinions. In addition to reading Shakespeare's plays aloud, club women wrote and presented such papers as "Are Shakespeare's Comedies Equal to His Tragedies," "Which Is the Greater Character in [*Hamlet*], King or Queen?" and "Something Gained from the Study of *Hamlet*."[65] Such topics necessitated presenting an opinion and argument about Shakespeare, and they would have offered club women the chance to develop their skills of presentation and argumentation while maintaining their focus on home responsibilities.[66]

The combination of domestic topics and Shakespeare was not confined to Kansas; in 1910 in South Dakota, for example, seven of the fifty-two clubs in the state federation studied Shakespeare, and "the study of household economics was taken up by nearly every club."[67] In Nebraska as well, the women in the Zetetic Club of Weeping Water combined study of Shakespeare in 1899–1900 with papers presented by members on topics such as "Problems of Today in American Politics," "The Business Education Required by the Women of Today," "Comparison of Men and Women as Story Writers," and "Kitchen Comforts versus Useless Incumbrances."[68] The Shakespeare Club of Devil's Lake, North Dakota, devoted the whole year of 1909 to study of "Domestic Science."[69]

Even clubs that were not specifically devoted to Shakespeare studied Shakespeare in connection with other topics; in 1925–26, the Nineteenth-Century

Club of Kingman, Kansas, covered such subjects as "Of what importance is the influence of a small woman's club on good citizenship?" as well as a reading of "Hermione's Defense" and scenes from *All's Well That Ends Well* and *The Tempest*, and discussion of "Shakespeare's Domestic Life." The club administered an intelligence test and conducted a debate on the topic "That woman is equal to, if she does not excel, man, in the business and professional world."[70] Women in the Elkhart, Kansas, Coterie Club were clearly aware of the impingement of their club work on their home life; in 1935, one topic for discussion was "What I Feed Hubby on Club Day." These women were taking time away from their household work to attend their club meetings and discuss literature, current events, and domestic improvements; topics for 1923–24 included Shakespeare, "How to Serve a Formal Dinner," "The Proper Age to Teach Sex," and "Corporal Punishment in the Home." Such activities helped to reshape ideologies about women's intellectual "work" and its place in the household. Through the structure of the Shakespeare club, women could maintain their responsibilities at home while engaging in "intellectual improvement." With Shakespeare as their subject, they could venture into topics such as women's equality, women in the workplace, and birth control. It is notable that Grover Cleveland did not single out Shakespeare clubs, even though, as we have seen, their meeting topics often involved discussion of what he called the "outside world" and their homework entailed perhaps a more significant time commitment than more general club work. We might also recall the Placerville, California, Shakespeare Club, discussed in the Introduction, whose members zeroed in on Shakespeare as a safe topic for their group when a more general women's club had been vetoed by local men.

Domestic Practices

Rather than separate home life and Shakespeare, some Shakespeare clubs sought to integrate Shakespeare into women's household labor, through such activities as cooking and baking for their Shakespeare club, compiling elaborate programs for club meetings, planning banquets and Shakespeare's birthday celebrations, and making detailed scrapbooks of club history and activities. Members of the Avon Club of Topeka, Kansas, for example, hosted an annual "banquet in honor of their Patron Saint" around Shakespeare's birthday, as did most clubs across the country.[71] The Woodland, California, Shakespeare Club held an annual birthday picnic with a trademark cake made by the same member for twenty years; other California clubs were often invited, and in 1904 the picnic was attended by more than 150 club women. The gathering was usually held on a club member's porch or in her yard, and "decorations were always Shakespearean flowers." One club member even recalled that "one time the floor was lightly strewn with leaves of herbs mentioned in his writings." The club had a special ceremony for cutting the birthday cake, which one member performed "in an original manner. With the knife in her hand transformed by her words and gestures into a sword, she became a Shakespearean character advancing upon the enemy."[72]

While we might see such domestic efforts as peripheral to the importance of these groups, the incorporation of practices familiar to women helped create what Kate Flint describes as "a safe space in which [women] could take the imaginative narratives as a jumping-off point for a discussion of what was happening in their lives, [and in] their country," much like the kitchen knife held by the club woman mentioned above, which momentarily "transformed" her from a housewife into a Shakespearean character.[73] One of the more unusual combinations of domestic labor and intellectual content comes from the Fredonia, New York, Shakespeare Club (founded 1885), which celebrated Shakespeare's birthday in 1888 with "an entertainment addressed to both the physical and mental nature." As part of the banquet, the club included a course called an "intellectual salad," which consisted of "lettuce leaves made of tissue paper of different tints of green," with a Shakespeare quotation written on each leaf. Members could take leaves as long as they continued to identify the source play correctly. The winner received a copy of the *Shakespeare Birthday Book*, and the others received copies of *Shakespeare Forget-Me-Nots*.[74] These various activities inserted Shakespeare into "a sphere of activity widely considered to be women's domain—cooking and entertaining."[75]

One club in particular might serve as a case study of how women could combine domestic practices, intellectual work, and domestic space. The Anne Hudgins Shakespeare Class of Marietta, Georgia, has been meeting for nearly eighty years, in the homes of members, most of whom are descendants of the founding families of the city of Marietta. The club was initiated by Anne Hudgins when she moved from Atlanta to the suburb of Marietta in 1931, as a way of maintaining her intellectual life. The current history of the club is kept in the home of one of the founding members of the club. In her living room is a bust of Shakespeare, along with numerous editions of the plays and works of Shakespeare criticism. Of particular interest is the "Shakespeare Closet," a closet filled with full runs of the journals *Shakespeare Quarterly* and *Shakespeare Survey*, Shakespeare games, a model of the Globe Theatre, and an extensive collection of scrapbooks.

Some of these scrapbooks are related to the club's history, but most of them contain various bits of Shakespeareana, organized alphabetically by play, from *Antony and Cleopatra* to *The Winter's Tale*. The contents include newspaper and magazine clippings about productions, works of Shakespeare criticism, and any items that could be tangentially related to a reference in one of the plays— articles on Epiphany are in the *Twelfth Night* scrapbook, for example. Family members recall that compiling the Shakespeare scrapbook was a task for the entire family on Sundays, when they would sit around the dining room table and paste in the clippings collected by their mother during the week.[76]

One recent history of scrapbooking describes it as "a female activity, linked to traditional female concerns of holding families together and preserving nostalgic items."[77] Shakespeare scrapbooks were certainly part of the construction of Shakespeare as an object of nostalgia, but they also constituted an important part of women's household work, diverting domestic labor away from household duties into the service of Shakespeare. Judy Giles points out that at the fin de siècle, women experienced contradictory domestic identities and were "sometimes pulled forward as agents of change but at others pushed back as symbolisations of continuity and tradition."[78] Scrapbooking responded to both initiatives; it was a means to preserve tradition but also a forward-looking way to devote household labor to intellectual work and to the preservation of a record of intellectual accomplishments.[79]

Certainly one of the objectives for the Anne Hudgins club member was to chronicle the history of her own Shakespeare club, in line with goals related to nostalgia and preservation. But we might see additional significance in the fact that Shakespeare occupied part of the household labor and space, not only for the woman of the house but for the whole family. Scrapbooking was also a way to produce something from Shakespeare, linking domestic labor to literary culture. As one scholar has described the practice of scrapbooking, "the reader becomes an author," and the scrapbook takes "place on the border between reading and authoring."[80] Through scrapbooking, women produced something with and from Shakespeare, thus establishing his place in the home as a product of domestic labor.

Because these scrapbooks resided in their own designated household space, such as "the Shakespeare Closet" in the formal dining room, the product of Shakespeare-centered labor was literally allocated space in the home.[81] According to one historian, "as the nineteenth century progressed, the well-to-do dedicated their homes to domesticity, consumption and reproduction rather than to domestic manufacturing or income production," and the home was "indicative of social and economic standing."[82] If domestic space can be linked to economic success, the allocation of domestic space to Shakespeare signified his association with economic stability and prosperity.[83] This particular house in Marietta has additional historical significance: this is not just any closet, for the previous house on that site was reported to be the last house General Sherman burned on his way to Atlanta from Kennesaw Mountain.[84] The current house is thus a memorial both to Shakespeare and to a piece of history that the family wants to preserve, again involving nostalgia and production and preservation of an artifact, all within a domestic setting.

Like the often carefully preserved minutes and other club relics, the practice of scrapbooking allowed women to create their own history of reading Shakespeare. The members of the Woman's Shakespeare Club of Flint, Michigan, for example, began to build their own history in 1896, three years after their founding. Members were asked each week to bring in "any criticism, or item of information found, which if it were in possible shape was put in a Shakespeare book which was being prepared."[85] The scrapbook of the Shakespeariana Club of Grand Rapids, Michigan, offers further insight into the significance of these domestic practices. This scrapbook contains club programs cut apart and interspersed with clippings from the Stratford, Ontario, Shakespeare Festival, reviews of books and articles on Shakespeare, and club photographs. The scrapbook places the club within a larger context of Shakespeare-related practices as a way to frame the importance of women's activities—club women were not just meeting privately to read Shakespeare, their scrapbook argues, but were part of a wider cultural movement involving international theater, publishing, and scholarship.[86]

Numerous other clubs chronicled their activities in similar ways. For Loula Kendall Rogers, keeping the records of the Woman's Shakespearean Club of Barnesville, Georgia, also served as a history of her personal reading; she wrote in the 1895 club minutes, "This contains also a list of the books I have read from time to time, quotations to be preserved, etc."[87] The Portia Club of Payette, Idaho, physically connected Shakespeare to domesticity by building a club house for Shakespeare study (complete with homemade curtains), finished in 1927. This Shakespeare-centered house included both a stage and a kitchen, with "everything the heart of any kitchen housewife could desire," yet dedicated to Shakespeare.[88]

We might derive additional meaning from the activities of these clubs—creating scrapbooks, celebrating Shakespeare's birthday, reciting Shakespeare's poetry at meetings, and the like—if we look at them as rituals of commemoration.[89] Such customs of Shakespeare clubs had lasting effects on members' lives. As Paul Connerton remarks, "Whatever is demonstrated in rites permeates also non-ritual behaviour and mentality. . . . Rites have the capacity to give value and meaning to the life of those who perform them."[90]

The Anne Hudgins Shakespeare Class of Marietta, Georgia, still engages in just such a ritualized practice. For its annual Twelfth Night ceremony, each woman prepares a passage from Shakespeare that summarizes her life in the previous year. After commemorating her year through Shakespeare, she takes a bough of greenery and throws it into the fireplace, signifying the end of one year and the start of another. Some women have been members of the club for more than fifty years and thus have marked half a century with this Shakespeare-centered ritual.[91] Similar practices occupied other clubs across the country; for example, the Shakespeariana Club of Grand Rapids, Michigan, reminded members to mark their year with Shakespeare by producing their own annual Shakespeare calendar.

Conclusion

For many American women in the early twentieth century, Shakespeare was appropriate subject matter for reading, performance, and analysis and, at the same time, provided an opportunity for women to produce something that simultaneously documented their activities, preserved Shakespeare for posterity, and involved Shakespeare in the production of a household object that occupied symbolic domestic space. Shakespeare became ensconced in the home—as material objects (books and busts) and as study material—but also brought women out of the home through the development of public libraries, gardens, and other projects connected to literacy, education, and civic improvement, as we saw in Chapter 1.

In a 1902 essay, Mrs. M. F. Pitts, who was involved in such activities in St. Louis, offered the following explanation of the value of club life to women: "the club can bring a mental stimulant to every careworn, tired housewife who has nothing to look forward to but the monotonous routine of farm life and its lonesome cares" and serves to "get the women to express themselves and take her outside of herself and of the care with which her life is filled; and saves the intellect from stagnation, as well as to awaken lofty thought in a dormant mind, which is only secondary to saving a soul."[92] For hundreds of American women, Shakespeare provided the "mental stimulant" and "save[d] the intellect from starvation." The next chapter discusses the farthest reaches of Shakespeare study, to some of the most remote areas of the United States.

❧ CHAPTER 3

The Outpost

"In a log-cabin in the woods of Southern Minnesota, on cold stormy nights in winter, after the ranch work is done," a group called the Snow Blockade Club met in the late 1880s to read Shakespeare in Lanesboro, a town of just over 1,000 people. Less than ten miles from the Canadian border, in Swanton, Vermont (population 1,200), a club of women gathered in 1893 to read Shakespeare. In a tiny village in northern Michigan that numbered between 400 and 600 citizens at the time, the Northport Shakespeare Club received its traveling library shipment of "Shakespeare and American Literature" to share among its eight readers in 1896.[1] Two years later, in 1898, the Woman's Shakespearean Club of Barnesville, Georgia, halfway between Atlanta and Macon, reported that its twenty-five women had not only studied Shakespeare but also established a public Shakespeare reference library, started a night school for factory hands and a girls' club for factory women, and sponsored a series of public lectures.[2] In this rural town, known as the "Buggy Capital of the South" for its production of buggies, wagons, carts, hearses, and coffins, the study of literature, public service, and community education were connected to reading Shakespeare.

From Florida to California, in cities and towns of every size, thousands of American men and women gathered to read Shakespeare.[3] Activities of urban Shakespeare clubs are relatively well known; Boston, New York, and Philadelphia all had active and fairly well documented Shakespeare clubs, and it is no surprise that Shakespeare provided reading material for women's clubs in these areas. But what role did reading Shakespeare have for Americans outside these cultural centers? This chapter concentrates on several representative rural and isolated communities and their Shakespeare reading groups, exploring how reading Shakespeare played a key part in civic life and in the formation of American literary culture in locales not usually considered crucial to literary history. The story of Shakespeare in the frontier West has been well documented, particularly in terms of performance history and male readers.[4] Yet a substantial population of women readers of Shakespeare in "outpost" areas made up a significant portion of Shakespeare's audience in the late nineteenth and early twentieth centuries.

These American women readers of Shakespeare, who pursued an agenda of self-education and instruction, suggest the need for further inquiry into the variety of readers in geographically distant locales and their often overlooked influence on a broad understanding of American literary culture and civic life. As one 1929 account put it, "The cultural standards of the towns in which these [Shakespeare] clubs have functioned owe something definite and fine to their continued presence. They buy new books on the general subject of the Shakespeare plays, they encourage 'Little Theatre' projects, they support stage revivals of the great plays."[5] A letter from "an earnest teacher in New England" likewise affirmed the need for intellectual inspiration across the country: "Many people are suffering for the lack of mental food to whom such a club would be a blessing. . . . My own experience shows me that a club might be formed in every town and village in our country, where two persons could be found to make a nucleus for it."[6] The women of the Zetetic Club in Weeping Water, Nebraska (population 1,150), would have agreed with this teacher's statement; located in sparsely populated Nebraska near the Iowa border, they spent two full years in the 1880s studying Shakespeare.[7] Likewise, an account of the clubs in the Black Hills of South Dakota boasted that "perhaps there is no section in the country with the same number of inhabitants where there are so many woman's literary organizations as there are in this district"; according to this history, there were nineteen women's clubs in the Black Hills, most of which studied Shakespeare.[8]

In many such areas of the country, starting a Shakespeare reading club was a way of reestablishing a cultural life from a former place of residence and an important part of community building. In his story of "the trying years of our mother's life," Owen P. White recalled the excitement his parents expressed when a traveling group came to present Shakespeare in 1890s Tucson, Arizona: "Tucson, being the kind of town it was, had several variety theaters, and when the largest of these advertised that some traveling barnstormer would present a series of Shakespeare's plays from its stage . . . classically educated parents, who hadn't seen a play since before the [Civil] war, were all agog with excitement." White and his brothers attended the performances with their father and noted

Figure 4. The Wednesday Morning Club of Pueblo, Colorado, 1911. Shakespeare's women readers could be found not only in major urban centers but also in smaller cities and towns, where establishing a reading club was an important part of community building. Photo courtesy of Scott Rubel

that "when the week of dramatic uplift was over a new element of excitement and interest had been added to the lives of all four of us." For his mother, however, access to Shakespeare was prohibited because the performances were held in an inappropriate venue for women, "a variety theater," though she still expressed her love for Shakespeare by teaching her children. White remembered, "We were taught whole passages of Shakespeare, especially passages wherein somebody kills somebody else . . . we fought and acted all over the place, and, although the bard of Avon must have tossed in his grave at the things we did to his immortal lines, it was not up to us to worry about Bill. Our audience always liked the show; our mother laughed and applauded, our father rewarded us liberally with nickels and dimes and, thus encouraged, we daily engaged in mortal combat."[9]

The choice of Shakespeare as reading material was both deliberate and consequential in the American frontier, particularly for women; Julie Roy Jeffrey has argued that frontier women "considered themselves responsible for civilization and morality," and this was often achieved through reading Shakespeare.[10] Thus, Leah Price's maxim that the "history of the book is also a geography of the book" takes a different shape across the country as women readers responded to their local, personal, and cultural needs.[11]

Even in areas not too distant from larger cities, reading Shakespeare was a way to extend cultural life beyond the metropolis. The Worcester, Massachusetts, club began when former actress Josephine Heard Cutter wanted to re-create the theater life she had known formerly in New York, less than two hundred miles away. Likewise, Anne Hudgins, a member of the Atlanta Shakespeare Class, started a second reading group in the northern suburb of Marietta when she moved there later in life, and Mrs. Beveridge Hill of Chicago was instrumental in the development of a reading club in Idaho Springs, Idaho.[12] As one club member from the Dakotas explained, "Our Western women are really Eastern women transplanted, and many of us look back to homes in dear old New York or New England. . . . So, in your thought of us, do not feel as if we were anything strange or far off."[13] The Shakespeare Club of Great Falls, Montana, was founded on just such a principle, because "its members yearned for eastern culture, either because they missed what they had known or wanted to acquire what they had never known." Anna Nelson, originally of the Israel Putnam family of Massachusetts and wife of a prosperous Montana sheep farmer, was voted in to the Shakespeare Club "because she could contribute 'Boston culture.'"[14] Similarly, the nineteen women's literary clubs in the Black Hills of South Dakota were composed of women who were "eastern born and educated, many of them college bred, with fine literary tastes," who have been "accustomed to the best in lectures, readings and musical entertainments" but after moving west, "have suffered some loss of privilege and opportunity" and thus decided to start clubs where they could study Shakespeare.[15] Reading Shakespeare was part of this civilizing process, a way to inject literary culture, learning, and social stability into a community. Shakespeare often functioned as both a necessity and a luxury; according to one pioneer wife in Woodward, Oklahoma, her husband helped organize a Shakespeare reading club "as soon as he washed his hands after driving the stake on his lot."[16] Shakespeare was part of this major theme of civilizing the American West, which had repercussions for Shakespeare's place in the American literary canon across the country.

Kansas: A Sample Outpost

A detailed focus on one area of America can illuminate the many ways women in nonurban communities found an outlet for their intellectual and philanthropic endeavors through reading groups centered on Shakespeare, and demonstrates what reading practices might tell us about cultural knowledge and its dissemination outside urban centers. One of the most intriguing places where Shakespeare clubs flourished is the nineteenth-century prairie frontier of Kansas. Kansas is not unique in terms of the number and variety of Shakespeare clubs, and it can serve as a typical example of the variety, scope, and influence of women readers and their unique relationship with Shakespeare.[17] Interest in Shakespeare clubs extended throughout the state, in a climate often inhospitable to the basics of survival. As historian Craig Miner points out, "Nothing has ever been automatic in Kansas nor ever would be . . . success on the prairie was a continuing responsibility, and it was a region where things that did not move died."[18] In fact, reading Shakespeare in a club may have been even more essential to women's intellectual survival in places such as Kansas, which, according to one description, "exemplifies everything that a civilized metropolitan or cosmopolitan mind despises," with few alternative intellectual outlets.[19]

Estimates range from one to two hundred active women's clubs in late nineteenth-century Kansas, with as many as thirteen clubs in Lawrence and at least eighteen in Topeka.[20] Women of vastly different political leanings were involved in Kansas club life in the late nineteenth century; an 1897 article reported that "all over the State to the westernmost limit of the Corn Belt are the homes of club women. . . . These homes, those of the suffragists, the reformers, the radicals, the conservatives—all show alike the high plane upon which the Kansas woman stands, from which she aspires to attain a yet higher, living the motto of her State, *ad astra per aspera*."[21] The combination of *aspera* (difficulties) and *astra* (stars) locates reading Shakespeare as the apex of intellectual achievement even in adverse conditions. Indeed, study of Shakespeare was a way to survive the often difficult circumstances of prairie life. Johnny Faragher and Christine Stansell have discussed the need for frontier women to "[carve] out a life of their own" and to fight "against the forces of necessity to hold together the few fragments of female subculture left to them."[22] Shakespeare was part of this "female subculture" and functioned as an essential component of intellectual survival and development for women. As we shall see, "Shakespeare" meant something particular for these women readers: a sense of intellectual achievement (still evident today) within the realm of material deemed appropriate for female study.

I identified more than twenty-four Kansas groups, in small and large towns alike, that were either solely devoted to reading Shakespeare or engaged in substantial study of Shakespeare.[23] Clubs that named themselves Shakespeare clubs, at least indicating by their title a commitment to Shakespeare, existed in every corner of Kansas, from the capital city of Topeka to towns such as Colby and Waterville, with populations between 600 and 700. In descending order by size of population, the following list illustrates the range of clubs; the number in parentheses is the population according to the census of 1900:

Topeka (33,608)

Lawrence (10,862)

Galena (10,155)

Ottawa (6,934)

Salina (6,074)

El Dorado (3,466)

Columbus (2,310)

Kingman (1,785)

Baxter Springs (1,641)

Belleville (1,371)

Pratt (1,213)

La Cygne (1,037)

Baldwin City (1,017)

Cottonwood Falls (842)

Colby (641)

Waterville (610)

The desire to read and study Shakespeare encompassed a wide cross-section of women in all geographical areas of Kansas; these data provide some indication of how many citizens were reading Shakespeare across America, in small towns like Cottonwood Falls, which supported both a Shakespeare Club and a Junior Shakespeare Club.[24]

Even in the often isolated prairie communities, Shakespeare was part of general cultural knowledge, disseminated via such publications as the *Kansas City Review*. The August–December 1885 issue, for example, focused on "Science, Art, Industry and Literature." Here readers could find such essays as "A Chinese Columbus," "A Fish Eating Plant," "Native American Dogs," and "Shakespeare's Childhood."[25] For rural Americans interested in reading and studying Shakespeare, geographical isolation was not necessarily an impediment; Mrs. Beardslee's circulating library of Hiawatha, Kansas, included Shakespeare's works in an 1879 list of books.[26]

Another indication of the widespread readership of Shakespeare comes from the *Kansas State Library Department of Traveling Libraries Bulletin* of 1916. The *Bulletin* reported, "In communities having no general reference library, or remote from libraries, club study is hampered by the lack of suitable books to supplement the personal knowledge of the members. To meet this want the Kansas Traveling Libraries Commission is now prepared to furnish literature relating to almost every topic embraced in the study outlines here presented."[27] It is no surprise that Shakespeare was a significant topic of study outlined in the bulletin. The Traveling Libraries had a collection of papers available for club use,

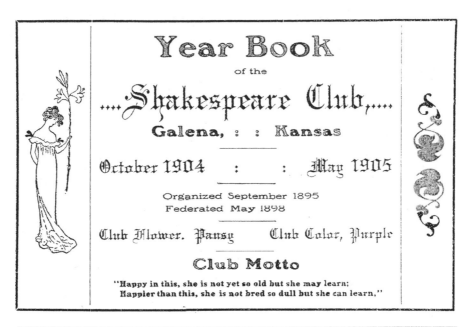

Year Book

of the

....Shakespeare Club,....

Galena, : : Kansas

October 1904 : : May 1905

Organized September 1895
Federated May 1898

Club Flower. Pansy   Club Color, Purple

Club Motto

"Happy in this, she is not yet so old but she may learn;
Happier than this, she is not bred so dull but she can learn."

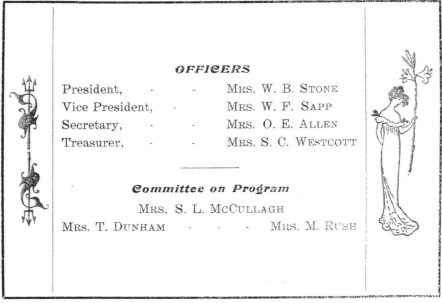

OFFICERS

President,   -   -   MRS. W. B. STONE
Vice President,   -   MRS. W. F. SAPP
Secretary,   -   -   MRS. O. E. ALLEN
Treasurer,   -   -   MRS. S. C. WESTCOTT

Committee on Program

MRS. S. L. McCULLAGH

MRS. T. DUNHAM   -   -   -   MRS. M. RUSH

FIGURE 5. Yearbook of the Shakespeare Club of Galena, Kansas, 1904–5. The Galena club was one of dozens of groups in Kansas at the turn of the century devoted to reading or studying Shakespeare. Courtesy of the Kansas State Historical Society

October Seventh

••

Henry V

"The roystering prince, that afterward
Belied his madcap youth and proved
A greatly simple warior lord
Such as our warrior fathers loved."

Home of Mrs. Allen

Roll Call   An Incident of the Summer
Date of Composition of the Play
The Sources of the Plot
Duration of Action
Argument   -   -   -   *Mrs. Hutchins*
Leader   -   -   -   *Mrs. Milliken*

Critic's Report

October Fourteenth

••

Home of Mrs. Arthur

Roll Call   Quotations from Act I Henry V
Paper   France and England   -   *Mrs. Rush*
Life and Character of Henry V   -   *Mrs. Stone*
Reading   Epic Elements of the Play   *Mrs. Sapp*
Paper   Manners and Customs of the
        Times   ·   -   *Mrs. McCullagh*

Critic's Report

for a fee of ten cents. In addition to essays such as "Hygiene of the Backward Child," "Rural Schools of Michigan," and "Needless Waste—Swat the Fly," clubs could order "Lear's Insanity" and "Shakespeare in Music."

The Traveling Libraries Commission also printed sample study programs from clubs across the state, confirming that Shakespeare was a significant component of more general club study. Kansas clubs devoted to Shakespeare of course had Shakespeare as part of their program, but so did clubs with a more general emphasis, such as the Traveler's Club of Burlington, which studied such topics as "Richard III of Shakespeare and of history," "Was Shakespeare a true historian?" and "Relative strength of his comedies and tragedies." The Entre Nous Club of Winfield had a serious concentration in Shakespeare, in one year covering *King Lear, The Winter's Tale,* and *Henry IV* part 2, and hosting an annual banquet "presenting 'The shades of Shakespeare's women': Portia, Juliet, Katherine (The shrew), Lady Macbeth, Miranda, Desdemona, Cordelia, Ophelia, and the Witches."[28] Shakespeare's works constituted a substantial share of the curriculum for numerous rural club women looking to develop their reading, study, and analytical skills, even in clubs with a more general educational mandate.[29]

To gauge the impact of these reading clubs on their local communities, one might imagine the scenario for the club in Waterville, Kansas, a small rural community in the northeast corner of the state, founded in 1867 along the banks of the Little Blue River as an end-of-the-line railroad stop. The Shakespeare Club began there in 1903, four years before the Waterville train depot was built. By 1905, the club included twenty-six women from a significant number of the households that made up the population of just over 600 citizens, meeting every Thursday for two hours to discuss such topics as "The effect on Hamlet of Ophelia's lack of strong character," "How does Ophelia compare, contrast with Juliet," "Biblical, classical and mythological allusions," and "Uses of verse and prose in this play, and where?"[30] In 1906, the club formed a committee to establish a public library and reading room, a year before the train depot was built. Club members began by sponsoring a traveling library that same year, which they kept in the local Eli Peterson store. The club worked for eight years to raise money for its own building, and in 1914 the library moved to a room in the City Hall.[31] That year, among its various topics such as "Peace," "Social problems," and "How to beautify Waterville," the club debated the proposition, "That Lady Macbeth's ambition was an outgrowth from her loyalty and love for her husband rather than from an inherent wickedness in herself."[32] Although the text of this discussion does not survive, one can surmise that it probably included dialogue about female ambition, spousal loyalty, and female wickedness. In this small community, meeting to study, debate, and analyze Shakespeare was a communal source of intellectual engagement and one of the bedrocks of social, cultural, and civic life, entwined with community betterment and concern for social welfare. Reading Shakespeare was not a passive solitary activity but a community enterprise that promoted philanthropy and social engagement.

Elsewhere in Kansas, groups like the Wakeeney Locust Club included Shakespeare as part of its study, producing papers such as the "Biography of

Shakespeare" and a roll call of Shakespearean quotations. The Prentis Study Club of Wellington did intensive study of *A Midsummer Night's Dream* along with papers on topics such as garbage disposal and neighborliness. The Saturday Club of Hiawatha also studied Shakespeare, presenting programs such as "Shakespeare, and English Art" and "Shakespeare, and French Art." Topics included "Compare Ibsen's dramatic construction with that of Shakespeare," "Lady Macbeth as interpreted by famous actresses," "Home influence as portrayed by Calpurnia and Portia," and "Shakespearean ethics in his dramas."

As we saw in the previous chapter, women's reading was often interwoven with improving domestic life and other topics related to the daily routines of women, perhaps as a way to justify their use of leisure time.[33] One group was ingenious enough to combine Shakespeare and domestic improvement into a product: at the Kansas state fair in 1912, women from the Good Government Club of Topeka offered "Lady Macbeth Spotbane," intended "for the removal of ink spots, iron rust and such, supposed to equal in power the strong language of Lady Macbeth when she washed her hands."[34] Such an invention relied on the common knowledge of Shakespeare's plays and characters among the general public.

The Ladies' Reading Club of Junction City, Kansas, is further testimony to the widespread popularity of reading Shakespeare as well as the challenges that women in rural locales faced when forming societies and carrying out intellectual work. The Ladies' Reading Club began in 1874 "in a little pioneer town of a few hundred inhabitants," when nine "good progressive pioneer women" joined together during the grasshopper season and drought of 1874, a time "when all vegetation was devoured and starvation and misery were threatening on every hand." Their initial mission was to distribute food, clothing, and supplies sent from the East Coast. According to one history of the club, "after having associated so closely in this work, [they] found themselves congenial in mind and purpose and consequently when Spring came and aid work was no longer incumbent," they decided to continue as a society for literary study.[35] The women "felt that in those days of strenuous exertion for material advancement, a special effort was necessary if the new homes were to maintain the intelligence and refinement of those which they had left behind."[36] Reading Shakespeare was part of this mission. In addition to their concentration on Shakespeare's plays, in 1876 they began to build a town hall and start a library with their own collection of books, which included the works of Shakespeare.[37] In Junction City, reading Shakespeare played a crucial part in establishing the "intelligence and refinement" that these women sought to establish in their homes and community.[38] Shakespeare was the foundation for their library and the means for maintaining their literary culture.

The benefits of reading Shakespeare and other literature extended beyond civic improvements. Shakespeare study also promoted personal intellectual development for rural club women, who had few other venues for such edification. Mary Vance Humphrey, one of the club founders, observed that "few of the women were accustomed to reading and speaking before others," but soon "some of these women became well known as ready speakers and able writers, but at that time they drew back with 'Oh, I never could read a paper—even if I could write one.'" Frequently relying on Shakespeare for their material, Humphrey and her cofounders worked with the other members to develop their intellectual skills until they were ready to participate in critical discussion. Humphrey modeled rhetorical skills for the club women, assuring the more reluctant, "We won't ask you to read or write until you are ready for it. We will do it for you. . . . Mrs. Boller and I read from a book or magazine, encouraging discussion afterward—until those new members learned to hear their own voices, and found it a greater pleasure to give their opinions on a literary topic than on a gown or a pudding."[39] The dual objectives of personal and public improvement characterize the role of Shakespeare clubs across the country, as reading Shakespeare became one of the main conduits for women's civic and intellectual pursuits, encouraging them to move beyond "gowns and puddings" and to engage in literary analysis and public works.[40] Such activities were especially crucial in geographical regions far from cultural centers, where women had few options for intellectual stimulation.

Other Outposts

Kansas was not unique in its abundance of Shakespeare clubs; women in numerous other rural locales engaged in similar plans of study and social activism based on their communal reading of Shakespeare. In Texas, for example, Kate Friend, director of the Waco Shakespeare Club, remarked, "There's more Shakespeare to the square inch studied in Texas than anywhere else in this country."[41] Records of Texas Shakespeare clubs substantiate her claim. According to one list of Texas literary clubs, there were twenty-seven Shakespeare clubs meeting in the first half of the twentieth century, from Lubbock to North Zulch.[42] In one district of the Texas Federation of Women's Clubs, there were six clubs devoted solely to reading Shakespeare and another eleven clubs that included Shakespeare.[43] In rural Waxahachie, Texas, two neighbors who lived far from town met to plan "more ambitious things than pretty handwork in their afternoon chats" and decided to organize a Shakespeare club. The club consisted of women in outlying areas as well as in the town of Waxahachie, including Miss Emma Davis, a "pioneer among women in the business world," who ran a millinery shop in town.[44] The members of the Waxahachie Shakespeare Club rented a cottage to be used as a room for rural women and children to stay in when in town, taking part in "rural reform efforts" in their community.[45]

Elsewhere in the United States, women were similarly occupied with Shakespeare. In the South, a report on the Kettledrum, an Alabama women's club that read Shakespeare, noted, "Too much cannot be said in praise of this delightful organization, which is a household word in the quiet refined little city" of Tuscaloosa.[46] Despite its reputation as "one of the most depressing places in the world," filled with "squalid shanties situated in the mud," the mining camp of Cripple Creek, Colorado, laid out in 1891 by gold prospectors, had a Shakespeare club that "studied carefully the plays of the dramatist whose name it bore."[47] In Eugene, Oregon, the activities of the Shakespeare Club were reported in the newspaper "in the early days when there were less things going on in town."[48]

The upper Midwest, too, had enclaves of Shakespeare clubs. In northern Michigan, the lumber town of Alpena became known as "the Athens of Northern Michigan," partly due to the reputation of its Ladies' Shakespeare Class, which met weekly beginning in 1894.[49] Likewise, the eight members of the Northport, Michigan, Shakespeare Club met every week to present papers and do readings; unsurprisingly, the women in this rural club admitted that they were "hampered somewhat in its work for the want of a reference library."[50] In Sodus, Michigan, a "Chicago lady rusticating in the country" set up the Clio Club when she "saw what the people of the town all realized, that they were in a fair way to grow rusty, narrow minded and dwarfed in intellect through inaction, for the members belong to that most monotonous of classes, farmers' wives."[51] Reading Shakespeare was a way to work against boredom and narrowmindedness.

We can also track Shakespeare clubs in the Northeast. Even though the seaside town of Camden, Maine, was several hours outside Boston, the commitment of the Camden Shakespeare Club was evident in the game it developed, "A Study of Shakespeare: An Instructive Game," designed for play by several people or for "study in the home." The game was advertised in magazines and received testimonials from W. J. Rolfe, Horace Howard Furness, and H. L. Chapman of Bowdoin College, who congratulated the club on its "ingenuity and good judgment." The description in the *Chautauquan* praised the game's combination of Shakespeare and local geography, with a "picture of the Camden mountains upon the reverse side of each card [which] does honor to the birthplace of the game."[52] This representation also served to link Camden, a town with fewer than a thousand residents, with the cultural cachet of Shakespeare.

For women in Montana, too, Shakespeare served a crucial purpose. According to one source, "The one constant in the lives of the majority of Montana women was work. Whether living on hardscrabble homesteads, in rowdy mining cities, in hastily built railroad towns, or on one of the new Indian reservations, women in early Montana faced a challenging landscape and a society that ranked them as second-class citizens." Even so, sparsely populated Montana had its share of Shakespeare clubs; one historian attests that "in virtually every Montana community, women formed church societies, cultural clubs, ethnic organizations, and ladies' auxiliaries for their own pleasure and edification, as well as to provide community social services."[53] In the mining town of Butte, Montana, for example, clubs "provided company and a means of molding their environment into a more familiar shape," and Shakespeare clubs were part of this move to create a cultural life in an unstable community where "the unpredictability of the price of copper and the dominance of mining in the economy encouraged a fluid society."[54] Such organizations were particularly important for women, who "had fewer opportunities for social recreation. Housekeeping was a lonely job and did not provide income or time for commercial pleasures." The West Side Shakespeare Club in Butte even tailored its schedule to members' needs, meeting in the evenings "because many of its schoolteacher members could not attend afternoon meetings."[55] In Great Falls, Montana, the Shakespeare Club was one of the groups women were "invited to join" as the community became more "stratified."[56] The Great Falls group offers evidence of how reading Shakespeare was a way to shape social status even in developing parts of the country and also how Shakespeare groups were often established in tandem with the founding of towns.

Local demand for Shakespeare study was high in the Midwest as well. Toledo, Ohio, had so many women apply for membership in the Arden Shakespeare Club in 1902 that three other women's Shakespeare clubs formed to meet the demand: Ye Shakespeare Study Class, the Ariel Class, and the Elizabethans. These four clubs joined together annually for more than twenty-five years as the Associated Shakespeare Clubs to celebrate Shakespeare's birthday. Their efforts during the tercentenary in 1916 were particularly impressive; in addition to promoting "a world-wide campaign for the observance of the tercentenary," they planted Shakespeare memorial trees "on the campuses of hundreds of High Schools and Colleges, on grounds of Art Institutes, on 'public squares,' in city parks." The group also celebrated by distributing over a million bookplates "used principally in public schools in New York, Boston, Philadelphia, Chicago, Pittsburgh, New Orleans, San Francisco, Seattle, Minneapolis." In an interesting reversal of cultural influence, the distribution of these bookplates to urban centers involved a celebration of Shakespeare: "each pupil brought to school his favorite book, wrote his own name on the line provided in the book-plate, and pasted the plate in the book while the teacher told the story of the significance of the event the anniversary of which all the world was observing."[57] Enthusiasm for Shakespeare study did not necessarily originate in densely populated urban areas and move to rural America; such passion could also develop in the heartland and travel to metropolitan locales.

Literacy in the Outpost

In Chapter 1, we saw how women's Shakespeare clubs were involved in the development of public libraries. Traveling libraries, which began in America in 1892, were also supported by women's clubs and disseminated books (including the works of Shakespeare) across the country, usually for free along railroad or coach lines.[58] According to one description from 1904, traveling libraries provided "the foundation for future public libraries" and targeted "the smaller communities, little villages, the farming regions, where books and magazines are few."[59] Shakespeare clubs were involved in traveling libraries in two ways: they helped organize and circulate traveling libraries and also used the libraries as resources for their own study. As Anna L. Meeker, president of the Pasadena, California, Shakespeare Club put it in a 1911 essay, "In California, before the state had developed so completely the library organization, much of the energy of the women's clubs was spent in sending traveling libraries to communities where there were no libraries."[60]

Traveling libraries often began with clubs sharing study materials but soon grew to be "a major force for general public education" and "a means for improving the lives of ordinary people living in harsh and relatively deprived conditions."[61] As Joanne E. Passet remarks, traveling libraries "thrived during an era in which reformers regarded the book as a curative for social ills."[62] According to one account, by the early 1900s, the traveling library extended to nearly every state and throughout Canada as well. Women's clubs were largely responsible for the traveling library movement, which reached "ranches, mining-camps, and country schools" in Colorado, the "rice-fields of Louisiana, the 'mountain whites' of Kentucky and Tennessee, the remote country districts of Georgia, and many isolated sections in Alabama, Missouri, and Texas."[63]

Traveling libraries extended literacy to remote regions of the country and allowed club women to "provide books to their sisters on the farms and in other isolated areas."[64] Though novels and other "questionable" items were often part of these collections, they also included works of Shakespeare and study guides. In fact, traveling libraries encouraged the formation of clubs and even provided study materials for rural Shakespeare groups to use. In California, for example, traveling libraries were designed to "encourage the foundation and maintenance of clubs for systematic study," and a 1906 report noted that Shakespeare was one of only four study club libraries.[65] Similarly, in Indiana, 163 traveling libraries were sent to "farm homes, country schools, Sunday schools, clubs and reading circles of all kinds." Shakespeare was the reading material of choice for

Indiana study clubs, along with Browning and American art.[66] The Wisconsin Free Library Commission also reported that study clubs were placing increasing demands on their traveling libraries, including the one on Shakespeare's plays.[67] In Minnesota, too, the works of Shakespeare made up one of the traveling club libraries available for clubs to borrow; in 1910–11, for example, clubs from rural Bald Eagle, Graceville, and Rockford (all with fewer than 1,000 residents) borrowed the Shakespeare traveling library.[68] The Shakespeare Club of Port Gamble, Washington, a mill town of fewer than 500 people on the shores of the Hood Canal, apparently used a traveling library; after the women had decided on their course of reading, their minutes stated, "Mrs. Ames was asked to send for the books so the reading could begin."[69] The effort involved for such groups to obtain Shakespeare study materials signals a deep commitment to making Shakespeare a part of their communities and underlines the important role Shakespeare played in the formation of American literary culture.

The infrastructure of traveling libraries also facilitated the spread of enthusiasm for group reading of Shakespeare. The Brimfield, Massachusetts, Public Library had its own extensive Shakespeare traveling library, including editions, criticism, and pictures, which it sent out to rural neighboring towns. The traveling library inspired a group of citizens in the nearby town of Wales to form a Shakespeare club. The Brimfield librarian reported that they "took up the study of Shakespeare, pursuing it more faithfully and profoundly than we did, and we sub-loaned some of the books of our travelling library to them." At the end of the winter, citizens of Wales and Brimfield celebrated with a joint Shakespeare banquet at which Shakespeare books and quotations were displayed on each table, in effect creating a local network of Shakespeare study in central Massachusetts.[70]

Culture and Public Activism in the Outpost

Although most clubs maintained a primary focus on reading Shakespeare, many groups broadened their mandate to develop greater cultural resources for a community—the establishment of a library (as discussed in Chapter 1), a scholarship, a public garden, a sponsored performance, a charitable act—inspired by an initial camaraderie about reading and particularly important in rural areas with few cultural amenities. We have already seen in earlier chapters the extensive role that Shakespeare clubs played in public libraries and various civic projects; such efforts had great effect in less populated areas.

In Wauseon, Ohio (population 2,148), for instance, the Stratford Shakespeare Club donated a complete set of the Furness Variorum Shakespeare "and many other valuable works of reference" to the public library and made annual contributions to the library fund for books. One description of its efforts attested in 1929 that "although Wauseon is a small town in the Middle-West its local library compares favorably with that of large cities" due to the efforts of the Shakespeare Club. These women further enriched their community by sponsoring a scholarship fund, doing hospital work, and patronizing stage productions of Shakespeare; members were "known to travel many miles in order to witness a performance."[71]

In Denton, Texas (population 4,187), in 1911, the Woman's Shakespeare Club raised money to provide every school in town with a drinking fountain,[72] and in Kearney, Nebraska (population 5,637), in April 1916, the Shakespeare Club helped put on a tercentenary celebration at the Opera House, where several local clubs performed scenes from Shakespeare. Many rural clubs extended their advocacy of Shakespeare to local schools. In Enid, Oklahoma (population 3,444), the Shakespeare Club encouraged the local study of Shakespeare by giving two awards a year for the best papers in the Shakespeare class at a local university.[73] The Shakespeare Club of Lawton, Oklahoma (a town with fewer than 1,000 people), founded in 1902 and apparently still meeting, endows a scholarship at Lawton's Cameron University for students who plan to teach English in high school. Such efforts suggest that it was not just communal reading but rather reading *Shakespeare* specifically that led to such extensive cultural and civic engagement. In rural America, the work of Shakespeare club women would have loomed large on the social and cultural landscape.

Conclusion

Small-town Shakespeare clubs across America helped spread the idea that reading Shakespeare was a democratic practice, available to everyone, not just privileged citizens in metropolitan areas, and that reading could be closely aligned with participation in intellectual and civic life. Shakespeare became a marker for learning, self-improvement, civilization, and entertainment for a broad array of populations across the country—cowboys, miners, and housewives alike. The combination of the club movement, with its push for self-education, and the availability of Shakespeare's plays democratized Shakespeare as reading material for all Americans, no matter their locale, and communal readers worked to improve their communities while simultaneously embedding Shakespeare as one of the foundations of American literary culture.

❧ Chapter 4

Shakespeare and Black Women's Clubs

In 1899, the front page of the Topeka, Kansas, black newspaper the *Plaindealer* reported on the tenth anniversary of a women's literary group called the Ladies' Coterie. Made up of eleven black women, including founding members the artist Fanny Clinkscale and prominent society woman Mrs. Robert Buckner, the group was described as "the nucleus around which modern Topeka society was formed."[1] The Coterie hosted a lecture by Ida Wells Barnett titled "The Evils of Lynching'" in 1895 during her antilynching tour, as well as "church suppers, whist parties, literature selections, relief work." It centered its literary work on "the best known writers of this country and England," with a goal of "advanced thought and knowledge and progressiveness generally in its members."[2] And it began by studying Shakespeare.

Like the members of the Coterie, black club women across the country saw knowledge of Shakespeare as a way to attain "advanced thought and knowledge and progressiveness" and frequently included Shakespeare as part of their educational programs, but they usually read Shakespeare in ways very different from those employed by the white women's clubs already discussed.[3] First, few black clubs read only Shakespeare. Rather, the most common practice was to read Shakespeare as part of a wider curriculum that included other classic authors, African American writers, women authors, and usually a substantial component of civic work, more so than for most white women's clubs.[4] In this context, reading Shakespeare was not the only goal for most black women readers, but it was a significant step in their commitment to education as a component of racial progress.[5] As this chapter shows, numerous black club women across the country claimed Shakespeare for their educational and social agendas.

Although black women had a long history of "organized self-help" before the formation of the National Association of Colored Women in 1896, the NACW expressed "the aspirations of a middle class that was better educated and more confident."[6] The NACW, aptly termed by one historian a "collective self-help project," began with 5,000 members in 1896, but by 1904 it had grown to 15,000 women in thirty-one states and added a department of literature.[7] According to one estimate, by 1910 black women may have formed even more voluntary associations than white women.[8]

The motto of the NACW, "Lifting as we climb," embodied the dictum of helping ("lifting") the entire "race," as opposed to improving individual women (thus the term "racial uplift"), and claimed for women the "moral leadership of the black community."[9] As one black woman put it, "we have more to do than other women. Those of us fortunate enough to have education must share it with the less fortunate of our race."[10] Similarly, Fannie B. Williams's oft-quoted description (from 1900) of the differences between white and black clubs was that white women focused on "the forward movement of the best women in the interest of the best womanhood" whereas black women concentrated on "the effort of the few competent in behalf of the many incompetent." This imperative left little time for the type of intensive reading and study that often occupied white women's clubs.[11] Even so, many black women discovered that Shakespeare could be an effective part of their agenda for "social uplift of a race."[12]

Education was one of the central tenets of the black women's club movement, and the NACW worked to promote "moral, mental, and material progress."[13] In an 1894 essay, Fannie Barrier Williams argued that black women "are eagerly demanding the best of education open to their race. They continually verify what President Rankin of Howard University recently said, 'Any theory of educating the Afro-American that does not throw open the golden gates of the highest culture will fail on the ethical and spiritual side.'"[14] The "golden gates of the highest culture" frequently included Shakespeare.[15]

Black women were charged with the imperative to improve education and thus uplift the race; as Deborah Gray White puts it, "the uplift of women was the means of uplifting the race," and clubs operated on the principle of "racial uplift through self-help."[16] Although black women agreed that racial progress was the goal of the club movement, progress "meant different things to different people, and not all black women, let alone black men, measured it the same way."[17]

Even so, black women may not have experienced the same domestic restrictions that white women did, perhaps due to the "sense of real equality with black men." Shirley J. Carlson has argued that black women did not encounter the same pressure to remain committed to the home as did white women in the early twentieth century, and because the black community had an "appreciation for a development of the feminine intellect," it urged women to become educated "for the same purposes as males": racial uplift and self-improvement.[18] Many black women felt that they "held the key to racial progress"; as one club woman put it, "It is to the Afro-American women that the world looks for the solution of the race problem."[19]

Given the female-centered agenda for racial uplift, the commitment to education, and the demand for access to "the golden gates of the highest culture," it is no surprise that Shakespeare was frequently used to address these goals around the fin de siècle. Across the country, black club women recognized the cultural power inherent in reading Shakespeare and in claiming him as part of their educational agenda. An 1895 essay in the periodical *Woman's Era* advised black club women to "not read about authors and imagine you have read the authors themselves, but with great care *study* the masters of the art of literature, authors like Milton, Dante, Shakespeare, Bacon, Goethe, Cervantes, Schiller, and others."[20] As "the pinnacle of high culture," Shakespeare could serve the interests of black club women in a variety of ways connected to education and racial uplift, prompting one writer in 1925 to argue the need for a "black Shakespeare or Dante."[21]

Shakespeare did not simply serve as pro forma material in a program of European cultural dominance. Like the clubs discussed in Chapter 1, black clubs tailored their use of literature such as Shakespeare to their own personal, collective, and community needs.[22] Black club women deliberately chose to include Shakespeare as study material because of his cultural cachet and importance, underlining Andrew Murphy's argument that "a knowledge and appreciation of Shakespeare . . . is part and parcel of a culture of success and, ultimately, a culture of power."[23]

Much evidence survives to suggest that for black club women in the decades around the turn of the century, from Boston to St. Louis to San Francisco, reading Shakespeare was part of a larger plan of empowerment, and his cultural capital was recognized and used in their educational programs.[24] Although Shakespeare helped fulfill the "dual purpose of self-improvement and community uplift" of black women's clubs, "Shakespeare" served different purposes for different groups.[25] The surviving accounts of black club women reading Shakespeare are more diverse and varied than for white club women (and less well documented), but they reveal a range of beneficial uses of Shakespeare by women.[26] As one black club woman remarked in 1895, black clubs had a special purview to address "things that are of especial interest to us as *colored* women," and they tailored Shakespeare to fit those needs.[27]

Shakespeare and Black Readers

In the late nineteenth century, a number of black communities across the country engaged in programs of racial uplift, through organized social activities such as clubs, much like the "outpost" communities discussed in the previous chapter. One survey of upper-class black clubs notes that these literary associations "devoted much attention to the study of classics, especially the works of Shakespeare."[28] In turn-of-the-century San Francisco, for example, many African Americans "joined societies and clubs to acquire social skills and poise" because "a refined, urbane life style symbolized the heights an Afro-American could attain, thus proving the equality of Black folk." According to one historian of the American West, "whether learning the 'fine art of dancing' for three dollars a month at Seales Hall in 1865 or exhibiting a flair for Shakespearean acting at the Charles H. Tinsley Drama Club four decades later, these [San Francisco] urbanites saw successful citizenship as linked to standards of Victorian civility."[29] The development of black urban cultural centers in a variety of early twentieth-century locales across America often involved Shakespeare as part of this cultured urbane lifestyle.[30]

In the West, black women's clubs "sprang up in virtually every western community that had a concentration of black women."[31] In Topeka, Kansas, for example, the explosion of population in the late 1870s, as "Southern blacks poured in at a rate of three hundred per month," created "profound, permanent changes" that led to an active population of African American women who ran "numerous religious, social, and cultural organizations," a development that may explain the profusion of clubs in Topeka, discussed later in this chapter.[32] Quintard Taylor remarks that black women's clubs in the urban West "engaged in 'racial uplift,' which usually meant encouraging education and moral rectitude among lower-class black women." They chose the content of their intellectual programs to promote this goal and "took charge of their collective lives and fates and avoided victimization by the world around them."[33] By association, Shakespeare was thus linked to racial uplift for black women as part of their curriculum of race improvement, civil rights, and women's rights.

African American literary societies were prevalent as early as the eighteenth century and "laid the foundation for a black female intellectual tradition in the United States."[34] Like the outpost clubs discussed in the previous chapter, where Shakespeare was a way to quickly establish a sense of culture, black clubs were "among the social institutions that reinforced the class consciousness of the black aristocracy in the decades after Reconstruction." The more exclusive upper-class black women's clubs "cultivated tastes for fine literature, music, and art; displayed elegant manners and other attributes of gentility; and manifested a paternalistic interest in what they viewed as the 'submerged masses.'"[35] In a

January 1902 speech to the Boston Literary and Historical Association, Reverend Frank F. Hall urged his listeners to "know something about the really great literature of Homer, Virgil, Dante, Shakespeare and don't slight the really great works for the latest publication."[36] If African American literary societies were "both agents for and products of an empowered black community," what does it mean that many of these groups read Shakespeare?[37]

It was not unusual for black families to include Shakespeare as a household symbol of upward mobility, at times physically establishing Shakespeare's works in the material goods of their homes. In his study of African American households around the turn of the century, for example, W. E. B. Du Bois described a representative black Georgia household as follows: "the furniture consists of one parlor suite, mahogany-finished and leather-bottomed, and two bookcases, one in oak and one in oil-finish, with books such as the works of George Eliot, Dickens, Shakespeare, Irving, Poe; Latin, Greek, German and French textbooks, and others."[38] Likewise, in the 1901 survey "Art in Negro Homes," Jerome Dowd inventoried the art and literature in the homes of twenty-five black residents of Durham, North Carolina, noting that "only one home was without a book." Dowd counted fifteen volumes of Shakespeare's works, second only to those of Dickens.[39]

Shakespeare occupied a significant space on the bookshelves of many African Americans, and reading Shakespeare was often part of household literate practice. Musician and writer Maud Cuney Hare recalled Shakespeare's place in the household reading of her childhood in Galveston, Texas, in the 1880s: "Father cared but little for current fiction. He read deeply, preferring early Hebrew, Greek and Roman history. He was fond of the classics, and in poetry, enjoyed Byron, perhaps next to Shakespeare. He often read aloud to us, and we liked to listen, although there were many things which we could not understand." Hare particularly remembered her father's devotion to Shakespeare, which affected the whole family: "Shakespeare was his beloved poet, and he knew him intimately. Father's enthusiasm awakened the interest of my boy cousins . . . [who] used to commit to memory long passages, and in the dining room made cheerful by an open fire, they rehearsed scenes from Shakespeare's plays. We young children of the family . . . composed the audience and thought the actors very wonderful." Shakespearean characters were so well known as common references in her family that they were often used to describe acquaintances; her father would "softly quote in an affectionate, quizzing undertone, passages" from *Richard III* in front of a family friend who walked with a limp.[40] This example suggests that for some black Americans, Shakespeare's characters circulated as common available frames of reference. Shakespeare functioned as something more than a symbolic book on the intellectual shelf; but rather represented a set of references that could be adopted and used as needed.[41]

Other black readers around the turn of the century recognized the inherent cultural power in having knowledge of Shakespeare and were able to use it to their advantage. Nick Moschovakis has argued that in this period Macbeth was "a figure for African-American self-empowerment and self-advancement."[42] Philip A. Bell, for example, who migrated to San Francisco from New York, "read selections from Shakespeare to help pay the court costs of the California fugitive slave, Archy Lee," in the nineteenth century.[43]

We might turn to the example of Ida B. Wells for a closer examination of the connections between Shakespeare and black women. According to several biographers, Shakespeare was part of Wells's middle-class life in Memphis. She "attended social gatherings at which guests recited Shakespeare, read poetry, and sang German songs—in German" and "was among a generation of educated Americans for whom mastery of English, symbolized by the mastery of the words of William Shakespeare, marked a new standard of cultural competence and class identification."[44] This background apparently influenced Wells; she was an avid reader of Shakespeare and a devoted theatergoer. Wells even quoted Shakespeare in casual conversation, complaining of "'the winter of my discontent' when a chill January day brought illness."[45]

Publicly, Wells often turned to Shakespeare as a topic for recitation and included him in her political speeches. Patricia A. Schechter points out that "figures and themes from *Macbeth* would echo across Wells's career through to the writing of her autobiography."[46] Wells was an accomplished orator of Shakespeare and recounted one memorable occasion in her diary for 4 July 1886: "Went to Mrs. H[ooks]'s concert & recited 'The Letter Reading' & Sleepwalking scenes from 'Lady McBeth.' The first was loudly applauded the last, given in my Mother Hubbard was not so effective as I could have wished."[47] An account in the black newspaper the *Chicago Conservator* praised her, using an analogy from Shakespeare: "God grant the race a few more Lady Macbeths like Ida Barnett to pump self respect into our loud-mouthed Negro leaders."[48] Later in her life, Wells again turned to the rhetorical power she found in Shakespeare; when giving a speech in protest of the "martyred Negro soldiers" in 1917, she declared, "I would consider it an honor to spend whatever years are necessary in prison as the one member of the race who protested, rather than to be with all the 11,999,999 Negroes who didn't have to go to prison because they kept their mouths shut." She ended her speech with a passage from Shakespeare: "Lay on, Macduff, and damn'd be him that first cries 'Hold enough!'"[49]

As one of the most prominent black women of her era, a well-known lecturer across the nation, and an integral part of the black women's club movement, Wells helped spread the idea among black communities that Shakespeare was rhetorically effective. According to one historian, Wells's antilynching lectures "in Boston, New Haven, Chicago, and elsewhere also provided the initial impetus for the formation of black women's clubs," which "then sustained Wells's antilynching work" by sponsoring lectures and meetings and raising money for her publications.[50] The Coterie Club of Topeka, discussed at the opening of this chapter, embodied the same values as Wells, in its reading of Shakespeare combined with a commitment to crucial issues such as antilynching.

Shakespeare in Black Women's Periodicals

Readers of black periodicals around the turn of the century would often have encountered Shakespeare as recommended reading, study, and performance material. The *Woman's Era*, the first periodical published for black women in America (1894–97), described itself as "the organ of the colored women's clubs" with "a large circulation in many of the large cities, notably Boston, New Bedford, Providence, New York, Chicago, Washington, and Kansas City."[51] The *Woman's Era* "did more than any other single agency to nationalize the club idea among the colored women of the country," and it contained numerous references to Shakespeare, both as study material for clubs and as general recommended cultural knowledge. As such, the newspaper circulated the idea nationally that Shakespeare was appropriate and desirable study material for black women.[52] For example, in the December 1894 issue, Dora J. Cole related that the Educational Club of Philadelphia, "composed of about thirty young women and girls who meet for real earnest study," sponsored a Shakespearean recital at which "Mr. R. Henri Strange showed his versatility in widely contrasted selections from Shakespeare, being especially happy in his rendition of scenes from *Hamlet*."[53] Likewise, in the May 1895 issue, the Round Table Club of Denver reported that it was devoting the year to studying Shakespeare's history plays.[54]

In addition to representing "knowledge and progressiveness" for black women, Shakespeare's heroines served as models for ideal womanhood. One black reader of the *Woman's Era* remarked that "throughout all fiction, aside from five ideal characters of Shakespeare, there is not a mother who is an admirable character." By asserting that the "duty of the wife and mother [is] to keep in touch with the world about her, and to represent the highest culture attainable,"[55] this reader linked Shakespeare to a desired ideal of African American womanhood.

The *Woman's Era* also influenced women's choices in reading material. An essay by Sarah E. Tanner appropriately titled "Reading" urged women to choose their reading material carefully because "the moment we enter the world of books that moment a great *personal* responsibility rests upon us." As we saw earlier, she implored her audience to "not read about authors and imagine you have read the authors themselves, but with great care *study* the masters of the art of literature, authors like Milton, Dante, Shakespeare, Bacon, Goethe, Cervantes, Schiller, and others."[56] The numerous readers of the journal were encouraged not to seek out just casual knowledge of Shakespeare but to immerse themselves in his writing, to "study" him with "great care."

Shakespeare was recommended reading in other African American publications as well. When J. Max Barber launched his new magazine *Voice of the Negro* in 1904, he trumpeted it as a sign that "culture is taking a deep hold upon our people. It is an indication that our people are becoming an educated, a reading people, and that is a thing of which to be proud."[57] In 1905, the magazine began a series of essays by African American writer Pauline Hopkins titled "The Dark Races of the Twentieth Century." From the start, Hopkins employed the cultural power of Shakespeare in her writing and "brought the power of inter-textuality to bear on her efforts to use literature to achieve political intervention and to provide her readers with substantial, though concise, access to valuable intellectual debate." It is no accident that her first article in the series began with "a lyrical and persuasive meditation on Shakespeare and his considerations of race and oppression."[58]

In addition to such periodicals as the *Woman's Era* and *Voice of the Negro*, the Chautauqua movement brought African American women into contact with Shakespeare. Many of the Chautauqua study programs used Shakespeare as primary material, which clubs often combined with an emphasis on social concerns related to race. The Chautauqua Circle of Atlanta, "one of the oldest African American women's clubs in the city," was founded in 1912 by Henrietta Curtis Porter, wife of dentist James Reynolds Clark, and the group espoused "strict adherence to the philosophies of the National Chautauqua Movement."[59] It is likely, then, that members read Shakespeare as part of the standard literature curriculum. According to the club's records, members discussed "race improvement after studying the Chautauqua courses," which may have placed Shakespeare study in the context of "race improvement."[60]

Shakespeare and Black Women's Clubs

Elsewhere in the African American community, the value of reading literature was touted as a panacea for women's intellectual needs. As we saw in Chapter 2, Josephine T. Washington argued in 1907 that "the most palpable gain is found in the club with a literary feature. Here the members study standard authors, read the latest books, discuss current events, and compare opinions on questions of interest." In addition to the intellectual benefits of reading, studying, and discussion, Washington stressed the importance of the literary club for helping women carve out time for intellectual activities from their home duties and for bringing women into the public sphere. She pointed out that clubs "cause many an active house-wife to find the time for study that she thought she did not have." Clubs also gave black women the opportunity to prove themselves outside the home: "Sometimes the husband has little faith in the ability of his wife to do anything outside of the domestic sphere," but women's desires extend beyond the home: "We feel that we owe something to those outside of the home-nest."[61]

The history of black women readers is much more difficult to trace than that of white women; few records of black clubs survive, and existing records can often be frustratingly scant. For example, on 7 April 1898, the newspaper *Colored Citizen* of Topeka reported the bare details of an unnamed Shakespeare club: "The Shakespeare club met with Mrs. W. I. Jamison last Monday evening." Likewise, the *Kansas State Ledger* for 25 May 1894 recounted that "four South Topeka young ladies have formed a class to study Shakespeare," but neither newspaper named the women or the club, nor did it provide any further details about these anonymous women readers.[62] The paucity of materials on black women's clubs leaves many questions unanswered. For example, there is simply no evidence that any groups read *Othello* or *Titus Andronicus*, both plays with obvious racial issues. Likewise, there is no evidence that black readers ignored these texts either. We can say for certain that Shakespeare's plays were an important and crucial part of the reading programs of numerous black women's clubs across the United States, but not enough information survives for us to make an argument about the particular texts that made up what most clubs simply recorded in their reading lists as "Shakespeare." As this chapter suggests, for black club women, the reputation of "Shakespeare" was as important as the texts themselves in terms of their reading, study, and social goals.

I found very few black women's clubs that were primarily devoted to studying Shakespeare; instead, Shakespeare was blended into a varied curriculum that included African American writers as well as texts addressing social and community needs of the early twentieth century.[63] The most common use of Shakespeare in black women's clubs was as part of a more general curriculum of literature and history, or, to use Washington's 1907 phrase, as part of "standard authors" and "the latest books."[64] As this chapter shows, black club women used Shakespeare in a variety of ways based on their various needs and goals— some read his plays, some listened to lectures on Shakespeare, some performed plays for their community—all evidence of what Elizabeth McHenry calls "a complex and differentiated black population" that counters "the myth of the monolithic black community."[65] It is worth underlining the fact that for black women, reading and studying Shakespeare was a conscious choice they made in light of his ideological and cultural cachet, and a move intended to take advantage of his cultural capital.[66]

Case Study: Black Women's Clubs and Shakespeare in Kansas

We have an unusually rich array of details about black women's clubs in Kansas, largely because Nick Chiles, the editor of the black newspaper the *Plaindealer*, was supportive of women's clubs and regularly printed their news in a column titled "The Club Woman: Of Interest to Women of Our Race in Kansas."[67] It is likely that reading groups in other areas of the country resembled those in Kansas, but their details did not get recorded; we might consider the variety of clubs in Kansas as a case study of the possible ways Shakespeare functioned in black women's clubs in other locales where records do not survive.

Several black women's clubs in Kansas had substantial Shakespearean components, and some were devoted completely to studying Shakespeare.[68] According to the black newspaper *Topeka Times-Observer*, there were enough black literary clubs in Kansas to merit a state convention of literary societies, which was held in December 1891: "In every town in Kansas there are a few persons, a very few in some, who constantly aim to gain a thorough knowledge of English and American literature and to become conversant with the great minds of modern and ancient history."[69] One such group was the Ladies' Coterie of Topeka, which began in 1889 with eleven black women. In its second year, the club joined the men of the Pleasant Hour Circle in a Chautauqua study club, but the women playfully noted that "the desire for, and pleasure taken in a woman's club was too great to be effaced even by the scintillating minds of our superiors—the men" and they returned to their women-only structure.[70] Though the club read primarily Shakespeare, members also covered current events: they "believed that to be progressive, they must advance not along one line of study alone, but that the topics of the day should receive attention too."[71] In their first year, they concentrated on Shakespeare's *Henry VIII* and Longfellow's poetry, and the second year focused on "Home and Fireside" and U.S. history.[72] Nonliterary topics included a lecture by civil rights advocate Josephine Silone Yates called "The Social Necessity of an Equal Standard of Morality for Men and Women," in which Yates advocated "a noble, conscious and ideal fatherhood" as well as "true and noble motherhood."[73]

Topeka artist Fanny Clinkscale hosted the club's final meeting of 1895 and provided the music, with Miss E. M. Glenn offering a "Character Study of Julius Caesar." Other women contributed as well; Mrs. F. E. Buckner reviewed the year's work, Mrs. Jamison provided instrumental music, and Mrs. Keith sang.[74] Their motto, "Life without Literature Is Death," speaks to the value this group placed on studying Shakespeare, and their literate practices resemble those of the white women's clubs discussed in Chapter 1. Records suggest that at some point the Coterie may have become biracial, including white women such as Martha Farnsworth, a politically and socially active woman in Topeka.[75]

Another black Topeka group known as the Arden Club gathered weekly to read Shakespeare, at times meeting in conjunction with the Coterie to take on various social and cultural projects. In 1901, the *Plaindealer* reported that the clubs met together "to perfect their plans for an entertainment to be given for the school picture fund. There will be an exhibit of pictures from one of the book stores and a program rendered by pupils from the public schools."[76] The Arden Club hosted elaborate annual celebrations of Shakespeare's birthday; in 1900, for example, each woman was asked "to suggest in some way, in dress, by pantomime or quotation, some Shakespearean character." In 1901, its celebration included five papers on Shakespeare: "Shakespeare as a Man," by Miss M. Jamison; "Shakespeare as a Dramatist," by Mrs. S. G. Watkins; "Favorite Characters from Shakespeare," by Mrs. R. H. Wade; "Familiar Sayings from Shakespeare," by Miss H. Hawkins; and "Selection from *King John,*" by Miss L. Thompson.[77] In 1902, the club played a game with questions about Shakespeare's life and works, with a souvenir of "a card with a small water color, tied with the club color and the word Shakespeare artistically written."[78] That same year, the women had a contest to answer questions about Shakespeare's life and work, in addition to a competition to form words from "Arden."[79]

The Arden Club appears to have included men, and it had some of the same members as the Ladies' Coterie; the *Plaindealer* reported that Mr. C. F. Clinkscale read a paper on Kenilworth Castle, followed by a reading of the last act of *Henry VI* part 2, and Mr. and Mrs. Clinkscale hosted the next meeting. Mrs. Robert Buckner, also a member of the Coterie, gave a "review" of Act 3 of *Henry VI*, and the club read and discussed Act 4.[80] Mr. Ira Guy reviewed the life of Henry V, as reported in the *Plaindealer* on 17 May 1901. That same year, the club began to preserve its work by printing its yearly programs in book form.[81] The fact that many members of the Arden Club also belonged to the Coterie suggests a vibrant black intellectual community in Topeka, one that was centered on reading Shakespeare.

It is likely that a third group in Topeka read Shakespeare as part of its literature program. The Ne Plus Ultra Club began in 1899 with a mandate of "inculcating the spirit of good will and unity among [women] so that various human needs and problems could be met intelligently and harmoniously," and to "stimulate the domestic interests of home life and make life in the home one of less drudgery but more beauty." The women began with various forms of sewing (embroidery, crocheting, tatting) and art, but because "each woman was eager to broaden her knowledge to the fullest extent," they soon added literature to their agenda.[82] Given the local interest in Shakespeare among Topekans, it is likely that he was part of their program.

Elsewhere in Topeka, Shakespeare was a component of other black clubs. When the Athenian Literary Society hosted a lecture on Shakespeare by the Rev. G. C. Booth, "one of the most scholarly gentlemen in our city, irrespective of race," the *Topeka Times-Observer* reported, "The Athenian bids fair to become one of the most progressive societies in the state."[83] Likewise, Shakespeare's plays were esteemed by the members of the Capital City Whist Club, who offered two volumes of Shakespeare, *The Merchant of Venice* and *Twelfth Night*, as prizes in 1898.[84]

Interest in Shakespeare among African Americans spread from Kansas to neighboring states. The Interstate Literary Association was founded in 1892 as an "outlet for cultural interests of black Topekans" as well as citizens from Nebraska and Missouri, predominantly "educators and other professionals." Thomas C. Cox notes that "in addition to readings from Shakespeare and Tennyson, the association sponsored lectures, art exhibitions, and musicals, all of which were carried off with some sophistication. Social consciousness and endorsement of race progress were evident in the association's active support of quality public education and in strident opposition to segregated schools"; by association, Shakespeare was part of this agenda.[85] Prominent black citizens were involved in the group: John Lewis Waller, the first African American consul to Madagascar, honed his debating skills as a member of the Interstate Literary Association.[86]

Shakespeare and Racial Uplift

The reading programs of numerous African American clubs reveal an important and recurring role of Shakespeare in relation to agendas of racial uplift and advancement of social ambitions. According to one historian of African American clubs in Chicago, for example, studying literature such as Shakespeare served to "join club women of like aspiration and social class."[87] Several examples of individual women and of representative clubs exemplify similar mandates linking Shakespeare to racial uplift through agendas of cultural education.

In earlier chapters, we saw how individual women were often the impetus behind forming clubs and setting their agendas (Anna Randall-Diehl of the Fortnightly Shakespeare Club of New York, or Agnes Filmore of the Zanesville, Ohio, Shakespeare Club). We might look to the example of Carrie Still Shepperson, of Little Rock, Arkansas, as a case study of the possibilities for black women's involvement in club life and for the ways Shakespeare could be influential in black communities. Shepperson, the mother of African American composer William Grant Still, was an active member of the Phyllis Wheatley

Club and the Bay View Reading Club, where she likely read Shakespeare. The Bay View educational system included a "School of Expression and Public Reading" with a special course on Shakespeare as well as an English literature course on Shakespeare.[88]

Around the turn of the century, Shepperson was a founding member of the Lotus Club, where members "read the classics and the latest 'best sellers,' and discussed books at meetings." The Lotus Club focused on both personal and public intellectual initiatives for women and resembled many typical white women's Shakespeare clubs in its reading and use of Shakespeare for the development of public literacy initiatives. According to her granddaughter, Shepperson's involvement in the Lotus Club "even led her to write a book herself," now lost, about "the prejudices against Negroes and women in her day."[89] Carrie Shepperson was "committed to a mission of service and racial uplift" and found that Shakespeare was one way to achieve those goals. She was "disturbed over the fact that there was no public library in Little Rock open to colored people, despite the fact that several colored residents had extensive private libraries."[90] Shepperson began to put on productions of Shakespeare, raising enough money to form a school library in 1916. She also organized several community initiatives around reading, including performances of Shakespeare with local students. Her shows were so successful that she began to stage an annual "extravaganza" held in 1918 in the Kempner Theatre, where performances were sold out "long before opening night."[91] When she helped her students perform *The Merchant of Venice* and *A Midsummer Night's Dream*, for example, she was renowned for her particular emphasis on "the intricacies of Shakespeare's vocabulary."[92] Judith Anne Still, granddaughter of Carrie Shepperson, remembers her teaching lines from *The Merchant of Venice* to a "slender, walnut-skinned Negro boy" by "holding a large volume of Shakespeare out in front of him."[93]

Shepperson's literary activities affected her son William Grant Still, later a famous composer, who recalled growing up "in an atmosphere of literary clubs, lectures, musical recitals [and] stage shows" and described his family as "people who were interested in intellectual matters."[94] Club meetings were also inspirational; he wrote, "Many times I had to escort my mother to club meetings when Mr. Shepperson wasn't at home," even recalling one meeting at which "Richard B. Harrison, later to win fame as The Lord in 'The Green Pastures,' read a Shakespearian play."[95] Like the activities of numerous women discussed in Chapter 2, Shepperson's intellectual work had an influence on her home and family, and her efforts serve as an example of the ways Shakespeare could function for black club women who were committed to racial uplift.

Like Carrie Still Shepperson, other influential black women saw the possibilities for the role of literature (and often specifically Shakespeare) in their social agendas. The activities of Margaret Murray Washington, wife of Booker T. Washington, underscore this function. In 1895, Washington founded the Tuskegee Women's Club, composed mainly of middle-class female teachers and faculty wives from the Tuskegee Institute.[96] Mary Washington, a founder and president of the National Association of Colored Women, began the club for the "general intellectual development of women" and to provide "a forum for their intellectual, educational, and spiritual growth."[97] The club was also involved in such social initiatives and community projects as the Russell Plantation, a settlement for former convicts, for whom club women instituted a reading program. The club organized "mothers' meetings" as well as reading groups for men.[98] For the Shakespeare Tercentenary in 1915–16, the club put on a lengthy, elaborate celebration with readings, music, and performances of plays. The *Southern Letter* newspaper advertised a week of events in honor of Shakespeare, including "a review of the life of Shakespeare," readings from several plays, and performances of *The Merchant of Venice* and *A Midsummer Night's Dream*.[99] The club's commemoration of the Shakespeare Tercentenary was an activity in a larger context of social programs: setting up mothers' meetings, improving the Russell Plantation, and engaging in women's "intellectual development," placing Shakespeare within their progressive social agenda.[100]

In addition to the importance of individual women and localized clubs for the history of Shakespeare study, several larger black organizations turned to Shakespeare as part of their public agendas of racial uplift and cultural edification. In Chicago, the Frederick Douglass Center held regular Sunday forums where cofounder Celia Parker Wooley "often introduced, read, and critiqued European and American writers whose works carried deliberate political and social themes." One program in 1906 included Rev. Joseph Stolz's paper "Shylock: A Study in Prejudice," and the forums drew people from a variety of economic levels.[101] The center also had a Woman's Club, "composed of prominent African American and native-born white women," who studied African American and European literature, including a class on English literature taught by Ida B. Wells.[102] Given Wells's affection for Shakespeare, it is likely that she included his works.

One of the more extensive literary groups in the country, the Bethel Literary and Historical Association of Washington, D.C., included Shakespeare as part of its educational program and had a significant influence on black clubs across America. The association was founded in 1881 and included "most of Washington's black elite."[103] According to the group's history, the original plan was to "make the Literary the intellectual center of Washington." After a successful first year, the Bethel Literary had clearly "met a popular need" in its "appeal to the intellect" and vowed "to supply all the people's intellectual needs."[104] This format disseminated material to a large group of people, often in the hundreds, and typically included a paper read by a speaker and followed by an open discussion.[105] As Michelle N. Garfield argues, this type of public lecture "demonstrated the way in which the black elite wanted to make education and knowledge available to the larger community": Shakespeare was part of this goal of upward mobility and "higher culture."[106] In 1893, for example, papers included "Race Problem—Theories Reviewed," "Woman's Suffrage," and "The Shakesperian School of Ethics."[107] The concluding exercise considered the questions "What has Bethel Literary done for the race?" and "What may it do?" Although the members were made up of the "black elite," the Bethel Literary was an important oral forum for spreading ideas about literature, politics, and culture to a population that was not necessarily literate.[108]

Indeed, the Bethel Literary provides evidence of a longer history of the relationship between African Americans, Shakespeare, and social aspirations. According to the 1896 account of the Bethel Literary, earlier African American groups had met to study Shakespeare and other literature in D.C.: "There was, indeed, a literary organization here in 1881, admission to which was based more on certain social tests rather than always on sound literary qualifications or ambitions." For almost a decade, "first under one name and then under another, in drawing-rooms, kindred spirits met, discussed Shakespeare and Tennyson and held conversations on art and music."[109] Given this history of linking Shakespeare to upward mobility, it is no surprise that the Bethel Literary program was successful; the group engendered "the establishment of other literary organizations, in different sections of our city, in connection with churches, all conducted on the same general plan as that of this foster mother," which made Shakespeare available for those who passed the "social tests."[110] Though the Bethel Literary involved men and women, women were active participants "not only as members but as central players" in the leadership of the group; Mary Church Terrell served as president in 1892. The activities of this group were circulated across the country in African American newspapers and through traveling speakers.[111]

Other black groups committed to racial uplift and education reveal similar uses of Shakespeare. The all-women Booklovers Club of Washington, D.C., founded in 1894, aimed to "pursue courses of reading and study for higher culture," covering Shakespeare, Wagner, and topics related to family life.[112] The club's influence is evident in the fact that it inspired outpost groups in Harlem; Kansas City, Missouri; and Kansas City, Kansas, where its program of reading and study material, including Shakespeare, was circulated to other parts of the United States.

Like several of the clubs already discussed, for which Shakespeare was part of a civic and intellectual agenda, two groups in Durham, North Carolina, used Shakespeare as an impetus for "cultural and social interaction" in the "small but growing educated class of black Durhamites."[113] Mary Pauline Fitzgerald Dame and her sister Sallie Fitzgerald founded the Volkamenia Literary Club in 1903 as "an organization to bring Durham's coterie of educated young adults together for cultural and social interaction."[114] With women as the "nucleus," Volkamenia had a mixed-gender membership drawn from the "elite and middle classes of Durham." At a typical meeting, "one member prepared a paper on an assigned topic for discussion, and all brought newspaper clippings about current events. In addition to art, music, and literature, the subjects of migration, segregation, and images of blacks were likely topics, and the role of women in a dynamic black community held the attention of club members." Shakespeare provided some of the literary content of this group, which "enlarged the number of 'public' places where women spoke across gender lines." The club also collected supplies for schoolteachers and taught literacy through a newspaper reading circle, which later developed into a forum to increase the number of working-class black voters.[115] Like the Tuskegee Women's Club, this mixed-gender group blended Shakespeare with a broader agenda of social and cultural activities.

Two examples highlight the importance for women of Volkamania, both as intellectual stimulation and as a venue for upward mobility. Lawyer and poet Pauli Murray relates her family's involvement in the Volkamania Literary Club. She writes in her autobiography that her "aunts, mother, and older cousins were among the most popular young women of their growing community and pioneered in its cultural beginnings," including starting the Volkamania club, a tennis club, and a drama club. Murray recalls that she was "acutely conscious of living outside the elite circle," and the women in her family worked to improve their status. Her aunt (who helped start Volkamenia) told her, "Your family stands with the best. It's not what you have but what you *are* that counts."[116] Participation in Volkamenia, and by extension reading Shakespeare, was part of this social agenda.

Susie V. Gille, a black northern woman who came to the South in 1906 to work for the black insurance company North Carolina Mutual and Provident Association, was part of this "new black elite." As an employee of Mutual, she was expected to "illustrate that African Americans were capable of being what whites believed they were not: worthy citizens who could uphold the ethical imperatives of the American mainstream." Joining the Volkamenia Literary Club, where she read Shakespeare, was part of this purpose.[117]

"Social betterment" was the main goal for another black club in Durham with a specific focus on Shakespeare. Founded at about the same time as the Volkamenia Club, the Schubert-Shakespeare Club comprised both men and women, who took part in "rigid reading programs, entertained lecturers, held debates, and engaged in self-evaluation"; they "imitated the white intelligentsia

at the same time they sought to organize the race for 'social betterment.'"[118]
Dr. Aaron Moore, a prominent Durham physician, was a partner in the North
Carolina Mutual Life Insurance Company as well as the "driving force of the
social and cultural life of the black community" in Durham. In the early years of
the twentieth century, he actively "encouraged the company to support a literary society that sponsored reading programs, offered lectures, and held debates,
and the Schubert-Shakespeare Club, which offered classical music, plays, and
lectures on 'social betterment' of the race."[119]

Case Study: The Detroit Study Club

We might look to the Detroit Study Club as an example of how black club
women focused on Shakespeare as study material and as a means of cultural
betterment, as well as for the repercussions of these activities for the women
involved. One of the longest-running clubs, the Detroit Study Club started
out as a Browning club in 1898 but soon widened its scope to include other
authors such as Shakespeare, under the rubric of studying "any author or subject that will contribute to the literary, civic, social and cultural growth of the
members."[120] The club included affluent black women who "studied issues,
literature and music" and was limited to forty-five members by invitation only,
often involving several generations of women. One member who used to attend meetings at age seven with her mother remarks on the influence of the
club: "The notion of lifelong learning, the cultivation of a wide range of interests and a connection to the community was the water in which I swam."[121]
A club history written in 1928 described the founding members as "earnest,
serious minded women of literary tendencies, who felt the need of keeping
their own minds bright and their schooling brushed up," who "eagerly grasped
the opportunity to study and make weekly excursions among the best poets
and authors of the world." Study of Shakespeare and other authors provided a
respite from domestic duties; as one member put it, women were "so engrossed
in the care and comfort of their families" that "they were apt to become dull
by the cobwebs collecting in their brain," and the club offered "an oasis in the
weekly routine of duties."[122] Their discussions often veered from literature to
the current status of women; one member recalled that around 1915 several
meetings were devoted to the history of the suffrage movement, and members
were "just becoming conscious of the change in women all over the world who
were clamoring for 'rights,' and forgetting to stay at home and rock the cradle
of the man child who would rule the world." The club thus changed its focus
in 1915 to include women's rights.[123] Later in the twentieth century, the group
undertook a biracial study of literature, including both black and white women
(and sometimes male guests) in their meetings.

The 1928 club history reports that in the early decades of the fin de siècle, "gradually the Club changed from just a self-culture club and branched out into the broader field of Philanthropy and civic and social work in our own city." Beginning in 1908, the club was able to have its programs printed, and it changed its meeting time to evenings "after many women began to be occupied in the world's work during the day." As well as entertaining women from white clubs, the Detroit Study Club hosted Booker T. Washington, the composer Nathaniel Dett, and avid reader Lucy Laney, all of whom would have shared in the appreciation of Shakespeare.[124] Members included the sopranos Maggie Porter Cole and Florence Cole Talbert and social activist Lucy Thurman. The club history records that over its hundred years, "the club has helped us to not only keep our own minds bright and latent talents in many developed, but best of all, it led us to the realization that our education was to be used in the service of our fellow men."

Like most black clubs, the Detroit Study Club left no specific details about its reading of Shakespeare—no play titles, discussion topics, or study guides. Its history simply lists "Shakespeare" as part of members' reading. However, club records offer a detailed picture of the importance and role of this group for its members and for its community; although we do not know exactly which plays of Shakespeare were read and discussed, it is clear that Shakespeare was part of the group's educational mandate.

In its effect on the families of members, the Detroit Study Club resembles many of the clubs discussed in Chapter 2. Deborah Duval Gates, a third-generation member, writes, "I can't remember a time when the Detroit Study Club was not a part of my life. As a very young girl I remember my grand-mother, Mabel Moore, and mother, Agnes Duval, dressing up every other Friday evening to attend 'The Study Club.' . . . The importance of the meeting was in the air and the wishes of a six or seven year old about wanting them to stay home were secondary." Gates notes that "as I grew a bit older I had to attend some of the meetings with my mother or grandmother. There I had to be a perfectly quiet observer to watch the elegant ladies discuss" literature and other topics. Gates recalls that although the Study Club "remained an important part of my family's life as I grew up," it was not until after she was married that her grandmother "told me that she felt it was time that I join the Study Club."

Other members of the club remember its influence on them as young children and the legacy of membership among generations of women. Dottie Pelton recollects, "My mother and grandmother preceded me and left a brilliant legacy. My childhood memories are highlighted with tutelage from many of their contemporaries," many of whom were members of the Detroit Study Club. Likewise, Karen H. Rucker joined the club along with her mother in the 1970s and recalls that there were other mother-daughter members; several of her aunts were members as well: "so many of the members were of my family," she observes. For member Louise Williams, who served as club president in the later twentieth century, the Detroit Study Club was intimately bound with her family history: "My earliest memory of the Detroit Study Club, from the mid 1930's, was sitting on the stairwell landing of our family home . . . and watching and listening to the members conduct their meeting. My sister Barbara and I quietly watched and listened to the ladies speaking so properly. Dinner would be served first, followed by the business meeting and then the subject presentations. Meetings were always held in the home then. We thought the ladies were elegant, intellectual, but ever so serious and proper." For her grandmother, Evangeline Aray Loomis, who served as president in 1938, the club was "the highlight" of her life, and "as far back as I can remember she was always planning and reading and talking about the Study Club."

The Study Club's influence in Detroit is evident in the numerous accolades that appear in the booklet published to commemorate the club's 100th anniversary in 1998. A letter from U.S. Senator Spencer Abraham, for example, attests that "the efforts and accomplishments of the club have touched many lives in the greater Detroit area, reaching far beyond the club's membership." Congresswoman Carolyn Kilpatrick wrote that "the Detroit Study Club understands that black women guard and nurture the intellectual and spiritual growth of our race," and the club even received a letter from then president Bill Clinton, congratulating members for "join[ing] together in a spirit of cooperation to realize a common vision." According to Darlene Clark Hine, clubs such as the Detroit Study Club "were safe spaces within which [black women] could plan their personal and collective agenda to affect social change."[125] Their study plans placed Shakespeare in a framework of texts and topics that advocated social change and also entailed upward mobility and upper-class aspirations.[126]

Social Change vs. Self-Education

The tension between achieving social change and attaining self-education created controversy for many black clubs. Though spending time reading Shakespeare fulfilled the imperative of "advanced thought and knowledge and progressiveness" (in the words of the Coterie of Topeka), it also took time away from more crucial social programs and thus came under criticism. An article in the black newspaper *Topeka Plaindealer* from 14 February 1902 denounced "the lack of closer sympathy between the educated Negro woman and her less fortunate sister. Not having that charity for her sister that should come with education, the educated Negro woman has sought refuge in Shakespearean clubs 'and sich' [*sic*] while the masses of the women of our race are suffering for the knowledge that makes home 'one glad sweet song.'"[127] The conflict is evident here between more urgent social issues and the "refuge" that study of Shakespeare may have provided for "the educated Negro woman." Likewise, in 1904 Booker T. Washington criticized a student who studied "the genius of Shakespeare" and "showered imperial Shakespeare with much eloquence." Because this student "came from a log cabin on the outskirts of a sleepy little town in Alabama, where her surroundings were the most wretched," Washington argued that she should have focused her education on "cooking and sewing and housekeeping and nursing and gardening, as are needed to make her father's cabin a home."[128] Such critiques ignore the reality that black women set their own agenda for education and racial uplift, determining the content of their educational programs themselves.[129] The fact that they often included Shakespeare speaks to his place as desirable material for women seeking self-improvement, and in the case of the black women's club movement, self-improvement translated into racial uplift.

The choice between personal advancement achieved through education, and racial uplift through social change, is captured by writer Charles Chesnutt, who himself belonged to a co-ed group in Cleveland called the Social Circle (founded 1869). It is likely that the Social Circle read Shakespeare; it "held formal meetings twice a month in the homes of members for evenings of debate, music, dramatic reading, discussion, and light refreshment."[130] Chesnutt's daughter wrote that after her parents had been in Cleveland for several years, "they were invited to join the Cleveland Social Circle. This little club had been organized in 1869 by a group of young colored people who wanted to promote social intercourse and cultural activities among the better-educated people of color. This was a very exclusive organization—membership in it was the *sine qua non* of social standing." The club met every other week, and "there was always a literary and musical program."[131]

In his stories "The Wife of His Youth" and "A Matter of Principle," Chesnutt creates a group called the "Blue Vein Society," described in "The Wife of His Youth" (1899) as "a little society of colored people, more white than black."[132] This "little society" met in a northern city called Groveland, and its purpose was to "establish and maintain correct social standards among a people whose social condition presented almost unlimited room for improvement." The society is both condemned and praised in the story, as "a glaring example of the very prejudice from which the colored race had suffered most," but later, "when such critics had succeeded in getting on the inside, they had been heard to maintain with zeal and earnestness that the society was a life-boat, an anchor, a bulwark and a shield . . . to guide their people through the social wilderness."[133]

The society was presided over by Mr. Ryder, the "dean of the Blue Veins," and "poetry was his passion."[134] He could "repeat whole pages of the great

English poets" and had a "good library, especially rich in poetry." At the end of "The Wife of His Youth," Ryder tells a story to a crowd at a party and then quotes from Shakespeare: "After we had looked upon the matter from every point of view, I said to him, in words that we all know:

'This above all: to thine own self be true,
And it must follow, as the night the day,
Thou canst not then be false to any man.'"[135]

At the story's climax, Ryder uses Polonius's lines from *Hamlet* as a way to resolve his dilemma of acknowledging his racial heritage and proving himself to be "a man of high principle."[136] For Ryder, Shakespeare serves as an ethical arbiter on whom he relies to make moral decisions, but also as common cultural content ("words we all know") for his upwardly mobile audience. In a 1930 letter, Chesnutt wrote about his sympathies for the character of Ryder: "I belonged to the 'Blue Vein Society,' and the characters in 'The Wife of His Youth' and 'A Matter of Principle' were my personal friends. I shared their sentiments to a degree, though I could see the comic side of them."[137] Chesnutt's depiction of the intellectual club underlines the resonance Shakespeare had for black readers in America. When seeking literary texts to provide self-education, offer cultural knowledge, and facilitate "racial uplift," black club women often turned to Shakespeare.

Conclusion

In many ways, black and white women's clubs were similar. Lynda F. Dickson points out that "both consisted of *women* who were interested in improving themselves through the study of literature; they were mothers who were interested in finding better methods of child and home care; they were hungry for regular social interactions with women of similar interests; and they were conscientious community participants who felt the need to help those less fortunate than themselves."[138] As this chapter has shown, we might add to that list the fact that many of these clubs saw in Shakespeare material that they could use to their advantage.

Some of the differences between black and white women's clubs can account for their contrasting emphases on literature and on Shakespeare. Black and white women's clubs had similar organizational structures, membership, and ideologies about the importance of women's moral authority in the home, but the mission of black clubs involved a much more urgent need for social reform.[139] Anne Firor Scott points out that black women felt responsible for the black community and that "certain issues that white women's associations rarely touched were central concerns of black women: lynching, rape, domestic violence, and the convict lease system."[140] Therefore, literature often had to take a back seat to more pressing concerns.

Activist and club woman Fannie Barrier Williams pointed this out in her 1900 essay "The Club Movement among Colored Women of America." Williams distinguished between white and black clubs, stating that "the club movement among colored women reaches into the sub-social condition of the entire race. Among white women clubs mean the forward movement of the best women in the interest of the best womanhood. Among colored women the club is the effort of the few competent in behalf of the many incompetent; that is to say that the club is only one of many means for the social uplift of a race. Among white women the club is the onward movement of the already uplifted."[141] As Williams noted, more was at stake in the activities of black clubs; their choice of Shakespeare as reading material is thus especially significant in light of the fact that black clubs often devoted substantial time to activities other than reading.

The availability of leisure time for study of literature may also have had an effect on the way black women approached their reading; according to one source, in comparison with white women, black women "lacked the financial resources necessary for equal leisure."[142] Black educator Charlotte Hawkins Brown made this point in a 1929 speech to the Volkamenia Club: "You know me surely as a very busy woman, and while I scorn not the delights of literature in all of its beauty and art, my utilitarian program has deprived me of that recent research and study sufficient to meet the demands of a literary organization."[143] Considering their time constraints, black club women thus had to be more deliberate in their reading choices.[144] Reading Shakespeare was often part of a well-crafted agenda to attain such goals as racial uplift, upward mobility, and self-education.

Conclusion

The women whose stories of reading Shakespeare I have related in this book were, for the most part, not well known, and their names have long since disappeared from the historical record, if they ever had a place there to begin with. Yet their sheer number means that Shakespeare had a substantial impact on the lives of ordinary women, who may not have achieved fame or fortune but who nevertheless influenced their own families and communities. They remind us of Shakespeare's role in the history of women's lives, particularly for ordinary women who were not famous authors, public figures, or well-known household names but who found a fulfilling and rewarding life of the mind by reading, studying, and performing Shakespeare. In addition, the women readers in this book do not fit into the narrative of the evolution of Shakespeare to an institutionalized academic highbrow author, and the politicized discussions of the canon have rarely associated Shakespeare with intellectual liberation for groups outside power structures.[1] Yet the women readers chronicled in these pages make a case for Joan Shelley Rubin's argument that "the meaning of texts [is] inseparable from the associations, longings, and purposes they acquired in the hands of readers."[2]

To say that Shakespeare was liberating for housewives, that his characters were inspiring, that he provided intellectual stimulation for women amid their domestic duties, that he energized common people who met in the evening after working all day, and that he was a basis for building communities for thousands of ordinary citizens across America does not fit the image of Shakespeare as the highbrow property of an elite and exclusive enclave.[3] Yet numerous women readers designed their own journey of self-education and found value in Shakespeare as an author who fulfilled their desire for knowledge and gave them a place in intellectual history.

The women who provide the basis for this book read Shakespeare of their own accord, separate from any established institution or academic setting. In doing so, they discovered subject matter that allowed them a remarkable autonomy to chart their own course of self-education and to express their own opinions through writing, analysis, discussion, performance, and adaptation. Many of these freedoms occurred for women in clubs with men as well as with women—this female intellectual space was not something that existed just with women, but rather was a concept that circulated in co-ed groups as well, where women were given equal opportunities to contribute.

The bias against giving ordinary readers (particularly women) agency for literary and cultural change may also explain the absence of these women from the historical record.[4] Further, these omissions speak to class and geographical biases in literary history. Indeed, one rarely hears of such places as Pocatello, Idaho; Jerseyville, Illinois; and Holden, Missouri, as noteworthy locations of literary activity, nor are housewives, farm women, and small-town teachers frequently given credit for effecting literary and cultural change.

★★★★★

If we return briefly to the Portia Club of Avon, Illinois, with which I began this book, we can trace a trajectory of the club's focus in its one-hundred-year history. The club began in 1894 with "at home reading and study," in which members were responsible for leading "discussions on authors, locations, art and music of that time." The club's main objective was initially studying Shakespeare, but as the twentieth century progressed, the aim of the club shifted according to the needs and interests of its members. In its second decade, social and political issues were still of interest; in 1905, the club's tenth anniversary was celebrated with a "toast to the 'New Woman,'" and in 1909–10 the club discussed the temperance movement. From 1911 to 1921, the women took particular interest in civic issues, with a "special concern" for "Boys on the Streets." Yet in this same decade, club historian Ruth M. Davis perceived a decline in the club: "How many 'modern' women would make and wear costumes and learn many lines just for the amusement of their friends? How many would walk to the library once a week during the winter? We know how few now are willing to study for and present programs with such enthusiasm." Davis celebrated the progress of women but lamented the loss of solidarity and camaraderie: "I am glad that our lot as women has much improved but I retain a bit of envy for these women who could study and present 'papers,' but also use the words gaiety, amusement, merriment and 'happy event' as a regular part of their reports." Shakespeare study was no longer a primary objective; by 1924–25, the club focus had shifted to "Travel, Drama, and Miscellaneous." In 1939, the club did away with the position of "Critic" (the member responsible for analysis and research), and the club historian again commented that the group was "slowing down." One meeting in 1942, for example, focused entirely on "the appropriateness of slacks." In 1944–45, the club records chronicled a further waning; the "'mad rush of the world today' was hurting the attendance. Sometimes only half of the members attended meetings." Programs focused on travel, politics, and philanthropic work but rarely on Shakespeare. The year 1965–66, for instance, was devoted entirely to speakers on travel, including "what to wear, what to do, how to act." By the 1980s, most programs were presented by nonmembers whereas "in the early years 100% of the programs were prepared by members and they worked countless hours to prepare them." The last years of the club's history, in the 1990s, show great pride and nostalgia for the "small group of young women hungry for education, culture and self improvement" who founded the club in 1894, yet current members insisted that they owed the "ghosts" of the club "no apology in this age of job-holding women, TV, automobiles and computers, though we still marvel at the quality of work done when modern conveniences were little known." The club seems to have fulfilled its purpose long ago and now exists as a tribute to a period of history when women's pursuits—intellectual, social, political, and civic—could be fulfilled with Shakespeare study.[5]

Like the Portia Club of Avon, the peak of Shakespeare clubs seems to have been the period from 1890 to 1940, but it is difficult to say exactly what happened to the majority of clubs chronicled in this book.[6] Most seem to have stopped meeting in the postwar period, but few clubs formally recorded a slow decline in membership, sparse turnout at meetings, and an eventual decision to disband (a likely trajectory).[7]

Major world events occurred just as a second generation of women were due to take over from club founders—the Depression, World War I, and World War II. During the two world wars, many clubs shifted to fewer meetings or became involved in more demanding war efforts. According to the history of the Eugene, Oregon, Shakespeare Club, "at times, due to the two World wars, it had been necessary to omit or sharply curtail plans for the club's social events."[8] Social concerns took precedence; the history also notes, "Meetings during World War I were discontinued by vote of the club in October 1917, and members gave their time to Red Cross work. The little money in the treasury was used to buy War Savings Stamps." Although meetings resumed in 1919, World War II again disrupted the club, and in the 1940s "club members were found answering the higher call of duty in connection with World problems . . . they enrolled for regular Red Cross work, helped with Bundles for Britain, made comfort kits and quilt tops for the use of soldiers and sailors, subscribed in 1942 and 1943 to LIFE magazine for soldiers at the filter center and contributed money for other supplies for enlisted men." Apparently, the club's efforts were so diffused that "serious consideration was given to discontinuing all club meetings until after the war."[9]

Other clubs followed a similar pattern. According to the history of the Silver Creek, New York, Shakespeare Club, "nearly everyone was knitting socks" in 1918. "Yes, the war made its way into the Shakespeare Club," noted its historian.[10] The Friday Shakespeare Club of Santa Cruz, California, was also involved in war efforts, as its records proudly note: "During both World Wars they contributed their time to the Red Cross, knitting, and sewing."[11] The Depression further curtailed socializing; according to one history of American family life, "club memberships and extracurricular school activities were also restricted, and fewer family members went to pool halls, bowling alleys, or boxing rings."[12] The break in continuity due to world events may have led some clubs to disband and may have interfered with a second wave of club women, who would have taken over around the time of World War I.

Entry into higher education and into the workforce became more common for women as the century progressed; as we saw in the Introduction, the number of women in higher education doubled between 1940 and 1960. The resultant decline in leisure time and the availability of new venues for women's intellectual pursuits may help explain the disappearance of many clubs. Members of the Portia Club of Payette, Idaho, founded in 1895, noted just such a shift when they had their last meeting in 1972 and voted to disband, due to "their advancing age and inability to attract new members."[13]

The decline in clubs may also be part of a larger national trend away from community activities. In his study of the decline of American's social connections and civic engagement, Robert D. Putnam offers several possible reasons: "generational change—the slow, steady, and ineluctable replacement of the long civic generation by their less involved children and grandchildren"; the privatization of leisure time by electronic media, particularly television; suburbanization; and pressures of time and money on two-career families.[14]

The history of the Woodland, California, Shakespeare Club (founded 1886) cited many of these causes for the club's decline: "As the years have passed by, less and less time has been devoted to the study of Shakespeare." By the late 1960s, the club spent only one program a year on Shakespeare. According to the club historian, "the evolving programs through the years have been a reflection of the changing position of women, the greater opportunities for higher education, the increase in other cultural and recreational outlets, and the consequent changing interests and needs of the Club members." The club historian noted that during World War II, meetings became less frequent (once a month) and continued that way after the war. By the 1960s, the group's purpose was primarily social, and it met chiefly to attend plays at the Oregon Shakespeare Festival. The historian reminisced that "in the early days the Club was the center of cultural being for its members. As the years have gone by, higher education for women has become commonplace and other cultural activities compete for the members' time and energies."[15] Although the club apparently still meets, its purpose and format are much different from those of "the early days."

★★★★★

Why were American women such supporters and promoters of Shakespeare? "Shakespeare" meant different things to different women, both individually and collectively. Some found models to emulate in characters such as Portia; others saw the opportunity to make an argument for a female president; some, like the women in the Zanesville, Ohio, club, enjoyed the chance to cross the line of acceptable decorum; many took pleasure in the female fellowship of a women's study club; some saw possibilities for a form of domestic feminism; others found an opportunity to infuse intellectual content into the home; some (particularly black club women) saw a way to achieve social progress; most sought a version of self-improvement they could tailor to their individual and collective needs and desires.

In fact, the association of Shakespeare with civic, cultural, and educational improvement still exists today: critiques of educational systems often focus on Shakespeare as a measure of respectable intellectual achievement, as in a 2007 report titled *The Vanishing Shakespeare* by the American Council of Trustees and Alumni, whose president declared that "a degree in English without Shakespeare . . . is tantamount to fraud."[16] The Shakespeare Behind Bars prison reading program in LaGrange, Kentucky, is based on a principle that we can trace back to these nineteenth-century clubs—that reading Shakespeare can make you a better person and can contribute to moral and intellectual progress.[17] The connection between reading Shakespeare and civic life has a long history, from the late nineteenth-century women in the Barnesville, Georgia, Woman's Shakespearean Club who taught factory workers in rural Georgia, to the contemporary prisoners in the Shakespeare Behind Bars program.

We can see traces of these women's activities in the fact that Shakespeare's role in American public life, cultural knowledge, and even "democratic principles" is now promoted by the U.S. government, financed at an estimated $75 million.[18] Most recently, Shakespeare has been the focus of a "We the People" grant from the National Endowment for the Humanities and the National Endowment for the Arts to fund the "Shakespeare in American Life" project (a website and radio documentary commemorating the 75th anniversary of the Folger Shakespeare Library).[19] The mandate of the "We the People" program is "to encourage and enhance the teaching, study, and understanding of

American history, culture, and democratic principles." As in many of the initiatives of women's Shakespeare clubs over the last century, the NEH operates on the premise that "cultivating the best of the humanities has real and tangible benefits for civic life."[20] The rationale for allocating funds from the NEH to the "Shakespeare in American Public Life" project is strikingly similar to the goals of the women's clubs in their quest for an alternative form of education and of civic and personal betterment: "Shakespeare's works weave like a bright thread through the history of American education and self-improvement."[21]

Even though most of the clubs that provide the evidence for this book have been left out of the historical record, they did not disappear. Vestiges of their work remain in both tangible and intangible forms—in the many public libraries, civic projects, and educational initiatives; in the influence on home life and women's intellectual achievements; and in the women themselves, who left a legacy of sustained engagement with Shakespeare, a writer who inspired their intellectual pursuits and encouraged them to read, study, analyze, discuss, write, build intellectual communities, and socialize. These women readers also make a case for an alternative narrative for Shakespeare in America—one in which he functioned as material for inspiration, adaptation, community building, and the life of the mind for ordinary readers in ordinary places.

 **APPENDIX**

Shakespeare Clubs in America

Key

★ All men

★★ Men and women

[no ★] All women

† African American club

This appendix includes clubs with a substantial focus on Shakespeare. The year of the club's founding, if known, is given in parentheses.

Alabama

Birmingham

Birmingham Fortnightly Shakespeare Club

Birmingham Shakespeare Club

Pierian Literary Society of Birmingham (1890)

Demopolis

Round Table (1892)

Greensboro

Saturday Shakespeare Club (1886)

Greenville

Inter Se Club (1890)

Mobile

Mobile Shakespeare Club (1897)

Montgomery

Montgomery Shakespeare Club

Selma

Thursday Literary Circle (c. 1894–95)

Tuscaloosa

Kettledrum of Tuscaloosa (1889)

Arizona

Flagstaff

Flagstaff Shakespeare Club (1903)

Fort Smith
Fortnightly Club (1888)

Arkansas

Conway
Conway Junior Shakespeare Club
(1926)
Conway Shakespeare Club★★ (1894)

Lake Village
Delta Shakespeare Club (1905)

Little Rock
Little Rock Shakespeare Club★
Philomathic Club (renamed Pacaha
Club in 1892) (1892)
Lotus Club†

Mena
Mena Women's Literary Club (1898)

California

Alameda
Alameda Shakespeare Club (1889)

Bellflower
Bellflower Mary Arden Club

Berkeley
Berkeley Shakespeare Club
Shakespeare Club of Berkeley★★

Culver City
Culver City Shakespeare Club★★

El Monte
Mountain View Shakespeare Club
(1902)

Los Angeles
Kate Tupper Galpin Shakespeare
Club (1892)

Modesto
Modesto Shakespeare Club (1916)

**Mountain View Acres (San
Bernardino County)**
Mountain View Shakespeare Club
(1902)

Nevada City
Nevada City Shakespeare Club

Nordhoff
Ojai Valley Shakespeare Club

Oakdale
Oakdale Shakespeare Club

Oakland
Ebell Women's Club
Locke Richardson Shakespeare
Class★★ (c. 1887)

Ojai
Ojai Shakespeare Club★★ (1880)

Ontario
Ontario Shakespeare Club

Pasadena
Pasadena Shakespeare Club (1888)

Placerville
Placerville Shakespeare Club (1897)

Pomona
Shakespeare Club of Pomona (1904)

Sacramento
Tuesday Club (1896)

San Diego
As You Like It Club (1910)
Portia Club of San Diego (1901)
San Diego Shakespeare Club
Stratford Shakespeare Club

San Francisco
Avon Shakespeare Society★★ (1886)
Channing Auxiliary Shakespeare
Class (1881)
East Bay Shakespeare Club
San Francisco Shakespeare Class

Sanger
Sanger Shakespeare Club

Santa Barbara
Santa Barbara Shakespeare Club★★
Melander Shakespeare Society

Santa Clara
Santa Clara Shakespeare Club (1893)

Santa Cruz
Friday Shakespeare Club (1903)

Ventura
Ventura Shakespeare Club

Willows
Willows Shakespeare Club (1900)

Woodland
Mutual Shakespeare Club★★
Woodland Shakespeare Reading
  Club★★ (1884)
Woodland Shakespeare Club (1886)

Colorado

Aspen
Aspen Shakespeare Club (1913)

Boulder
Fortnightly Club (1884)

Colorado Springs
Anne Hathaway Shakespeare Club
  (1895)
Portia Club

Cripple Creek
Cripple Creek Shakespeare Club

Delta
Delta Shakespeare Study Club

Denver
Pleasant Hour (renamed Monday
  Literary Club in 1889) (1881)
Round Table Club (1888)

Georgetown
Georgetown Shakespeare Club

Idaho Springs
Idaho Springs Shakespeare Club
  (1887)

Leadville
Home Reading Club (1889)
Leadville Shakespeare Club

Pueblo
Wednesday Morning Club

Connecticut

Hartford
Hartford Shakespeare Club (renamed
  Four Corners Club in 1892)
  (1878)
H. G. L. Shakespeare Club (1883)

New Haven
The Delia Bacon Club (1850)

Norwich
Norwich Shakespeare Club (1881)

Waterbury
Waterbury Shakespeare Class (St.
  Margaret's School)★★

D.C.

Robert Downing Shakespeare Club
  (1886)
Shakespeare Class★★ (1882)
Shakespeare Club (1872)
Shakespeare Society of Washington★★
Uniontown Shakespeare Club★★

Delaware

Dover
Dover Shakespeare Club (1898)

Florida

Milton
Shakespeare Club of Milton (1912)

Palm Beach
Palm Beach Shakespeare Club

Tampa
Tampa Shakespeare Study Club
  (1952/53)

Georgia

Atlanta
Atlanta Shakespeare Class (1896)

Barnesville
Barnesville Woman's Shakespearean
  Club (1895)

Cuthbert
Cuthbert Shakespeare Club

Marietta
Anne Hudgins Shakespeare Class
(1931)

Savannah
Wednesday Morning Study Club
(1932)

Idaho

Idaho Springs
Idaho Springs Shakespeare Club
(1888)

Moscow
Pleiades Club (1892)

Payette
Portia Club (1895)

Pocatello
Study League

Illinois

Albion
Albion Shakespeare Club

Avon
Portia Club of Avon (1894)

Chicago
Argyle Park Portia Club
Hull House Shakespeare Club
Shakespeare Club of Chicago★★
(1879)

Chrisman
Chrisman Shakespeare Club

Decatur
Decatur Women's Club (1887)

Fairbury
Fairbury Shakespeare Club

Farmer City
Farmer City Shakespeare Club

Greenville
Greenville Shakespeare Club (1888)

Hoopeston
Hoopeston Shakespeare Club (1898)

Jacksonville
Jacksonville Shakespeare Club

Jerseyville
Jerseyville Shakespeare Club (1895)

Mount Vernon
Mount Vernon Shakespeare Club
(1893)

Peoria
Peoria Shakespeare Class (1888)

Quincy
Friends in Council Shakespeare
Club (1869)
The Round Table Club
Quincy Shakespeare Class

Springfield
Authors' Club

Indiana

Columbus
Columbus Shakespeare Reading
Club

Decatur
Ladies' Shakespeare Club (1882)
Shakespeare Club of Decatur

Des Moines
Des Moines Shakespeare Class

Fort Wayne
Fort Wayne Shakespeare Club (1892)
Thursday Afternoon Shakespeare
Club

Huntington
Huntington Shakespeare Club

Indianapolis
Indianapolis Shakespeare Club★★
(1895)

Kendallville
Kendallville Shakespeare Club

Knightstown
Avon Club
Knightstown Shakespeare Club
    (1889)
Priscilla Club (1898)

Laporte
Indiana Shakespeare Class★★
Laporte Shakespeare Society
Viginti★★ (1887)

Mishawaka
The Reviewers★★ (1933)

Monticello
Monticello Shakespeare Club (1892)

New Albany
New Albany Shakespeare Club
    (1885)

Noblesville
Noblesville Shakespeare Club (1890)

Richmond
The Shakespeare Club (1893)

Rosedale
Rosedale Shakespeare Club

Iowa

Algona
Algona Shakespeare Club

Belle Plaine
Belle Plaine Portia Club

Burlington
Burlington Shakespeare Club (1892)

Calamus
Calamus Shakespeare Study Club

Cedar Rapids
Wednesday Shakespeare Club

Des Moines
Des Moines Shakespeare Society
Vincent Circle (1883)

Eldon
Eldon Shakespeare Club

Hampton
As You Like It Club

Indianola
Indianola Shakespeare Club

Lake City
Lake City Shakespeare Club (1897)

Marion
Shakespeare Club of Marion (1909)

Marshallton
Marshallton Shakespeare Club (1885)

Mason City
Maria Mitchell Club (1879)

Osage
Osage Shakespearean Club (1881)

Ottumwa
Ottumwa Shakespeare Club (1882)

Sioux City
Bard of Avon Club
Shakespeare Section of the Unity
    Club (1889)

Union
Union Shakespeare Club

Waverly
Waverly Shakespeare Club

Kansas

Abilene
Ladies' Literary League (1885)

Atchison
Friday Afternoon Club (1880)

Baldwin
Baldwin City Shakespeare Club

Baxter Springs
Baxter Springs Shakespeare Club

Belleville
Belleville Shakespeare Club

Clay Center
Ladies' Library Club (1899)

Colby
Colby Shakespeare Club (1907)

Columbus
Columbus Shakespeare Club

Cottonwood Falls
Cottonwood Falls Shakespeare Club
  (1902)
Junior Shakespeare Club

El Dorado
El Dorado Shakespeare Club (1894)

Elkhart
Coterie Club (1922)

Galena
Galena Shakespeare Club (1895)

Holden
Holden Shakespeare Club

Junction City
Ladies' Reading Club (1874)

Kingman
Kingman Shakespeare Club (1897)

La Cygne
La Cygne Shakespeare Club (1903)

Lawrence
Friends in Council Shakespeare
  Class (1871)
Zodiac Club (1878)

Norton
Avon Club of Norton (1886)

Ottawa
Columbian Shakespeare Club (1893)

Pratt
Coterie Club

Prentis
Prentis Study Club (1898)

Salina
Salina Shakespeare Club (1900)

Timkin
Coterie Club

Topeka
Arden Shakespeare Club†
Avon Club of Topeka★★ (1869)
Chaldean Club (1888)
Coterie Club† (1904?)
Friends in Council
Interstate Literary Association†
  (Topeka area)
Occidental Club (1887)
Portia Club (1897)

Waterville
Waterville Shakespeare Club (1903)

Kentucky

Fulton
Fulton Shakespeare Club

Louisiana

New Orleans
Round Table Club
New Orleans Shakespeare Club★★
  (1872)
New Orleans Shakespeare Society

Maine

Bangor
Bangor Shakespeare Club

Brunswick
Brunswick Shakespeare Club (1876)

Calais
Calais Shakespeare Club

Camden
Camden Shakespeare Club (1897)

Cherryfield
Cherryfield Shakespeare Club (1893)

Lewiston
Mount David Shakespeare Club
  (1889)

Lisbon Falls
Lisbon Falls Shakespeare Club (1897)

Portland
Portland Shakespeare Class

Rockland
Rockland Shakespeare Society (1889)

Maryland

Baltimore
Baltimore Shakespeare Club★★
(1885)

Cumberland
Cumberland Reading Club (1886)

South Kensington
Baconian Society

Massachusetts

Amherst
Amherst Shakespeare Club

Berlin
Berlin Shakespeare Club

Boston
Athenas Therapes★★ (1884)
The Furness Club★★ (1888)
Boston Bar Association Shakespeare
   Club★
Boston Shakespeare Class★★
Boston Shakespeare Class
Wednesday Morning Club

Brimfield
Brimfield Shakespeare Club

Cambridge
Cambridge Shakespeare Club★★
(1882)
Old Cambridge Shakespeare
   Association★★ (1882)
Old Shakespeare Club (1880)

College Hill
College Hill Shakespeare Club
(1878)

Florence
Florence Shakespeare Class

Grafton
Grafton Shakespeare Club (1880)

Great Barrington
Great Barrington Shakespeare Class
(1887)

Lexington
Shakespeare Club of Lexington
(1898)

Lynn
Shakespeare Club of Lynn

Medford
Medford Shakespeare Club (1867)

Natick
Natick Shakespeare Club (1876)

Newton
Newton Highlands Shakespeare Club

Stockbridge
Stockbridge Shakespeare Club

Wales
Wales Shakespeare Club

Wellesley
Shakespeare Society of Wellesley
   College (1877)

Worcester
Shakespeare Club of Worcester
(1887)

Michigan

Alpena
Alpena Ladies' Shakespeare Class
(1894)

Benton Harbor
Ossoli Club (1894)

Charlevoix
Charlevoix Shakespeare Club

Detroit
Clio Club
Detroit Shakespeare Study Club
Detroit Study Club† (1898)
Shakespeare Coterie (1886)

Fenton
Monday Evening Club (1890)

Flint
Bangs Shakespeare Club
Flint Shakespeare Club** (1889)
Shakespeare Club of Genessee
    County** (1889)
Woman's Shakespeare Club of Flint
    (1893)

Grand Haven
Grand Haven Shakespeare Class
    (1896)
Grand Haven Woman's Club (1891)

Grand Rapids
Avon Shakespeare Club
Grand Rapids Shakespeariana Class
    (1887)

Greenville
Greenville Shakespeare Club (1890)

Hart
Ladies' Literary Club

Hastings
Hastings Shakespeare Class** (1885)

Ionia
Ionia Literary Club** (1875)

Lansing
Lansing Shakespeare Club (1894)

Manchester
Manchester Shakespeare Reading
    Club (1897)

Mason
Tourist Club**

Muskegon
Muskegon Woman's Club

Niles
Ladies' Reading Club (1882)

Northport
Northport Shakespeare Club (1895)

Petoskey
Petoskey Shakespeare Club

Potterville
Potterville Shakespeare Club

Romeo
Monday Club (1880)

Spring Lake
Spring Lake Shakespeare Club

Minnesota

Lanesboro
The Snow Blockade Club

Minneapolis
Girls' Shakespeare Club of the
    Y.M.C.A.
Ladies' Shakespeare Club of
    Minneapolis (1891)

Northfield
Pioneer Club (renamed Shakespeare
    Club in 1875) (1870)

Sleepy Eye
Sleepy Eye Women's Club (1888)

St. Charles
St. Charles Shakespeare Club

Winona
Winona Shakespeare Club

Mississippi

Jackson
Jackson Shakespeare Club (1911)

Missouri

Bowling Green
Bowling Green Shakespeare Club

Carthage
Junior Shakespeare Society (1892)

Clinton
Clinton Shakespeare Club (1886)

Holden
Holden Shakespeare Club (1904)

Kansas City
Bancroft Club (1888)
Portia Club
Strictly Shakespeare Club (1882)

Lebanon
Lebanon Shakespeare Club (1882)

Maysville
Maysville Shakespeare Club

Moberly
Moberly Shakespeare Club

Salisbury
Salisbury Shakespeare Club

Springfield
Springfield Friends in Council Club
Springfield Shakespeare Club (1887)

Trenton
Trenton Shakespeare Club

Washington
Shakespeare Club of Washington/
Fort Nightly Club (1894)

Montana

Butte
Butte Shakespeare Club
Westside Shakespeare Club

Dillon
Dillon Shakespeare Club

Great Falls
Great Falls Shakespeare Club

Missoula
Missoula As You Like It Club

Nebraska

Atkinson
Avon Shakespeare Club

Falls City
Falls City Shakespeare Club

Kearney
Shakespeare Club of Kearney (1902?)

Omaha
Fremont Shakespeare Club★★ (1878)

Weeping Water
Zetetic Club (1884)

Nevada

Las Vegas
Las Vegas Shakespeare Club (1909)

New Hampshire

Concord
The Amateurs★★ (1878)
Avon Club (1883)
Hathaway Shakespeare Club (1894)
Junior Club (or As You Like It)
   (1883)
Monday Evening Shakespeare Club
   (renamed Hathaway Club in 1894)
   (1888)
Concord Shakespeare Club★★ (1877)
Stratford Club (1881)
Twelfth Night Club (1895)
Warwick Club★★

Manchester
Manchester Shakespeare Club (1873)

Nashua
Nashua Shakespeare Club (1887)

Newington
Newington Shakespeare Club

New Jersey

Bayonne
Athena Club (1892)

Beverly
Beverly Shakespeare Club★★ (1885)

Elizabeth
Elizabeth Shakespeare Club
Sisters' Shakespeare Society
The Shakespeare (1883)

Elmora
Elmora Literary and Social Club

Morristown
Morristown Shakespeare Club★★
   (1886)

Plainfield
Plainfield Shakespeare Club★★
   (1887)

New Mexico

Roswell
Roswell Shakespeare Club

New York

Albion
Historical Conversation Club★★ (1878)

Aurora
Shakespeare Reading Club (Wells College)

Binghamton
Shakespeare Dramatic Club

Brooklyn
Portia Reading Group (1879)
Brooklyn Shakespeare Club

Buffalo
Buffalo Shakespeare Club

Canisteo
Shakespeare Club of Canisteo (1887)

Clinton
Shakespeare Club of Hamilton College★★

Cooperstown
Shakespeare Reading Club★★ (1880)

Cortland
Ladies' Literary Club (1880)

Cuba
Cuba Shakespeare Club (1887)
Shakespeare Amateur Society

Dansville
Shakespeare Club of Dansville (1902)

Eden
Shakespeare Club of Eden (1899)

Endicott
Shakespeare Club of Endicott (1934)

Flushing
Flushing Reading Club (1880)

Fredonia
Fredonia Shakespeare Club (1895)
Shakespeare Club (State Normal School) (1886)

Garden City
Garden City Shakespeare Class★★ (1885)

Gouverneur
Shakespeare Club of Gouverneur (1893)

Granville
Granville Shakespeare Club

Horseheads
Horseheads Shakespeare Club

Ilion
Ilion Shakespeare Club (1908)

Kinderhook
Shakespeare Club of Kinderhook (1910)

LeRoy
Local Circle Shakespeare Study Club (1881)

Lewiston
P. V. K. Shakespeare Club★★ (1877)

Monticello
Monticello Shakespeare Society

New Rochelle
Avon Bard Club (1908)
New Rochelle Shakespeare Club

New York City
Columbia College Shakespeare Club★★ (1884)
Fortnightly Shakespeare Club (1875)
Mary Arden Shakespeare Club (1895)
Shakespeare Society of New York★★ (1885)
Twelfth Night Shakespeare Club (1889)

Oneida
Avon Shakespeare Club (1893)

Ovid
Ovid Shakespeare Club

Pawling
Pawling Shakespeare Club (1898)

Penn Yan
Penn Yan Shakespeare Class

Queens
Queens Shakespeare Club

Rochester
Rochester Shakespeare Club (1865)
Rochester Shakespeare Society★★
    (1865)

Saratoga Springs
Saratoga Springs Shakespeare Club

Seneca Falls
Shakespeare Club of Seneca Falls
    (1883)
Shakespeare Society of Seneca Falls
    (1882)

Silver Creek
Silver Creek Shakespeare Club
    (1889)

Sing Sing
Stratford Club of Sing Sing (1893)

Syracuse
Danforth Shakespeare Club (1895)

Tonawanda
Women's Shakespeare Club of
    Tonawanda (1908)

Troy
Monday Evening Shakespeare Club

Waterville
Every Saturday Night Club (1886)

Whitney Point
Whitney Point Shakespeare Club

Location uncertain (New York)
As You Like It Club (1884)
Club of Two
Shakespeare's Amateurs (1891)

North Carolina

Chapel Hill
Shakespeare Club of Univ. of North
    Carolina★★ (1886)

Durham
Durham Shakespeare Club★★ (1880s)
Schubert-Shakespeare Club† (1903)
Volkamenia Club†

Oxford
Shakespeare Club of Oxford (1898)

Raleigh
Raleigh Shakespeare Club
Univ. of North Carolina Shakespeare
    Club★ (1886/87)
Tuesday Afternoon Book Club
    (1903)

Tarboro
Shakespeare Club of Tarboro★★

North Dakota

Devil's Lake
Devil's Lake Shakespeare Club

Huron
Huron High School Club★★ (1888)

Ohio

Akron
Akron Shakespeare Class

Bowling Green
Shakespeare Round Table of Bowling
    Green (1904/5)

Cadiz
Ladies' Shakespeare Club (1875)

Celina
Celina Shakespeare Club (1894)

Cincinnati
Cincinnati Shakespeare Club
Progress Club

Columbus
Shakespeare Dramatic Club (1871)
Vassar Correspondence Club

Crestline
Crestline Shakespeare Club

Delaware
Delaware Shakespeare Club★★ (1878)

Findlay
William Shakespeare Club

Hamilton
Hamilton Shakespeare Class★★
(1879)

Lima
Shakespeare Study Club (1905)

Maumee
Shakespeare Club of Maumee (1930)

Napoleon
Shakespeare Club of Napoleon
(1930)

Pomeroy
Pomeroy Shakespeare Club

Springfield
Springfield Shakespeare Club

Sidney
Sidney Junior Shakespeare Club
(1887)
Sidney Shakespeare Club

St. Clairesville
St. Clairesville Shakespeare Circle

Toledo
Agnes Morris Class
Arden Shakespeare Club (1902)
Ariel Shakespeare Class
The Elizabethans
Toledo Shakespeare Club
Ye Shakespeare Study Class

Wauseon
Stratford Shakespeare Club (1908)

Zanesville
Zanesville Shakespeare Club (1877)

Oklahoma

Claremore
Claremore Shakespeare Sunshine
Club

Collinsville
Collinsville/Comedy of Errors
Shakespeare Club (1904)

Conneautville
Conneautville Shakespeare Club

Enid
Enid Shakespeare Club (1905)

Gotebo
Gotebo Arden Study Club

Guthrie
Guthrie Shakespeare Club

Kingfisher
Kingfisher Shakespeare Club

Lawton
Lawton Shakespeare Club (1902)

Muskogee
Muskogee Shakespeare Club (1908)

Oklahoma City
Shakespeare Club of Oklahoma City
(1924)

Pawhuska
Pawhuska Shakespeare Club

Pond Creek
Pond Creek Shakespeare Club

Sayre
As You Like It Club

Shawnee
Shawnee Shakespeare Club

Tulsa
Tulsa Shakespeare Club (1913)

Woodward
Woodward Shakespeare Club★★

Oregon

Albany
Albany Shakespeare Club

Eugene
Monday Afternoon Shakespeare Club
Shakespeare Club of Eugene (1909)

McMinnville
McMinnville Shakespeare Club
(1902)

Portland
Portland Reading Club
Portland Shakespeare Club★★
Portland Shakespeare Study Club

Pennsylvania

Ashland
Ashland Shakespeare Club★★
(1882)

Canonsburg
Canonsburg Shakespeare Club

Clearfield
Clearfield Shakespearian Society★★
(1887)

Conneautville
Conneautville Shakespeare Club

Germantown
Germantown Shakespeare Club
(1910)
Murdoch Shakespeare Club

Greensburg
Greensburg Shakespeare Club★★

Grove City
Shakespeare Club of Grove City
(1931)

Indiana
Shakespeare Club of Indiana, Pa.★★
(1879)

Lockhaven
Lockhaven Shakespeare Reading
Club

Northumberland
Shakespeare Class (Normal High
School)

Philadelphia
Crescent Literary Society
Hathaway Shakespeare Club (1923)
Murdoch Shakespeare Club
The IX Shakespeare Club (1881)

New Shakespeare Society of
Philadelphia
Philadelphia Shakespeare Society★★
(1872)
Round Table Shakespeare Club of
Roxborough
Rufus Adams Shakespeare Class★★
(1883)
Senior Electrical Engineering Class
(Univ. of Pa.)★★
Shakespeare Literature Class (New
Century Guild) (1882)
Shakespeare Reading Club (1888)
Shakespeare Society of
Philadelphia★★ (1852)
Shakespeare Society of the New
Century Guild
West Philadelphia Junior Shakespeare
Club (1893)
West Philadelphia Shakespeare Club
(1882)

Port Allegheny
Port Allegheny Shakespeare Club

Pottsville
Schuylkill Students' Shakespeare
Society★★ (1875)

Roxborough
Round Table Shakespeare Club

Tidioute
Tidioute Shakespeare Club

Towanda
Towanda Shakespeare Club

Warren
Warren Shakespeare Club★★ (1884)

Wilkes-Barre
Shakespeare Society★★ (1880)

Rhode Island

Newport
Newport Shakespeare Club
Shakespeare Club of the First
Congregational Church

Providence
Providence Shakespeare Club (1887)

South Carolina

Charleston
Charleston Shakespeare Club (1886)

Greenville
Senior Literature Class (Greenville College)★★ (1880)

Union
Union Shakespeare Club (1887)

South Dakota

Aberdeen
Shakespeare Club of Aberdeen (1901)

Hot Springs
Hot Springs Shakespeare Club (1893)

Huron
Huron High School Club★★
Huron Shakespeare Club

Watertown
Woman's Club of Watertown (1889)

Tennessee

Clarksville
Clarksville Shakespeare Club★★ (1885)

Knoxville
Knoxville Shakespeare Club

Lebanon
Shakespeare Class (College for Young Ladies)
Shakespeare Class (Lebanon University)★★ (1885)

Lexington
Lexington Shakespeare Club (1877)

Maryville
Maryville Shakespeare Class★★ (1886)

Memphis
Howe Institute Shakespeare Club†

Nashville
Buford College Shakespeare Club
Nashville Shakespeare Club (1886)
Query Club (1885)

Texas

Abilene
Abilene Shakespeare Club (1883)

Arlington
Arlington Shakespeare Club

Austin
Austin Shakespeare Club (1898)
Shakespeare Class (Univ. of Texas)★★ (1883)

Ballinger
Ballinger Shakespeare Club

Beaumont
Beaumont Shakespeare Club

Bryan
Bryan Shakespeare Club

Calvert
Calvert Shakespeare Club

Cleburne
Cleburne Shakespeare Club

Clifton
Clifton Shakespeare Society

Coleman
Coleman Shakespeare Club

Colorado City
Shakespeare Club of Colorado City

Como
Como Shakespeare Club

Crockett
Crockett Shakespeare Club

Dallas
Dallas Shakespeare Club (1886)
Shakespeare Followers
Stratford Club (two clubs) (1911)

DeLeon
DeLeon Shakespeare Club

Del Rio
Del Rio Shakespeare Club

Denton
Denton Women's Shakespeare Club
(1899)

Edna
Edna Shakespeare Club

Flatonia
Flatonia Shakespeare Club

Fort Worth
Woman's Shakespeare Club of Fort
Worth (1905)

Giddings
Giddings Shakespeare Club

Groesbeck
Groesbeck Shakespeare Club

Hearne
Hearne Shakespeare Club

Honey Grove
Honey Grove Shakespeare Club

Itaska
Itaska Woman's Shakespeare Club

Lancaster
Lancaster Shakespeare Club

Longview
Longview Shakespeare Club

Lubbock
Lubbock Shakespeare Club

Lufkin
Lufkin Shakespeare Club

Marlin
Marlin Shakespeare Society★★ (1889)

Marshall
Marshall Shakespeare Club

Morgan
Morgan Shakespeare Club

Mount Vernon
Mount Vernon Shakespeare Club
(1902)

Nacogdoches
Nacogdoches Shakespeare Club

Nixon
Nixon Shakespeare Club

North Zulch
North Zulch Shakespeare Club

Oak Cliff
Oak Cliff Shakespeare Club (two
clubs)

Rockwall
Rockwall Shakespeare Club

San Antonio
San Antonio Shakespeare Club
(1898)

Seguin
Seguin Shakespeare Club

Sherman
Kidd-Key Shakespeare Club (1895)

Smithville
Smithville Shakespeare Club

Texarkana
Texarkana Shakespeare Club

Tyler
Tyler Shakespeare Club

Vernon
Vernon Shakespeare Club

Waco
Waco Shakespeare Club

Waxahachie
Shakespeare Club of Waxahachie
(1889)

Wichita Falls
Wichita Falls Shakespeare Club

Vermont

Burlington
Burlington Shakespeare Club

Lyndonville
Lyndonville Shakespeare Club

Rutland
Rutland Progressive Shakespeare
Club
Rutland Shakespeare Club

Swanton
Swanton Shakespeare Club
(1893)

Virginia

Christiansburg
Shakespeare Society (Montgomery
Female College)

Danville
Danville Junior Shakespeare Club
Shakespeare Study Club

Harrisonburg
Harrisonburg Shakespeare Club
(1878)

Hollins
Shakespeare Reading Club (Hollins
Inst. pupils) (1887)
Shakespeare Reading Club (Hollins
Inst. teachers)★★ (1886)

Lynchburg
Shakespeare Class (Lynchburg High
School)★★ (1885)

Montvale
Montvale Shakespeare Club

Norfolk
Norfolk Shakespeare Club★★

Smithfield
Smithfield Shakespeare Class
(1905)

Suffolk
Suffolk Literary Club (1894)

Washington

North Yakima
Portia Club

Port Gamble
Port Gamble Shakespeare Club

Spokane
Spokane Shakespeare Class
(1892)

Walla Walla
Walla Walla Shakespeare Club
(1892)

West Virginia

Wheeling
Wheeling Shakespeare Club★★
(1874)

Wisconsin

Berlin
Athena Club (1890)

Cambria
Cambria Shakespeare Club

De Pere
De Pere Shakespeare Club

Fort Atkinson
Tuesday Club (1880)

Green Bay
Monday Shakespeare Club of Green
Bay
Neville Shakespeare Club
Shakespeare Club of Green Bay
(1877)

Kenosha
Shakespeare Society of Kenosha★
(1878)

Kewaunee
Kewaunee Shakespeare Club

Marinette
William Shakespeare Club of
Marinette (1897)

Superior
Mary Arden Shakespeare Club
Shakespeare-Browning Club

Tomah
Tomah Shakespeare Club
(1895)

Waterloo

Shakespeare Club of
  Waterloo

Waukesha

Waukesha Shakespeare
  Club

Wyoming

Cheyenne

Cheyenne Shakespeare Club

Whitney Point

Whitney Point Shakespeare Club

✍ NOTES

Preface

1. The History of Portia Club of Avon, Illinois, 1894–1994, Illinois State Historical Library, i; *Historical Encyclopedia of Illinois and History of Mercer County*, ed. Newton Bateman and Paul Selby (Chicago: Munsell Publishing, 1903). Bateman and Selby list the 1890 population of Avon as 692.

2. The evidence in this book runs counter to many of Lawrence W. Levine's oft-quoted claims about Shakespeare in America. Levine contends that around the end of the nineteenth century "the increasing separation of Shakespeare from 'every-day' people becomes more evident"; "Shakespearean oratory" was "a part of life" in the nineteenth century, he maintains, but by the end of the century the decline of oratory and the growth of literacy undermined Shakespeare's place in American culture, making him "archaic and inaccessible." See *Highbrow/Lowbrow: The Emergence of Cultural Hierarchy in America* (Cambridge, Mass.: Harvard University Press, 1988), 33, 36, 80. The more than five hundred clubs that form the basis for this book offer substantial evidence that Shakespeare was far from archaic or inaccessible to a wide variety of Americans across the country, and especially for women.

3. The report of the Stratford Club of Concord in 1959 notes that there were once ten Shakespeare clubs in Concord. "Notes and Comments: Shakespeare in New Hampshire," *Shakespeare Quarterly* 10.3 (1959): 456. The popularity of Shakespeare clubs in Concord spread to other locales; when Mrs. Jacob G. Cilley moved from Concord to Cambridge, Massachusetts, she brought with her the idea for a Shakespeare club—thus the Old Cambridge Shakespeare Association. See "Old Cambridge Shakespeare Association, 1882–2006: A Finding Aid," Brinkler Library, Cambridge Historical Society.

4. Autograph Letters of Joseph Crosby, Y.c. 1372, Folger Shakespeare Library, Letter of 27 January 1876. When I inquired about the records of the Lexington, Massachusetts, Shakespeare Club, the reference librarian at the Cary Memorial Library responded, "We are especially happy to share materials that are rarely (ever?) used." Personal communication, 2007.

5. Shakespeare clubs existed in many parts of the world, including Germany, England, Scotland, Australia, and Canada. See, for example, Heather Murray, *Come, Bright Improvement: The Literary Societies of Nineteenth-Century Ontario* (Toronto: University of Toronto Press, 2002); Ken Stewart, "Much Ado About Everything: The Melbourne Shakespeare Society, 1884–1904," *Australian Literary Studies* 19.3 (2000): 269–78. For Shakespeare's relationship to Victorian women in Britain, see Gail Marshall, *Shakespeare and Victorian Women* (Cambridge: Cambridge University Press, 2009). Women's clubs in Britain did not multiply as quickly as those in the States. Christine Bolt points out that the American club movement was "not matched" in Britain: "the 1870s and 1880s produced no proliferation of high-profile female clubs, combining cultural, social and civic purposes with a distinctive conception of the role of women." This was due in

part to the strength of men's clubs and also to the tradition of "co-operating with men rather than organising entirely separately from them in reform endeavours." Christine Bolt, *The Women's Movements in the United States and Britain from the 1790s to the 1920s* (Amherst: University of Massachusetts Press, 1993), 168–69. I heed Sara M. Evans's call to examine how women "affected and transformed the dynamic interplay of public and private life in our past and how the experience of women in America actively shaped the broader history that we, women and men, all claim as our own." *Born for Liberty: A History of Women in America* (New York: Free Press, 1989), 6.

6. Anne Ruggles Gere counters the negative perception of women's clubs as limited to white, middle-class women; she points out, "Difference as well as similarity marked the groups clustered under the term *women's club*, creating a diverse and multifaceted social movement." *Intimate Practices: Literacy and Cultural Work in U.S. Women's Clubs, 1880–1920* (Urbana: University of Illinois Press, 1997), 6.

7. The groundbreaking work of Ann Thompson and Sasha Roberts in *Women Reading Shakespeare, 1660–1900: An Anthology of Criticism* (Manchester, U.K.: Manchester University Press, 1997) offers the most extensive discussion of women readers of Shakespeare in Britain and the United States and was one of the central inspirations for this book. Recent works such as Andrew Murphy, *Shakespeare for the People: Working-Class Readers, 1800–1900* (Cambridge: Cambridge University Press, 2008), which focuses on readers in Britain, suggest that the late nineteenth century is fertile ground for analysis of reading practices related to Shakespeare.

8. McGuffey's readers were circulated around the United States, with Shakespeare as a preferred source of citation. According to one description, "Time and again the memoirs of pioneers across three thousand miles are studded with saws and instances from the Bible, *Pilgrim's Progress*, and Shakespeare." Alistair Cooke, "Shakespeare in America," in *Shakespeare: Pattern of Excelling Nature*, ed. David Bevington and Jay L. Halio (Newark: University of Delaware Press, 1978), 20.

9. In making this argument, I follow the work of a number of historians of women and reading, such as Catherine Kerrison, who elucidates "how literacy is directly linked with power and authority" for women. *Claiming the Pen: Women and Intellectual Life in the Early American South* (Ithaca: Cornell University Press, 2006), 4.

10. Kim C. Sturgess, *Shakespeare and the American Nation* (Cambridge: Cambridge University Press, 2004), claims to "tell the story of America's relationship with Shakespeare" without making a single reference to a Shakespeare club. In addition to omitting Shakespeare clubs, Michael Bristol, in *Shakespeare's America, America's Shakespeare* (London: Routledge, 1990), focuses on institutional structures; my concern with literate practices outside institutional structures constitutes the major difference between our approaches. Perry Miller, *The Raven and the Whale: The War of Words and Wits in the Era of Poe and Melville* (New York: Harcourt, Brace, 1956), chronicles the challenge Shakespeare presented to mid-nineteenth-century American literati. See especially the section "A Greater Than Shakespeare?" 221–34. Stephen J. Brown argues that Shakespeare was used "in America as an instrument of WASP cultural domination" and makes a case for Shakespeare as "the poet of an emerging ruling class." "The Uses of Shakespeare in America: A Study in Class Domination," in Bevington and Halio, *Shakespeare*, 230–38. As we shall see in this book, however, Shakespeare was also read by frontier settlers, housewives, black women, and other Americans who do not fit the description of a "ruling class." Several Shakespeare clubs were associated with educational institutions, but I have left major consideration of that material for another work.

11. In the Conclusion, I discuss some of the possible reasons for the omission of these readers from history. Elizabeth McHenry argues that "new directions in the study of readers and reading need . . . to decenter formal education as the primary institutional force behind the reading of literature." *Forgotten Readers: Recovering the Lost History of African-American Literary Societies* (Durham, N.C.: Duke University Press, 2002), 10. Similarly, Elizabeth Long criticizes "the disjuncture between women's feelings about the importance of reading groups in their lives and the groups' relative invisibility—or dismissability—to most men and historically male-dominated scholarship." *Book Clubs: Women and the Uses of Reading in Everyday Life* (Chicago: University of Chicago Press, 2003), 219. Book historians have lamented the absence of materials about the reading habits of ordinary people; fortunately, records of numerous women readers of Shakespeare are plentiful. See David Perkins, *Is Literary History Possible?* (Baltimore: Johns Hopkins University Press, 1992), 25–27.

12. Most histories of Shakespeare in America have been performance-based, such as Frances Teague, *Shakespeare and the American Popular Stage* (Cambridge: Cambridge University Press, 2006); Helene Wickham Koon, *How Shakespeare Won the West: Players and Performances in America's Gold Rush, 1849–1865* (Jefferson, N.C.: McFarland, 1989); and Philip C. Kolin's collection *Shakespeare in the South: Essays on Performance* (Jackson: University Press of Mississippi, 1983). Essays by Levette J. Davidson, "Shakespeare in the Rockies," *Shakespeare Quarterly* 4 (1953): 39–49, and Richard A. Van Orman, "The Bard in the West," *Western Historical Quarterly* 5 (1974): 29–38, help provide a wider picture of Shakespeare across America. The exhibit on Shakespeare and American life curated at the Folger Shakespeare Library in 2007 by Virginia Mason Vaughan and Alden Vaughan (and the accompanying volume, *Shakespeare in American Life*) is the most substantial discussion of Shakespeare in America to date; the exhibition included a display case on Shakespeare clubs. In "Making Shakespeare American: Shakespeare's Dissemination in Nineteenth-Century America," V. Vaughan discusses both the performance history of Shakespeare and the circulation of Shakespeare's texts. *Shakespeare in American Life*, ed. Virginia Mason Vaughan and Alden T. Vaughan (Washington, D.C.: Folger Shakespeare Library, 2007), 23–33. Other works on Shakespeare in America include Esther Dunn, *Shakespeare in America* (New York: Macmillan, 1939); Alfred Westfall, *American Shakespearean Criticism, 1607–1865* (New York: H. W. Wilson, 1939); Brown, "Uses of Shakespeare in America"; Charles Shattuck, *Shakespeare on the American Stage* (Washington, D.C.: Folger Press, 1976, 1987); Scott L. Newstok and Ayanna Thompson, eds., *Weyward Macbeth: Intersections of Race and Performance* (New York: Palgrave Macmillan, 2010); Gay Smith, *Lady Macbeth in America: From the Stage to the White House* (Basingstoke, U.K.: Palgrave, 2010); and Nigel Cliff, *The Shakespeare Riots: Revenge, Drama, and Death in Nineteenth-Century America* (New York: Random House, 2007). The collection *Shakespearean Educations: Power, Citizenship, and Performance*, ed. Coppélia Kahn, Heather S. Nathans, and Mimi Godfrey (Newark: Delaware University Press, 2011), was published just as this book was going into production.

13. Many of the women readers I discuss in this book wrote their own history; in his study of memoirs of working-class readers in Britain, Jonathan Rose remarks that such records are significant because "they represent an effort by working people to write their own history"; these readers "decided what to include" about their reading experiences. *The Intellectual Life of the British Working Classes* (New Haven, Conn.: Yale University Press, 2001), 2.

14. I build on Gere's argument that women's clubs were "one of the *competing* publics at the turn of the century" rather than evidence of a binary separation between public and private. *Intimate Practices*, 13.

15. Gere points out that "clubwomen often identified their literacy practices as the source of their capacity to carry out projects of social welfare," and Shakespeare was part of this agenda. *Intimate Practices*, 12.

16. The article "How to Promote a Shakespeare Club," published in London in *Cassell's Family Magazine* (1880), argued that "it is desirable to eschew all such fancy terms as 'The Falstaff,' 'The Hamlet,' and most ultimate satisfaction will be found in either a name indicating the place where the club meets (as the Clifton Shakespeare Club, Bristol) or the time, the date at which the Club is to meet" (415). Most American women's Shakespeare clubs followed this formula; see the appendix.

17. Many clubs followed the pattern of the Grove City, Pennsylvania, Club. Its former president (and thirty-five-year member) Hilda Kring writes, "Through the years, all the works of Shakespeare have been studied, researched, acted (I was Cleopatra once!), reported, etc. His period and contemporaries have been explored; famous quotes have been discussed as to their eternal impact. In short, no stone has been left unturned." Hilda Kring, personal communication, 1999.

18. This section is indebted to Murphy's insightful comments in his afterword to *Shakespeare for the People*.

19. Lillian Bateman, "A Review of the Work of the Detroit Study Club for the Last 5 Yrs," 9 April 1908, MS, Burton Historical Collection, Detroit Public Library.

Introduction

1. Anne Ruggles Gere points out that club women "interacted, as daughters, mothers, sisters, wives, or friends, with a circle of others [and] club influence extended to a good portion of the population." *Intimate Practices: Literacy and Cultural Work in U.S. Women's Clubs, 1880–1920* (Urbana: University of Illinois Press, 1997), 5. Several historians have charted the rise and progress of women's clubs. See Elizabeth Long, *Book Clubs: Women and the Uses of Reading in Everyday Life* (Chicago: University of Chicago Press, 2003); Elizabeth McHenry, *Forgotten Readers: Recovering the Lost History of African American Literary Societies* (Durham, N.C.: Duke University Press, 2002); Theodora Penny Martin, *The Sound of Our Own Voices: Women's Study Clubs, 1860–1910* (Boston: Beacon Press, 1987); and Karen J. Blair, *The Clubwoman as Feminist: True Womanhood Redefined, 1868–1914* (New York: Holmes and Meier, 1980), *The Torchbearers: Women and Their Amateur Arts Associations in America, 1890–1930* (Bloomington: Indiana University Press, 1994), and *Joining In: Exploring the History of Voluntary Organizations* (Malabar, Fla.: Krieger Publishing, 2006). Jane Cunningham Croly, *The History of the Woman's Club Movement in America* (New York: Henry G. Allen, 1898), remains the main source of information on women's clubs.

2. Anne Firor Scott, *Natural Allies: Women's Associations in American History* (Urbana: University of Illinois Press, 1991), 2. For the importance of women's networks in the first half of the nineteenth century, see Mary Kelley, *Learning to Stand and Speak: Women, Education, and Public Life in America's Republic* (Chapel Hill: University of North Carolina Press, 2006). Catherine Kerrison discusses the intellectual life of early southern women in *Claiming the Pen: Women and Intellectual Life in the Early American South* (Ithaca: Cornell University Press, 2006).

3. Anne Ruggles Gere, "Common Properties of Pleasure: Texts in Nineteenth-Century Women's Clubs," in *The Construction of Authorship: Textual Appropriation in Law and Literature*, ed. Martha Woodmansee and Peter Jaszi (Durham, N.C.: Duke University Press, 1994), 385.

4. This chapter is influenced by Niko Besnier's argument that "the cultural meaning of a written text must be understood in terms of its relationship with [the sociocultural] context, i.e. in terms of who the readers are, what their position is in society, how they use and judge the texts, and so on." *Literacy, Emotion, and Authority: Reading and Writing on a Polynesian Atoll* (Cambridge: Cambridge University Press, 1995), 10.

5. *Michigan State Library Bulletin* No. 1 (May 1896): 1–2.

6. *Shakespeariana* 4 (1887): 329.

7. In addition, Kate Flint argues that "what distinguishes the reading group from . . . other sites of shared discussion is the fact that its members continually, at some level, return to a text and to their encounter with it, both as individuals and as members of a community." "Women and Reading," *Signs* 31.2 (2006): 517.

8. For critiques of women's clubs, see Martin, *Sound of Our Own Voices*, 117–24.

9. "Kate Tupper Galpin Shakespeare Club," *Who's Who among the Women of California*, ed. Louis S. Lyons and Josephine Wilson (San Francisco: Security Publishing, 1922), 158.

10. The Placerville, California, Shakespeare Club began its civic work by putting garbage cans on street corners and paying for removal of garbage and grass clippings, which was the start of their county's "current sanitation system." They later began a campaign to preserve trees along a local highway, founded the first Parent Teacher Association in Placerville, started a free kindergarten, and established the first city library. "Placerville Society Began with the Shakespeare Club," undated newspaper clipping, Club History Collection, CH CA 054, General Federation of Women's Clubs Archives.

11. *Michigan State Library Bulletin* No. 1 (May 1896): 74–75. The Traverse City Woman's Club joined the Michigan State Federation of Women's Clubs in 1895.

12. *Michigan State Library Bulletin* No. 1 (May 1896): 95–96.

13. *Michigan State Library Bulletin* No. 1 (May 1896):120–21. The Unity Club of Sioux City, Iowa, had a Shakespeare section, in which they read *King Lear* and *A Midsummer Night's Dream* in 1888. See *Shakespeariana* 6 (1889): 286.

14. It is impossible give an exact number of the general women's clubs that read Shakespeare, but several thousand would be a conservative estimate.

15. "The Club Forum," *Shakespeare Association Bulletin* 1.3 (1926): 19.

16. Furness is probably best known for his pioneering work with the variorum Shakespeare editions. See James M. Gibson, *The Philadelphia Shakespeare Story: Horace Howard Furness and the New Variorum Shakespeare* (New York: AMS Press, 1990), 57. Agnes Lincoln, a member of the Medford, Massachusetts, Shakespeare Club, founded in 1867 by twenty women, wrote in her diary of 1880, "No one has yet disputed our claim to being the oldest continuing Shakespeare Club in the U.S.A." Gladys N. Hoover, "The First Hundred Years of the Medford Shakespeare Club," MS 369, Medford Public Library, Medford, Massachusetts. The Natick, Massachusetts, Shakespeare Club boasted that it was "the oldest literary club in the country to have pursued the study of Shakespeare continuously for over half a century." *Shakespeare Association Bulletin* 3.2 (1928): 13.

17. Henry L. Savage, "The Shakspere Society of Philadelphia," *Shakespeare Quarterly* 3 (1952): 346, 350. See also Gibson, *Philadelphia Shakespeare Story*, and Matt Kozusko,

"The Shakspere Society of Philadelphia" *Borrowers and Lenders: The Journal of Shakespeare and Appropriation* 2 (Fall/Winter 2006), http://www.borrowers.uga.edu/cocoon/borrowers/request?id=781462.

18. *The Shakespeare Society of New York: Articles of Association* (New York: Shakespeare Press, 1895), 3. An earlier group also known as the Shakespeare Society of New York was established in 1852 and survived for about a year and a half.

19. Andrew Murphy points out that "the increasing accumulation of early Shakespeare texts in American libraries may be reflected in a publishing programme initiated under the auspices of the New York Shakspere Society in 1888 and running through to 1908." *Shakespeare in Print: A History and Chronology of Shakespeare Publishing* (Cambridge: Cambridge University Press, 2003), 163.

20. *Shakespeare Society of New York: Articles of Association,* 8–9; *New Shakespeareana* 4.3 (1905): 85.

21. Honorary memberships were reserved for Europeans such as J. O. Halliwell-Phillipps, who left the society his collection of "plates, cuts, wood blocks, and electros of wood blocks of Shakespearean vestiges and details, illustrating his home and his history." *Shakespeare Society of New York: Articles of Association,* 15.

22. The account of the Wheeling club in *Shakespeariana* 2 (1885) states that "the interest in the readings diminished, and the members, business men, all of them, had little time for more thorough study, and hence the inevitable result." "Shakespeare Societies of America: Their Methods and Work," 484.

23. The Shakespeariana Club of Grand Rapids, Michigan, for example, included in its program for 1914 a talk called "Shakespeare in Club Work," by Lucy White Williams, the treasurer-general of the General Federation of Women's Clubs. Folger scrapbook 243553, Folger Shakespeare Library. Club women's position on suffrage varied according to geography; Carolyn Stefanco points out that in western states such as Colorado, literary clubs "provided intellectual stimulation for house-bound women, as well as a forum for suffrage proponents." "Networking on the Frontier: The Colorado Women's Suffrage Movement, 1876–1893," in *The Women's West*, ed. Susan Armitage and Elizabeth Jameson (Norman: University of Oklahoma Press, 1987), 265–76, at 270.

24. *Historical Encyclopedia of Illinois and History of Peoria County*, ed. David McCulloch, vol. 2 (Chicago: Munsell Publishing Co., 1902), 19.

25. *Shakespeare Association Bulletin* 4.4 (1929): 119.

26. *Shakespeare Association Bulletin* 4.4 (1929): 77. Such testimonies (which occur frequently in club records) support Jonathan Rose's argument that "the same books recommended by intellectual elites brought aesthetic joy, political emancipation, and philosophical excitement" to "ordinary readers." *The Intellectual Life of the British Working Classes* (New Haven, Conn.: Yale University Press, 2001), 4.

27. Nan Johnson, *Gender and Rhetorical Space in American Life, 1866–1910* (Carbondale: Southern Illinois University Press, 2002), 15. See also Aileen S. Kraditor, ed., *Up from the Pedestal: Selected Writings in the History of American Feminism* (Chicago: Quadrangle Books, 1968), and Barbara Welter, *Dimity Convictions: The American Woman in the Nineteenth Century* (Athens: Ohio University Press, 1976).

28. *Shakespeariana* (1883): 159. The Lexington, Massachusetts, Shakespeare Club also did extensive reading of Shakespeare in which male and female members were equally prominent. See "Minutes of the Meetings of the Lexington Shakespeare Club," MS, Cary Memorial Library, Lexington, Mass.

29. *Shakespeariana* 5 (1888): 218–20.

30. Brooklyn Shakespeare Club minutes, MS AM 1675, Houghton Library, Harvard University.

31. Croly, *History of the Woman's Club Movement*, 612; "Old Cambridge Shakespeare Association, 1882–2006: A Finding Aid," Brinkler Library, Cambridge Historical Society.

32. Esther Bickmore Clark, *The Woodland Shakespeare Club: A History, 1886–1967* (Woodland, Calif.: privately printed, 1968), 7.

33. Lupton's essay was published in Mary LaFayette Robbins, *Alabama Women in Literature* (Selma, Ala.: Selma Printing Co., 1895), 194–98. In her essay "Shakespeare as the Girl's Friend," Mary Cowden Clarke argued that Shakespeare was "a valuable friend of woman-kind." Reprinted in *Shakespeariana* 4 (1887): 355–69, originally published in *The Girl's Own Paper* (London, June 1887).

34. See Kathryn Sport and Bert Hitchcock, *De Remnant Truth: The Tales of Jake Mitchell and Robert Wilton Burton* (Tuscaloosa: University of Alabama Press, 1991), 4. Lupton also translated François Fénelon's *The Education of Girls* (1681) from the French. Lupton House is now a dormitory at Vanderbilt. See Alexander Heard, *Speaking of the University: Two Decades at Vanderbilt* (Nashville, Tenn.: Vanderbilt University Press, 1995), 303. The club was probably sponsored by her father, Nathaniel Thomas Lupton, a chemistry professor at Vanderbilt and later president of the University of Alabama. Thomas McAdory Owen, *History of Alabama and Dictionary of Alabama Biography*, vol. 4 (Chicago: S. J. Clarke, 1921), 1077. It is perhaps not entirely coincidental that Lupton's son, Lupton Allemong Wilkinson, became a poet and essayist. See "The Alumni of Vanderbilt University," *American University Magazine,* November/December 1897, 182.

35. Autograph Letters of Joseph Crosby, Y.c. 1372, Folger Shakespeare Library, letter of 7 September 1877. See also *One Touch of Shakespeare: Letters of Joseph Crosby to Joseph Parker Norris, 1875–1878*, ed. John W. Velz and Frances N. Teague (Washington, D.C.: Folger Shakespeare Library, 1986).

36. The Zanesville club is now in its second incarnation. The Silver Creek, New York, Shakespeare Club offered similar matchmaking opportunities. After six years, the club switched from co-ed to women only; the club history notes, "As a woman's club it was bound to take on a different aspect. Some of the stimulus was gone, naturally, and possibly some of the romance. True it is that the teacher, Miss Mareenus married Mr. Van Schoonover, and Jenny McAndrew married William Fuller. Could the Shakespeare Club have been responsible to any degree?" Silver Creek Shakespeare Club Records, 1889–1990, MS 53, University Archives, State University of New York at Buffalo. The Shakespeare Club of Chicago met for seven years, until 1886, when meetings were suspended due to too many marriages among members. The club history records, "It was never supposed on the organizing of the club that it would degenerate into a matrimonial bureau. But such seemed to be the irresistible tendency." Arthur Woodcock, *The Shakespeare Club, a Sketch* (Chicago: privately printed, 1896), 21.

37. William Taylor Thomas advocated Shakespeare study for both sexes: Shakespeare "must be studied by the American boys and girls." "The Introduction of Shakespeare into the Schools," *Shakespeariana* 1 (1883): 11. Blair (*Clubwoman as Feminist*, 69) asserts that in clubs, "the male presence intimidated women and hampered them from acquiring the public speaking skills they desired," but this does not seem to have been the case with most Shakespeare clubs.

38. On the occasion of its first anniversary in 1888, the Shakespeariana Club of Grand Rapids, Michigan, received letters of congratulation from Mrs. J. W. Shoemaker,

vice president of the National School of Elocution and Oratory; Appleton Morgan, president of New York Shakespeare Society; and Charlotte Porter, editor of the monthly magazine *Shakespeariana*.

39. Johnson, *Gender and Rhetorical Space*, 14.

40. Sara M. Evans, *Born for Liberty: A History of Women in America* (New York: Free Press, 1989), 3.

41. J. W. Wood, *Pasadena, California: Historical and Personal* (Pasadena, Calif.: J. W. Wood, 1917), 478–79.

42. According to Christine Bolt, "The creation of the General Federation of Women's Clubs in the United States in 1890, and of state federations in 1894, indicates how far American club creation had proceeded since the 1860s, and how far American women had drawn ahead of their British sisters in this aspect of the women's movement." *The Women's Movements in the United States and Britain from the 1790s to the 1920s* (Amherst: University of Massachusetts Press, 1993), 220. For the history of reading Shakespeare in Britain, see Andrew Murphy, "Shakespeare among the Workers," in *Shakespeare Survey 58: Writing about Shakespeare*, ed. Peter Holland (Cambridge: Cambridge University Press, 2005), 107–17, and *Shakespeare for the People: Working-Class Readers, 1800–1900* (Cambridge: Cambridge University Press, 2008).

43. For the history of the GFWC, see Mary Jean Houde, *Reaching Out: A Story of the General Federation of Women's Clubs* (Chicago: Mobium Press, 1989).

44. *Lewiston Daily Sun*, 19 April 1927, 3. On the publications of women's national organizations in relation to women's clubs, and clubs' use of mainstream magazines and newspapers, see Gere, *Intimate Practices*, 8–9.

45. "The Club Forum," *Shakespeare Association Bulletin* 1.3 (1926): 19.

46. Larry Grove, *Dallas Public Library: The First 75 Years* (Dallas: Dallas Public Library, 1977), 18.

47. Mrs. William D. Faris and Mrs. Bernard Peters of the Portia Reading Club of Brooklyn, and Mrs. M. R. Silsby and Mrs. C. Lester of the Seneca Falls, New York, Shakespeare Club.

48. Clark, *Woodland Shakespeare Club*, 22.

49. George W. Kingsbury, *History of Dakota Territory*, vol. 3 (Chicago: S. J. Clarke, 1915), 778.

50. Chandler Lyons and Sharon Atteberry, *Women of Peoria, 1620 to 1920* (Peoria, Ill.: Wilde Press, 2003), 76–77. Lyons notes that the club was divided on the issue in 1906 but united behind suffrage the following year.

51. As Gere points out, "clubs explored suffrage, but they gave it little public support." *Intimate Practices*, 273n12. The women in the Silver Creek, New York, Shakespeare Club also discussed suffrage in 1917. Silver Creek Shakespeare Club Records, 1889–1990, MS 53, University Archives, State University of New York at Buffalo. For geographical variations in women's involvement in social issues, see Nancy A. Hewitt, *Women's Activism and Social Change: Rochester, New York, 1822–1872* (Ithaca: Cornell University Press, 1984), and Sandra Haarsager, *Organized Womanhood: Cultural Politics in the Pacific Northwest, 1840–1920* (Norman: University of Oklahoma Press, 1997).

52. Croly, *History of the Woman's Club Movement*, 798.

53. Clark, *Woodland Shakespeare Club*, 22.

54. Robert F. Sperry, "A History of Barnesville, Georgia, 1865–1900," typescript, Old Jail Museum and Archives, Barnesville–Lamar County Historical Society; Andrea Knecht, "'We Are from the City, and We Are Here to Educate You': The Georgia Fed-

eration of Women's Clubs and Tallulah Falls School," in *The Educational Work of Women's Organizations, 1890–1960,* ed. Anne Meis Knupfer and Christine Woyshner (New York: Palgrave Macmillan, 2008), 216–17.

55. *Michigan State Library Bulletin* No. 1 (May 1896): 34–35.

56. http://www.shakespeareclub.org/history.htm.

57. Clark, *Woodland Shakespeare Club*, 32.

58. "Placerville Society Began with the Shakespeare Club," undated newspaper clipping, Club History Collection, CH CA 054, General Federation of Women's Clubs Archives. A member of the Shakespeare Club of San Diego felt differently about prostitution; Mrs. L. K. Lanier remarked in 1912 after a police raid, "I do not think that the redlight district ought to have been abolished. . . . The women will only go to infect another city." Clare V. McKanna, Jr., "Prostitutes, Progressives, and Police: The Viability of Vice in San Diego 1900–1930," *Journal of San Diego History* 35.1 (1989): unpaginated.

59. See the chapter on criticism of women's clubs in Patricia Marks, *Bicycles, Bangs, and Bloomers: The New Woman in the Popular Press* (Lexington: University Press of Kentucky, 1990), 117–46. Gere points out that "one of the most frequent attacks [on club women] emphasized the selfishness inherent in study or self-improvement." *Intimate Practices*, 10. In her history of women's clubs, Croly remarked that "there was little sympathy with organizations of women not expressly religious, charitable, or intended to promote charitable objects." *History of the Women's Club Movement*, 9.

60. "Ladies Shakespeare Club, 1882–1982," typescript, Indiana State Library, Indianapolis. The club also had a humorous club song with the refrain "All Baconites to eschew" and to Shakespeare "be true." *Shakespeariana* 6 (1888): 286.

61. See William Enfield, *The Speaker* (1782), and Gerald Graff, *Professing Literature: An Institutional History* (Chicago: University of Chicago Press, 1987, 2007), 41; Nan Johnson, *Nineteenth-Century Rhetoric in North America* (Carbondale: Southern Illinois University Press, 1991), 82–83. Kevin J. Hayes notes that Shakespeare was typical reading material for colonial women. *A Colonial Woman's Bookshelf* (Knoxville: University of Tennessee Press, 1996), 13. See also Heather S. Nathans, "'A Course of Learning and Ingenious Studies': Shakespearean Education and Theater in Antebellum America"; Sandra M. Gustafson, "Eloquent Shakespeare"; and Nan Johnson, "Shakespeare in American Rhetorical Education, 1870–1920"; all in *Shakespearean Educations: Power, Citizenship, and Performance*, ed. Coppélia Kahn, Heather S. Nathans, and Mimi Godfrey (Newark: University of Delaware Press, 2011), 54–70, 71–91, 112–27.

62. William Taylor Thomas remarked that "Shakespeare is a fine text-book" for studying rhetoric. "The Introduction of Shakespeare into the Schools," *Shakespeariana* 1 (1883): 10–11.

63. Randall-Diehl was the author of *Reading and Elocution: Theoretical and Practical* (New York: Ivison, Blakeman, Taylor, 1869), *Carleton's Popular Readings: Prose and Poetry* (New York: G. W. Carleton, 1879), *Elocutionary Studies and New Recitations* (New York: E. S. Werner, 1887, reprinted 1903), and *Two Thousand Words and Their Definitions, not in Webster's Dictionary* (New York: J. S. Ogilvie, 1888).

64. Margherita Arlina Hamm, "The Fortnightly Shakespeare Club." *American Shakespeare Magazine* 3 (1897): 319.

65. Philip H. Christensen, "McGuffey's Oxford (Ohio) Shakespeare," *Journal of American Studies* 43 (2009): 102. See also Jonathan Burton, "Lay on, McGuffey:

Excerpting Shakespeare in Nineteenth-Century Schoolbooks," in Kahn et al., *Shakespearean Educations*, 95–111.

66. Christensen, "McGuffey's Oxford (Ohio) Shakespeare," 104.

67. Dolores P. Sullivan, *William Holmes McGuffey: Schoolmaster to the Nation* (Rutherford, N.J.: Fairleigh Dickinson University Press, 1994), 91. It's worth pointing out that Shakespeare clubs weren't alone in promoting Shakespeare as a figure of American culture.

68. Charlotte M. Canning, *The Most American Thing in America: Circuit Chautauqua as Performance* (Iowa City: University of Iowa Press, 2005), 1.

69. *Shakespeariana* 1 (1883): 93. See Victoria Case and Robert Ormond Case, *We Called It Culture: The Story of Chautauqua* (New York: Doubleday, 1948); Theodore Morrison, *Chautauqua: A Center for Education, Religion, and the Arts in America* (Chicago: University of Chicago Press, 1974); and Jeffrey Simpson, *Chautauqua: An American Utopia* (New York: Henry N. Abrams, 1999); Canning discusses Chautauqua performances of Shakespeare in *Most American Thing in America,* 186, 189, 196–98, 200. For Shakespeare in the lyceum, see Carl Bode, *The American Lyceum: Town Meeting of the Mind* (New York: Oxford University Press, 1956), 232–33. The well-known American editor Henry Hudson's lectures on Shakespeare were part of this program.

70. Mary Bowden Carroll, *Ten Years in Paradise: Leaves from a Society Reporter's Note-Book* (San Jose, Calif.: Popp and Hogan, 1903), 109; *Michigan State Library Bulletin* No. 1 (May 1896): 69. Likewise, the Indiana, Pennsylvania, Shakespeare club did four years of the Chautauqua Home Study Course before returning to only Shakespeare. The Records of the Shakespeare Club of Indiana County, MS 85, Special Collections and University Archives, Indiana University of Pennsylvania.

71. *Michigan State Library Bulletin* No. 1 (May 1896): 41. Many clubs also took part in the Bay View Reading Circle program, which extended its study plans across the country, including the Friday Shakespeare Club of Santa Cruz, California. "A Brief History of the Friday Shakespeare Club on the Seventy-Fifth Anniversary," MS 104, University Library, University of California, Santa Cruz. The Ladies' Shakespeare Club of Decatur, Indiana, even split its club into two groups so some members could take the C.L.S.C. course. "Ladies Shakespeare Club, 1882–1982," typescript, Indiana State Library, Indianapolis.

72. See Canning, *Most American Thing in America.*

73. Gere explores some of the links between these study groups and the professionalization of the study of English. *Intimate Practices*, 212, 217–19. See also Elizabeth Renker, "Shakespeare in the College Classroom, 1870–1920," and Coppélia Kahn, "Poet of America: Charles Mills Gayley's Anglo-Saxon Shakespeare," both in Kahn, *Shakespearean Educations*, 131–56, 201–15.

74. Graff, *Professing Literature,* 66. As Murphy notes, "Shakespeare entered the American university curriculum at a time when the academic world was becoming increasingly professionalised." *Shakespeare in Print*, 160.

75. Evans, *Born for Liberty*, 139. Martin points out that in the late 1800s, "even with an increasing number of college doors open to them, women did not rush through." *Sound of Our Own Voices,* 42–47, 112–16, at 43. See also *Women and Higher Education in American History*, ed. John Mack Faragher and Florence Howe (New York: W. W. Norton, 1988), and Frederick Rudolph, *The American College and University: A History* (New York: Alfred A. Knopf, 1965), 307–28. Rudolph writes, "Given the conditions of American life, it was inevitable that the college classroom should one day be blessed with the

charms of femininity and graced by the presence of aspiring American womanhood. But it would take time" (307). Barbara Miller Solomon offers a more enlightened discussion of women's place in higher education. See *In the Company of Educated Women: A History of Women and Higher Education in America* (New Haven, Conn.: Yale University Press, 1985).

76. Solomon, *In the Company of Educated Women*, 62.

77. Gere maintains that women's clubs "offered a cultural other against which a professionalized version of English studies could be established," and that between 1880 and 1920, in order to "justify its place in the academy," English studies had to wrestle "control of the field away from women." Gere, *Intimate Practices*, 212. Gere argues that "anxieties engendered by professionalized English studies led many clubwomen, particularly those in white middle-class groups, to emulate the practices and terms of the academy." *Intimate Practices*, 217.

78. Croly, *History of the Woman's Club Movement*, 368.

79. "Woman's Shakespearean Club Celebrates Its Anniversary," *Barnesville News-Gazette*, 10 September 1896, clipping from Loula Kendall Rogers Papers, Robert W. Woodruff Library, Emory University.

80. Kristin L. Hoganson traces a similar trajectory in women's imaginary travel clubs; she notes that the Albert Lea, Minnesota, Travel Class began "when a local doctor departed for a long trip to Europe, without his wife," who then gathered some friends together for "imaginary ramblings, thus refusing to be left behind." Hoganson notes that "the tourist mentality encouraged women to see their ability to travel, if only vicariously, as a mark of women's increasing freedoms and rising status." *Consumers' Imperium: The Global Production of American Domesticity, 1865–1920* (Chapel Hill: University of North Carolina Press, 2007), 187, 205. In founding the Peoria Shakespeare Class, Clara Bourland sought to "bring the music, art and literature she had enjoyed in Europe to audiences in Central Illinois." Lyons and Atteberry, *Women of Peoria*, 68.

81. Clark, *Woodland Shakespeare Club*, 9.

82. The Shakespeare Study Club of Detroit, for example, began in 1906 with "a group of earnest women, longing for a greater knowledge of Shakespeare's works." "The Progress of the Clubs: History and a Garden in Detroit," *Shakespeare Association Bulletin* 3.2 (1928): 13. These examples support Jonathan Rose's argument that "again and again we find classic literature embraced by working people who thoroughly lacked literary education." *Intellectual Life of the British Working Classes*, 5. Although not all these women readers lacked literary education, their reading and study took place outside the formal structures of literary education in America. Women readers of Shakespeare give us a chance to answer Kate Flint's call to study "the actual reading habits and experiences of those whose access to print has not necessarily been shaped by dominant institutions." "Women and Reading," 529.

83. Robbins, *Alabama Women in Literature*, 55; "Kate Tupper Galpin Shakespeare Club," 158. Whereas Gere characterizes women's clubs' approach to literature as "literary study as a means of informing philanthropic projects by enhancing their understanding of humanity," with a goal of "more effective benevolence and enhanced life experiences," she describes the male scholarly tradition as aiming "to strengthen the mind and develop intellectual capacities." Men privileged "knowledge of language, while clubwomen often looked to the knowledge of their own experience." *Intimate Practices*, 216.

84. According to Solomon, there were 601,000 women enrolled in higher education in 1940 and 1,223,000 by 1960. *In the Company of Educated Women*, 63. I discuss the decline of clubs further in my conclusion.

85. *Shakespeariana* 4 (1887): 177–78; Clark,*Woodland Shakespeare Club,* 7; *Shakespeariana* 3 (1886): 367. The Sisters' Shakespeare Society of Elizabeth, New Jersey, required each member to "memorize and give a quotation from some play at each meeting." *Shakespeariana* 1 (1883–84): 159.

86. *Shakespeariana* 4 (1887): 329. Member Frances M. Abbott noted that "the sonnets have been found of particular interest."

87. Even in the most haphazardly organized club, the journal *Shakespeariana* optimistically noted, "some good does not fail to get done . . . if it is merely the good of turning the attention of some one of the members to the rich browsing ground within Shakespearian pastures." *Shakespeariana* 3 (1886): 461.

88. Published from 1936 to 1950, the *Shakespeare Association Bulletin* was the precursor to *Shakespeare Quarterly.* Christy Desmet provides a discussion of *Shakespeariana* in "*Shakespeariana* and Shakespeare Societies in North America, 1883–1893," *Borrowers and Lenders: The Journal of Shakespeare and Appropriation* 2 (Fall/Winter 2006). Gere lists numerous women's publications that circulated news of women's clubs nationwide. See *Intimate Practices*, 8–9.

89. Mary Cowden Clarke's *The Girlhood of Shakespeare's Heroines* (1851) and Anna Jameson's *Characteristics of Women: Moral, Poetical and Historical* (1832), based on Shakespeare's heroines, were among the most popular works of Shakespeare criticism for club women.

90. *Shakespeare Society of New York: Articles of Association,* 15.

91. Porter later started the monthly journal *Poet Lore* with Helen Clarke in 1889, which focused on Shakespeare, Browning, and literary study. See *Famous American Women: A Biographical Dictionary from Colonial Times to the Present*, ed. Robert McHenry (New York: Dover, 1980), 73.

92. This is Rose's phrase for describing "the expanding culture of print," which applies as much to American women as it does to the working-class British in his work. *Intellectual Life of the British Working Classes*, 10. As early as 1883, *Shakespeariana* was influential for club study; the men and women in the Cooperstown, New York, Shakespeare Club reported that they "thoroughly enjoyed" *Shakespeariana* as part of their study program. *Shakespeariana* 1 (1883): 200.

93. *Shakespeariana* 2 (1885): 450.

94. *Shakespeariana* 3 (1886): ii, 456; *Shakespeariana* 4 (1887): 176–77; *Shakespeariana* 5 (1888): 28–30, 218; *Shakespeariana* 6 (1889): 47.

95. *American Shakespeare Magazine* 3 (1897): 376. The first volume was issued as the *Fortnightly Shakespeare.* Randall-Diehl's questions were used by the Bryant Shakespeare Correspondence School, whose members submitted their work to her "for examination and criticism."

96. *American Shakespeare Magazine* 3 (1897): 357–64.

97. *Midland Monthly* 9 (January–June 1898): 471.

98. The Reviewers Club of Mishawaka, Indiana, would have helped Daly's cause in the early twentieth century. Made up of six husbands and their wives who met monthly "to read and enjoy Shakespeare," they often traveled to Chicago to attend theater performances. "Shakespeare Clubs and Study Groups," *Shakespeare Quarterly* 2 (1951): 274.

99. "The Shakespeare Club Forum," *Shakespeare Association Bulletin* 1.2 (1925): 7. Further evidence of the journal's success comes from the women of the Shakespeare Club in Eugene, Oregon, who used "reports from the *Shakespeare Bulletin*" regularly in their meetings and also belonged to the Shakespeare Association of America. Effie R.

Knapp, "History of the Eugene Shakespeare Club," MS 227, Special Collections and University Archives, University of Oregon Library.

100. *Shakespeare Association Bulletin* 4.4 (1929): 120. In 1929, the "Club Forum" was taken over by Mrs. Robert Carlton Morris of the Toledo Shakespeare Club.

101. *Shakespeare Association Bulletin* 4.4 (1929): 78.

102. *Shakespeare Association Bulletin* 5.3 (1930): 142.

103. "Brief History of the Friday Shakespeare Club." Marie Davis was the club secretary.

104. Browning societies were a distant second in popularity to Shakespeare clubs. An editorial in the 1889 issue of *Shakespeariana* asked, "Will the study of Browning cast out the study of Shakespeare?" It answered the query: "The limitations of Browning study alone forbid it. How can we debate the meaning of a phrase, the tendency of a thought, the trend of a story, the morals of an episode, night after night, week after week, overhauling libraries for the least hint or suggestion so as to help us in our search, when the rare old poet himself is alive, and a postage-stamp will settle our quandary from the very pen of the poet himself?" *Shakespeariana* 6 (1889): 92–93. The Kate Tupper Galpin Shakespeare Club, for example, "once changed its course of study to Browning and gave some thought to Greek literature, but returned to the inexhaustible resources of the Beloved Bard." "Kate Tupper Galpin Shakespeare Club," 158.

105. *Shakespeare Quarterly* 1 (1950): 121; *Shakespeare Quarterly* 3 (1952): 78. I discuss this shift further in the Conclusion.

106. "Shakespeare for Everyman," *Proceedings of the American Philosophical Society* 106.5 (1962): 393–400, at 400. Ronald J. Zboray lists Shakespeare as one of the popular items in Homer Franklin's New York bookstore in 1840–41. *A Fictive People: Antebellum Economic Development and the American Reading Public* (New York: Oxford University Press, 1993), 140, 149.

107. Murphy, *Shakespeare in Print*, 153, 159–60.

108. *Shakespeariana* 4 (1887): 330. Similarly, the women in the Round Table Club of Demopolis, Alabama, used "Rolfe's and Kellogg's editions, and all the outside help at our command." Robbins, *Alabama Women in Literature*, 36.

109. *Shakespeariana* 3 (1886): 463.

110. *How to Organize a Shakespeare Club* (New York: Doubleday and McClure, 1898), 4, 10.

111. Many clubs read these works; the Columbus, Kansas, Shakespeare Club included Anna Jameson's *Characteristics of Women* in its program for 1900–1901.

112. *Shakespeariana* 4 (1887): 355–56; originally published in *The Girl's Own Paper* (London, June 1887).

113. Elizabeth Wormeley Latimer, *Familiar Talks on Some of Shakespeare's Comedies* (Boston: Roberts Brothers, 1886), v–vi. Latimer's other works include the novel *Our Cousin Veronica: or, Scenes and Adventures over the Blue Ridge* (1856), translations from French and Italian, and histories, among them *France in the Nineteenth Century, England in the Nineteenth Century, Europe in Africa in the Nineteenth Century, Italy in the Nineteenth Century*; see *Shakespeariana* 3 (1886): 579.

114. The passage comes from Furnivall's introduction to *The Leopold Shakspere: The Poet's Works in Chronological Order* (London: Cassell, 1877).

115. This is in contrast to the parlor rhetoric movement, which identified "men and not women" as "rhetorical agents in the public and professional spheres." Johnson, *Gender and Rhetorical Space*, 28.

116. *The Shakespeare Cyclopaedia and New Glossary* (New York: Industrial Publication Co., 1902), 7. Edward Dowden provided the introduction. Phin was apparently an expert in a number of areas in addition to Shakespeare: he was the author of *The Practical Dictionary of Apiculture, How to Use the Microscope,* and *How to Become a Good Mechanic.*

117. In Texas, the Shakespeare Club of Sherman, the Woman's Wednesday Club of Fort Worth, and the XXI Club of Denison followed Ticknor's plan. Stella L. Christian, ed., *The History of the Texas Federation of Women's Clubs* (Houston: Dealy-Adey-Elgin, 1919), 12. See Anna E. Ticknor, *Society to Encourage Studies at Home* (Cambridge, Mass.: Riverside Press, 1897), for a history. The daughter of a Harvard professor, Ticknor began the society in 1873 to gratify "the aspirations of the large number of women throughout the country who would fain obtain an education, and who had little, if any hope of obtaining it," whose "homes were far away from the centres of learning and instruction, and yet who craved educational advantages for themselves and their families" (2, 4). Women of "all classes," not just "the wealthy class," were her audience (9). One female student attested to the value of the society: "I do not know where I should stop, if I tried to tell how much they have helped me . . . in my isolated life. I craved so much, and there seemed no access possible to anything I wanted." (18). Another student from Chicago testified that the study course gave her "a love for Shakespeare, which will be a pleasure and comfort to me through life" (166).

118. Ticknor, *Society to Encourage Studies at Home,* "Acting Secretary's Report," 209–10.

119. Ticknor, *Society to Encourage Studies at Home,* 172. The magazine *Self Culture* also advertised papers on Shakespeare, as well as a section called "Woman and the Home," which "will as usual contain bright and breezy paragraphs, and from time to time will give reports of the work accomplished by women's clubs in various sections of the country." *Book Reviews: A Monthly Journal Devoted to New and Current Publications* 8.1 (1900): 1–2. For extended discussion of Ticknor's society, see Harriet F. Bergmann, "'The Silent University': The Society to Encourage Studies at Home, 1873–1897," *New England Quarterly* 74.3 (2001): 447–77.

120. *Shakespeariana* 4 (1887): 328–30. Scott points out that "with respect to the much disputed notion that in their associations middle-class women were attempting to assert control over the behavior of the 'lower classes,' I think the evidence does not support any simple hypothesis." She argues that club women "did not always draw distinctions in terms of economic or social class." *Natural Allies,* 4. In *Intimate Practices,* Gere counters the perception that women's clubs were made up only of white middle-class women by analyzing a variety of women's clubs of differing ethnic, racial, class, and religious composition.

121. A survey of homemakers in the 1920s by the Bureau of Home Economics, Department of Agriculture, described typical club women as "middle-class homemakers." Anna E. Richardson, "The Woman Administrator in the Modern Home," *Annals of the American Academy of Political and Social Science* 143 (May 1929): 21–32, at 22.

122. As Anne Meis Knupfer puts it, the "intimacy and privacy" of club meetings "allowed access only for those who were present" and "indicate that women consciously created and defined a literary space for themselves." *Toward a Tenderer Humanity and Nobler Womanhood: African American Women's Clubs in Turn-of-the-Century Chicago* (New York: New York University Press, 1996), 122.

123. Robbins, *Alabama Women in Literature*, 56.

124. http://www.shakespeareclub.org/Shakespeare.htm, accessed 4 December 2007.

125. Charles R. Heventhal, *Readers of the Bard: The Shakespeare Club of Worcester, a Centennial Sketch* (privately printed, 1990).

126. Although the club began with Shakespeare, it also read works of Dickens, Dante, and Longfellow, and Ibsen's *Doll's House*. In 1912, it changed its name to the Fort Knightly Reading Club. "The Shakespeare Club to the Fort Knightly Reading Club of Washington, Missouri," Tibbe-Cuthbertson Family Papers, 1849–1975, MS C3711, Western Historical Manuscript Collection, University of Missouri/State Historical Society of Missouri. In Eugene, Oregon, the Shakespeare Club was organized by Mrs. P. K. Hammond, wife of the Episcopal rector; she "invited a group of women to the rectory to read Shakespeare's plays with her," but the club history explains that "it has not been the custom to confine the membership to Episcopalians." Knapp, "History of the Eugene Shakespeare Club."

127. *Shakespeariana* 2 (1885): 48. See http://www.ah.dcr.state.nc.us/archives/ead/eadxml/org_tuesdayafternoonbook_raleigh.xml.

128. "Woman's Shakespearean Club Celebrates Its Anniversary."

129. For further discussion of women's groups in the South, see Darlene Rebecca Roth, *Matronage: Patterns in Women's Organizations, Atlanta, Georgia, 1890–1940* (Brooklyn, N.Y.: Carlson Publishing, 1994).

130. *Shakespeariana* 4 (1887): 177.

131. Clark, *Woodland Shakespeare Club*, 5, 2–3.

132. Croly, *History of the Woman's Club Movement,* 796.

133. Its first president, Alice Ayres (one of four Ayres sisters who were members), was only twenty-nine when elected. Hoover, "First Hundred Years of the Medford Shakespeare Club."

134. Clark, *Woodland Shakespeare Club*, 17. The Friday Shakespeare Club of Santa Cruz, California, capped its membership at twenty women and had a waiting list of women who wanted to join. "Brief History of the Friday Shakespeare Club."

135. Wood, *Pasadena*, 480.

136. *Shakespeariana* 4 (1887): 327–38. The article "How to Promote a Shakespeare Club," published in London in *Cassell's Family Magazine* (June 1880): 415–16, advocated a similar membership policy of excluding anyone who received one negative vote in seven, aimed at preventing "the admission not only of obviously unsuitable persons, but of any whose presence might prove embarrassing to even a small minority of its members." The piece amusingly ends by adding that "although we have throughout used the words 'him' and 'his,' yet many Shakespeare Clubs contain ladies, and find the arrangement convenient and pleasant" (416). The Old Cambridge (Massachusetts) Shakespeare Association had a clever way of voting on potential members; votes were cast by either kernels of corn or black beans in a ballot box. "Old Cambridge Shakespeare Association, 1882–2006: A Finding Aid," Brinkler Library, Cambridge Historical Society.

137. The Shakespeare Club of Indiana, Pennsylvania, also built social cohesion by including only married couples in its membership. The Records of the Shakespeare Club of Indiana County, MS 85, Special Collections and University Archives, Indiana University of Pennsylvania.

138. "Shakespeare Clubs and Study Groups," *Shakespeare Quarterly* 4 (1953): 368.

139. Mae Wenger, *Centennial History: GFWC Kansas Federation of Women's Clubs* (Shawnee Mission, Kan.: Kes-Print, 1988), 144.

140. *The Encyclopedia of New Jersey*, ed. Maxine N. Lurie and Marc Mappen (New Brunswick, N.J.: Rutgers University Press, 2004), 734. The Anne Hudgins Shakespeare Class of Marietta, Georgia, began meeting in 1931 and still meets every other Thursday; members include many descendants of the founding families of Marietta. This information comes from the private records of the Anne Hudgins Shakespeare Class. I am grateful to the current president, Candace Azermendi, and to the club for access to these records.

141. Willie Newbury Lewis, *History of the Dallas Shakespeare Club, 1886–1970* (N.p., [197–?]), 3, 14. Copy in the Dallas Public Library.

142. Club records often note women who resigned, however.

143. Flint points out that in the nineteenth century "it continues to be more difficult to discern what women felt and thought when they were reading than it is to arrive at ideas of men's responses to the written word" because women "had less occasion or impetus to record their lives and to reflect on the range of texts that formed a role in their self-fashioning." "Women and Reading," 523. Shakespeare Clubs are an exception; most left well-documented lists of their texts, study questions, minutes, and even personal reflections.

144. Robbins, *Alabama Women in Literature*, 49; "1886: Queen of Clubs," *Texas Monthly* (January 1986): 151.

145. Papers of the Shakespeare Society of Plainfield, N.J., Local History Department, Plainfield Public Library, Plainfield, N.J. The Shakespeare Club of Eugene, Oregon, voted to donate its club minutes to the University of Oregon library and planned to "continue doing this if the University Library is willing to take them." Leila Stafford, "Recollections of People and Events in the Earlier Days of the Eugene Shakespeare Club," MS 227, Special Collections and University Archives, University of Oregon Library.

146. Medford Shakespeare Club, 1867–1967; Hoover, "First Hundred Years of the Medford Shakespeare Club."

147. Hoover, "First Hundred Years of the Medford Shakespeare Club."

148. Letter of 20 May 1987, Folger Scrapbook 243553, Folger Shakespeare Library.

149. Thomas W. Higginson, "Women and Men: A Typical Club," *Harper's Bazaar* 22 (30 March 1880): 826–27. Gere contends that club women "began to conceal or minimize their own reading and writing projects in favor of emphasizing their service to the community as it became clear that self-improvement attracted negative attention." Shakespeare, however, seems to have provided immunity from such criticism; clubs publicized their reading accomplishments and engaged in public service projects as well. Gere, *Intimate Practices*, 10. See also her comments on p. 6 and the chapter on club women in Marks, *Bicycles, Bangs, and Bloomers*, 117–46.

150. "Shakespeare Round Table of Bowling Green, Ohio," *Shakespeare Quarterly* 7 (1956): 462–63. The Friday Shakespeare Club of Santa Cruz, California, knitted and sewed for the Red Cross during both world wars and donated books to the Shakespeare collection at the local library. "Brief History of the Friday Shakespeare Club." In addition to celebrating Shakespeare's birthday every year, the Waxahachie, Texas, Shakespeare Club started an "Empty Stocking Crusade" to deliver gifts to needy children at Christmas and a "Christmas Cheer" project to gather packages for children of workers at nearby cotton mills, furnished a room in the local sanitarium, and worked for the Red

Cross during World War II. Maude Wilson, "Highlights of 54 Years Listed by City, State Federated Shakespeare Club," newspaper clipping dated 1951, Waxahachie vertical file, Nicholas P. Sims Library, Waxahachie, Texas; "The Shakespeare Club of Waxahachie, Texas," MS CH TX 003, General Federation of Women's Clubs Archive. Similarly, the Shakespeare Club of Aberdeen, South Dakota, collected food for a poor family, donated jelly to local hospitals, and supported the Girl Scouts. See Lysbeth Em Benkert, "Shakespeare on the Prairie: The Shakespeare Club of Aberdeen, South Dakota," *Borrowers and Lenders: The Journal of Shakespeare and Appropriation* 2.2 (2006), http://www.borrowers. uga.edu/cocoon/borrowers/request?id=781465.

151. *Shakespeare Association Bulletin* 5.4 (1930): 188.

152. *Lewiston Daily Sun*, 19 April 1927, p. 3. The article mentions Shakespeare gardens in New York City, Cleveland, and Toronto. In Oklahoma City, the local Shakespeare Club sponsored a Shakespeare Garden in one of the city's parks, with a bust of Shakespeare and a public celebration of Shakespeare's birthday every April. "Shakespeare Club of Oklahoma City," *Shakespeare Quarterly* 7 (1956): 462. Apparently, the club also planned a Shakespeare Center furnished with Elizabethan period furniture. Although the account in *Shakespeare Association Bulletin* 4.4 (1929) reports that "they have already laid aside a substantial sum for this purpose," it does not appear to have materialized (79).

153. *Shakespeare Association Bulletin* 5.4 (1930): 186.

154. Clark, *Woodland Shakespeare Club*, 21, 23.

155. J. Torrey Connor, *Saunterings in Summerland* (Los Angeles: Ernest K. Foster, 1902), 78. The building was known as Cumnock Hall.

156. *Shakespeare Association Bulletin* 4.4 (1929): 77.

157. "Shakespeare Clubs and Study Groups," *Shakespeare Quarterly* 2 (1951): 274. Phillips University unfortunately went bankrupt and closed in 1998. "Shakespeare Clubs and Study Groups," *Shakespeare Quarterly* 3 (1952): 394; "Shakespeare Clubs and Societies," *Shakespeare Quarterly* 7 (1956): 462. The Dallas Shakespeare Club had an endowment fund from which it awarded a scholarship every year. See "Shakespeare Clubs and Study Groups," *Shakespeare Quarterly* 2 (1951): 179–80.

158. Wilson, "Highlights of 54 Years." The Toledo, Ohio, Shakespeare Club, "following its custom of stimulating the interest of the children," offered three $20 prizes "for the best description of a Shakespeare garden in picture, in poetry or in prose," open only to residents of northwestern Ohio under eighteen. *Shakespeare Association Bulletin* 5.4 (1930): 187. In South Dakota, the Aberdeen Shakespeare Club collected funds for a scholarship for a girl to study in Oxford, U.K. Benkert, "Shakespeare on the Prairie."

159. Hamm, "Fortnightly Shakespeare Club," 320.

160. *Shakespeare Association Bulletin* 4.4 (1929): 78.

161. According to U.S. Census records, Payette had 396 citizens in 1890 and 614 in 1900.

162. See http://www.portiaclub.com/, recollection of Florence Steigerwalt Lattig Bigelow, 13 October 2001.

163. "Portia Club Restoration Begins," *Mountain Light: The Newsletter of the Idaho State Historical Society,* Spring 2005, 6.

164. The club disbanded in 1972 but is currently undergoing a revival. See http://portiaclub.com/history/cleo.html.

165. Public enthusiasm for Shakespeare suggests that these clubs were taking part (and helping to create) a larger phenomenon of Shakespeare's growing cultural value in America. In 1914, the 350th birthday celebration of Shakespeare in New York City

involved 800,000 schoolchildren and a week of public events, culminating in discussion of founding a national Shakespeare Association. Mary C. Hyde, "The Shakespeare Association of America to the Folger Shakespeare Library on Its 40th Anniversary, 23 April 1972," *Shakespeare Quarterly* 23 (1972): 220. For the history of the Shakespeare Association of America, see Mrs. Donald F. Hyde, "The Shakespeare Association of America," in *Shakespeare 400: Essays by American Scholars on the Anniversary of the Poet's Birth*, ed. James G. McManaway (New York: Holt, Rinehart and Winston, 1964), 313–19.

166. *Americans on Shakespeare, 1776–1914*, ed. Peter Rawlings (Aldershot, U.K.: Ashgate, 1999), 165, 282.

167. This description comes from a member of the Shakespeariana Club of Grand Rapids, Michigan, in "Cordelia," 23 April 1908, p. 7, private pamphlet, Folger Scrapbook 243553, Folger Shakespeare Library.

Chapter 1

1. Such evidence runs counter to Robert Darnton's claim that "the experience of the great mass of readers lies beyond the range of historical research." "First Steps towards a History of Reading," in *The Kiss of Lamourette* (London: Faber and Faber, 1990), 177. Likewise, Kate Flint remarks that nineteenth-century women's responses to reading are more difficult to track because women "had less occasion or impetus to record their lives and to reflect on the range of texts that formed a role in their self-fashioning." "Women and Reading," *Signs* 31.2 (2006): 523. Shakespeare clubs are an exception to this. The evidence they left allows us to answer Janice Radway's call, in her study of romance readers, to locate "real readers in order to discern exactly what romances they read or how they understand and respond to the texts they choose." *Reading the Romance: Women, Patriarchy, and Popular Literature* (Chapel Hill: University of North Carolina Press, 1984), 7. Women's Shakespeare clubs provide us with opportunities to study reading practices based on real readers as opposed to readers constructed through methodological or theoretical models, ideal readers, or implied readers. See Daniel Allington and Joan Swann's discussion of different types of readers in "Researching Literary Reading as Social Practice," *Language and Literature* 18.3 (2009): 220, and Christine Pawley, "Seeking 'Significance': Actual Readers, Specific Reading Communities," *Book History* 5 (2002): 143–60. I should underline the fact that not every reader, or even the majority of readers, left detailed responses to her reading.

2. I have taken the phrase "potentially transformative activity" from Elizabeth McHenry's work on African American literary societies and relocated it specifically in reading Shakespeare; she argues that "reading was a potentially transformative activity, not only for individuals but for society as a whole." *Forgotten Readers: Recovering the Lost History of African American Literary Societies* (Durham, N.C.: Duke University Press, 2002), 3. Many scholars of book history have argued for the power of reading. Jennifer Phegley and Janet Badia discuss "the act of reading for women as one of opportunity, enlightenment, and self-transformation" but also one that produces "cultural anxieties." *Reading Women: Literary Figures and Cultural Icons from the Victorian Age to the Present* (Toronto: University of Toronto Press, 2005), 10. Bonnie Gunzenhauser remarks, "To say that reading is transformative, that reading can change the direction of a culture or a life, is to assert that reading has power." Introduction to *Reading in History: New Methodologies in the Anglo-American Tradition* (London: Pickering and Chatto, 2010), 1. Niko Besnier has argued that literacy can "help members of society to distance themselves from disad-

vantageous positions in these relations, and thus resist them in small but significant ways." *Literacy, Emotion, and Authority: Reading and Writing on a Polynesian Atoll* (Cambridge: Cambridge University Press, 1995), 10. Flint points out that reading can be "a site of personal expansion, both emotional and intellectual," and can lead to "personal insights, to reassessments of the social order, and to the exploration of disjunctions between social strictures and women's own experiences and/or ideals." "Women and Reading," 513, 515. Long argues that reading groups offer "social and intellectual empowerment." "Textual Interpretation as Collective Action," in *The Ethnography of Reading*, ed. Jonathan Boyarin (Berkeley: University of California Press, 1993), 194. In *Book Clubs: Women and the Uses of Reading in Everyday Life* (Chicago: University of Chicago Press, 2003), Long focuses on women's reading groups in Houston, Texas.

3. This chapter follows one of the central aspects of reader-response criticism; as Radway puts it, "Literary meaning is not something to be found *in* a text. It is, rather, an entity produced by a reader in conjunction with the text's verbal structure. The production process is itself governed by reading strategies and interpretive conventions that the reader has learned to apply as a member of a particular interpretive community." *Reading the Romance*, 11. In *Intimate Practices: Literacy and Cultural Work in U.S. Women's Clubs, 1880–1920* (Urbana: University of Illinois Press, 1997), Anne Ruggles Gere makes a similar argument for more general women's clubs, that they "enacted cultural work through their literacy practices" (2), but she does not focus on Shakespeare.

4. I hope it becomes evident throughout this book that the relationship between women readers and Shakespeare runs counter to Patrocinio P. Schweickart's argument that "the literary canon is androcentric" and "has a profoundly damaging effect on women readers," and that "a literary education may very well cause [women] grave psychic damage." "Towards a Feminist Theory of Reading," in *Gender and Reading: Essays on Readers, Texts, and Contexts*, ed. Elizabeth A. Flynn and Patrocinio P. Schweickart (Baltimore: Johns Hopkins University Press, 1986), 40–41. Rather, the evidence of women readers of Shakespeare supports Jonathan Rose's claim that the canon "seems to have had precisely the opposite effect." *The Intellectual Life of the British Working Classes* (New Haven, Conn.: Yale University Press, 2001), 18. The women readers I discuss do, however, "take control of the reading experience" as advocated by Schweickart (49).

5. Flint, "Women and Reading," 512, 533.

6. Nan Johnson, *Gender and Rhetorical Space in American Life, 1866–1910* (Carbondale: Southern Illinois University Press, 2002), 6.

7. The connections between Shakespeare, literacy, and education are still evident today, as discussed further in the Conclusion.

8. The Shakespeare Room in the Concord, New Hampshire Public Library, was given to the library in 1888 for the exclusive use of Shakespeare clubs. The room was run by a committee composed of women from the Shakespeare clubs, who added furnishings, books, and even souvenirs of European travel to it every year. Clubs rotated their meeting schedules to share the room and celebrated Shakespeare's birthday there as well: "On April 23, 1894, there was a gathering of the clans, the only time that the whole Shakespeare population of the town has ever been summoned to the tinkling of the teacups." See Jane Cunningham Croly, *The History of the Woman's Club Movement in America* (New York: Henry G. Allen, 1898), 799–800.

9. William St. Clair raises useful questions, such as how histories of reading can "help us to understand how knowledge was constituted and diffused, how opinions were formed and consolidated, how group identities were constructed," as well as the

"links between texts, books, reading, changing mentalities, and wider historical effects." *The Reading Nation in the Romantic Period* (Cambridge: Cambridge University Press, 2004), 1. For a good summary of the scholarship on the history of reading, see Leah Price, "Reading: The State of the Discipline," *Book History* 7 (2004): 303–20, and "From *The History of a Book* to a 'History of the Book,'" *Representations* 108 (2009): 120–38. Other relevant works on book history include Carl Kaestle et al., *Literacy in the United States: Readers and Reading since 1880* (New Haven, Conn.: Yale University Press, 1991); Cathy N. Davidson, ed., *Reading in America: Literature and Social History* (Baltimore: Johns Hopkins University Press, 1989); James L. Machor, *Readers in History* (Baltimore: Johns Hopkins University Press, 1993); Barbara Ryan and Amy M. Thomas, eds., *Reading Acts: U.S. Readers' Interactions with Literature, 1800–1950* (Knoxville: University of Tennessee Press, 2002); and the work of Roger Chartier. Andrew Murphy argues that Shakespeare "gained a political value" for nineteenth-century working-class British readers who were "involved in the various radical, reform and labour movements." *Shakespeare for the People: Working-Class Readers, 1800–1900* (Cambridge: Cambridge University Press, 2008), 5.

10. Long, "Textual Interpretation," 190 (emphasis in original). The scholarship on nineteenth-century women readers is extensive; for some of the most useful works, see Badia and Phegley, eds., *Reading Women*; Nina Baym, *Woman's Fiction: A Guide to Novels By and About Women in America, 1820–1870* (Ithaca: Cornell University Press, 1978) and *Feminism and American Literary History* (New Brunswick, N.J.: Rutgers University Press, 1992); Kate Flint, *The Woman Reader, 1837–1914* (Oxford: Clarendon, 1993); Jacqueline Pearson, *Women's Reading in Britain, 1750–1835* (Cambridge: Cambridge University Press, 1999); Barbara Sicherman, *Well-Read Lives: How Books Inspired a Generation of American Women* (Chapel Hill: University of North Carolina Press, 2010).

11. *Shakespeariana* 4 (1887): 175. Such comments underline Gere's point that "textual exchanges strengthened bonds among women separated by distance and/or time, adding an affective dimension to their literacy practices." *Intimate Practices*, 8.

12. *Michigan State Library Bulletin* No. 1 (May 1896): 17.

13. Mary LaFayette Robbins, *Alabama Women in Literature* (Selma, Ala.: Selma Printing Co., 1895), 57. Reading Shakespeare in a club created what Barbara Sicherman calls a "culture of reading," an "environment or way of life that fostered intense engagement with literacy in its diverse forms." *Well-Read Lives*, 3.

14. Estelle Freedman argues that "any female-dominated activity that places a positive value on women's social contributions, provides personal support, and is not controlled by antifeminist leadership has feminist political potential." This description seems to apply to women's Shakespeare clubs. See "Separatism as Strategy: Female Institution Building and American Feminism, 1870–1930," *Feminist Studies* 5 (1979): 527n7. Long argues that reading groups offer "a socially negotiated process of cultural reflection" that encourages "insight and innovation in the arena of identity, values, and meanings." Long, "Textual Interpretation," 202. Work on book clubs has expanded in the last decade. In addition to the work of Elizabeth Long, see Kathleen Rooney, *Reading with Oprah: The Book Club That Changed America* (Fayetteville: University of Arkansas Press, 2005), and Cecilia Konchar Farr, *Reading Oprah: How Oprah's Book Club Changed the Way America Reads* (Albany: State University of New York Press, 2004), for discussion of contemporary clubs.

15. This section is inspired by Besnier's point that "the first aim of an ethnographically informed approach to literacy is descriptive: before claiming to understand the general meaning of literacy for a particular social group, one must characterize the range and diversity of literacy experiences and contextualize each one of them in its historical antecedents, its contemporary associations, and its links to other forms of literacy." *Literacy, Emotion, and Authority,* 5.

16. Flint, "Women and Reading," 517; Long, *Book Clubs,* 221. Geoff Hall points out that "reading aloud and reading silently require and develop different practices and cognitive processing, and will have reciprocal effects on writers' use of language, as well as possible major ramifications for social history itself." "Texts, Readers—and Real Readers," *Language and Literature* 18.3 (2009): 335. Hall cites Paul Saenger, *Space between Words: The Origins of Silent Reading* (Stanford, Calif.: Stanford University Press, 1997), for the origin of this comment. Clubs also offer us a unique opportunity to examine Flint's description of women's literate practices as "poised between an intensely private, inward experience, on the one hand, and, on the other, as inseparable from a social world." "Women and Reading," 512.

17. As Jane Greer points out, "shared texts and common reading strategies can lay the groundwork for forging connections among otherwise isolated individuals." "'Some of Their Stories Are Like My Life, I Guess': Working-Class Women Readers and Confessional Magazines," in *Reading Sites: Social Difference and Reader Response,* ed. Patrocinio P. Schweickart and Elizabeth A. Flynn (New York: Modern Language Association, 2004), 157.

18. Clubs provided women with what Sara M. Evans calls "important training grounds for public activity." *Born for Liberty: A History of Women in America* (New York: Free Press, 1989), 140. Gere explores some of the links between these study groups and the professionalization of the study of English. *Intimate Practices,* 212, 217–19. Karen J. Blair writes that club women "began to acquire the speaking, organizational, and leadership skills that enabled them to develop and express their ideas." The clubs "gave participants important skills that would enable them to grow out of their self-consciousness and isolation . . . to share news and companionship with women like themselves." These clubs took on the difficult task of "freeing women from inhibitions about speaking publicly." *The Clubwoman as Feminist: True Womanhood Redefined, 1868–1914* (New York: Holmes and Meier, 1980), 66–67.

19. Robbins, *Alabama Women in Literature,* 31. The report on the Kettledrum club adds that "lasting friendships have been formed." One member of the Eugene, Oregon, Shakespeare Club was "very interested in the study of the play but suffered greatly from shyness and could never bring herself to lead a study." Instead, she got together with another member of the club "in her little house, and they would read together the play that was being studied at the time." Effie R. Knapp, "Recollections of People and Events in the Earlier Days of the Eugene Shakespeare Club," MS 227, Special Collections and University Archives, University of Oregon Library.

20. Jonathan Boyarin's important collection of essays works to dissolve "the stereotype of the isolated individual reader, showing that not only is all reading socially embedded, but indeed a great deal of reading is done in social groups." *The Ethnography of Reading* (Berkeley: University of California Press, 1993), 4. See also Davidson's work on reading and social history in *Reading in America.* Schweickart and Flynn point out that "we read with the anticipation of discussing our responses with others and that the

meaning of a text is not the product of isolated readers but the collaborative project of a community of readers." *Reading Sites*, 6. Likewise, Long has emphasized the need to examine "the collective nature of reading." "Textual Interpretation" 185.

21. The Thursday Literary Circle of Selma, Alabama, used the similar term of "home reading" for such activities. Robbins, *Alabama Women in Literature*, 55–56.

22. *Michigan State Library Bulletin* No. 1 (May 1896): 54.

23. Maude Wilson, "Highlights of 54 Years Listed by City, State Federated Shakespeare Club," newspaper clipping dated 1951, Waxahachie vertical file, Nicholas P. Sims Library, Waxahachie, Texas.

24. The Dallas Shakespeare Club must hold the record for the lengthiest and most intensive method of study: six months for a scene-by-scene analysis of a single play. Theodora Penny Martin, *The Sound of Our Own Voices: Women's Study Clubs, 1860–1910* (Boston: Beacon Press, 1987), 106–8.

25. "The Progress of the Clubs," *Shakespeare Association Bulletin* 2.3 (1927): 19.

26. "Kate Tupper Galpin Shakespeare Club," *Who's Who among the Women of California*, ed. Louis S. Lyons (San Francisco: Security Publishing, 1922), 158.

27. *Shakespeariana* 3 (1886): 464–65.

28. Long points out the problems with assumptions that "significant social development and change occur only within the public realm" and emphasizes the need to look at private life as a source of social change. "Textual Interpretation," 187.

29. *Shakespeariana* 5 (1888): 359. The women in the San Antonio, Texas, Shakespeare Club printed their own guidelines for preparing a play for a meeting, including the following: "1. Read the play, 2. Mark favorite/memorable passages, 3. Be prepared to read parts when requested by leader, 4. Take part in general discussion." San Antonio Shakespeare Club program for 1973–74, San Antonio Shakespeare Club Folder, VF-SA 4004657, The Daughters of the Republic of Texas Library, The Alamo.

30. Such serious study methods should counter Michael Bristol's depiction of clubs as "often more preoccupied with the social etiquette of club meetings or with the menus planned for club dinner than with serious critical scrutiny of the plays." *Big-Time Shakespeare* (London: Routledge, 1996), 3.

31. William Taylor Thomas, "The Introduction of Shakespeare into the Schools," *Shakespeariana* 1 (1883): 11 (emphasis in original).

32. *Shakespeariana* 5 (1888): 362.

33. *Shakespeariana* 3 (1886): 367.

34. *Shakespeariana* 4 (1887): 179. The women in the Shakespeare Society of Seneca Falls, New York, relied on Rolfe's edition of Shakespeare and recommended his "invaluable little books" for Shakespeare study.

35. *Shakespeariana* 3 (1886): 523.

36. *Shakespeariana* 3 (1886): 464.

37. *Shakespeariana* 4 (1887): 326.

38. *Shakespeariana* 2 (1885): 49.

39. See Christy Desmet, "'Intercepting the Dew-Drop': Female Readers and Readings in Anna Jameson's Shakespearean Criticism," in *Women's Re-visions of Shakespeare: On Responses of Dickinson, Woolf, Rich, H.D., George Eliot, and Others*, ed. Marianne Novy (Urbana: University of Illinois Press, 1990), 41–57.

40. *Shakespeariana* 1 (1883): 99.

41. Andrew Murphy, *Shakespeare in Print: A History and Chronology of Shakespeare Publishing* (Cambridge: Cambridge University Press, 2003), 164. Murphy calls Porter

and Clarke "the first women not to have worked in conjunction with a male associate" and concludes that "their contribution to Shakespeare scholarship was indeed significant." The Zetetic Club of Weeping Water, Nebraska, used the handbook of a local professor, L. A. Sherman (professor of English literature at the University of Nebraska), for its study of Shakespeare. Sherman's book *Shakespeare: Artist and Man* (1901) provided an introduction to Shakespeare but left it "to the reader to do his own discerning, and so far as possible his own work" in studying Shakespeare. Zetetic Club of Weeping Water, Nebraska State Historical Society MS RG 4513. Sherman's book was advertised in *Book Reviews: A Monthly Journal Devoted to New and Current Publications* (New York: Macmillan, 1900), 16. Other resources for clubs included Mary Grafton Moberly's *Hints for Shakespeare-Study* (1884), designed to prepare women readers for the Cambridge (England) Higher Local Examination for Women but recommended as a study guide by the American journal *Shakespeariana*. See *Shakespeariana* 3 (1886): 564–68.

42. *Shakespeariana* 5 (1888): 29, 264.

43. *Shakespeariana* 5 (1888): 415; Croly, *History of the Woman's Club Movement*, 797.

44. Esther Bickmore Clark, *The Woodland Shakespeare Club: A History, 1886–1967* (Woodland, Calif.: privately printed, 1968), 9.

45. Douwe Draaisma, *Metaphors of Memory: A History of Ideas about the Mind*, trans. Paul Vincent (Cambridge: Cambridge University Press, 1995), 207. See also Harald Weinrich, who describes memory as "an art that can serve to overcome forgetting." *Lethe: The Art and Critique of Forgetting*, trans. Steven Rendall (Ithaca: Cornell University Press, 2004), 10. Mary Carruthers notes that "in rhetoric, memory craft is a stage in composing a work; presupposed is the axiom that recollection is an act of investigation and recreation in the service of conscious artifice." *The Book of Memory: A Study of Memory in Medieval Culture*, 2nd ed. (Cambridge: Cambridge University Press, 2008), x. Carruthers states that in the medieval period, *memoria* "signifies the process by which a work of literature becomes institutionalized—internalized within the language and pedagogy of a group . . . a work is not truly read until one has made it part of oneself" (11). Michael Rowlands points out that "memory traces exist as marks which are not conscious, but by appropriate stimuli they might be energized long afterwards." He adds that "object traditions" such as "heirlooms, souvenirs and photographs" can "establish continuities with past experience" because "as a material symbol rather than verbalized meaning, they provide a special form of access to both individual and group unconscious processes." "The Role of Memory in the Transmission of Culture," *World Archaeology* 25.2 (1993): 141–51, at 144.

46. Rowlands remarks that "building memorials and monuments are part of the material culture of remembering." "Role of Memory," 144.

47. Louis B. Wright, "Shakespeare for Everyman," *Proceedings of the American Philosophical Society* 106.5 (1962): 393–400, at 399. For discussion of the function of memorization and recitation in the nineteenth century, see Catherine Robson, "Standing on the Burning Deck: Poetry, Performance, History," *PMLA* 120.1 (2005): 148–62.

48. Price argues that "the scene of one person reading to others restores a social dimension to an activity now more often parsed as individual or even individualistic." "Reading," 310. Similarly, many scholars have pointed out the importance of studying communities of readers rather than individual readers. See, for example, Natalie Davis, "Printing and the People," in *Society and Culture in Early Modern France: Eight Essays* (Stanford, Calif.: Stanford University Press, 1975); Brian Stock, *The Implications of Literacy: Written Language and the Models of Interpretation in the Eleventh and Twelfth Centuries*

(Princeton, N.J.: Princeton University Press, 1983); and Rebecca Krug, *Reading Families: Women's Literate Practice in Late Medieval England* (Ithaca: Cornell University Press, 2002). McHenry likewise points out in *Forgotten Readers* that "reading in early black communities was not always an individual enterprise" (13). *PMLA* (125.3 [2010]: 418–42) recently published a cluster of articles on community reading.

49. This is in contrast to Janice A. Radway's interpretation of the Book-of-the-Month Club, which she argues "consolidate[d]" the views of subscribers and advocated that knowledge needed to be "parsed according to the authority" of the club. *A Feeling for Books: The Book-of-the-Month Club, Literary Taste, and Middle-Class Desire* (Chapel Hill: University of North Carolina Press, 1999), 297–99.

50. *Shakespeare Association Bulletin* 4.4 (1929): 119. Similarly, the Atlanta Shakespeare Club reported in 1883 that in its study of Shakespeare "much is learned, inquiries are awakened and discussions ensue." *Shakespeariana* 1 (1883): 28. The Shakespeare Study Club of Detroit "showed a lively interest in each play and would study the plot and development of characters, having discussion and also debates and presenting scenes for practice." "The Progress of the Clubs: History and a Garden in Detroit," *Shakespeare Association Bulletin* 3.2 (1928): 13.

51. Zetetic Club minutes for 23 April 1898, MS RG 4513, Nebraska State Historical Society.

52. Clark, *Woodland Shakespeare Club*, 3–4, 18.

53. In New England, the men and women in the Norwich, Connecticut, Shakespeare Club structured their meetings around the study questions in *Shakespeariana*, which produced "a general discussion, and sometimes . . . interesting arguments." *Shakespeariana* 4 (1887): 177. The Shakespeare Society of Seneca Falls, New York, attested that "opinions and criticisms are in order at every meeting, and often animated discussions arise." *Shakespeariana* 4 (1887): 179. In describing its process of choosing plays, Clara E. Masters, the secretary of the co-ed Brooklyn Shakespeare Club, cited *Hamlet* as the play "that gives them the most scope for argument, for agreements and disagreements, and seems to open them, as no other play does, to put forth all their best powers of interpretation in thought and reading." The club's meeting on *1 Henry IV* was equally conducive for argument and produced "a fierce debate about the table, the fiercest the Shakespeare club has had in months and months," even in a group that described its typical meeting format as "heated discussion" involving both men and women. Brooklyn Shakespeare Club minutes, MS AM 1675, Houghton Library, Harvard University. A meeting of the Norwich, Connecticut, Shakespeare Club in 1888 listed the following debate topic as its "Discussion" for *Twelfth Night*: "Resolved, That Shakespeare's men are more constant in love than his women." *Shakespeariana* 5 (1888): 32. In their first year of study, the women in the Barnesville, Georgia, Woman's Shakespearean Club noted several examples of intellectual debate centered on Shakespeare: "The question of Hamlet's sanity called forth a vigorous intellectual battle. . . . Whether jealousy or honor was Othello's ruling motive caused an exciting contest." "Woman's Shakespearean Club Celebrates Its Anniversary," *Barnesville News-Gazette*, 10 September 1896, clipping from Loula Kendall Rogers Papers, Robert W. Woodruff Library, Emory University.

54. *Shakespeariana* 3 (1886): 465.

55. *Shakespeariana* 2 (1885): 400–401.

56. Robbins, *Alabama Women in Literature*, 28–30. The Kettledrum Club of Tuscaloosa also set up debates and appointed a judge to evaluate the outcome. See Waldo W.

Braden, *Oratory in the New South* (Baton Rouge: Louisiana State University Press, 1999), 214, and Croly, *History of the Woman's Club Movement,* 232. The Kettledrum Club met from 1888 until at least 1965 (the last date of its papers, held at the University of Alabama archives).

57. *Shakespeariana* 1 (1883): 93.

58. *Shakespeariana* 2 (1885): 49.

59. Papers of the Shakespeare Society of Plainfield, N.J., Local History Department, Plainfield Public Library, Plainfield, N.J.

60. *Shakespeariana* 4 (1887): 177–78. The club also took great pride in its "rendering of the stage songs as they occur in the play, in their quaint and antique settings."

61. Rose points out that the "tradition of collective reading pervasively reinforced the importance of literature and education, even in the many working-class families that were indifferent or even hostile to culture." *Intellectual Life of the British Working Classes,* 87.

62. *Shakespeariana* 3 (1886): 367.

63. *Shakespeariana* 2 (1885): 48–49. The women in the Woodland Shakespeare Club read each play twice, and members had to read aloud to the club "four of the most impressive passages" of each play, followed by "a thorough discussion of the whole." Clark, *Woodland Shakespeare Club,* 7.

64. Folger Scrapbook 243553, Folger Shakespeare Library. References listed included "Shakespeare Commentaries, Prof. Gervinus. Shakespeare Key, C. & M. Cowden Clarke. Dr. Abbott's *Shakesperian Grammar. Mind and Art of Shakespeare,* E. Dowden."

65. *Shakespeariana* 4 (1887): 177–78.

66. *Shakespeariana* 5 (1888): 122–25.

67. *Shakespeariana* 4 (1887): 179.

68. *Shakespeariana* 3 (1886): 522–23.

69. Folger Scrapbook 243553.

70. *Shakespeariana* 2 (1885): 49.

71. Hall, "Texts, Readers—and Real Readers," 334. Besnier argues, "Talk frequently provides a contextual frame for literacy . . . an investigation of literacy as social practice must . . . pay attention to oral dimensions of literacy events." *Literacy, Emotion, and Authority,* 13–14. Similarly, in his study of the relationship between literacy and social structure in nineteenth-century America, Harvey J. Graff maintains that oral relations are "vital to the livelihood of the community and those within it," for connecting "individuals and groups to each other and to their larger society." *The Literacy Myth: Cultural Integration and Social Structure in the Nineteenth Century* (New Brunswick, N.J.: Transaction, 1979, 1991), 306.

72. Croly, *History of the Woman's Club Movement,* 796.

73. Papers of the Shakespeare Society of Plainfield, N.J.

74. "Woman's Shakespearean Club Celebrates Its Anniversary," *Barnesville News-Gazette,* 10 September 1896.

75. Shakespeare Club, Clinton, Missouri, minutes, 1892–1911, MS C2477, Western Historical Manuscript Collection, University of Missouri/State Historical Society of Missouri.

76. *Shakespeare Association Bulletin* 4.4 (1929): 119.

77. *Buffalo Tales* 6.7 (1983): 5. Judge Hostetler was also known for quoting "Shakespeare both at work and at leisure." The co-ed Shakespeare Club of Indiana, Pennsylvania, held a "social hour following dinner" (but before reading Shakespeare), during

which "the men and women repaired to separate rooms of the house." Records of the Shakespeare Club of Indiana County, MS 85, Special Collections and University Archives, Indiana University of Pennsylvania.

78. Shakespeare Club, Clinton, Missouri, minutes.

79. Brooklyn Shakespeare Club minutes, MS AM 1675, Houghton Library, Harvard University.

80. Brooklyn Shakespeare Club minutes.

81. Papers of the Shakespeare Society of Plainfield, N.J.

82. *Shakespeariana* 2 (1885): 481.

83. *Shakespeariana* 4 (1887): 178–79. Croly, *History of the Woman's Club Movement*, 1076.

84. Clark, *Woodland Shakespeare Club*, 19.

85. Charles R. Heventhal, *Readers of the Bard: The Shakespeare Club of Worcester, a Centennial Sketch, 1887–1987* (Worcester, Mass.: privately printed, 1990), 8.

86. "Cordelia," dated April 23, 1908, 7–8.

87. For the idea of "talking back" to Shakespeare, see Martha Tuck Rozett's *Talking Back to Shakespeare* (Newark: University of Delaware Press, 1994); Julie Sanders's *Novel Shakespeares: Twentieth-Century Women Novelists and Appropriation* (Manchester, U.K.: Manchester University Press, 2002); and Marianne Novy's work (*Engaging with Shakespeare: Responses of George Eliot and Other Women Novelists* [Athens: University of Georgia Press, 1998]; *Women's Re-visions of Shakespeare*; *Cross-Cultural Performances: Differences in Women's Re-visions of Shakespeare* [Chicago: University of Illinois Press, 1993]; and *Transforming Shakespeare: Contemporary Women's Re-visions in Literature and Performance* [New York: St. Martin's Press, 1999]). The history of Shakespeare adaptation has been treated extensively; see, for instance, Daniel Fischlin and Mark Fortier, eds., *Adaptations of Shakespeare: A Critical Anthology of Plays from the Seventeenth Century to the Present* (London: Routledge, 2000), and Margaret Jane Kidnie, *Shakespeare and the Problem of Adaptation* (London: Routledge, 2009). In connection with women specifically, see works by Sanders and Novy listed above.

88. As Sanders points out, women "frequently 'talk back' to Shakespeare, to use [Margaret] Atwood's phrase, questioning the silence or marginalisation of female characters, according voices or rewriting endings, and even providing explanatory prequels to events. The act of engagement is rarely passive." *Novel Shakespeares*, 3, 13.

89. Besnier points out that "everyday reading and writing practices (as examples of everyday social practices in general) contribute to the maintenance of power or the emergence of resistance." *Literacy, Emotion, and Authority*, 15. Some women readers engaged in resistance; others did not. Besnier points out that "literacy can have a multiplicity of seemingly contradictory meanings that depend crucially on the social contexts of reading and writing practices" (20).

90. This is Rose's analysis of the role of amateur theatricals in *Intellectual Life of the British Working Classes*, 79. Rose points out that Shakespeare "dominated the repertory of amateur dramatic groups" in Britain (81). For a discussion of women's amateur art clubs, see Karen J. Blair, *The Torchbearers: Women and Their Amateur Arts Associations in America, 1890–1930* (Bloomington: Indiana University Press, 1994). See also Michael Dobson, *Shakespeare and Amateur Performance: A Cultural History* (Cambridge: Cambridge University Press, 2011).

91. Karen Haltunnen points out that "the abundance of guides to parlor theatricals published in the 1850s and 1860s clearly suggests a new middle-class interest in the

use of the parlor as a stage." *Confidence Men and Painted Women: A Study of Middle-Class Culture in America, 1830–1870* (New Haven, Conn.: Yale University Press, 1982), 175; see also 153–90.

92. The transformative power of performance has been theorized extensively; see Erika Fischer-Lichte, *The Transformative Power of Performance: A New Aesthetics*, trans. Saskya Iris Jain (London: Routledge, 2008), especially Marvin Carlson's introduction, for an overview of recent work. Although few works deal with the type of amateur performance enacted in women's clubs, similar studies include Jessica Brantley's discussion of the connections between private reading and performance in the fifteenth century in *Reading in the Wilderness: Private Devotion and Public Performance in Late Medieval England* (Chicago: University of Chicago Press, 2007), and Shannon Jackson, *Lines of Activity: Performance, Historiography, Hull-House Domesticity* (Ann Arbor: University of Michigan Press, 2000).

93. *Shakespeariana* 5 (1888): 314; *Shakespeare Quarterly* 5.1 (1954): 103. The club reported in 1954 that Character Day became a guest-speaker night when the group grew too large.

94. *Shakespeare Association Bulletin* 4.3 (1929): 90.

95. Clark, *Woodland Shakespeare Club,* 10.

96. *Shakespeare Association Bulletin* 5.3 (1930): 142.

97. *Fortnightly Shakespeare* 1 (1895): 2.

98. Chandler Lyons and Sharon Atteberry, *Women of Peoria, 1620 to 1920* (Peoria, Ill.: Wilde Press, 2003), 76. The club had 360 members in 1900.

99. Frances A. Wittick, "Founders' Day 1946," MS, Peoria Historical Society. Wittick recounts a dress rehearsal when the club janitor "appeared suddenly on the stage. There were shrieks and a quick dispersal of actors but he took it very calmly and merely said, 'Aw you don't need to mind me, Ladies. I've seen Mrs. Monahan lots of times.'"

100. Elizabeth Greenfield, "Shakespearean 'Culture' in Montana, 1902," *Montana: The Magazine of Western History* 22.2 (1972): 49–50.

101. On the "political power" involved in women's turn-of-the-century performances, see Pamela Cobrin, *From Winning the Vote to Directing on Broadway: The Emergence of Women on the New York Stage, 1880–1927* (Newark: University of Delaware Press, 2009). Cobrin argues that "every time a woman was on public display during this era, whether as a marcher in a parade, an actress on stage, a playwright who crafted parts for women, a stage 'tech,' or a director, her performance threatened to fall outside the conventional Victorian models of womanhood, thus projecting an absent ideal; therein lay the political power of these performances" (17–18).

102. *Fortnightly Shakespeare* 1 (1895): 4.

103. Florence Earl, "Recollections of People and Events in the Earlier Days of the Eugene Shakespeare Club," MS 227, Special Collections and University Archives, University of Oregon Library.

104. *Shakespeare Association Bulletin* 3.3 (1928): 15. Unfortunately, the play does not survive.

105. "Followers of the Bard," undated clipping, San Antonio Shakespeare Club Folder, VF-SA 4004657, The Daughters of the Republic of Texas Library, The Alamo.

106. San Antonio Shakespeare Club program, 1973–74, San Antonio Shakespeare Club Folder, VF-SA 4004657, The Daughters of the Republic of Texas Library, The Alamo.

107. "The Progress of the Clubs," *Shakespeare Association Bulletin* 2.3 (1927): 19.

108. Mary Porter, *Place aux Dames, or The Ladies Speak at Last* (Chicago: Dramatic Publishing Co., 1910), 4.

109. Porter, *Place aux Dames,* 14.

110. Porter, *Place aux Dames,* 17.

111. *Fortnightly Shakespeare* 1 (1895): 2.

112. The play was deposited at the Library of Congress on 29 December 1902 but does not contain any information about the club from which it came. Library of Congress, Copyright Office, Drama Deposits Collection, Manuscript Division, reel #60, copyright registration number 2853.

113. "Shakespeare's Heroines in Club Life": A One Act Play by Mrs. Will Madders, 1902, Microfilm MS, Library of Congress.

114. Marianne Novy, "Introduction: Women's Re-visions of Shakespeare, 1664–1988," in *Women's Re-visions of Shakespeare,* 1.

115. Shakespeare's bawdy content has been discussed extensively; see Eric Partridge's seminal work *Shakespeare's Bawdy* (London: Routledge, 1947), now in its fourth edition (2001), as well as Pauline Kiernan's more recent *Filthy Shakespeare: Shakespeare's Most Outrageous Sexual Puns* (New York: Gotham, 2007). The Bowdler's Family Shakespeare editions attempted to address this problematic content in the nineteenth century.

116. Not all club women were comfortable with unseemly material; when the Shakespeare Club of San Antonio, Texas, decided to put some modern plays on its program, "one little lady was aghast at a certain new play she had to review" and "she struggled through the afternoon by omitting certain portions of it." "Followers of the Bard."

117. Autograph Letters of Joseph Crosby, Y.c. 1372, Folger Shakespeare Library, letter of 8 January 1878.

118. Shakespeare Club, Clinton, Missouri, minutes.

119. Clark, *Woodland Shakespeare Club,* 4.

120. *Shakespeariana* 4 (1887): 330. Abbott was active in the suffrage movement and successfully debated the pro-suffrage position in 1913. *The History of Woman Suffrage,* ed. Ida Husted Harper, vol. 6. (New York: J. J. Little and Ives, 1922), 404. One of the original members of the Stratford Club, she also wrote the chapter "Domestic Customs and Social Life" for the *History of Concord.*

121. Papers of the Shakespeare Society of Plainfield, N.J., Box 1, Folder 1, Volume 1, p. 291. Selection from 1909. The club noted that members must be "at least half a century old. Sufficient discretion to eliminate the very human element from the poet's writings seldom is found in younger people."

122. Shakespeare's plays have had a long and complex rapport with women readers and writers. As Juliet Fleming puts it, "women have regularly taken pleasure in, and understood the contemporary material benefits of, the enterprise of arguing the case for women's special relation to England's national poet." "The Ladies' Shakespeare," in *A Feminist Companion to Shakespeare,* ed. Dympna Callaghan (Malden, Mass.: Blackwell, 2001), 4. Women's adulation of Shakespeare's heroines often began at a young age. The "Shakespeare's Amateurs" Club of New York recognized the importance of Shakespeare's heroines as role models for young women. Organized in 1889, this group of twelve-year-old girls began by reading Lamb's *Tales of Shakespeare.* They also consulted "essays on the plays themselves, their individual merits, critical studies of the characters, sketches of the places in which the scenes are laid, and of the times which they delineate." The "character test" encompassed another club activity.

In this exercise, "the name of a character from Shakespeare was given to each girl, and she was required to tell in what play it was found." Croly, *History of the Woman's Club Movement*, 913. The Pieria Literary Society of the Pollock-Stephens Institute in Birmingham, Alabama, a private school for girls, had a "Shakespearean Women" contest in 1891 and specialized in memorizing Shakespeare. Robbins, *Alabama Women in Literature*, 26–28. The Inter Se Club of Greenville, Alabama, was formed for young girls and included character analysis of Shakespeare. Robbins, *Alabama Women in Literature*, 51.

123. "Woman's Shakespearean Club Celebrates Its Anniversary," *Barnesville News-Gazette*, 10 September 1896.

124. Clark, *Woodland Shakespeare Club*, 4.

125. Heventhal, *Readers of the Bard*, 5. Other publications circulated the idea that American women readers should connect with Shakespeare. In his essay "Shakespeare Study for American Women," William Taylor Thomas noted that Shakespeare provided particularly apt educational material for women in his "pictures of noble womanhood," women who are "not poetic abstractions, nor yet creatures of angelic perfection; they are living, breathing women, with faults and virtues and strengths and weaknesses." He wrote that "no other man has drawn such female characters as Shakespeare," concluding that if "the women of our race would know and be what the men of our race love as their ideals, let them study Shakespeare and be what he makes his women." William Taylor Thomas, "Shakespeare Study for American Women," *Shakespeariana* 1 (1883): 97–102, at 100–101. Editor and critic Norman Hapgood's book *Why Janet Should Read Shakespeare* (New York: Century, 1929) originated from an argument for the value of reading Shakespeare for women. Hapgood attributed his love of Shakespeare to his mother's love of reading Shakespeare, and recalled that he and his siblings "would sit around in the evening, or sprawl on the floor, while my mother with strong emotion read 'Macbeth,' 'Lear' or any one of a dozen of the plays" (8).

126. As Long argues, for women's reading groups, "reflection usually takes place through the lens of character, a category that link texts to individual members' lives." "Textual Interpretation," 199.

127. Undated letter from Ella A. Perry to Mrs. Lorraine Immen, Folger Scrapbook 243553, Folger Shakespeare Library.

128. One wonders how club women reacted to the 1929 film of this play starring Mary Pickford and Douglas Fairbanks, but I found no evidence of responses.

129. *Fortnightly Shakespeare* 1 (1895): 2–3.

130. Patricia Marks, *Bicycles, Bangs, and Bloomers: The New Woman in the Popular Press* (Lexington: University Press of Kentucky, 1990), 19.

131. *New York Truth*, 23 March 1895, 3. Martha J. Cutter discusses this poem in *Unruly Tongue: Identity and Voice in American Women's Writing, 1850–1930* (Jackson: University Press of Mississippi, 1999), 21. She points out that it "links the New Woman's verbal candor with her willingness to fight for social and educational equality" (21).

132. *Fortnightly Shakespeare* 1 (1895): 1.

133. Georgianna Ziegler writes, "It is surely no accident that Queen Victoria's reign, 1837–1901, corresponded to a heightened cult of womanhood which revealed itself in a focus on the heroines of that other idol of the period, Shakespeare." "Queen Victoria, Shakespeare, and the Ideal Woman," in *Shakespeare's Unruly Women*, ed. Georgianna Ziegler, Frances A. Dolan, and Jeanne Addison Roberts (Washington, D.C.: Folger Shakespeare Library, 1997), 11.

134. Portia Club History, http://www.portiaclub.com/.

135. The San Diego Portia Club is listed in *Club Women of California Official Directory and Register* (San Francisco: Calkins Publishing House, 1906–7), 183. The Shakespeare Club of Clinton, Missouri, held a "Conversation" in 1910 on the topic "Compare Portia's Wit and Lancelot's."

136. Shakespeare Club, Clinton, Missouri, 1910–11 program, C2477, Western Historical Manuscript Collection, University of Missouri/State Historical Society of Missouri.

137. The paper was subsequently published in *American Shakespeare Magazine* 3 (November 1897): 331–35.

138. *American Shakespeare Magazine* 3 (1897): 334.

139. *American Shakespeare Magazine* 3 (1897): 369–72. See Fleming, "Ladies' Shakespeare," 3–20.

140. Ann Thompson and Sasha Roberts point this out in *Women Reading Shakespeare, 1660–1900: An Anthology of Criticism* (Manchester, U.K.: Manchester University Press, 1997), 232.

141. Robbins, *Alabama Women in Literature*, 34.

142. Thomas Augst, Introduction to *Institutions of Reading: The Social Life of Libraries in the United States*, ed. Thomas Augst and Kenneth E. Carpenter (Amherst: University of Massachusetts Press), 4.

143. Paula Watson notes that "libraries were among the very earliest objects of club interest in community development" and that women's clubs were involved in 50 to 75 percent of libraries across the country, exerting what she calls a "massive nationwide influence" on libraries, particularly outside the urban Northeast. Paula D. Watson, "Founding Mothers: The Contribution of Women's Organizations to Public Library Development in the United States," *Library Quarterly* 64.3 (1994): 235, 238. Anne Firor Scott points out that despite these statistics, "except for an old article by Mois Coit Tyler, none of the standard works in library history so much as mentions" the fact that over 75 percent of public libraries were originated by women. "Women and Libraries," *Libraries, Books, and Culture*, ed. Donald G. Davis Jr. (Austin: University of Texas Press, 1986), 400. See also Gere, *Intimate Practices*, 122. Haynes McMullen provides a list of libraries for women as early as 1795 in "A Note on Early American Libraries for Women," *Journal of Library History* 13.4 (1978): 464–65. Given the large number of libraries founded by club women, it seems strange for Daniel F. Ring to blame women's clubs for failed library campaigns in four cities, failures that he ascribes to women "leading inept campaigns" and being "so politically unsophisticated that they didn't even know when they had been out-witted." Based on his study of four libraries, he concludes that "women's clubs, or at least those that I studied, did not have the political sophistication to mount successful campaigns for a Carnegie library." "Women's Club Culture and the Failure of Library Development in Illinois, Michigan and Ohio," in *Carnegie Denied: Communities Rejecting Carnegie Library Construction Grants, 1898–1925*, ed. Robert Sidney Martin (Westwood, Conn.: Greenwood Press, 1993), 72–73.

144. Carl K. Bennett, "The Librarian of a Small Library" (paper read at the Mankato meeting of the Minnesota Library Association), *Minnesota State Library Commission Library Notes and News* 1 (December 1904): 3.

145. *Report of Officers of the Public Library to the City Council* (Concord: Rumford Press, 1907), 9. Similarly, J. N. Nicholsen, Trustee of the Blue Earth Public Library, remarked that "the local library should be a storehouse for the literature of the commu-

nity." *Minnesota Public Library Commission Library Notes and News* 9 (December 1906): 16. A later historian of public libraries noted, "A history of a library reflects clearly the history of the community it serves." Frank Woodford, "Second Thoughts on Writing Library History," *Journal of Library History* 1.1 (1966): 34–42, at 41. Public libraries "sought to standardize and personalize the meaning of reading as a practice of citizenship," with books functioning as "a public good, whose benefit to community required popular circulation and use." Augst, Introduction to *Institutions of Reading*, 11. Augst argues that "the history of libraries is also a history of taste" (11); Shakespeare was a part of this.

146. Shakespeare clubs also supported traveling libraries, discussed in greater length in Chapter 4. On the history of circulating libraries in America, see David Kaiser, *A Book for a Sixpence: The Circulating Library in America* (Pittsburgh: Beta Phi Mu, 1980).

147. The Shakespeare Club of Lyndon contributed $5 to the library, slightly more than the Leap Year Party ($4.50). The main contributors were the "local entertainment" groups of the Ladies' Minstrels and Merry Milkmaids, which contributed $24 and $178, and the Whist Club, which gave $48.08. *Second Biennial Report of the Board of Library Commissioners of Vermont, 1897–98* (St. Johnsbury, Vt.: Caledonian Co., 1898), 64–65. Women from the Shakespeare club in Queens, New York, began the Queens Village Library with a traveling library and then helped raise money for a permanent library. http://www.queenslibrary.org/index.aspx?page_nm=CL-CommunityInfo&branch_id=Q#.

148. Five of the six clubs (Shakespeare, Stratford, Avon, Juniors, Monday Evening) were women-only; the Warwick Club was the exception. *Poet Lore* 1 (1889): 274–75. See *The History of Concord, New Hampshire*, vol. 1, ed. James O. Lyford (Concord: Rumford Press, 1903), 572, 606. The report of the Stratford Club of Concord in 1959 noted that there were once ten Shakespeare clubs in Concord. *Shakespeare Quarterly* 10.3 (1959): 456. According to the library dedication, the room was designated "as a place of meeting and study for any club or association, and the several members thereof, now or hereafter formed in said Concord for the purpose of reading and studying the works of William Shakespeare." *Exercises at the Dedication of the Fowler Library Building* (Concord, N.H.: Republican Press Association, 1889), 78. By 1911, the report of the Public Library lamented that "even the Shakespeare Room is no longer used by eight clubs, and the girls of the present will hardly meet there as women to read the author whom one young person of today dismissed with, Yes, I've glanced through Shakespeare but I don't like the way it ends." *Report of Officers of the Public Library to the City Council* (Concord, N.H.: Ira C. Evans, 1912), 8.

149. *Report of Officers of the Public Library to the City Council* (Concord: Rumford Press, 1901), 9. The Shakespeare Clubs of Concord also united to provide books for the Shakespeare Room. *Shakespeariana* 6 (1889): 369.

150. http://www.stmarys.lib.oh.us/information/history.

151. *Chautauquan* 35 (April–September 1902): 206; *Chautauquan* 44 (September–November 1906): 128. Likewise, the Shakespeare Study Club of Lima, Ohio, presented a check to the town's public library "sufficient to buy ten volumes of the new variorum edition of Shakespeare." *Shakespeare Association Bulletin* 4.4 (1929): 120.

152. "Shakespeare Clubs and Societies," *Shakespeare Quarterly* 7 (1956): 462–43.

153. *Shakespeare Quarterly* 7 (1956): 462–63. See also http://wcdpl.lib.oh.us/wcdplhistory.asp. In Hammond, Indiana, the Shakespeare club began a public library with only fifty books, housed in the Bloomhoff and Company Millinery Store and later supported by a Carnegie grant for a permanent building. http://www.hammondindiana.

com/old_main.html. In Decatur, Indiana, Shakespeare club women were instrumental in starting a public library and were rewarded for their perseverance by positions on the first library board. http://www.genevapl.lib.in.us/About_Us/history.html.

154. http://www.mtvbrehm.lib.il.us/about-us/copy_of_director-s-message. When the Choral Club of Spring Valley, Minnesota, disbanded, members decided to use their remaining money to purchase a bust of Shakespeare for the local library. *Minnesota Public Library Commission Library Notes and News* 7 (April 1906): 16. For further information on the development of public libraries in Minnesota, see Paul John Ostendorf, "The History of the Public Library Movement in Minnesota from 1849 to 1916" (PhD diss., University of Minnesota, 1984).

155. The women in the Eugene, Oregon, Shakespeare Club used the library of the University of Oregon but could study only two plays a year because that is all the library had. According to one member, "We used to borrow from the public library one of the two or three volumes of the Variorum edition of Shakespeare's plays when we were leading the study of a play and we gained a great deal from them." Florence Earl, "Recollections of People and Events in the Earlier Days of the Eugene Shakespeare Club," MS 227, Special Collections and University Archives, University of Oregon Library. By 1942, the club was purchasing volumes from the Variorium Shakespeare to donate to the city library. Effie R. Knapp, "History of the Eugene Shakespeare Club," MS 227, Special Collections and University Archives, University of Oregon Library.

156. R. Anna Morris Clark, "Women's Literary and Social Clubs of the Black Hills," *Bits and Pieces* 11.1 (1976): 26. Abigail A. Van Slyck argues that "in contrast to the industrialized East where a wealthy man often endowed the town library, throughout the West it was more common for middle-class women to take responsibility for establishing town libraries." *Free to All: Carnegie Libraries and American Culture, 1890–1920* (Chicago: University of Chicago Press, 1995), 125.

157. Cleo Dolphus Thompson, "The Portia Club of Payette: Then and Now," http://www.portiaclub.com/history/cleo.html.

158. Leila Stafford, "Recollections of People and Events in the Earlier Days of the Eugene Shakespeare Club," MS 227, Special Collections and University Archives, University of Oregon Library.

159. See http://www.uca.edu/archives/m8924.php. Scott notes that in Arkansas "at least 14 libraries had been founded in one decade" around 1902–3. "Women and Libraries," 403. "Shakespeare Club Celebrates Bard's Creativity." *Palm Beach Post-Times,* 19 April 1969, 10. The club donates an award to a high school student for literary achievement. See also Junius Elmore Dovell, *Florida: Historic, Dramatic, Contemporary,* vol. 4 (New York: Lewis Historical Publishing, 1952), 546–48.

160. "Woman's Shakespearean Club Celebrates Its Anniversary," *Barnesville News-Gazette,* 10 September 1896.

161. See http://www.lancastertxlib.org/history/index.htm.

162. See http://38.106.4.184/index.aspx?page=381. The Jacksonville, Texas, Shakespeare Club members helped organize the efforts to form a public library and served as librarians. See http://www.jacksonvillelibrary.com/about-us. The women of the Shakespeare Club in Cleburne, Texas, donated a collection of books to the Cleburne Public Library. *Handbook of Texas Libraries* no. 2 (Houston: Texas Free Library Association, 1908), 16. Other Texas Shakespeare clubs involved with public libraries include those in Longview, Marshall, and Honey Grove. The Flatonia, Texas, Shakespeare Club began the public library with a book donated by each member. Stella L. Christian, *The*

History of the Texas Federation of Women's Clubs (Houston: Dealy-Adey-Elgin, 1919), 172–73. In rural Texas, the Waxahachie Shakespeare Club had a custom of presenting books to the local library in honor of deceased members. Wilson, "Highlights of 54 Years."

163. "History of the DeLeon Shakespeare Club," MS CH TX 048, General Federation of Women's Clubs Archives.

164. For the details of this story, I am grateful to Frank Mowery, head of conservation at the Folger Shakespeare Library, who restored the Folio for the club and helped it design a special case and room in the Dallas Public Library. See also Michael V. Hazel, *The Dallas Public Library: Celebrating a Century of Service, 1901–2001* (Denton: University of North Texas Press, 2001), 177, 219.

165. Scott, "Women and Libraries," 404.

166. Christian, *History of the Texas Federation of Women's Clubs*, 172–73.

167. Watson, "Founding Mothers," 265.

Chapter 2

1. Frances A. Wittick, "Founders' Day 1946," MS, Peoria Historical Society. Maud Benner Nixon was the wife of Charles E. Nixon, who owned a printing company in Peoria. See James Montgomery Rice, *Peoria City and County, Illinois: A Record of Settlement, Organization, Progress, and Achievement*, vol. 2 (Chicago: S. J. Clarke, 1912), 644. The Shakespeare Class met at the home of President Clara Bourland. See Jane Cunningham Croly, *The History of the Woman's Club Movement in America* (New York: Henry G. Allen, 1898), 402.

2. Maud Nixon apparently did this quite often, even taking on male roles such as Orsino and Sir Toby Belch in *Twelfth Night* and Duke Frederick in *As You Like It*.

3. As Judy Giles notes, the parlor was one of "the physical spaces in which [women] experienced the effects of modernization. These were also the spaces that shaped the imaginations from which came their expressions of modernity." *The Parlour and the Suburb: Domestic Identities, Class, Femininity and Modernity* (Oxford: Berg, 2004), 11. See also Eleanor McD. Thompson, ed., *The American Home: Material Culture, Domestic Space, and Family Life* (Hanover, N.H.: University Press of New England, 1998), and Francesca Sawaya, *Modern Women, Modern Work: Domesticity, Professionalism, and American Writing, 1890–1950* (Philadelphia: University of Pennsylvania Press, 2004).

4. According to Margaret Gibbons Wilson, "Within the cities of late nineteenth- and early twentieth-century America significant changes were occurring in what remained the major focus of most women's lives, the day-to-day running of the household." *The American Woman in Transition: The Urban Influence, 1870–1920* (Westport, Conn.: Greenwood Press, 1979), 76. Anne Firor Scott remarks, "By the 1870s a perceptive observer would have noticed that the changes in women's literacy and educational opportunity were part of a whole complex of social and economic changes that were altering the face of the country." "Women and Libraries," in *Libraries, Books, and Culture*, ed. Donald G. Davis Jr. (Austin: University of Texas Press, 1986), 402. As Sara M. Evans puts it, women "changed the meaning of public life itself . . . while simultaneously shaping and adapting their own private sphere, the family, to changing times. . . . By pioneering in the creation of new public spaces—voluntary associations located between the public world of politics and work and the private intimacy of family—women made possible a new vision of active citizenship." *Born for Liberty: A History of Women in America* (New York: Free Press, 1989), 3. Anne Ruggles Gere describes women's clubs

as "intermediate institutions located between the family and the state." *Intimate Practices: Literacy and Cultural Work in U.S. Women's Clubs, 1880–1920* (Urbana: University of Illinois Press, 1997), 13. On the effects of reading on the lives of nineteenth-century American men, see Thomas Augst, *The Clerk's Tale: Young Men and Moral Life in Nineteenth-Century America* (Chicago: University of Chicago Press, 2003). On women and participation in public life, see Mary P. Ryan, *Women in Public: Between Banners and Ballots, 1825–1880* (Baltimore: Johns Hopkins University Press, 1990).

5. Robyn Warhol's discussion of the effects of reading on the body underlines my points here, in that reading was a significant activity that produced a number of repercussions for domestic life. Warhol remarks, "Reading is a physical act. Depending on how you look at it, reading is also a cognitive activity, a psychological process, a political engagement, an intertextual encounter, an aesthetic exercise, an academic discipline, a communitarian endeavor, a spiritual practice, a habit. But whatever else it may entail, reading always happens in and to a body." *Having a Good Cry: Effeminate Feelings and Pop-Culture Forms* (Columbus: Ohio State University Press, 2003), ix. In this chapter, I also take inspiration from Niko Besnier's argument that literacy "is crucially tied to the social practices that surround it and to the ideological system in which it is embedded." *Literacy, Emotion, and Authority: Reading and Writing on a Polynesian Atoll* (Cambridge: Cambridge University Press, 1995), 3. For women at the fin de siècle, domesticity was a crucial social practice and ideological system that became intertwined with Shakespeare. Kristin L. Hoganson discusses how women's travel clubs used imaginary travel to subvert domesticity and "turned homes into points of departure and points of encounter," and how "imaginary travel fostered nondomestic aspirations." *Consumers' Imperium: The Global Production of American Domesticity, 1865–1920* (Chapel Hill: University of North Carolina Press, 2007), 207–8. Douglas Anderson remarks that "American spiritual and intellectual life was 'feminized'—or at least domesticated—long before the nineteenth century." *A House Undivided: Domesticity and Community in American Literature* (Cambridge: Cambridge University Press, 1990), 5. We might relate these clubs to discussions of the "feminization of Shakespeare" studies; see, for example, Charles H. Shattuck, "The Feminization of Shakespeare," in *Shakespeare on the American Stage*, vol. 2 (Washington, D.C.: Folger Shakespeare Library, 1987), 93–141. According to one historian of women's clubs in Texas, women were responsible for teaching men "to cease being merely a cog in a machine ceaselessly grinding out money" and to appreciate art, music, and culture. Stella Christian, ed., *The History of the Texas Federation of Women's Clubs* (Houston: Dealy-Adey-Elgin, 1919), 4. In *The Feminization of American Culture* (New York: Alfred A. Knopf, 1977), Ann Douglas contends that women "were becoming the prime consumers of American culture" (8).

6. Kathryn Kish Sklar, *Catharine Beecher: A Study in American Domesticity* (New Haven, Conn.: Yale University Press, 1973), 158–60; Catharine Beecher, *A Treatise on Domestic Economy* (New York: Harper and Brothers, 1841), 180–81. For the history of women's struggles to meet family demands and have equality, see Carl N. Degler, *At Odds: Women and the Family in America from the Revolution to the Present* (New York: Oxford University Press, 1980). Nancy F. Cott argues that for middle-class New England women, "the canon of domesticity required women to sustain the milieu of task-oriented work that had characterized earlier family organization. This requirement made service to others and the diffusion of happiness in the family women's tasks." *The Bonds of Womanhood: "Woman's Sphere" in New England, 1780–1835*, 2nd ed. (New Haven, Conn.: Yale University Press, 1977), 71.

7. Julie A. Matthaei, *An Economic History of Women in America: Women's Work, the Sexual Division of Labor, and the Development of Capitalism* (New York: Schocken Books, 1982), 159. See also Alice Kessler-Harris, *Out to Work: A History of Wage-Earning Women in the United States* (New York: Oxford University Press, 1982), 49–56.

8. Ida M. Tarbell, "The Cost of Living and Household Management," *Annals of the American Academy of Political and Social Science* 48 (July 1913): 130.

9. Clarence W. Taber, *The Business of the Household* (Philadelphia: J. B. Lippincott, 1918), 1.

10. Anna E. Richardson, "The Woman Administrator in the Modern Home," *Annals of the American Academy of Political and Social Science* 143 (May 1929): 21–32, at 23.

11. Janice Radway underlines the need to explore "what precisely is 'getting said,' both to readers and to others each time a woman turns her attention away from her ordinary routine and immerses herself in a book." *Reading the Romance: Women, Patriarchy, and Popular Literature* (Chapel Hill: University of North Carolina Press, 1984), 8–9.

12. Evans, *Born for Liberty*, 139. Giles notes that "the first half of the twentieth century was a moment when the forces of modernisation that swept across Europe and North America transformed domestic life and, in doing so, produced opportunities for change that were beneficial for millions of women" but also brought "anxiety, loss and insecurity." *Parlour and the Suburb,* 4–5. Although Giles's book focuses mainly on Britain, some of her points apply to the United States as well.

13. See Karen J. Blair, *The Clubwoman as Feminist: True Womanhood Redefined, 1868–1914* (New York: Holmes and Meier, 1980), 4, 117. The movement of women into the public sphere has been labeled a variety of things: "domestic feminism" by Daniel Scott Smith in "Family Limitation, Sexual Control, and Domestic Feminism," *Feminist Studies* 1 (Winter/Spring 1973); "social housekeeping" by Mary P. Ryan in *Womanhood in America: From Colonial Times to the Present* (New York: New Viewpoints, 1975); "social feminism" by William O'Neill in *Everyone Was Brave: The Rise and Fall of Feminism in America* (Chicago: Quadrangle Books, 1969); and "social homemaking" by Matthaei in *Economic History of Women in America*, 173–77. For "municipal housekeeping," see Madeline Stein Wortman, "Domesticating the American City," *Prospects* 3 (1978): 531–72, and Karen J. Blair, *The Torchbearers: Women and Their Amateur Arts Associations in America, 1890–1930* (Bloomington: Indiana University Press, 1994), 32–33. Abigail A. Van Slyck argues that "women's involvement with shaping cultural institutions in the public realm calls into question the possibility of applying the concept of the separate spheres (common in discussions of Victorian gender ideology) directly to an analysis of the cultural landscape." *Free to All: Carnegie Libraries and American Culture, 1890–1920* (Chicago: University of Chicago Press, 1995), 241. See also Linda K. Kerber, "Separate Spheres, Female Worlds, Woman's Place: The Rhetoric of Women's History," *Journal of American History* 75 (June 1988): 9–39.

14. R. Anna Morris Clark, "Women's Literary and Social Clubs of the Black Hills," *Bits and Pieces* 11.1 (1976): 26. Hoganson looks at how middle-class American households reflected "international sensibilities as manifested through imported household objects, fashion, cooking and entertaining, armchair travel clubs, and the immigrant gifts movement" in *Consumers' Imperium*, 9.

15. "Women's Clubs to Unite," *New York Times*, 20 November 1894, p. 8. Such a statement resembles Radway's conclusion that "romance reading constitutes a 'declaration of independence' from these women's duties and responsibilities as wives and mothers" and "is a beneficial form of escape because it sparks hope, provides much-needed

reassurance, and helps them to learn about the world around them." *Reading the Romance*, 14. It should come as no surprise that Jessie Lozier Payne was a voice for activism; her grandmother, Clemence Lozier (1813–88), was a health reformer, founded the homeopathic New York Medical College and Hospital for Women, and was a public speaker whose New York City home was a "mecca for reform activity, filled to overflowing with documents and pamphlets protesting women's inequality under the law, as well as petitions on behalf of suffrage, antislavery, temperance, sanitary reform, improvement of conditions for American Indians, moral education, and reform of prisons and insane asylums." See Anne Taylor Kirschmann, *A Vital Force: Women in American Homeopathy* (New Brunswick, N.J.: Rutgers University Press, 2004), 39.

16. Silver Creek Shakespeare Club Records, 1889–1990, MS 53, University Archives, State University of New York at Buffalo.

17. One could argue that women's participation in these clubs and their influence on domesticity were important for the development of feminism; Anderson contends that "the emergence of American feminism depended to a significant degree on the ideology of domesticity as a means of developing a sense of the collective importance of women and a sense of their shared destiny." *House Undivided*, 7.

18. *How to Organize a Shakespeare Club* (New York: Doubleday and McClure, 1898), 7–8.

19. Mary LaFayette, Robbins, *Alabama Women in Literature* (Selma, Ala.: Selma Printing Co., 1895), 55.

20. "The Shakespeare Club to the Fort Knightly Reading Club of Washington, Missouri," Tibbe-Cuthbertson Family Papers, 1849–1975, C3711, Western Historical Manuscript Collection, University of Missouri/State Historical Society of Missouri.

21. *Shakespeare Quarterly* 5.1 (1954): 103.

22. *Shakespeariana* 4 (1887): 327. For a history of the parlor as a feminine space, see Katherine Grier, "The Decline of the Memory Palace: The Parlor after 1890," in *American Home Life, 1880–1930: A Social History of Spaces and Services*, ed. Jessica H. Foy and Thomas J. Schlereth (Knoxville: University of Tennessee Press, 1992), 49–74. Grier describes the parlor as the space "where many of [Victorian] culture's dynamics were most clearly expressed" (50).

23. Robbins, *Alabama Women in Literature*, 55–56.

24. History of Portia Club of Avon, Illinois, 1894–1994, Illinois State Historical Library.

25. *Shakespeariana* 5 (1888): 30; *Shakespeariana* 4 (1887): 329.

26. *Shakespeariana* 3 (1886): 522–23.

27. *Michigan State Library Bulletin* No. 1 (May 1896): 32.

28. Mary Church Terrell, "Washington," *Woman's Era*, December 1894, 7.

29. *Huntington County, Indiana: History and Families, 1834–1993* (Paducah, Ky.: Turner Publishing, 1993), 123.

30. *Shakespeare Quarterly* 3 (1952): 78.

31. Indeed, these women readers may have had an experience similar to that of Lynne Sharon Schwartz, who recalls her solitary reading as "an act of reclamation. This and only this I did for myself. This was the way to make my life my own." *Ruined by Reading: A Life in Books* (Boston: Beacon, 1996), 119. For women and reading in the home, see Anne Scott MacLeod, "Reading Together: Children, Adults, and Literature at the Turn of the Century," in *The Arts and the American Home, 1890–1930*, ed. Jessica H. Foy and Karal Ann Marling (Knoxville: University of Tennessee Press, 1994), 111–23.

32. Naomi Greenfield, *History of the Shakespeare Round Table*, MS 249, Center for Archival Collections, Bowling Green State University, 18.

33. Josephine T. Washington, "What the Club Does for the Club-Woman," *Colored American Magazine* 12 (February 1907): 122–25.

34. Richardson, "Woman Administrator in the Modern Home," 31. Richardson also remarked that women "as administrators of modern homes are gaining relief from the countless activities which used to be connected with the responsibility for the family's physical welfare, and gradually they are arriving at the place where they can, by choice, determine how they will expend their effort and time" (30).

35. History of Portia Club of Avon, Illinois, 6.

36. Edna Stephenson, "A Brief History of Portia Club," 1965, http://portiaclub. com/history/history2.html. Barbara Sicherman gives a gendered view of the home library that does not seem to apply to the female-centered libraries discussed in this section. She argues that men "were the principal buyers of books for home libraries, which, with their leather chairs, port, and cigars, often exuded the atmosphere of a men's club." "Reading and Middle Class Identity," in *Reading Acts: U.S. Readers' Interaction with Literature, 1800–1950*, ed. Barbara Ryan and Amy M. Thomas (Knoxville: University of Tennessee Press, 2002), 144. See also Linda M. Kruger, "Home Libraries: Special Spaces, Reading Places," in Foy and Schlereth, *American Home Life*, 94–119. In Waxahachie, Texas, the children of Shakespeare Club members were involved in the club's civic work, delivering gifts in their red wagons to needy children at Christmas. Maude Wilson, "Highlights of 54 Years Listed by City, State Federated Shakespeare Club," newspaper clipping dated 1951, Waxahachie vertical file, Nicholas P. Sims Library, Waxahachie, Texas.

37. History of Portia Club of Avon, Illinois, 12. Sasha Roberts points out the difficulties of tracing individual reading habits: "more often than not it is impossible to pursue the detail of either women's or men's reading acts, let alone how a book or library may have formed or transformed a woman's life." "Reading in Early Modern England: Contexts and Problems," *Critical Survey* 12.2 (2000): 5.

38. Elizabeth Greenfield, "Shakespearean 'Culture' in Montana, 1902," *Montana: The Magazine of Western History* 22.2 (1972): 49–50.

39. Greenfield, "Shakespearean 'Culture' in Montana," 49–51. The Great Falls club is also of interest due to class diversity; member Anna Nelson had a cook whereas Mrs. Heisey scrubbed her own floors. Heisey's husband ran a wholesale grocery store in Great Falls. Anna Nelson, originally from Boston, was also the author of the story "The Cowboy Artist, a Story of the Medicine Arrow," published in 1898 in *Sports Afield*. See Elizabeth Greenfield, "The Cowboy Artist as Seen in Childhood Memory," in *Charlie Russell Roundup: Essays on America's Favorite Cowboy Artist*, ed. Brian W. Dippie (Helena: Montana Historical Society Press, 1999), 154–62. Her husband, H. H. Nelson, was a railroad contractor in Great Falls.

40. Scrapbook 258624, Folger Shakespeare Library.

41. "Mrs. Maude Wilson Gives Sketch of the Personalities of Shakespeare Founders," *Waxahachie Daily Light*, 16 February 1955, Waxahachie vertical file, Nicholas P. Sims Library, Waxahachie, Texas.

42. Croly, *History of the Woman's Club Movement*, 612.

43. Mary Ellen Lamb, personal communication, 2010.

44. *Shakespeariana* 2 (1885): 48. On the legacy of club women to future generations of women, see Gwen Athene Tarbox, *The Clubwomen's Daughters: Collectivist Impulses in Progressive-Era Girls' Fiction* (New York: Garland, 2000).

45. Information on the San Antonio Shakespeare Club is taken from "All the World's a Stage for Club," *San Antonio Express,* clipping of 7 September 1976; and "Followers of the Bard," undated clipping, both from San Antonio Shakespeare Club Folder, VF-SA 4004657, The Daughters of the Republic of Texas Library, The Alamo.

46. The Shakespeare memorabilia in Lida Baskin's living room fits Grier's argument that "the contents of parlors were the medium for expressing a family's position in [a] web of values." "Decline of the Memory Palace," 54. Janet Field Baskin published a poem based on *Hamlet* titled "Hamlet at a 'Spoon River' Banquet of Shakespeare's Characters Reveals Himself as Interpreted by the Modern Critics," *University of California Chronicle* 29 (1927): 308–9.

47. Vivian Anderson Castleberry, *Daughters of Dallas: A History of Greater Dallas through the Voices and Deeds of Its Women* (Dallas: Odenwald Press, 1994), 146.

48. The Shakespeare Round Table of Bowling Green, Ohio, included mothers and daughters, grandmothers and granddaughters, aunts and nieces, mothers-in law and daughters-in law. Greenfield, *History of the Shakespeare Round Table.* The Shakespeare Club of Smithfield, Virginia, recorded that "membership, which is limited to twenty, is much coveted, especially by the daughters of the charter members." *Shakespeare Quarterly* 4 (1953): 368.

49. *New Hampshire Women: A Collection of Portraits and Biographical Sketches* (Concord, N.H.: New Hampshire Publishing Co., 1895), 145. The grandchild of the president of the Shakespeare Club of Manchester, New Hampshire, Edward Scott Snazey, "has been in touch with the club since his babyhood, and is held in admiring regard by every member as a youth of great promise and as a mascot of great generosity." Croly, *History of the Woman's Club Movement,* 795.

50. *Huntington County, Indiana,* 123.

51. Entry for 10 April 1885, diary of Mary Freeman, MS, Clarke Historical Library, Central Michigan University.

52. Entry for 25 April 1885, diary of Mary Freeman.

53. Wegia Hope Hall Tracy, "Women's Clubs in Nebraska," *Midland Monthly* 5.3 (1896): 262–71, at 268.

54. Entry for 9 March 1906, *Plains Woman: The Diary of Martha Farnsworth, 1882–1922,* ed. Marlene Springer and Haskell Springer (Bloomington: Indiana University Press, 1986), 163. As Blair points out, "For a few hours each month the study of culture took precedence over motherhood" for club women. *Clubwoman as Feminist,* 68. Though I have found surprisingly few criticisms of women's Shakespeare clubs, according to one source, "some men blamed women's clubs for the decrease in America's output of home-made pies." Blair, *Clubwoman as Feminist,* 70.

55. Anne Firor Scott, *Natural Allies: Women's Associations in American History* (Urbana: University of Illinois Press, 1991), 2.

56. *Shakespeariana* 4 (1887): 278.

57. Willie Newbury Lewis, *History of the Dallas Shakespeare Club, 1886–1970* (N.p. [197-?]), ii. Copy in the Dallas Public Library.

58. Hull House founder and activist Jane Addams expressed the frustration of women's "search for a purpose for life"; she described herself as "filled with shame that with all my apparent leisure I do nothing." Anne Firor Scott, *Making the Invisible Woman Visible* (Urbana: University of Illinois Press, 1984), 112.

59. History of Portia Club of Avon, Illinois, i.

60. As Hoganson argues, "Social reform did not necessarily imply a rejection of domesticity" but instead could be done by reconfiguring public and private space. *Consumers' Imperium*, 206.

61. Grover Cleveland, "Woman's Mission and Woman's Clubs," *Ladies Home Journal*, May 1905, 4.

62. For criticism of Cleveland, see Gere, *Intimate Practices*, 31–32.

63. This was particularly true of the outpost clubs I discuss in the next chapter, possibly because women in such locales "may have felt the demands of feminine propriety even more keenly" than women on the more populated East Coast. Mary Ann Irwin, "'Going About and Doing Good': The Politics of Benevolence, Welfare, and Gender in San Francisco, 1850–1880," *Pacific Historical Review* 68.3 (1999): 372.

64. Ann Thompson argues that "women in the nineteenth century used play-reading groups to educate themselves and others and to develop their self confidence about speaking in public." "A Club of Our Own: Women's Play Readings in the Nineteenth Century," *Borrowers and Lenders: The Journal of Shakespeare and Appropriation* 2.2 (2006). http://www.borrowers.uga.edu/cocoon/borrowers/request?id=781461.

65. Information on Kansas clubs comes from the General Federation of Women's Clubs of Kansas Collection, MS Coll. 780, Kansas State Historical Society.

66. Likewise, in 1916–17 the women in the Shakespeare Club of Kingman, Kansas, wrote and presented papers such as "Juliet Compared with Shakespeare's Other Heroines," "Was Banquo Responsible for the Death of Duncan?" and "What Indications Are There That Macbeth and His Wife Had Thought of the Murder of Duncan before the Play?" In 1923–24, as well as reading Shakespeare, the club debated "Can a Woman Run a Home and a Job, Too?" For 1926–27, the club acted scenes from Shakespeare and presented a paper on Hamlet titled "Was He Insane?" Like the Library Club of Clay Center, the Kingman club offered women opportunities for intellectual discussion and debate centered on Shakespeare, folded into their acceptable domestic concerns. The Shakespeare Club of Colby, Kansas, also combined study of Shakespeare with a number of domestic topics, including "Religion in the Home," "Books in the Home," "Character Building in the Home," "Why Educate Women," "Shakespeare's Picture of Domestic Life," and a whole program in 1930 called "The Emancipation of the House Wife," covering topics such as "Who'll Wash Our Dishes?" "Is the Modern Housewife a Lady of Leisure?" and "Creative Housekeeping."

67. George W. Kingsbury, *History of Dakota Territory*, vol. 3 (Chicago: S. J. Clarke, 1915), 778.

68. Zetetic Club program for 1899–1900, MS RG 4513, Nebraska State Historical Society.

69. *The General Federation of Women's Clubs: Tenth Biennial Convention, Official Report* (Newark, N.J.: General Federation of Women's Clubs, 1910), 180.

70. Other clubs combined their emphasis on Shakespeare with topics of current interest. The Portia Club of Avon, Illinois, had a theme of "The Changing World" for 1943, and in 1935, members combined study of *Henry V* with meetings on "Birth Control." Edra Singleton, "Highlights of Portia, 1930–1937," History of Portia Club of Avon, Illinois, 18.

71. *Shakespeariana* 1 (1883): 29. The San Antonio Shakespeare Club had an annual banquet for which a "white marble bust of Shakespeare that is a fixture of the Shakespeare Club meetings was draped in pink roses for the organization's Twelfth Night Revel" at a club member's home. *North San Antonio Times*, 21 January 1982, clipping

from San Antonio Shakespeare Club Folder, VF-SA 4004657, The Daughters of the Republic of Texas Library, The Alamo.

72. Esther Bickmore Clark, *The Woodland Shakespeare Club: A History, 1886–1967* (Woodland, Calif.: privately printed, 1968), 19, 21. The Peoria Women's Club more formally combined food and performance of Shakespeare with an annual "Shakespeare Breakfast" prepared by a committee that served shrimp salad every year. Frances A. Wittick's handwritten reminiscences noted, "After the breakfast we entertained ourselves by giving scenes from the different plays, first in the dining-room and later here on the stage in costume." Frances A. Wittick, "Founders' Day 1946," MS, Peoria Historical Society.

73. Kate Flint, "Women and Reading," *Signs* 31.2 (2006): 513.

74. *Shakespeariana* 5 (1888): 312. *The Shakespeare Birthday Book* was edited by Mary F. P. Dunbar and published by Thomas Whittaker in 1883. *Shakespeare Forget-Me-Nots: A Text Book of Shakespeare Quotation* was published in New York by E. P. Dutton in the 1880s. The Nashville, Tennessee, Query Club engaged in a similar practice; for their final meeting of the year, members filled a china bowl "full of the thick, dark southern magnolia leaves: the first member of the class who took one of these leaves finding upon it a pasted slip bearing a quotation. If she could not tell the play from whence it was chosen it was passed on to the next, and a fresh leaf offered her, and so on and on, until the whole group were putting their heads together over these living leaves of poetry. She who finally placed the most quotations and had the biggest heap of leaves in her lap was given the bowl to hold her laurels." *Shakespeariana* 5 (1888): 314. The Fredonia, New York, club may have gotten its tradition of using Shakespeare mottoes from its founder, Alice D. Smith, who sent a bouquet of flowers to the club a few days before her death, including with it a "Shakespearean motto which she had selected, to each guest." Oscar W. Johnson, *Addresses, Essays and Miscellanies* (Fredonia, N.Y., 1890), 323.

75. Hoganson, *Consumers' Imperium*, 123. Hoganson discusses how women in the early twentieth century explored food as a way to internationalize their domestic realm.

76. Personal communication, 2007.

77. Katherine Ott, Susan Tucker, and Patricia Buckler, "An Introduction to the History of Scrapbooks," in *The Scrapbook in American Life*, ed. Susan Tucker, Katherine Ott, and Patricia Buckler (Philadelphia: Temple University Press, 2006), 10.

78. Giles, *Parlour and the Suburb*, 22.

79. Leigh Anne Palmer points out that "the sheer number [of scrapbooks] dedicated to Shakespeare that are preserved in the Folger Library's collection remains a very real reminder of his popularity in America in this period." "'A Thing of Shreds and Patches': Memorializing Shakespeare in American Scrapbooks," in *Shakespeare in American Life*, ed. Virginia Mason Vaughan and Alden T. Vaughan (Washington, D.C.: Folger Shakespeare Library, 2007), 145.

80. Ellen Gruber Garvey, "Scissorizing and Scrapbooks: Nineteenth-Century Reading, Remaking, and Recirculating," in *New Media, 1740–1915*, ed. Lisa Gitelman and Geoffrey B. Pingree (Cambridge, Mass.: MIT Press, 2003), 210, 214.

81. The closet has a long history of connection to women's private spaces. See, for example, Katherine R. Larson, "Reading the Space of the Closet in Aemilia Lanyer's *Salve Deus Rex Judaeorum*," *Early Modern Women* 2 (2007): 73–93.

82. S. J. Kleinberg, "Gendered Space: Housing, Privacy and Domesticity in the Nineteenth-Century United States," in *Domestic Space: Reading the Nineteenth-Century Interior*, ed. Inga Bryden and Janet Floyd (Manchester, U.K.: Manchester University Press, 1999), 143.

83. The prevalence of Shakespeare in the household libraries of African Americans, discussed in Chapter 4, taps into similar connotations of stability and prosperity. See also Foy and Schlereth, *American Home Life.*

84. I have been unable to verify this story, which was told to me by a member of the Anne Hudgins Shakespeare Class.

85. *Michigan State Library Bulletin* No. 1 (May 1896): 33.

86. The Shakespeariana Club of Grand Rapids, Michigan, had a Shakespeare Chest containing, among other items, "a luncheon cloth on which the early members inscribed their names in embroidery," further uniting Shakespeare with female domestic labor. From a clipping dated 1949, Folger Scrapbook 258624, Folger Shakespeare Library.

87. Records of the Woman's Shakespearean Club of Barnesville, Georgia, MS 696, Loula Kendall Rogers Papers, Robert W. Woodruff Library, Emory University.

88. Mrs. P. H. Brown, "How We Furnished the New Club House," http://portiaclub.com/history/history4.html.

89. Paul Connerton has argued that "images of the past and recollected knowledge of the past . . . are conveyed and sustained by (more or less ritual) performances" and that performative commemorative ceremonies work to construct "social memory." *How Societies Remember* (Cambridge: Cambridge University Press, 1989), 3–4. The Kate Tupper Galpin Shakespeare Club, for example, printed commemorative programs every year, as did many clubs. "Kate Tupper Galpin Shakespeare Club," *Who's Who among the Women of California*, ed. Louis S. Lyons and Josephine Wilson (San Francisco: Security Publishing, 1922), 158.

90. Connerton, *How Societies Remember*, 44–45. Connerton uses Steven Lukes's definition of ritual as a "rule-governed activity of a symbolic character which draws the attention of its participants to objects of thought and feeling which they hold to be of special significance" (44).

91. Personal communication, 2007.

92. M. F. Pitts, "How Can the National Federation of Colored Women Be Made to Serve the Best Interests and Needs of Our Women?" in *A History of the Club Movement among the Colored Women of the United States of America* (n.p., 1902), 64. Pitts helped establish the Women's Christian Temperance Union among black women in St. Louis and was active in the St. Louis Colored Orphan's Home.

Chapter 3

1. Rev. A. S. Kemper reported the Snow Blockade Club in *Shakespeariana* 5 (1888): 88. The Northport, Michigan, Shakespeare Club is listed in the *Michigan State Library Bulletin* No. 3 (September 1898), "Study Clubs," 90. Northport, 168 miles north of Grand Rapids, is not even in the 1900 census, although it was incorporated as a village (which status it still retains) in 1849. It now has 630 residents. In comparison, a village of comparable size 12 miles away, Suttons Bay, had 398 residents in 1900.

2. Details of the Barnesville club are from Jane Cunningham Croly, *The History of the Woman's Club Movement in America* (New York: Henry G. Allen, 1898), 368. The factory hands were likely part of the buggy industry; Barnesville produced 9,000 buggies in 1900 at the height of the industry. The town history notes, "Nearly everyone in the community was employed in an industry that was in some way connected with the manufacturing and shipping of the buggies, wagons, carts,

hearses, and coffins." http://www.cityofbarnesville.com/site/page588.html, accessed 15 September 2009.

3. Many of the towns with Shakespeare clubs listed in the appendix, such as Northport, Michigan, and Camden, Maine, were too small to be listed in the 1900 census—that is, they had fewer than 1,000 residents. Numerous other towns with Shakespeare clubs had barely more than 1,000 citizens in 1900, such as Cuba, New York, with a population of 1,502, and Elkland, Pennsylvania, with a population of 1,109.

4. Helene Koon, *How Shakespeare Won the West: Players and Performances in America's Gold Rush, 1849–1865* (Jefferson, N.C.: McFarland, 1989), established a solid nineteenth-century performance base for Shakespeare in the frontier West. Likewise, Richard A. Van Orman, "The Bard in the West," *Western Historical Quarterly* 5 (1974): 29–38, covers Shakespeare for mountain men, soldiers, miners, and cowboys—mostly a male audience—with only a brief paragraph on women's Shakespeare clubs in the West. Levette J. Davidson also focuses mainly on performance and on the reading habits of men in "Shakespeare in the Rockies," *Shakespeare Quarterly* 4 (1953): 39–49. See also Philip C. Kolin, ed., *Shakespeare in the South: Essays on Performance* (Jackson: University Press of Mississippi, 1983).

5. *Shakespeare Association Bulletin* 4.3 (1929): 86. For the effect of voluntary associations on "the long struggle of a town's first generation to achieve urban greatness and construct a viable social order" (ix), see Don Harrison Doyle, *The Social Order of a Frontier Community: Jacksonville, Illinois, 1825–70* (Urbana: University of Illinois Press, 1978), 156–93.

6. *Shakespeariana* 3 (1886): 458.

7. Louis B. Wright, "Shakespeare for Everyman," *Proceedings of the American Philosophical Society* 106.5 (1962): 393–400, at 400.

8. R. Anna Morris Clark, "Women's Literary and Social Clubs of the Black Hills," *Bits and Pieces* 11.1 (1976): 26. On print culture in South Dakota, see Lisa Lindell, "Bringing Books to a 'Book-Hungry Land': Print Culture on the Dakota Prairie," *Book History* 7 (2004): 215–38. On print culture in the frontier West, see Jen A. Huntley-Smith, "Print Cultures in the American West," in *Perspectives on American Book History: Artifacts and Commentary*, ed. Scott E. Casper, Joanne D. Chaison, and Jeffrey D. Groves (Amherst: University of Massachusetts Press, 2002), 255–84.

9. Owen P. White, *A Frontier Mother* (New York: Minton, Balch, and Co., 1929), 87–89. The use of Shakespeare for a cultural and educational respite from frontier work was common: "A day of panning in the placers or hitching up teams of horses might be followed by reading *The Merchant of Venice*, acting out a scene from *Henry VI*." Elliott West, "Heathens and Angels: Childhood in the Rocky Mountain Mining Towns," *Western Historical Quarterly* 14.2 (1983): 159. See also his chapter "Beyond Baby Doe: Child Rearing on the Mining Frontier," in *The Women's West*, ed. Susan Armitage and Elizabeth Jameson (Norman: University of Oklahoma Press, 1987), 179–92.

10. Julie Roy Jeffrey, *Frontier Women: "Civilising" the West? 1840–1880*, rev. ed. (New York: Hill and Wang, 1998), 5. Wright remarks, "The goal of many literary clubs, organized by men and women on the frontier who were determined to reproduce the best of the civilization that they had left, was the reading and enjoyment of Shakespeare. Not many communities in the West were too barbaric or remote to have a few citizens who treasured their editions of Shakespeare." "Shakespeare for Everyman," 400.

11. Leah Price, "Reading: The State of the Discipline," *Book History* 7 (2004): 308. See also Miles Ogborn and Charles W. J. Withers, *Geographies of the Book* (Farnham,

U.K.: Ashgate, 2010). Sallie McMurry points out that "by the 1880s, the farm population was rapidly being outstripped by the urban population. Information on city life reached the progressive farm, oriented as it was to urban markets, by a variety of means. Lower postal rates, new subscription systems, club plans, and direct selling to local booksellers all allowed urban-based publications to reach rural markets." *Families and Farmhouses in Nineteenth-Century America: Vernacular Design and Social Change* (New York: Oxford University Press, 1988), 100. For extended discussion of reading in rural Iowa, see Christine Pawley, *Reading on the Middle Border: The Culture of Print in Late Nineteenth-Century Osage, Iowa* (Amherst: University of Massachusetts Press, 2001).

12. In her study of women's roles in the frontier West, Jeffrey points out that women felt responsible for morality and culture: "Even if it was impossible initially to live up to domestic and cultural ideals, these ideals helped women retain their sense of self and offered them hope of an ever-improving life." *Frontier Women,* 6. For further discussion of women on the western frontier, see Ruth B. Moynihan, Susan Armitage, and Christiane Fischer Dichamp, eds., *So Much to Be Done: Women Settlers on the Mining and Ranching Frontier* (Lincoln: University of Nebraska Press, 1990), and Sandra L. Myres, *Westering Women and the Frontier Experience, 1800–1915* (Albuquerque: University of New Mexico Press, 1982). Peggy Pascoe suggests the phrase "the search for female moral authority" as opposed to "social feminism" to describe women in the American West. See *Relations of Rescue: The Search for Female Moral Authority in the American West, 1874–1939* (New York: Oxford, 1990), xviii.

13. Croly, *History of the Woman's Club Movement,* 318.

14. Elizabeth Greenfield, "Shakespearean 'Culture' in Montana, 1902," *Montana: The Magazine of Western History* 22.2 (1972): 49. See also John Taliaferro, *Charles M. Russell: The Life and Legend of America's Cowboy Artist* (Boston: Little, Brown, 1996), 122.

15. Clark, "Women's Literary and Social Clubs of the Black Hills," 26.

16. Jane Jayroe, *Oklahoma 3* (Portland, Ore.: Graphic Arts Center Publishing, 2006), 18.

17. On literary societies in Kansas, see Clarence Robert Haywood, *Victorian West: Class and Culture in Kansas Cattle Towns* (Lawrence: University Press of Kansas, 1991), 126–32.

18. Craig Miner, *Kansas: The History of the Sunflower State, 1854–2000* (Lawrence: University Press of Kansas, 2005), 17.

19. Miner, *Kansas,* 2. Miner cites a 1937 letter from journalist Charles Edson for this source. June Underwood remarks, "Bonding among women, so important in eastern women's existence, did not seem to break down in the remote villages of Kansas. In fact, the general sense of isolation may have helped make organization come easy." "Civilizing Kansas: Women's Organizations, 1880–1920," *Kansas History: A Journal of the Central Plains* 7 (1984/85): 296. Similarly, in Nebraska during the drought of 1894, "Many a woman has told of the blessing the Club was to her during those dark days when everything was tinged with gloom. So many luxuries had to be given up that the women turned gladly to the Club, which permitted them to meet with others without having the hard times the only topic of conversation." Wegia Hope Hall Tracy, "Women's Clubs in Nebraska," *Midland Monthly* 5.3 (1896): 262–71, at 270–71.

20. Croly reports that in the late nineteenth century, Kansas "counts up nearly two hundred strictly women's clubs, the majority 'study' or 'literary' clubs.'" *History of the Woman's Club Movement,* 487.

21. Lillian Walker Hale, "The Club Movement in Kansas," *Midland Monthly* 7 (1897): 428–29. Clubs existed for a variety of religious backgrounds as well; according to Hale, Leavenworth had a Jewish women's club and a Catholic Literary Club (429). For a good overview of women's clubs in Kansas, see Patricia A. Michaelis, "The Meeting Will Come to Order," *Kansas Heritage* 14.1 (2006): 17–21.

22. Johnny Faragher and Christine Stansell, "Women and Their Families on the Overland Trail to California and Oregon, 1842–1867," *Feminist Studies* 2 (1975): 150–66, at 151–52.

23. Unless otherwise noted, information on Kansas clubs comes from the General Federation of Women's Clubs of Kansas Collection, MS Coll. 780, Kansas State Historical Society.

24. It is worth pointing out that several of these towns were railroad towns, including Pratt, Waterville, Galena, and El Dorado, which likely facilitated book distribution. See James R. Shortridge, *The Evolution of Urban Kansas* (Lawrence: University Press of Kansas, 2004), and Ronald J. Zboray, *A Fictive People: Antebellum Economic Development and the American Reading Public* (New York: Oxford University Press, 1993).

25. *Kansas City Review* 9.1 (1885). In 1875, the Topeka Reading and Spelling Association was formed, with "spellings" every Monday night, beginning with readings from Dickens and Shakespeare. See D. Thompson Peterson, "A Roster of 19th-Century Clubs and Societies of North Topeka from *North Topeka Times,*" in *The Clubs of Shawnee County from A to Z*, ed. John W. Ripley (Topeka, Kan.: Shawnee County Historical Society, 1984), 74.

26. "Mrs. Beardslee's Library," *Dispatch* (Hiawatha, Kansas), 9 January 1879.

27. *Kansas State Library Department of Traveling Libraries Bulletin* (1916): 4. The relationship between traveling libraries and clubs is made clear in Carrie M. Watson and Edith M. Clarke, eds., *Handbook of Kansas Libraries* (Lawrence, Kan., 1903): "As in most states, the traveling-library movement in Kansas was begun by club women" (89). See also Thomas Augst and Ken Carpenter, eds., *Institutions of Reading: The Social Life of Libraries in the United States* (Amherst: University of Massachusetts Press, 2007).

28. Entre Nous Club of Winfield, Kansas, Program, Kansas State Historical Society, 48–49.

29. Kansas was not the only state where study outlines for Shakespeare were available for women. Mrs. Charles Tidwell Phelan, organizer and leader of the Dallas Shakespeare Followers, published a series of study outlines titled *Keys to Shakespeare's Treasure House: A Series of Questions Covering Certain of the Bard's Plays, Designed to Aid Students and to Point a Way for the Desultory Reader* (Dallas, 1906).

30. The Shakespeare Club of Waterville, Kansas, program for 1905–6, General Federation of Women's Clubs of Kansas Collection, MS Coll. 780, Kansas State Historical Society.

31. In 1941, the club bought a bank building, and the next year it opened the Waterville Public Library. See http://waterville.mykansaslibrary.org/?page_id=7. Likewise, the Coterie of Pratt, which focused mainly on Shakespeare, founded the Pratt County Library. *Kansas Library Bulletin* 27.1 (1958): 19.

32. Shakespeare Club of Waterville, Kansas, program for 1913–14, General Federation of Women's Clubs of Kansas Collection, MS Coll. 780, Kansas State Historical Society.

33. Michaelis points out, "Rather than focusing only on the home and partaking in regular housekeeping and mothering duties, women now had the chance to develop

skills such as conducting meetings, establishing and monitoring budgets, fund raising, and even lobbying on behalf of political objectives." "Meeting Will Come to Order," 18.

34. Zula Bennington Greene, "Hair-Raising Tales," *Topeka County Journal*, 26 June 1982, 4.

35. "Junction City Ladies Club," *Kansas Woman's Journal* 1 (February 1922): 1–2.

36. Mary Vance Humphrey, "Junction City Reading Club," in "Clubs and Club Women," ed. Clara Teague Burch, *The Souvenir* (Salina, Kan.: Ladies Aid Society of the First Presbyterian Church, 1901), 89–90.

37. *Union*, 2 June 1883. *L.R.C. Library: An Alphabetical List of the Books Belonging to the Ladies' Reading Club of Junction City, Kansas* (Junction City, Kan.: Tribune Books and Job Printing House, 1886). By 1901, the library had grown to more than a thousand volumes. *Souvenir*, 90.

38. Reading Shakespeare was but one of many ways to improve Kansas households through club work; in 1904, for example, the Highland Beef Club was founded in To-peka to help provide beef to rural members in the summer. See Minnie D. Millbrook, "The Highland Beef Club," in Ripley, *Clubs of Shawnee County*, 52–55.

39. Mary Vance Humphrey, "Ladies' Reading Club Nears 40th Anniversary," *Topeka Capital*, 20 June 1915. The papers from the Lilla Day Monroe collection at the Kansas State Historical Society include several accounts of the founding of this group and its importance to Junction City. Mary Humphrey's daughter, Adele Humphrey, wrote that the club "has been a large force in making Junction City a town where wealth and fashion were never criteria of judgment." Other Kansas Shakespeare clubs improved their communities in various ways; the Colby, Kansas, Shakespeare Club lobbied for a library and a community room and urged the district judge "to close the doors to the public when immoral cases are being tried." See "Shakespeare Club, Colby, Kansas," MS CH KS 002, General Federation of Women's Clubs Archive.

40. Ann Thompson makes a similar point in "A Club of Our Own: Women's Play Readings in the Nineteenth Century," *Borrowers and Lenders: The Journal of Shakespeare and Appropriation* 2.2 (2006). http://www.borrowers.uga.edu/cocoon/borrowers/request?id=781461.

41. *Shakespeare Association Bulletin* 5.3 (1930): 142.

42. The appendix to Betty Holland Wiesepape's *Lone Star Chapters: The Story of Texas Literary Clubs* (College Station: Texas A&M University Press, 2004) includes Shakespeare clubs in Abilene, Arlinger, Ballinger, Coleman, Dallas (two clubs), DeLeon, Denton, Flatonia, Fort Worth, Groesbeck, Hearne, Lancaster, Longview, Lubbock, Mount Vernon, Nixon, North Zulch, Oak Cliff (two clubs), Seguin, Sherman, Smithville, Vernon, Waco, Waxahachie, and Wichita Falls.

43. Stella Christian, ed., *The History of the Texas Federation of Women's Clubs* (Houston: Dealy-Adey-Elgin, 1919), 174.

44. "Mrs. Maude Wilson Gives Sketch of the Personalities of Shakespeare Founders," *Waxahachie Daily Light*, 16 February 1955, Waxahachie vertical file, Nicholas P. Sims Library, Waxahachie, Texas.

45. Rebecca Sharpless, *Fertile Ground, Narrow Choices: Women on Texas Cotton Farms, 1900–1940* (Chapel Hill: University of North Carolina Press, 1999), 225.

46. Mary LaFayette Robbins, *Alabama Women in Literature* (Selma, Ala.: Selma Printing Co., 1895), 31–32.

47. Amanda M. Ellis, *The Strange, Uncertain Years: An Informal Account of Life in Six Colorado Communities* (Hamden, Conn.; Shoe String Press, 1959), 296. Copies of

Shakespeare were among the books that miners exchanged for reading. See Elizabeth Jameson, *All that Glitters: Class, Conflict, and Community in Cripple Creek* (Urbana: University of Illinois Press, 1998), 95.

48. Florence Earl, "Recollections of People and Events in the Earlier Days of the Eugene Shakespeare Club," MS 227, Special Collections and University Archives, University of Oregon Library.

49. *Michigan State Library Bulletin* No. 1 (May 1896): 9–10.

50. *Michigan State Library Bulletin* No. 1 (May 1896): 64–65.

51. *Michigan State Library Bulletin* No. 1 (May 1896): 74.

52. *Chautauquan* 40 (September 1904–February 1905): 485. The testimonials come from the copy of the game I examined at the Folger Shakespeare Library, Sh. Misc. 363.

53. Mary Murphy, "Votes and Violets: Montana Women in the Twentieth Century," in *Montana Century: 100 Years in Pictures and Words*, ed. Michael P. Malone (Helena, Mont.: Falcon Publishing, 1999), 95, 100. Murphy lists the Great Falls Shakespeare Club, the As You Like It Club of Missoula, the Kalispell Nineteenth Century Club, and literary societies in Stevensville, Red Lodge, Bozeman, Billings, and Laurel.

54. Mary Murphy, *Mining Cultures: Men, Women, and Leisure in Butte, 1914–41* (Urbana: University of Illinois Press, 1997), 136, 142. On women's lives in a Nevada mining town, see C. Elizabeth Raymond, "'I Am Afraid We Will Lose All We Have Made: Women's Lives in a Nineteenth-Century Mining Town," in *Comstock Women: The Making of a Mining Community*, ed. Ronald J. James and C. Elizabeth Raymond (Reno: University of Nevada Press, 1998), 3–16.

55. Murphy, *Mining Cultures,* 139–40.

56. Taliaferro, *Charles M. Russell,* 122.

57. *Shakespeare Association Bulletin* 4.3 (1929): 86–87. The clubs also banded together to set up a Shakespeare Garden in Toledo.

58. See Melvin Dewey, *Field and Future of Traveling Libraries* (Albany, N.Y., 1901), and Katherine Louise Smith, "Railroad Traveling Libraries," *New Outlook* 67 (1901): 961–63.

59. Helen E. Haines, "The Growth of Traveling Libraries," *World's Work* 8.5 (1904): 5231.

60. *Library Journal* 36 (July 1911): 353. On nineteenth-century subscription publishing, see Michael Hackenberg, "The Subscription Publishing Network in Nineteenth-Century America," in *Getting the Books Out: Papers of the Chicago Conference on the Book in 19th-Century America* (Washington, D.C.: Library of Congress, 1987), 45–75.

61. Paula D. Watson, "Founding Mothers: The Contribution of Women's Organizations to Public Library Development in the United States," *Library Quarterly* 64.3 (1994): 240.

62. Joanne E. Passet, "Reaching the Rural Reader: Traveling Libraries in America, 1892–1920," *Libraries and Culture* 26.1 (1991): 113. On books as moral and cultural uplift, see Dee Garrison, *Apostles of Culture: The Public Librarian and American Society, 1876–1920* (New York: Free Press, 1979), 67–87.

63. Haines, "Growth of Traveling Libraries," 5233. Kate Hutcheson Morrissette, of the No Name Club of Montgomery, noted that "the great effort of the women's clubs of Alabama is the creation of a public sentiment favorable to the Traveling Library." "Traveling Libraries in Alabama," *Sewanee Review* 6.3 (1898): 346. One account of a reader in Manitoba attests to the importance of these libraries in isolated communities. She wrote that while she was waiting for her reading material to arrive, "the loneliness was so great, the isolation so unendurable, the enforced idleness of the long, dreary win-

ter so hideous, that she unpicked and remade, unpicked and remade her scanty wardrobe over and over again, unraveled and reknit, unraveled and reknit her stockings so as to keep the balance of her mind." Haines, "Growth of Traveling Libraries," 5234.

64. Passet, "Reaching the Rural Reader," 102.

65. *News Notes of California Libraries* 1.5 (1906): 279.

66. *Library Occurrent* [Public Library Commission of Indiana] 1 (1906–8): 8.

67. *Library Journal* 35 (1910): 77. For details on traveling libraries in other states around the turn of the century, see *Public Libraries: A Monthly Review of Library Matters and Methods* 10 (1905): 76–81.

68. *Minnesota Public Library Commission Library Notes and News* 3 (1910–12): 41–42. The list of study club libraries for 1907–8 and 1908–9 also included Shakespeare.

69. "Secretaries Book of the Shakespeare Club," MS 0031, Special Collections Division, University of Washington Library. Port Gamble was never incorporated; in 1880, the population was 421. Calvin F. Schmid and Stanton E. Schmid, *Growth of Cities and Towns: State of Washington* (Olympia: Washington State Planning and Community Affairs Agency, 1969), 74.

70. Mary Anna Tarbell, *A Village Library in Massachusetts: The Story of Its Upbuilding*, Library Tract 8 (Boston: American Library Association Publishing Board, 1905), 13.

71. *Shakespeare Association Bulletin* 4.4 (1929): 77.

72. See Judith N. McArthur, *Creating the New Woman: The Rise of Southern Women's Progressive Culture in Texas, 1893–1918* (Urbana: University of Illinois Press, 1998), 63.

73. *Shakespeare Quarterly* 2 (1951): 274.

Chapter 4

1. *Plaindealer*, 30 November 1899, 1. A later issue of the *Plaindealer* (22 June 1900, 3) described the Coterie as "the oldest club in Topeka." At some point in the early twentieth century, the Coterie admitted white women such as Martha Farnsworth. See Marilyn Dell Brady, "Kansas Federation of Colored Women's Clubs, 1900–1930," *Kansas History* 9.1 (1986): 19–30. Buckner's husband, Robert, was described as "a leader of society." Robert Buckner emigrated from Canada after the Civil War and in 1900 was "a poor unlettered colored boy who has developed by his own efforts into one of the most prominent and successful Afro-American mechanics and contractors in this city"; only twelve years later, he was described as "one of the wealthiest blacks in the state." Thomas C. Cox, *Blacks in Topeka, Kansas, 1865–1915* (Baton Rouge: Louisiana State University Press, 1982), 161, 179. Ann Thompson and Sasha Roberts report that this group's members "were likely to be literate and relatively wealthy black women." *Women Reading Shakespeare, 1660–1900: An Anthology of Criticism* (Manchester, U.K.: Manchester University Press, 1997), 154.

2. Cox, *Blacks in Topeka*, 97; *Plaindealer*, 30 November 1899, 1.

3. In *Aristocrats of Color: The Black Elite, 1880–1920* (Fayetteville: University of Arkansas Press, 2000), Willard B. Gatewood summarizes the development of national organizations for black women's clubs and their philanthropic goals (249–50). The Colored Women's League was founded in 1892; the Federation of Afro-American Women was founded in 1896 and merged that same year with the league as the National Association of Colored Women. Paula Giddings, *When and Where I Enter: The Impact of Black Women on Race and Sex in America* (New York: Bantam, 1984), provides an excellent overview of the black women's club movement. Most scholarship on Shakespeare and

African Americans has focused either on performance or on the early modern history of race; I have found no sustained discussions of black women reading Shakespeare in the late nineteenth and early twentieth centuries. Performance-based studies include the collection *Weyward Macbeth: Intersections of Race and Performance*, ed. Scott L. Newstok and Ayanna Thompson (New York: Palgrave Macmillan, 2010), and Francesca T. Royster, "Playing with (a) Difference: Early Black Shakespearean Actors, Blackface and Whiteface," in *Shakespeare in American Life*, ed. Virginia Mason Vaughan and Alden T. Vaughan (Washington, D.C.: Folger Shakespeare Library, 2007), 35–48. Heather S. Nathans explores the meanings of *Macbeth* for white and black audiences in American culture before the Civil War, in "'Blood Will Have Blood': Violence, Slavery, and Macbeth in the Antebellum American Imagination," in Newstok and Thompson, *Weyward Macbeth*, 23–33. For the long history of Shakespeare and black actors, see Errol Hill, *Shakespeare in Sable: A History of Black Shakespearean Actors* (Amherst: University of Massachusetts Press, 1984). Hill discusses black actors who "persevered in their desire to reach the highest realms of the actor's art" by performing Shakespeare (xxv). The place of Shakespeare in black women's reading groups further supports my argument about reading practices taking place in nonacademic locales; as Elizabeth McHenry points out, such venues "have, since the nineteenth century, been sites for the dissemination of literacy and for literary interaction for members of the black community traditionally excluded from the nation's elite liberal arts colleges and universities." *Forgotten Readers: Recovering the Lost History of African American Literary Societies* (Durham, N.C.: Duke University Press, 2002), 10.

4. With a couple of exceptions (the Arden Club of Topeka, Kansas, and the Schubert-Shakespeare Club of Durham, North Carolina), no black women's club was devoted solely to reading Shakespeare. McHenry discusses other literary societies with an emphasis on the classics, such as the Colored Reading Society of Philadelphia for men. See *Forgotten Readers*, 50–52.

5. See McHenry, *Forgotten Readers*, 225, and Deborah Gray White, "The Cost of Club Work, the Price of Black Feminism," in *Visible Women: New Essays on American Activism*, ed. Nancy Hewitt and Suzanne Lebsock (Urbana: University of Illinois Press, 1993), 261.

6. Adam Fairclough, *Better Day Coming: Blacks and Equality, 1890–2000* (New York: Viking Penguin, 2001), 35. Black women were excluded from the General Federation of Women's Clubs. See Anne Ruggles Gere, *Intimate Practices: Literacy and Cultural Work in U.S. Women's Clubs, 1880–1920* (Urbana: University of Illinois Press, 1997), 5–6. Glenda Elizabeth Gilmore points out that black women's clubs had origins in church work: "Women brought to club work the skills they had learned the hard way in their church work." *Gender and Jim Crow: Women and the Politics of White Supremacy in North Carolina, 1896–1920* (Chapel Hill: University of North Carolina Press, 1996), 190.

7. Elizabeth Lindsay Davis, *Lifting as They Climb* (1933; New York: G. K. Hall, 1996), 44; Deborah Gray White, *Too Heavy a Load: Black Women in Defense of Themselves, 1894–1994* (New York: W. W. Norton, 1999), 35. "Collective self-help project" is Sieglinde Lemke's phrase from her introduction to Davis, *Lifting as They Climb*, xvii.

8. Anne Firor Scott, "Most Invisible of All: Black Women's Voluntary Associations," *Journal of Southern History* 56.1 (1990): 5. Scott points out that "by the turn of the century there were associations of some sort in nearly every black community, North and South, in cities, towns, and villages, and a very fat book would not encompass their detailed history" (16). For an extensive list of early black literary societies, see

Dorothy Porter, "The Organized Educational Activities of Negro Literary Societies, 1828–1846," *Journal of Negro Education* 5 (1936): 555–76. Of the many sources on black women's clubs, I have found the following helpful for providing a context for this chapter: Giddings, *When and Where I Enter;* Brady, "Kansas Federation of Colored Women's Clubs"; Davis, *Lifting as They Climb;* and Charles H. Wesley, *The History of the National Association of Colored Women's Clubs: A Legacy of Service* (Washington, D.C.: Associated Publishers, 1984).

9. Fairclough, *Better Day Coming,* 35. Lynda F. Dickson remarks that "the most important function of club affiliation was to provide a support system that could continually reinforce the belief that the task at hand—uplifting the race, and improving the image of black womanhood—was possible." "Toward a Broader Angle of Vision in Uncovering Women's History: Black Women's Clubs Revisited," *Frontiers* 9.2 (1987): 67. Mary Martha Thomas observes, "White women might talk about going onward, but they were already uplifted." *The New Woman in Alabama: Social Reforms and Suffrage, 1890–1920* (Tuscaloosa: University of Alabama Press, 1992), 89. White points out that "because the context of black and white women's effort was different, so were the implications of their respective movements, even when they pursued similar goals and used similar rhetoric." *Too Heavy a Load,* 39. She notes that most white women's club associations were "openly antiblack," including the General Federation of Women's Clubs, which was "hostile" to black women (40–41). For women involved in interracial clubs in Texas, see Ruthe Winegarten, *Black Texas Women: A Sourcebook* (Austin: University of Texas Press, 1996), 193–95.

10. Mamie Garvin Fields and Karen Fields, *Lemon Swamp and Other Places: A Carolina Memoir* (New York: Free Press, 1983), 189. Fields was recalling a speech by Mary Church Terrell but did not give a date. See Scott, "Most Invisible of All," 18, for further discussion. V. P. Franklin covers the topic of clubs and race vindication in *Living Our Stories, Telling Our Truths: Autobiography and the Making of the African American Intellectual Tradition* (New York: Oxford University Press, 1995), 73–75.

11. Lemke, introduction to *Lifting as They Climb,* xx; Thomas, *New Woman in Alabama,* 69. Gerda Lerner points out that "unlike white club women, the members of black women's clubs were often working women, tenant farmwives or poor women." *Black Women in White America: A Documentary History* (New York: Vintage Books, 1972), 437.

12. Fannie Barrier Williams, "The Club Movement among Colored Women of America" (1900), originally published in *A New Negro for a New Century: An Accurate and Up-to-Date Record of the Upward Struggles of the Negro Race,* ed. Booker T. Washington (Chicago: American Publishing House, 1900), 379–405, in *The New Negro: Readings on Race, Representation, and African American Culture, 1892–1938,* ed. Henry Louis Gates Jr. and Gene Andrew Jarrett (Princeton, N.J.: Princeton University Press, 2007), 54. Black women's clubs also had state federations; the Texas Federation of Colored Women's Clubs, for example, was formed in 1905. For black women's clubs in Texas, see Ruthe Winegarten, *Black Texas Women: 150 Years of Trial and Triumph* (Austin: University of Texas Press, 1995).

13. Davis, *Lifting as They Climb,* 41. According to Lemke, the NACW served clubs that wanted independence from both the Baptist Church and the white women's club movement. Introduction to Davis, *Lifting as They Climb,* xviii. Lizzie A. Davis, president of the Phillis Wheatley Club of Chicago, argued that women should be taught that "there are things more important than fine clothes and that their brains are not located in their heels" (*Lifting as They Climb,* 15). See Shirley J. Carlson, "Black Ide-

als of Womanhood in the Late Victorian Era," *Journal of Negro History* 77.2 (1992): 64. For black women and the "Cult of True Womanhood," see Shirley J. Yee, *Black Women Abolitionists: A Study in Activism, 1828–1860* (Knoxville: University of Tennessee Press, 1992), 40–59.

14. Fannie Barrier Williams, "The Intellectual Progress of the Colored Women of the United States since the Emancipation Proclamation" (1894), in Gates and Jarrett, *New Negro*, 61.

15. As Christopher M. Span argues, African Americans "were committed to acquiring an education because they collectively equated knowledge with power, autonomy, and social mobility." "'Knowledge Is Light, Knowledge Is Power': African American Education in Antèbellum America," in *Surmounting All Odds: Education, Opportunity, and Society in the New Millennium,* vol. 1, ed. Carol Camp Yeakey and Ronald D. Henderson (Greenwich, Conn.: Information Age Publishing, 2003), 4. Jacqueline M. Moore points out that "since most black elite women had taught at some point in their lives, they also realized the importance of education to racial uplift, and their own responsibilities as educated women to lead the reform." *Leading the Race: The Transformation of the Black Elite in the Nation's Capital, 1880–1920* (Charlottesville: University Press of Virginia, 1999), 162. McHenry remarks that "although greater literary appreciation was one outcome of organized literary activities, it was not the only goal of African American literary societies." *Forgotten Readers*, 17–18. Michelle N. Garfield likewise suggests that "the concept that 'knowledge is power' for blacks was one of the most important ideas developed in the 1830s," and it was later adopted by early literary societies and by the black women's club movement. "Literary Societies: The Work of Self-Improvement and Racial Uplift," in *Black Women's Intellectual Traditions: Speaking Their Minds,* ed. Kristin Waters and Carol B. Conaway (Hanover, N.H.: University Press of New England, 2007), 115–16.

16. White, *Too Heavy a Load,* 24, 27. White cites several statements supporting the point that women were seen as the solution: for example, "It is to the Afro-American women that the world looks for the solution of the race problem," and "The Negro woman has been the motive power in whatever has been accomplished by the race" (36–37). Other statements from black men and women at the end of the nineteenth century include "The status of its womanhood is the measure of the progress of the race," "A race can rise no higher than its women," and "The criterion for Negro civilization is the intelligence, purity and high motives of its women" (42–43).

17. White, *Too Heavy a Load,* 44. Scott points out that black women's clubs were not "simply pale copies [of] the white women's associations." "Most Invisible of All," 3.

18. White, *Too Heavy a Load,* 39; Carlson, "Black Ideals of Womanhood," 61–73, esp. 69. See also Wilson Jeremiah Moses, "Domestic Feminism, Conservatism, Sex Roles, and Black Women's Clubs, 1893–1896," *Journal of Social and Behavioral Sciences* 24.4 (1987): 166–76.

19. Gatewood, *Aristocrats of Color,* 245; Gertrude Culvert, president of the Iowa State Federation of Colored Women's Clubs, quoted in White, *Too Heavy a Load,* 36.

20. Sarah E. Tanner, "Reading," *Woman's Era,* June 1895, 13. Numerous black clubs listed English literature among their readings, which probably included Shakespeare. I have refrained from assuming that, however, and in this chapter I have included only clubs for which Shakespeare was specifically mentioned.

21. Cited in Henry Louis Gates, *The Signifying Monkey: A Theory of African-American Literary Criticism* (Oxford: Oxford University Press, 1988), 132. Shakespeare as the "pinnacle of high culture" is McHenry's term from *Forgotten Readers,* 227.

22. Scott points out that "the motivations for black women to organize were quite different" from those for white club women. "Most Invisible of All," 9. Dickson offers a useful reminder to avoid the "tendency to view white women's club activities as the 'norm' and black activities in terms of how well (or poorly) they conformed to this norm." "Toward a Broader Angle of Vision," 65.

23. Andrew Murphy, *Shakespeare for the People: Working-Class Readers, 1800–1900* (Cambridge: Cambridge University Press, 2008), 203. Although the context of Murphy's comment is working-class readers in nineteenth-century Britain, it applies equally to black women readers in America.

24. Margaret Washington's efforts to include Negro history in the school curriculum are indicative of this blending; she remarked, "We are not trying to displace any other literature or history, but trying to get all children of the country acquainted with the Negro." Margaret M. Washington to Lugenia Burns Hope, September 15, 1922, in Jacqueline Anne Rouse, "Out of the Shadow of Tuskegee: Margaret Murray Washington, Social Activism, and Race Vindication," *Journal of Negro History* 81 (1996): 41.

25. Anne Meis Knupfer, *Toward a Tenderer Humanity and a Nobler Womanhood: African American Women's Clubs in Turn-of-the-Century Chicago* (New York: New York University Press, 1996), 121.

26. Details about black club women's reading of Shakespeare are scarce, particularly in comparison to the extensive records kept by most white women's clubs. It is rare to find even a list of plays read, let alone topics discussed in meetings. Although in this chapter I discuss only those clubs that definitively included Shakespeare, the actual number of African American clubs that read and studied Shakespeare is probably much higher. Likely clubs to add to the discussion in this chapter include the following: clubs in Newport, Brinkley, and Searcy, Arkansas; the Pierian Club of Kansas City, Kansas; the Ladies' Reading Circle of Dallas; the Inquirer's Club and the Chautauqua Circle in Atlanta; the Ladies Literary and Dorcas Society of Rochester, New York; the Ladies' Literary Society of the City of New York; the Idle Hour Literary Society of St. Louis; the Adelphai Club of St. Paul, Minnesota; the Rowfant Club and the Social Circle of Cleveland; the Round Table Club of Denver; Semper Fidelis of Davenport, Iowa; the Athenaeum Club, Monday Night Literary Club, and Iroquois Literary and Social Club of New Orleans; the Woman's Club of Baton Rouge; the Baltimore Literary and Historical Association and the Monumental Literary and Scientific Association of Baltimore.

27. Josephine St. Pierre Ruffin, "Address," *Woman's Era*, August 1895, 14.

28. Gatewood, *Aristocrats of Color,* 221.

29. Douglas Henry Daniels, *Pioneer Urbanites: A Social and Cultural History of Black San Francisco* (Philadelphia: Temple University Press, 1980), 124–28, 132–40; Quintard Taylor, *In Search of the Racial Frontier: African Americans in the American West, 1528–1990* (New York: W. W. Norton, 1998), 200.

30. Daniels, *Pioneer Urbanites,* 126. Clubs such as the Cosmos Social Club were praised for their "uplift of the morale and standards of our western civilization" and for setting a "tone of refinement." The club was extolled for providing "a necessary medium, through which a higher status for its members—the communities in which they live, and the pursuits in which they engage,—may be reached." *California Voice*, 4 March 1927, 1. Quoted in Daniels, *Pioneer Urbanites*, 131–32. This club included men and women, black and white. See also Albert S. Broussard, *Black San Francisco: The Struggle for Racial Equality in the West, 1900–1954* (Lawrence: University Press of Kansas, 1993), 65. Taylor similarly comments that many black San Franciscans "sought

through reading, 'refinement,' and knowledge of the world" to gain "civility" and "respect of their fellow citizens." *In Search of the Racial Frontier,* 200.

31. Taylor, *In Search of the Racial Frontier,* 219. For black women in the West, see Glenda Riley, "American Daughters: Black Women in the West," *Montana: The Magazine of Western History* 38.2 (1988): 14–27.

32. Taylor, *In Search of the Racial Frontier,* 213–14. These clubs included the Interstate Literary Association and the Coterie, two clubs that studied Shakespeare.

33. Taylor, *In Search of the Racial Frontier,* 219. McHenry similarly argues that the history of middle and upper-class black Americans has been oversimplified "as indicative of one of two things: the desire to assimilate into the white middle class, or passive acceptance of white domination and accommodation to racial segregation." *Forgotten Readers,* 17.

34. Garfield, "Literary Societies," 117. The first black female literary society was formed as early as 1831; this was the Female Literary Association of Philadelphia, one of three black women's literary societies in the city (the Minerva Literary Association was founded in 1834 and the Edgeworth Literary Association a few years later). See Garfield, "Literary Societies," 119–22.

35. Gatewood, *Aristocrats of Color,* 217, 244. Black women's clubs organized into state federations in the early twentieth century. See Taylor, *In Search of the Racial Frontier,* 220, and Wesley, *History of the National Association of Colored Women's Clubs,* 406–519.

36. Quoted in McHenry, *Forgotten Readers,* 172.

37. McHenry, *Forgotten Readers,* 24.

38. W. E. Burghardt Du Bois, *The Negro American Family* (Atlanta: Atlanta University Press, 1908), 77. This example underlines Sarah Luria's description of "the home as a contested site of racial equality." "Racial Equality Begins at Home: Frederick Douglass's Challenge to American Domesticity," in *The American Home: Material Culture, Domestic Space, and Family Life,* ed. Eleanor McD. Thompson (Hanover, N.H.: University Press of New England, 1998), 27.

39. Jerome Dowd, "Art in Negro Homes," *Southern Workman* 30 (1901): 92. On the role of African Americans in the formation of libraries, see Rosie L. Albritton, "The Founding and Prevalence of African-American Social Libraries and Historical Societies, 1828–1918," in *Untold Stories: Civil Rights, Libraries, and Black Librarianship,* ed. John Mark Tucker (Urbana: University of Illinois Press, 1998), 23–46.

40. Maud Cuney Hare, *Norris Wright Cuney: A Tribune of the Black People* (New York: Crisis Publishing Co., 1913), 80–81. Heather S. Nathans argues that the image of "'brave Macbeth' resonated among both black and white communities, and within both pro- and antislavery factions." "Blood Will Have Blood," 27. Nathans observes that in the antebellum period, "the fact that African Americans performed and cited *Macbeth* so frequently in speeches or newspaper articles demonstrates a certain cultural familiarity with the text" (30). Likewise, John C. Briggs points out that Frederick Douglass used references to at least fifteen plays of Shakespeare throughout his career. See "The Exorcism of Macbeth: Frederick Douglass's Appropriation of Shakespeare," in Newstok and Thompson, *Weyward Macbeth,* 35–43.

41. McHenry notes that "many free blacks [believed] that literary texts and the ability to gain access to them could galvanize the black community." *Forgotten Readers,* 24.

42. Nick Moschovakis, "Reading *Macbeth* in Texts by and about African Americans, 1903–1944: Race and the Problematics of Allusive Identification," in Newstok and Thompson, *Weyward Macbeth,* 71.

43. Daniels, *Pioneer Urbanites*, 114.

44. Richard Wormser, *The Rise and Fall of Jim Crow* (New York: St. Martin's Press, 2003), 64; Patricia Ann Schechter, *Ida B. Wells-Barnett and American Reform, 1880–1930* (Chapel Hill: University of North Carolina Press, 2001), 48–49. Moschovakis discusses Wells-Barnett as a "problematic" reader of *Macbeth*. See "Reading *Macbeth*," 70.

45. James West Davidson, *"They Say": Ida B. Wells and the Reconstruction of Race* (Oxford: Oxford University Press, 2007), 37, 39. In her biography of Wells, Linda O. McMurry remarks that Wells was an avid theatergoer and often saw productions of Shakespeare. *To Keep the Waters Troubled: The Life of Ida B. Wells* (New York: Oxford University Press, 1998), 36.

46. Schechter, *Ida B. Wells-Barnett*, 48.

47. *The Memphis Diary of Ida B. Wells: An Intimate Portrait of the Activist as a Young Woman*, ed. Miriam Decosta-Willis (Boston: Beacon Press, 1995), 84.

48. *Chicago Conservator*, 21 April 1906, quoted in Schechter, *Ida B. Wells-Barnett*, 132.

49. This speech is quoted in Schechter, *Ida B. Wells-Barnett*, 157.

50. Fairclough, *Better Day Coming*, 34.

51. *Woman's Era*, December 1894, 10. For extended discussion of the *Woman's Era*, see McHenry, *Forgotten Readers*, 217–35.

52. Williams, "Club Movement," 56.

53. *Woman's Era*, December 1894. Julie Winch covers early black women's literary societies in Philadelphia in "'You Have Talents—Only Cultivate Them': Philadelphia's Black Female Literary Societies and the Abolitionist Crusade," in *The Abolitionist Sisterhood: Women's Political Culture in Antebellum America*, ed. Jean Fagan Yellin and John C. Van Horne (Ithaca: Cornell University Press, 1994), 101–18.

54. *Woman's Era*, May 1895.

55. Medora Gould, "Literature," *Woman's Era*, June 1894, 11. For more information on black women's clubs and their adherence to moral values, see Carlson, "Black Ideals of Womanhood," 61–73; Moses, "Domestic Feminism," 166–77; and Dickson, "Toward a Broader Angle of Vision."

56. Tanner, "Reading."

57. Michael Fultz, "'The Morning Cometh': African-American Periodicals, Education, and the Black Middle Class, 1900–1930," in *Print Culture in a Diverse America*, ed. James P. Danky and Wayne A. Wiegand (Urbana: University of Illinois Press, 1998), 129–48, at 129.

58. Lois Brown, *Pauline Elizabeth Hopkins, Black Daughter of the Revolution* (Chapel Hill: University of North Carolina Press, 2008), 473–74, at 473.

59. Theodore Morrison, *Chautauqua: A Center for Education, Religion, and the Arts in America* (Chicago: University of Chicago Press, 1974), 166. The Chautauqua Circle records are in the Trevor Arnett Library, Atlanta University. See Karen L. Jefferson, "The Chautauqua Circle Collection: Preliminary Inventory," from the Guide to Manuscripts and Archives in the Negro Collection of Trevor Arnett Library, Atlanta University, 1971. See also John Dittmer, *Black Georgia in the Progressive Era, 1900–1920* (Urbana: University of Illinois Press, 1977), 60–61. Knupfer remarks that African American women in Chicago participated in clubs and lyceums more than in Chautauquas. *Toward a Tenderer Humanity*, 113.

60. Knupfer, *Toward a Tenderer Humanity*, 112.

61. Josephine T. Washington, "What the Club Does for the Club-Woman," *Colored American Magazine* 12 (February 1907): 122–25. Jacqueline Jones Royster argues that in

clubs, African American women "acquired and refined skills as writers and orators that were unique for their day" and prepared them to be "writers and speakers in public domains." *Traces of a Stream: Literacy and Social Change among African American Women* (Pittsburgh: University of Pittsburgh Press, 2000), 210. See also the chapter "Community" in Phyllis M. Belt-Beyan, *The Emergence of African American Literacy Traditions: Family and Community Efforts in the Nineteenth Century* (Westport, Conn.: Praeger, 2004), 115–51.

62. *Colored Citizen* (7 April 1898), 4; *Kansas State Ledger* (25 May 1894).

63. Knupfer remarks, "The preponderance of European literature [in black women's clubs], however, did not imply a dearth of African American writing." *Toward a Tenderer Humanity,* 114.

64. Washington, "What the Club Does," 222.

65. McHenry, *Forgotten Readers*, 14–15.

66. This evidence supports Janice Radway's caution against assuming that readers are "passive, purely receptive individuals who can only consume the meanings embodied within cultural texts, [that] they are understood to be powerless in the face of ideology." *Reading the Romance: Women, Patriarchy, and Popular Literature* (Chapel Hill: University of North Carolina Press, 1984), 6. For further discussion of cultural capital, see John Guillory, *Cultural Capital: The Problem of Literary Canon Formation* (Chicago: University of Chicago Press, 1993).

67. Brady, "Kansas Federation of Colored Women's Clubs," 22. Cox notes that in Topeka "there were also Shakespeare, Beethoven, and Handel clubs as well as art appreciation societies" (*Blacks in Topeka,* 98), but they have left no public record. The section printed in the *Plaindealer* on 12 April 1901 (p. 2) included an epigraph from Shakespeare's *3 Henry VI*: "'Tis beauty that doth oft make woman proud; / 'Tis virtue, that doth make them most admired; / 'Tis modesty, that doth make them seem divine."

68. See Brady, "Kansas Federation of Colored Women's Clubs" and "Organizing Afro-American Girls' Clubs in Kansas in the 1920's," *Frontiers* 9.2 (1987): 69–73. See also Porter, "Organized Educational Activities of Negro Literary Societies." Other black clubs in Topeka incorporated Shakespeare into their programs in a variety of ways; according to Marilyn Dell Brady, many club women "responded to roll calls with quotations from Shakespeare, Longfellow, and Dunbar." "'Rowing Not Drifting': The Topeka Federation of Colored Women's Clubs," in *The Clubs of Shawnee County from A to Z,* ed. John W. Ripley (Topeka, Kan.: Shawnee County Historical Society, 1984), 30.

69. *Topeka Times-Observer,* 21 December 1891, 2.

70. *Plaindealer,* 30 November 1899, 1.

71. Although Moses sees a divide between black women's clubs that "favored agitation and a vigorous anti-lynching campaign, and those who emphasized racial uplift and domestic feminism," Shakespeare seems to have been a part of both agendas; the Coterie Club in Topeka, for example, read Shakespeare and hosted Ida Wells-Barnett on her antilynching tour in 1895. "Domestic Feminism," 173.

72. *Plaindealer,* 30 November 1899, 1.

73. *Plaindealer,* 1 February 1901, 1.

74. Husbands were apparently invited to attend the meeting as well. The notice in the *Kansas State Ledger* (14 June 1895, 1) lists the following as present: Mr. and Mrs. Jamison; Mr. and Mrs. Joe Page; Mr. and Mrs. Clinkscale, Mesdames Robt. Keith, W. W. Buckner, Jennie Vernella, F. E. Buckner; Messrs. A Sawyer, J. M. Wright, J. G. Guy; Misses Maggie Simpson, Nora Hines, E. M. Glenn, and Sadie Guy.

75. It is not clear when the Coterie became biracial. It is possible (but highly un-likely) that there were two clubs called the Coterie meeting in Topeka around 1900. Farnsworth's diary provides a window on the type of woman active in prairie club life around the turn of the century, and it contains several entries pertaining to the Coterie Club. Given the racial history of Topeka, a biracial group like the Coterie would have been remarkable. For discussion of Topeka's racial history, see Cox, *Blacks in Topeka*.

76. *Plaindealer,* 22 March 1901, 4.

77. *Plaindealer,* 3 May 1901, 3.

78. *Plaindealer,* 3 May 1900, 3; *Plaindealer,* 2 May 1902, 3.

79. *Plaindealer,* 2 May 1902, 3.

80. *Plaindealer,* 29 November 1901, 3; 27 June 1901, 3. The entry for 14 June 1901 in the *Plaindealer* similarly uses the phrase "read and discussed" for Act 3 of *Henry VI.* The club news was reported in the "Club Woman" section of the *Plaindealer,* which suggests the club was made up primarily of women.

81. *Plaindealer,* 17 May 1901, 4; *Plaindealer,* 11 October 1901, 3.

82. Ne Plus Ultra history, RH MS 679, Box 1, Folder 2, University Archives, University of Kansas Libraries.

83. *Topeka Times-Observer,* 19 December 1891, 3.

84. *Colored Citizen,* 7 April 1898.

85. Cox, *Blacks in Topeka,* 161.

86. Randall Bennett Woods, *A Black Odyssey: John Lewis Waller and the Promise of American Life, 1878–1900* (Lawrence: Regents Press of Kansas, 1981), 45–46. Waller also belonged to the Pleasant Hour Association. The Interstate Literary Association was also "one of the first 'legitimate' platforms for the public presentation of piano rags." Lynn Abbott and Doug Seroff, *Out of Sight: The Rise of African American Popular Music, 1889–1895* (Jackson: University Press of Mississippi, 2002), 452.

87. See Knupfer, *Toward a Tenderer Humanity,* 108–22, at 114. Knupfer provides a list of African American Women's Clubs in Chicago (139–43). See also *The Negro in Chicago: A Study of Race Relations and a Race Riot* (Chicago: University of Chicago Press, 1922), 141–42, which mentions more than seventy women's clubs in the Chicago Federation of Colored Women's Clubs; and Anne Meis Knupfer, *The Chicago Black Renaissance and Women's Activism* (Urbana: University of Illinois Press, 2006), 93–115.

88. See *Bay View Magazine* 17.8 (1910): 575. Little Rock clubs were connected through the NACW (1897) and the City Federation of Little Rock (1905). Jeannie Whayne and Willard B. Gatewood, eds., *The Arkansas Delta: Land of Paradox* (Fayetteville: University of Arkansas Press, 1993), 119.

89. Judith Anne Still, "Carrie Still Shepperson: The Hollows of Her Footsteps," *Arkansas Historical Quarterly* 42.1 (1983): 37–46, at 42. Jeannie M. Whayne offers a general discussion of black and white women's clubs in Arkansas in "Prosperity Eluded: Era of Transition, 1880–1900," in *Arkansas: A Narrative History,* ed. Jeannie M. Whayne, Thomas A. Deblack, George Sabo III, and Morris S. Arnold (Fayetteville: University of Arkansas Press, 2002), 251–54. See also Whayne and Gatewood, *Arkansas Delta,* 119; and "Arkansas," in *The Encyclopedia of African-American Culture and History,* ed. Jack Salzman, David Lionel Smith, and Cornel West, vol. 1 (New York: Simon and Schuster, 1996), 190.

90. William Grant Still, "My Arkansas Boyhood," *Arkansas Historical Quarterly* 26.3 (1967): 285–93, at 290. See also Willard B. Gatewood, "The Formative Years of William

Grant Still," in *William Grant Still: A Study in Contradictions*, ed. Catherine Parsons Smith (University of California Press, 2000), 32–33.

91. Fon Louise Gordon, "Black Women in Arkansas," *Pulaski County Historical Review* 35 (Summer 1987): 28–29.

92. J. Still, "Carrie Still Shepperson," 44. See also W. Still, "My Arkansas Boyhood," 290.

93. J. Still, "Carrie Still Shepperson," 37.

94. Gatewood, "Formative Years," 33; William Grant Still to Mary D. Hudgins, 3 February 1967. Quoted in Florence Price, *Symphonies Nos. 1 and 3*, ed. Rae Linda Brown and Wayne Shirley (Middleton, Wis.: A-R Editions, 2008), xviii.

95. W. Still, "My Arkansas Boyhood," 290.

96. George Hutchinson, *In Search of Nella Larsen: A Biography of the Color Line* (Cambridge, Mass.: Belknap Press of Harvard University Press, 2006), 100. Rouse notes that "the preservation of African-American history and culture" and "the incorporation of 'Negro History' into community affairs and academic curricula were among her most cherished priorities." "Out of the Shadow of Tuskegee," 38.

97. Cynthia Neverdon-Morton, *Afro-American Women of the South and the Advancement of the Race, 1895–1925* (Knoxville: University of Tennessee Press, 1989), 133; Rouse, "Out of the Shadow of Tuskegee," 33. For further discussion of the Tuskegee Woman's Club, see Thomas, *New Woman in Alabama,* 72–80. For the club's involvement in suffrage, see 85.

98. Rouse, "Out of the Shadow of Tuskegee," 33. For Mary Church Terrell's club work, see Mary Church Terrell, *A Colored Woman in a White World* (Washington, D.C.: Randsell Publishers, 1940), 148–56.

99. See *Southern Letter* 33 (April 1916): 2; "The Shakespeare Ter-Centenary," *Tuskegee Student*, 1 April 1916, 8; "Tuskegee Woman's Club," *Tuskegee Student*, 29 April 1916, 1. It is curious that these are the same plays that Carrie Still Shepperson taught.

100. Neverdon-Morton, *Afro-American Women of the South,* 133.

101. Knupfer, *Toward a Tenderer Humanity*, 116. The Shylock reference is from *Broad Ax,* 10 March 1906, 2.

102. See Knupfer, *Toward a Tenderer Humanity,* 117.

103. See the entry in *Organizing Black America: An Encyclopedia of African American Associations*, ed. Nina Mjagkij (New York: Garland, 2001), 93–94. On the Bethel Historical and Literary Association, see McHenry, *Forgotten Readers*, 141–65; Kim Roberts, "The Bethel Literary and Historical Society," *Beltway Poetry Quarterly* 11.2 (2010), http://washingtonart.com/beltway/bethel.html; Moore, *Leading the Race,* 19–20, 66–69.

104. John W. Cromwell, *History of the Bethel Literary and Historical Association* (Washington, D.C.: R. L. Pendelton, 1896), 6, 9.

105. See Roberts, "Bethel Literary and Historical Society."

106. Garfield, "Literary Societies," 125.

107. Cromwell, *History of the Bethel Literary and Historical Association,* 24.

108. McHenry discusses the paradoxical situation of Frederick Douglass's wife, Anna, who belonged to the East Baltimore Mental Improvement Society but was illiterate; McHenry points out that "some black Americans participated actively in the activities sponsored by African American literary societies without ever acquiring the ability to read or write for themselves." *Forgotten Readers*, 13.

109. Cromwell, *History of the Bethel Literary and Historical Association,* 26. Cromwell also traces the organization's roots to the antebellum lyceums. Garfield points out that

many of these early literary societies "were interested in reading classical works as well as those of contemporary authors." Garfield, "Literary Societies," 119.

110. Cromwell, *History of the Bethel Literary and Historical Association,* 27.

111. See Roberts, "Bethel Literary and Historical Society." It might be worth comparing this group with Du Bois's "Talented Tenth" (1903) of educated African Americans who were to become cultural leaders of their race (published as the second chapter in *The Negro Problem*).

112. Gatewood, *Aristocrats of Color,* 248. Passage quoted from *Encyclopedia of the Harlem Renaissance,* ed. Cary D. Wintz and Paul Finkelman (New York: Routledge, 2004), 1:172–73.

113. Leslie Brown, *Upbuilding Black Durham: Gender, Class, and Black Community Development in the Jim Crow South* (Chapel Hill: University of North Carolina Press, 2008), 105, 78. Brown notes that in post–Civil War Durham there were at least three literary clubs meeting weekly to study Shakespeare and other topics. She remarks that "from the bay windows of the black elite homes, the music of Schubert and readings of Shakespeare competed with the sounds of street culture that swelled to create another more shadowy reputation for black Durham" (252–53). See also Glenda Elizabeth Gilmore, *Gender and Jim Crow: Women and the Politics of White Supremacy in North Carolina, 1896–1920* (Chapel Hill: University of North Carolina Press, 1996).

114. Brown, *Upbuilding Black Durham,* 112, 105. See Valinda W. Littlefield, "A Yearly Contract with Everybody and His Brother: Durham County, North Carolina, Black Female Public School Teachers, 1885–1927," *Journal of Negro History* 79.1 (1994): 37–53, for a profile of Mary Pauline Fitzgerald.

115. See Brown, *Upbuilding Black Durham,* 105, 173. See also 183–84, 283, 324.

116. Pauli Murray, *Song in a Weary Throat: An American Pilgrimage* (New York: Harper and Row, 1987), 60.

117. Brown, *Upbuilding Black Durham,* 110–13.

118. Walter B. Weare, *Black Business in the New South: A Social History of the North Carolina Mutual Life Insurance Company* (Urbana: University of Illinois Press, 1973), 101. William K. Boyd, *The Story of Durham: The City of the New South* (Durham, N.C.: Duke University Press, 1927), 296, mentions the Volkamenia Society as well as the Schubert-Shakespeare Club.

119. Richard Wormser, *The Rise and Fall of Jim Crow* (New York: St. Martin's Press, 2003), 95.

120. Linda Williams Bowie and Dorothy Anne Lee, *A Commemorative Booklet: The Detroit Study Club (1998),* TS, Burton Historical Collection, Detroit Public Library. Unless otherwise noted, further quotations and history come from this source. See also Paul Sporn, *Against Itself: The Federal Theater and Writers' Projects in the Midwest* (Detroit: Wayne State University Press, 1995), 125–26.

121. Desiree Cooper, "Club's Name Is Its Goal for 110 Years," *Detroit Free Press,* 7 May 2008.

122. L. E. Johnson, "Reminiscences, Detroit Study Club, 30th Anniversary," 2 March 1928, TS, Burton Historical Collection, Detroit Public Library.

123. Johnson, "Reminiscences."

124. Lucy Laney, principal of the Haines Institute in Augusta, Georgia, "had read several of George Eliot's books, Charles Lamb's Tales of Shakespeare before reading several of Shakespeare's plays and she had read other standard literature long before she left home to go to school. Years after when she was at her best in developing her

school she would enjoy telling me how she would get away with the other children in the family by her love for reading. She would sit on the woodpile reading while the sisters were washing the dishes and the boys carrying in the wood for the night." Mary Jackson McCrorey, "Lucy Laney," *The Crisis,* June 1934, 161.

125. Darlene Clark Hine, "The Detroit Study Club and the Voluntary Tradition of Women," in *Commemorative Booklet: The Detroit Study Club.* For more on the Detroit Study Club, see Darlene Clark Hine, *Hine Sight: Black Women and the Reconstruction of American History* (Brooklyn, N.Y.: Carlson Publishing, 1994), 74–77.

126. Elsewhere in the country, Shakespeare appeared on black women's club reading lists in the late nineteenth and twentieth centuries. Memphis's Howe Institute, a Baptist college, hosted a Shakespeare Club. See "Memphis," in Mjagkij, *Organizing Black America,* 328. In the May 1895 issue of *Woman's Era,* the Round Table Club of Denver reported that it was devoting the year to studying Shakespeare's history plays. *Woman's Era,* May 1895. Women's clubs in Denver were clearly divided racially; the Denver Public Library has the records of the Women's Club of Denver, run by Mrs. Gano Senter. According to the library archivist, "she and her husband were prominent members of Denver society, and very active members of the Klan. We have their papers. And their robes." Personal communication, 2009. See also Lynda F. Dickson, "Lifting as We Climb: African-American Women's Clubs of Denver, 1890–1925," *Essays in Colorado History* 13 (1991): 70–107.

127. *Topeka Plaindealer,* 14 February 1902.

128. Booker T. Washington, "The Tuskegee Idea," *World To-Day* 6 (1904): 513. Even recent historians have been critical of the black women's club movement. Fairclough, for example, argues that "black clubwomen commanded too little political influence and mustered too few financial resources to effect much overall improvement in lives of the poor." Concerned more with "middle-class respectability," black club women would rather "listen to Beethoven, read Shakespeare, discuss Socrates, and study the Bible" instead of "gambling, drinking, and sensual dancing." *Better Day Coming,* 37.

129. As Anne Ruggles Gere and Sarah R. Robbins argue, black club women "constructed an alternative ideology of literacy, fashioned themselves as managers of textual production, and appropriated authority for their own projects of self-education and cultural change." "Gendered Literacy in Black and White Turn-of-the-Century African-American and European-American Club Women's Printed Texts," *Signs* 21 (1996): 645.

130. David A. Gerber, *Black Ohio and the Color Line, 1860–1915* (Urbana: University of Illinois Press, 1976), 130. The Social Circle of Cleveland even had connections with whites in Cleveland (131–32).

131. Helen M. Chesnutt, *Charles Waddell Chesnutt* (Chapel Hill: University of North Carolina Press, 1952), 61.

132. See *The Marcus Garvey and Universal Negro Improvement Association Papers,* vol. 5, ed. Robert A. Hill (Berkeley: University of California Press, 1986), 441n3.

133. Charles Duncan, ed., *The Northern Stories of Charles W. Chesnutt* (Athens: Ohio University Press, 2004), 62, 66. Duncan points out that Groveland is "Chesnutt's semi-disguised name for Cleveland" (100).

134. Duncan, *Northern Stories,* 65–66. According to Duncan, Ryder "constituted an entirely new African American subject: businessman, landowner, and social creature" (64).

135. Duncan, *Northern Stories,* 66–67, 75.

136. Duncan, *Northern Stories,* 63.

137. *An Exemplary Citizen: Letters of Charles W. Chesnutt, 1906–1932,* ed. Joseph R. McElrath Jr., Jesse C. Crisler, and Robert C. Leitz III (Stanford, Calif.: Stanford University Press, 2002), 258.

138. Dickson, "Toward a Broader Angle of Vision," 66.

139. See Giddings, *When and Where I Enter,* 95–102.

140. Scott, "Most Invisible of All," 19. Scott discusses the separation between white and black women's clubs on 19.

141. Williams, "Club Movement," 54.

142. Gatewood, *Aristocrats of Color,* 216, 244.

143. Quoted in Brown, *Upbuilding Black Durham,* 270, from a 1929 speech, "The Quest for Culture," in the Schlesinger Library.

144. Knupfer remarks that in Chicago, for example, "white women's literary study was considered more formal and systematic, especially through course instruction and lectures." *Toward a Tenderer Humanity,* 115. Black and white women's clubs sometimes mixed in Chicago for literary discussions.

Conclusion

1. The notion that canonical authors might have meaning for readers outside structures of power is not often heard, despite Jonathan Rose's monumental study of working-class British readers, which makes exactly this point. See *The Intellectual Life of the British Working Classes* (New Haven, Conn.: Yale University Press, 2001).

2. Joan Shelley Rubin, *Songs of Ourselves: The Uses of Poetry in America* (Cambridge, Mass.: Belknap Press of Harvard University Press, 2007), 2.

3. Critics such as Barbara Herrnstein Smith have asserted that such authors as "Homer, Dante, and Shakespeare do not figure significantly in the personal economies" of people like those chronicled in this book, and "do not perform individual or social functions that gratify their interest, *do not have value for them,* [and] might properly be taken as qualifying the claims of transcendent universal value made for such works." *Contingencies of Value: Alternative Perspectives for Critical Theory* (Cambridge, Mass.: Harvard University Press, 1988), 53 (emphasis in original).

4. Nina Baym remarks that literary criticism in America has had "a bias in favor of things male—in favor, say, of whaling ships rather than the sewing circle as a symbol of the human community." *Woman's Fiction: A Guide to Novels By and About Women in America, 1820–1870* (Ithaca: Cornell University Press, 1978), 14.

5. Details of the Portia Club history are taken from History of Portia Club of Avon, Illinois, 1894–1994, Illinois State Historical Library.

6. Anne Ruggles Gere traces the decline of more general clubs to the 1920s. *Intimate Practices: Literacy and Cultural Work in U.S. Women's Clubs, 1880–1920* (Urbana: University of Illinois Press, 1997), 271n1.

7. Perhaps indicative of this decline, the "Club Forum" section in the *Shakespeare Association Bulletin* lapsed in the late 1930s. Mrs. Donald F. Hyde, "The Shakespeare Association of America," in *Shakespeare 400: Essays by American Scholars on the Anniversary of the Poet's Birth,* ed. James G. McManaway (New York: Holt, Rinehart and Winston, 1964), 315. The Monday Afternoon Club of Blair, Nebraska, might be an exception; after meeting for 133 years, the club voted to disband in 2009. See RG5661.AM: Monday Afternoon Club, Nebraska State Historical Society. Even though most of the clubs chronicled in this book no longer meet, there are several

that still do, including Shakespeare clubs in Worcester, Massachusetts; Concord, New Hampshire; Grove City, Pennsylvania; Marietta, Georgia (the Anne Hudgins Shakespeare Class); Santa Cruz, California (the Friday Shakespeare Club); Pasadena, California; Culver City, California; and Pomona, California.

8. Effie R. Knapp, "History of the Eugene Shakespeare Club," MS 227, Special Collections and University Archives, University of Oregon Library.

9. Knapp, "History of the Eugene Shakespeare Club." It is not clear when the club disbanded; the records continue until 1957.

10. Silver Creek Shakespeare Club Records, 1889–1990, MS 53, University Archives, State University of New York at Buffalo.

11. Friday Shakespeare Club of Santa Cruz, MS 104, University of California, Santa Cruz Library.

12. Steven Mintz and Susan Kellog, *Domestic Revolutions: A Social History of American Family Life* (New York: Free Press, 1988), 138.

13. See http://www.portiaclub.com/history/cleo.html. According to Glenna Matthews, "as the veterans of the nineteenth-century women's movement were dying off, they were not being replaced by educated young women with a similar commitment to solidarity among women or to social change in general." *The Rise of Public Woman: Woman's Power and Woman's Place in the United States, 1630–1970* (New York: Oxford University Press, 1992), 177. See also Joanne Meyerowitz, ed., *Not June Cleaver: Women and Gender in Postwar America, 1945–1960* (Philadelphia: Temple University Press, 1994).

14. Robert D. Putnam, *Bowling Alone: The Collapse and Revival of American Community* (New York: Simon and Schuster, 2000), 283–84. In an appendix titled "The Rise and Fall of Civic and Professional Associations," Putnam lists 1956 as the year of peak membership in the General Federation of Women's Clubs, and records an 84 percent decline in membership between 1956 and 1997. *Bowling Alone*, 438.

15. Esther Bickmore Clark, *The Woodland Shakespeare Club: A History, 1886–1967* (Woodland, Calif.: privately printed, 1968), 10, 16, 26.

16. *The Vanishing Shakespeare: A Report by the American Council of Trustees and Alumni*, April 2007, http://www.vanishingshakespeare.org/.

17. Shakespeare Behind Bars was formed in 1995 by Curt Tofteland as an "outlet for artistic expression and as a tool for learning literacy and social skills such as tolerance and conflict resolution." See Amy Scott-Douglass, *Shakespeare Inside: The Bard Behind Bars* (London: Continuum, 2007), 1. Scott-Douglass remarks that "Shakespeare programs can provide an intellectually stimulating environment and emotionally enriching community, a fraternity or sorority of friends who are there to offer their support" (129). See also Peter Holbrook, "Shakespeare as a Force for Good," *Shakespeare Survey* 56 (2003): 203–14. Holbrook argues that Shakespeare has been "frequently associated with an oppositional outlook on society and a relativizing one on morality" (206).

18. See "We the People Fact Sheet," at http://www.wethepeople.gov/about/We_the_People_Fact_Sheet.pdf.

19. See http://www.shakespeareinamericanlife.org/documentary/sponsors.cfm for a full list of financial supporters of this project.

20. See http://www.wethepeople.gov/about/index.html; http://www.neh.gov/wtp/about/index.html.

21. See http://www.shakespeareinamericanlife.org/education/index.cfm.

✿ Bibliography

Archival Material and Periodicals

Alabama Department of Archives and History, Montgomery
American Citizen (Topeka, Kansas)
American Shakespeare Magazine (New York)
Anne Hudgins Shakespeare Class, Marietta, Georgia, records, private collection
Arizona Historical Society, Tucson
Arkansas History Commission
Baptist Headlight (Topeka, Kansas)
Bentley Historical Library, University of Michigan
Bowling Green State University, Center for Archival Collections
Brinkler Library, Cambridge, Massachusetts, Historical Society
Broad Ax (Chicago)
Butte–Silver Bow Public Archives, Butte, Montana
California Historical Society, San Francisco
Cary Memorial Library, Lexington, Massachusetts
The Chautauquan (Springfield, Idaho)
Clark Historical Library, Central Michigan University
Colored Citizen (Topeka, Kansas)
Dallas Historical Society
Dallas Public Library
Danville Public Library, Danville, New York
Daughters of the Republic of Texas Library, The Alamo
Detroit Public Library
    Burton Historical Collection
The Dispatch (Hiawatha, Kansas)
Folger Shakespeare Library
    Autograph letters of Joseph Crosby, Zanesville, Ohio, to various recipients,
    1870–84
Free Library of Philadelphia
General Federation of Women's Clubs Archive
    Club History Collection
Houghton Library, Harvard University
Ilion Public Library, Ilion, New York
Illinois State Historical Library
Indiana University of Pennsylvania, Special Collections and University Archives
Kansas City Review
Kansas Herald (Wakarusa, Kansas)
Kansas Library Bulletin

Kansas State Historical Society
    General Federation of Women's Clubs of Kansas Collection
    Lilla Day Monroe Collection
Kansas State Ledger (Topeka, Kansas)
Lewiston Daily Sun (Lewiston, New York)
Library Journal
Library Occurrent, Public Library Commission of Indiana, 1906–8
Library of Congress
    Drama Deposits Collection, Manuscript Division
Medford Public Library, Medford, Massachusetts
Morristown and Morris Township Library, Morristown, New Jersey
Nebraska State Historical Society
Neville Public Museum of Brown County, Wisconsin
News Notes of California Libraries
New York Truth
Nicholas P. Sims Library, Waxahachie, Texas
North Carolina State Archives
Old Jail Museum and Archives, Barnesville-Lamar County, Georgia Historical Society
Onandaga Historical Association, Syracuse, New York
Peoria, Illinois, Historical Society
The Plaindealer (Topeka, Kansas)
Plainfield, New Jersey, Public Library, Local History Department
Powers Museum of Carthage History, Carthage, Missouri
Robert W. Woodruff Library, Emory University
    Loula Kendall Rogers Papers
Shakespeare Association Bulletin
Shakespeare Quarterly
Shakespeariana (New York and Philadelphia)
Shawnee County Historical Society, Topeka, Kansas
The Southern Letter (Tuskegee, Alabama)
State University of New York at Buffalo, University Archives
Texas Women's University Library (Denton)
Tibbe-Cuthbertson Family Papers, State Historical Society of Missouri Manuscript
    Collection
Topeka and Shawnee County Public Library (Topeka, Kansas)
Topeka Times-Observer (Topeka, Kansas)
Trevor Arnett Library, Atlanta University, Negro Collection
Tuskegee Student (Tuskegee, Alabama)
University of California–Santa Cruz Library, Special Collections
University of Central Arkansas Archives
University of Colorado–Boulder Library
University of Iowa Library
University of North Carolina Library, Chapel Hill
University of Oregon Library, Special Collections and University Archives
University of Pennsylvania Rare Book and Manuscript Library
University of Washington Library, Special Collections Division
Western Historical Manuscript Collection, University of Missouri–Columbia/State
    Historical Society of Missouri

William Allan Neilson Library, Smith College
Wisconsin Historical Society, Madison
The Woman's Era

Books and Articles

Abbott, Lynn, and Doug Seroff. *Out of Sight: The Rise of African American Popular Music, 1889–1895*. Jackson: University Press of Mississippi, 2002.

Albritton, Rosie L. "The Founding and Prevalence of African-American Social Libraries and Historical Societies, 1828–1918." In *Untold Stories: Civil Rights, Libraries, and Black Librarianship*, edited by John Mark Tucker, 23–46. Urbana: University of Illinois Press, 1998.

Allington, Daniel, and Joan Swann. "Researching Literary Reading as Social Practice." *Language and Literature* 18.3 (2009): 219–30.

American Council of Trustees and Alumni. *The Vanishing Shakespeare: A Report by the American Council of Trustees and Alumni*. 2007. https://www.goacta.org/publications/PDFs/VanishingShakespeare.pdf.

American University Magazine, November/December 1897.

Anderegg, Michael. *Orson Welles, Shakespeare, and Popular Culture*. New York: Columbia University Press, 1999.

Anderson, Douglas. *A House Undivided: Domesticity and Community in American Literature*. Cambridge: Cambridge University Press, 1990.

Augst, Thomas. *The Clerk's Tale: Young Men and Moral Life in Nineteenth-Century America*. Chicago: University of Chicago Press, 2003.

Augst, Thomas, and Kenneth Carpenter, eds. *Institutions of Reading: The Social Life of Libraries in the United States*. Amherst: University of Massachusetts Press, 2007.

Baskin, Janet Field. "Hamlet at a 'Spoon River' Banquet of Shakespeare's Characters Reveals Himself as Interpreted by the Modern Critics." *University of California Chronicle* 29 (1927): 308–9.

Bateman, Newton, and Paul Selby, eds. *Historical Encyclopedia of Illinois and History of Mercer County*. Chicago: Munsell Publishing, 1903.

Baym, Nina. *Feminism and American Literary History*. New Brunswick, N.J.: Rutgers University Press, 1992.

———. *Woman's Fiction: A Guide to Novels By and About Women in America, 1820–1870*. Ithaca: Cornell University Press, 1978.

Beecher, Catharine. *A Treatise on Domestic Economy*. New York: Harper and Brothers, 1856.

Belt-Beyan, Phyllis M. *The Emergence of African American Literacy Traditions: Family and Community Efforts in the Nineteenth Century*. Westport, Conn.: Praeger, 2004.

Benkert, Lysbeth Em. "Shakespeare on the Prairie: The Shakespeare Club of Aberdeen, South Dakota." *Borrowers and Lenders: The Journal of Shakespeare and Appropriation* 2 (2006). http://www.borrowers.uga.edu/cocoon/borrowers/request?id=781465.

Bennett, Carl K. "The Librarian of a Small Library." *Minnesota State Library Commission Library Notes and News* 1 (December 1904): 3.

Berggren, Paula. "The Woman's Part: Female Sexuality as Power in Shakespeare's Plays." In *The Woman's Part: Feminist Criticism of Shakespeare*, edited by Carolyn Ruth Swift Lenz, Gayle Greene, and Carol Thomas Neely, 17–55. Champaign, Ill.: Illini Books, 1983.

Bergmann, Harriet F. "'The Silent University': The Society to Encourage Studies at Home, 1873–1897." *New England Quarterly* 74.3 (2001): 447–77.

Besnier, Niko. *Literacy, Emotion, and Authority: Reading and Writing on a Polynesian Atoll.* Cambridge: Cambridge University Press, 1995.

Blair, Karen J. *The Clubwoman as Feminist: True Womanhood Redefined, 1868–1914.* New York: Holmes and Meier, 1980.

———. *Joining In: Exploring the History of Voluntary Organizations.* Malabar, Fla.: Krieger Publishing, 2006.

———. *The Torchbearers: Women and Their Amateur Arts Associations in America, 1890–1930.* Bloomington: Indiana University Press, 1994.

Bode, Carl. *The American Lyceum: Town Meeting of the Mind.* New York: Oxford University Press, 1956.

Bolt, Christine. *The Women's Movements in the United States and Britain from the 1790s to the 1920s.* Amherst: University of Massachusetts Press, 1993.

Bowie, Linda Williams, and Dorothy Anne Lee. *A Commemorative Booklet: The Detroit Study Club (1998).* Privately printed. TS, Burton Historical Collection, Detroit Public Library.

Boyarin, Jonathan, ed. *The Ethnography of Reading.* Berkeley: University of California Press, 1993.

Boyd, William K. *The Story of Durham: The City of the New South.* Durham, N.C.: Duke University Press, 1927.

Braden, Waldo W. *Oratory in the New South.* Baton Rouge: Louisiana State University Press, 1999.

Brady, Marilyn Dell. "Kansas Federation of Colored Women's Clubs, 1900–1930." *Kansas History* 9 (1986): 19–30.

———. "Organizing Afro-American Girls' Clubs in Kansas in the 1920's." *Frontiers* 9.2 (1987): 69–73.

———. "'Rowing Not Drifting': The Topeka Federation of Colored Women's Clubs." In *The Clubs of Shawnee Country from A to Z,* edited by John W. Ripley. Topeka, Kan.: Shawnee County Historical Society, 1984.

Brantley, Jessica. *Reading in the Wilderness: Private Devotion and Public Performance in Late Medieval England.* Chicago: University of Chicago Press, 2007.

Briggs, John C. "The Exorcism of Macbeth: Frederick Douglass's Appropriation of Shakespeare." In *Weyward Macbeth: Intersections of Race and Performance,* edited by Scott L. Newstok and Ayanna Thompson, 35–43. New York: Palgrave Macmillan, 2010.

Bristol, Michael. *Big-Time Shakespeare.* London: Routledge, 1996.

———. *Shakespeare's America, America's Shakespeare.* London: Routledge, 1990.

Broussard, Albert S. *Black San Francisco: The Struggle for Racial Equality in the West, 1900–1954.* Lawrence: University Press of Kansas, 1993.

Brown, Leslie. *Upbuilding Black Durham: Gender, Class, and Black Community Development in the Jim Crow South.* Chapel Hill: University of North Carolina Press, 2008.

Brown, Lois. *Pauline Elizabeth Hopkins, Black Daughter of the Revolution.* Chapel Hill: University of North Carolina Press, 2008.

Brown, Stephen J. "The Uses of Shakespeare in America: A Study in Class Domination." In *Shakespeare: Pattern of Excelling Nature,* edited by David Bevington and Jay L. Halio, 230–38. Newark: University of Delaware Press, 1978.

Burt, Richard. *Unspeakable Shaxxxspeares: Queer Theory and American Kiddie Culture.* New York: St. Martin's Press, 1998.

Canning, Charlotte M. *The Most American Thing in America: Circuit Chautauqua as Performance.* Iowa City: University of Iowa Press, 2005.

Carlson, Shirley J. "Black Ideals of Womanhood in the Late Victorian Era." *Journal of Negro History* 77.2 (1992): 61–73.

Carroll, Mary Bowden. *Ten Years in Paradise: Leaves from a Society Reporter's Note-Book.* San Jose, Calif.: Popp and Hogan, 1903.

Carruthers, Mary. *The Book of Memory: A Study of Memory in Medieval Culture.* 2nd ed. Cambridge: Cambridge University Press, 2008.

Cartelli, Thomas. *Repositioning Shakespeare: National Formations, Postcolonial Appropriations.* London: Routledge, 1999.

Case, Victoria, and Robert Ormond Case. *We Called It Culture: The Story of Chautauqua.* New York: Doubleday, 1948.

Castleberry, Vivian Anderson. *Daughters of Dallas: A History of Greater Dallas through the Voices and Deeds of Its Women.* Dallas: Odenwald Press, 1994.

C. E. Brehm Memorial Public Library District. "A Brief History of the C. E. Brehm Memorial Public Library District." http://www.mtvbrehm.lib.il.us/about-us/copy_of_director-s-message.

Chesnutt, Helen M. *Charles Waddell Chesnutt.* Chapel Hill: University of North Carolina Press, 1952.

Chicago Commission on Race Relations. *The Negro in Chicago: A Study of Race Relations and a Race Riot.* Chicago: University of Chicago Press, 1922.

Christensen, Philip H. "McGuffey's Oxford (Ohio) Shakespeare." *Journal of American Studies* 43 (2009): 101–15.

Christian, Stella L., ed. *The History of the Texas Federation of Women's Clubs.* Houston: Dealy-Adey-Elgin, 1919.

Clark, Esther Bickmore. *The Woodland Shakespeare Club: A History, 1886–1967.* Woodland, Calif.: privately printed, 1968.

Clark, R. Anna Morris. "Women's Literary and Social Clubs of the Black Hills." *Bits and Pieces* 11.1 (1976): 26.

Cleveland, Grover. "Woman's Mission and Woman's Clubs." *Ladies Home Journal,* May 1905, 4.

Cliff, Nigel. *The Shakespeare Riots: Revenge, Drama, and Death in Nineteenth-Century America.* New York: Random House, 2007.

Cobrin, Pamela. *From Winning the Vote to Directing on Broadway: The Emergence of Women on the New York Stage, 1880–1927.* Newark: University of Delaware Press, 2009.

Connerton, Paul. *How Societies Remember.* Cambridge: Cambridge University Press, 1989.

Connor, J. Torrey. *Saunterings in Summerland.* Los Angeles: Ernest K. Foster, 1902.

Cooke, Alistair. "Shakespeare in America." In *Shakespeare: Pattern of Excelling Nature,* edited by David Bevington and Jay L. Halio, 17–25. Newark: University of Delaware Press, 1978.

Cooper, Desiree. "Club's Name Is Its Goal for 110 Years." *Detroit Free Press,* 7 May 2008.

Cott, Nancy F. *The Bonds of Womanhood: "Woman's Sphere" in New England, 1780–1835.* 2nd ed. New Haven, Conn.: Yale University Press, 1977.

Cowden Clarke, Charles, and Mary Cowden Clarke, eds. *The Works of William Shakespeare.* London, 1864–69.

Cox, Thomas C. *Blacks in Topeka, Kansas, 1865–1915: A Social History*. Baton Rouge: Louisiana State University Press, 1982.

Croly, Jane Cunningham. *The History of the Woman's Club Movement in America*. New York: Henry G. Allen, 1898.

Cromwell, John W. *History of the Bethel Literary and Historical Association*. Washington, D.C.: R. L. Pendelton, 1896.

Cutter, Martha J. *Unruly Tongue: Identity and Voice in American Women's Writing, 1850–1930*. Jackson: University Press of Mississippi, 1999.

Daniels, Douglas Henry. *Pioneer Urbanites: A Social and Cultural History of Black San Francisco*. Philadelphia: Temple University Press, 1980.

Danky, James P., and Wayne A. Wiegand, ed. *Print Culture in a Diverse America*. Urbana: University of Illinois Press, 1998.

Darnton, Robert. *The Kiss of Lamourette*. London: Faber and Faber, 1990.

Davidson, Cathy N., ed. *Reading in America: Literature and Social History*. Baltimore: Johns Hopkins University Press, 1989.

Davidson, James West. *"They Say": Ida B. Wells and the Reconstruction of Race*. Oxford: Oxford University Press, 2007.

Davidson, Levette J. "Shakespeare in the Rockies." *Shakespeare Quarterly* 4 (1953): 39–49.

Davis, Elizabeth Lindsay. *Lifting as They Climb*. 1933. New York: G. K. Hall, 1996.

Davis, Natalie Zemon. *Society and Culture in Early Modern France: Eight Essays*. Stanford, Calif.: Stanford University Press, 1975.

Decosta-Willis, Miriam, ed. *The Memphis Diary of Ida B. Wells: An Intimate Portrait of the Activist as a Young Woman*. Boston: Beacon Press, 1995.

Degler, Carl N. *At Odds: Women and the Family in America from the Revolution to the Present*. New York: Oxford University Press, 1980.

Denton Public Library. "History of Denton Public Library." http://38.106.4.184/index.aspx?page=381.

Desmet, Christy. "*Shakespeariana* and Shakespeare Societies in North America, 1883–1893." *Borrowers and Lenders: The Journal of Shakespeare and Appropriation* 2.2 (2006). http://www.borrowers.uga.edu/cocoon/borrowers/request?id=781464.

Dewey, Melvin. *Field and Future of Traveling Libraries*. Albany, N.Y., 1901.

Dickson, Lynda F. "Lifting as We Climb: African-American Women's Clubs of Denver, 1890–1925." *Essays in Colorado History* 13 (1991): 70–107.

———. "Toward a Broader Angle of Vision in Uncovering Women's History: Black Women's Clubs Revisited." *Frontiers* 9.2 (1987): 62–68.

Dittmer, John. *Black Georgia in the Progressive Era, 1900–1920*. Urbana: University of Illinois Press, 1977.

Dobson, Michael. *Shakespeare and Amateur Performance: A Cultural History*. Cambridge: Cambridge University Press, 2011.

Douglas, Ann. *The Feminization of American Culture*. New York: Alfred A. Knopf, 1977.

Dovell, Junius Elmore. *Florida: Historic, Dramatic, Contemporary*. Vol. 4. New York: Lewis Historical Publishing, 1952.

Dowd, Jerome. "Art in Negro Homes." *Southern Workman* 30 (1901): 92.

Doyle, Don Harrison. *The Social Order of a Frontier Community: Jacksonville, Illinois, 1825–70*. Urbana: University of Illinois Press, 1978.

Draaisma, Douwe. *Metaphors of Memory: A History of Ideas about the Mind*. Trans. Paul Vincent. Cambridge: Cambridge University Press, 1995.

Du Bois, W. E. Burghardt. *The Negro American Family*. Atlanta: Atlanta University Press, 1908.

Dunbar, Mary F. P. *The Shakespeare Birthday Book*. New York: Thomas Whittaker, 1883.

Duncan, Charles, ed. *The Northern Stories of Charles W. Chesnutt*. Athens: Ohio University Press, 2004.

Dunn, Esther. *Shakespeare in America*. New York: Macmillan, 1939.

Ellis, Amanda M. *The Strange, Uncertain Years: An Informal Account of Life in Six Colorado Communities*. Hamden, Conn.: Shoe String Press, 1959.

Evans, Sara M. *Born for Liberty: A History of Women in America*. New York: Free Press, 1989.

Exercises at the Dedication of the Fowler Library Building. Concord, N.H.: Republican Press Association, 1889.

Fairclough, Adam. *Better Day Coming: Blacks and Equality, 1890–2000*. New York: Viking Penguin, 2001.

Faragher, John Mack, and Florence Howe, eds. *Women and Higher Education in American History*. New York: W. W. Norton, 1988.

Faragher, Johnny, and Christine Stansell. "Women and Their Families on the Overland Trail to California and Oregon, 1842–1867." *Feminist Studies* 2 (1975): 150–66.

Farr, Cecilia Knochar. *Reading Oprah: How Oprah's Book Club Changed the Way America Reads*. Albany: State University of New York Press, 2004.

Fields, Mamie Garvin, and Karen Fields. *Lemon Swamp and Other Places: A Carolina Memoir*. New York: Free Press, 1983.

Fischer-Lichte, Erika. *The Transformative Power of Performance: A New Aesthetic*, Trans. Saskya Iris Jain. London: Routledge, 2008.

Fischlin, Daniel, and Mark Fortier, eds. *Adaptations of Shakespeare: A Critical Anthology of Plays from the Seventeenth Century to the Present*. London: Routledge, 2000.

Fleming, Juliet. "The Ladies' Shakespeare." In *A Feminist Companion to Shakespeare*, edited by Dympna Callaghan, 3–20. Malden, Mass.: Blackwell, 2001.

Flint, Kate. *The Woman Reader, 1837–1914*. Oxford: Clarendon, 1993.

———. "Women and Reading." *Signs* 31.2 (2006): 511–36.

Flynn, Elizabeth A., and Patrocinio P. Schweickart, eds. *Gender and Reading: Essays on Readers, Texts, and Contexts*. Baltimore: Johns Hopkins University Press, 1986.

Folger Shakespeare Library. "Shakespeare in American Life." http://www.shakespeareinamericanlife.org/.

Foy, Jessica H., and Thomas J. Schlereth, eds. *American Home Life, 1880–1930: A Social History of Spaces and Services*. Knoxville: University of Tennessee Press, 1992.

Franklin, V. P. *Telling Our Stories, Telling Our Truths: Autobiography and the Making of the African American Intellectual Tradition*. New York: Oxford University Press, 1995.

Fraser, Nancy. *Unruly Practices: Power, Discourse and Gender in Contemporary Social Theory*. Minneapolis: University of Minnesota Press, 1989.

Freedman, Estelle. "Separatism as Strategy: Female Institution Building and American Feminism, 1870–1930." *Feminist Studies* 5 (1979): 512–29.

Fultz, Michael. "'The Morning Cometh': African-American Periodicals, Education, and the Black Middle Class, 1900–1930." In *Print Culture in a Diverse America*, edited by James P. Danky and Wayne A. Wiegand, 129–48. Urbana: University of Illinois Press, 1998.

Furnivall, F. J. *The Leopold Shakspere: The Poet's Works in Chronological Order*. London: Cassell, 1877.

Garfield, Michelle N. "Literary Societies: The Work of Self-Improvement and Racial Uplift." In *Black Women's Intellectual Traditions: Speaking Their Minds*, edited by Kristin Waters and Carol B. Conaway. Hanover, N.H.: University Press of New England, 2007.

Garrison, Dee. *Apostles of Culture: The Public Librarian and American Society, 1876–1920*. New York: Free Press, 1979.

Garvey, Ellen Gruber. "Scissorizing and Scrapbooks: Nineteenth-Century Reading, Remaking, and Recirculating." In *New Media, 1740–1915*, edited by Lisa Gitelman and Geoffrey B. Pingree, 207–28. Cambridge, Mass.: MIT Press, 2003.

Gates, Henry Louis, Jr. *The Signifying Monkey: A Theory of African-American Literary Criticism*. Oxford: Oxford University Press, 1988.

Gates, Henry Louis, Jr., and Gene Andrew Jarrett, eds. *The New Negro: Readings on Race, Representation, and African American Culture, 1892–1938*. Princeton, N.J.: Princeton University Press, 2007.

Gatewood, Willard B. *Aristocrats of Color: The Black Elite, 1880–1920*. Fayetteville: University of Arkansas Press, 2000.

Gerber, David A. *Black Ohio and the Color Line, 1860–1915*. Urbana: University of Illinois Press, 1976.

Gere, Anne Ruggles. "Common Properties of Pleasure: Texts in Nineteenth-Century Women's Clubs." In *The Construction of Authorship: Textual Appropriation in Law and Literature*, edited by Martha Woodmansee and Peter Jaszi, 383–400. Durham, N.C.: Duke University Press, 1994.

———. *Intimate Practices: Literacy and Cultural Work in U.S. Women's Clubs, 1880–1920*. Urbana: University of Illinois Press, 1997.

Gere, Anne Ruggles, and Sarah R. Robbins. "Gendered Literacy in Black and White Turn-of-the-Century African-American and European-American Club Women's Printed Texts." *Signs* 21 (1996): 643–78.

Gibson, James M. *The Philadelphia Shakespeare Story: Horace Howard Furness and the New Variorum Shakespeare*. New York: AMS Press, 1990.

Gibson, John William, James Lawrence Nichols, and William Henry Crogman. *Progress of a Race*. New York: Arno Press, 1969.

Giddings, Paula. *When and Where I Enter: The Impact of Black Women on Race and Sex in America*. New York: Bantam Books, 1984.

Giles, Judy. *The Parlour and the Suburb: Domestic Identities, Class, Femininity and Modernity*. Oxford: Berg, 2004.

Gilmore, Glenda Elizabeth. *Gender and Jim Crow: Women and the Politics of White Supremacy in North Carolina, 1896–1920*. Chapel Hill: University of North Carolina Press, 1996.

Glasrud, Bruce A., and Merline Pitre, eds. *Black Women in Texas History*. College Station: Texas A&M University Press, 2008.

Gordon, Fon Louise. "Black Women in Arkansas." *Pulaski County Historical Review* 35 (Summer 1987): 28–29.

Graff, Gerald. *Professing Literature: An Institutional History*. Chicago: University of Chicago Press, 1987, 2007.

Graff, Harvey J. *The Literacy Myth: Cultural Integration and Social Structure in the Nineteenth Century*. New Brunswick, N.J.: Transaction, 1979, 1991.

Greene, Zula Bennington. "Hair-Raising Tales." *Topeka County Journal,* 26 June 1982, 4.

Greenfield, Elizabeth. "Shakespearean 'Culture' in Montana, 1902." *Montana: The Magazine of Western History* 22.2 (1972): 49–50.

Grier, Katherine. "The Decline of the Memory Palace: The Parlor after 1890." In *American Home Life, 1880–1930: A Social History of Spaces and Services*, edited by Jessica H. Foy and Thomas J. Schlereth, 49–74. Knoxville: University of Tennessee Press, 1992.

Grove, Larry. *Dallas Public Library: The First 75 Years*. Dallas: Dallas Public Library, 1977.

Guillory, John. *Cultural Capital: The Problem of Literary Canon Formation*. Chicago: University of Chicago Press, 1993.

Gunzenhauser, Bonnie, ed. *Reading in History: New Methodologies in the Anglo-American Tradition*. London: Pickering and Chatto, 2010.

Haarsagar, Sandra. *Organized Womanhood: Cultural Politics in the Pacific Northwest, 1840–1920*. Norman: University of Oklahoma Press, 1997.

Hackenberg, Michael. "The Subscription Publishing Network in Nineteenth-Century America." In *Getting the Books Out: Papers of the Chicago Conference on the Book in 19th-Century America*, 45–75. Washington, D.C.: Library of Congress, 1987.

Haines, Helen E. "The Growth of Traveling Libraries." *World's Work* 8.5 (1904): 5231.

Hale, Lilian Walker. "The Club Movement in Kansas." *Midland Monthly* 7 (1897): 423.

Hall, Geoff. "Texts, Readers—and Real Readers." *Language and Literature* 18.3 (2009): 331–37.

Haltunnen, Karen. *Confidence Men and Painted Women: A Study of Middle-Class Culture in America, 1830–1870*. New Haven, Conn.: Yale University Press, 1982.

Hamm, Margherita Arlina. "The Fortnightly Shakespeare Club." *American Shakespeare Magazine* 3 (1897): 319.

Handbook of Texas Libraries. Houston: Texas Free Library Association, 1908.

Hapgood, Norman. *Why Janet Should Read Shakespeare*. New York: Century, 1929.

Hare, Maud Cuney. *Norris Wright Cuney: A Tribune of the Black People*. New York: Crisis Publishing Co., 1913.

Harper, Ida Husted. *The History of Woman Suffrage*. 6 vols. New York: J. J. Little and Ives, 1922.

Hayes, Kevin J. *A Colonial Woman's Bookshelf*. Knoxville: University of Tennessee Press, 1996.

Haywood, Clarence Robert. *Victorian West: Class and Culture in Kansas Cattle Towns*. Lawrence: University Press of Kansas, 1991.

Hazel, Michael V. *The Dallas Public Library: Celebrating a Century of Service, 1901–2001*. Denton: University of North Texas Press, 2001.

Heard, Alexander. *Speaking of the University: Two Decades at Vanderbilt*. Nashville, Tenn.: Vanderbilt University Press, 1995.

Heventhal, Charles R. *Readers of the Bard: The Shakespeare Club of Worcester, a Centennial Sketch, 1887–1987*. Worcester, Mass.: privately printed, 1990.

Hewitt, Nancy A. *Women's Activism and Social Change: Rochester, New York, 1822–1872*. Ithaca: Cornell University Press, 1984.

Hewitt, Nancy A., and Suzanne Lebsock, eds. *Visible Women: New Essays on American Activism*. Urbana: University of Illinois Press, 1993.

Higginson, Thomas W. "Women and Men: A Typical Club." *Harper's Bazaar* 22 (30 March 1880): 826–27.

Hill, Errol. *Shakespeare in Sable: A History of Black Shakespearean Actors*. Amherst: University of Massachusetts Press, 1984.

Hill, Robert A., ed. *The Marcus Garvey and Universal Negro Improvement Association Papers*. 10 vols. Berkeley: University of California Press, 1983–.

Hine, Darlene Clark. *Hine Sight: Black Women and the Re-construction of American History*. Brooklyn, N.Y.: Carlson Publishing, 1994.

Hoganson, Kristin L. *Consumers' Imperium: The Global Production of American Domesticity, 1865–1920*. Chapel Hill: University of North Carolina Press, 2007.

Holbrook, Peter. "Shakespeare as a Force for Good." *Shakespeare Survey* 56 (2003): 203–14.

Houde, Mary Jean. *Reaching Out: A Story of the General Federation of Women's Clubs*. Chicago: Mobium Press, 1989.

How to Organize a Shakespeare Club. New York: Doubleday and McClure, 1898.

"How to Promote a Shakespeare Club." *Cassell's Family Magazine* (June 1880): 415.

Humphrey, Mary Vance. "Junction City Reading Club." In *The Souvenir*, 89–90. Salina, Kan.: Ladies Aid Society of the First Presbyterian Church, 1901.

Huntington County, Indiana: History and Families, 1834–1993. Paducah, Ky.: Turner Publishing, 1993.

Huntley-Smith, Jen A. "Print Cultures in the American West." In *Perspectives on American Book History: Artifacts and Commentary*, edited by Scott E. Casper, Joanne D. Chaison, and Jeffrey D. Groves, 255–84. Amherst: University of Massachusetts Press, 2002.

Hutchinson, George. *In Search of Nella Larsen: A Biography of the Color Line*. Cambridge, Mass.: Belknap Press of Harvard University Press, 2006.

Hyde, Mary C. "The Shakespeare Association of America to the Folger Shakespeare Library on Its 40th Anniversary, 23 April 1972." *Shakespeare Quarterly* 23.2 (1972): 220.

Irwin, Mary Ann. "'Going About and Doing Good': The Politics of Benevolence, Welfare, and Gender in San Francisco, 1850–1880." *Pacific Historical Review* 68.3 (1999): 365–96.

Jackson, Shannon. *Lines of Activity: Performance, Historiography, Hull-House Domesticity*. Ann Arbor: University of Michigan Press, 2000.

Jacksonville Public Library. "History of the Library." http://jacksonvillepublicli brary.org/JPL_History.html.

James, Ronald J., and C. Elizabeth Raymond, eds. *Comstock Women: The Making of a Mining Community*. Reno: University of Nevada Press, 1998.

Jameson, Elizabeth. *All That Glitters: Class, Conflict, and Community in Cripple Creek*. Urbana: University of Illinois Press, 1998.

———. "Women as Workers, Women as Civilizers: True Womanhood in the American West." *Frontiers* 7.3 (1984): 1–8.

Jayroe, Jane. *Oklahoma 3*. Portland, Ore.: Graphic Art Center Publishing, 2006.

Jeffrey, Julie Roy. *Frontier Women: 'Civilising' the West? 1840–1880*. Rev. ed. New York: Hill and Wang, 1998.

Johnson, Nan. *Gender and Rhetorical Space in American Life, 1866–1910*. Carbondale: Southern Illinois University Press, 2002.

———. *Nineteenth-Century Rhetoric in North America*. Carbondale: Southern Illinois University Press, 1991.

"Junction City Ladies Club." *Kansas Woman's Journal* 1 (February 1922): 1–2.

Kaestle, Carl F. "The History of Readers." In *Literacy in the United States: Readers and Reading since 1880*, edited by Carl F. Kaestle et al., 60–62. New Haven, Conn.: Yale University Press, 1993.

Kahn, Coppélia, Heather S. Nathans, and Mimi Godfrey, eds. *Shakespearean Educations: Power, Citizenship, and Performance.* Newark: University of Delaware Press, 2011.

Kaiser, David. *A Book for a Sixpence: The Circulating Library in America.* Pittsburgh: Beta Phi Mu, 1980.

"Kate Tupper Galpin Shakespeare Club." In *Who's Who among the Women of California,* edited by Louis S. Lyons and Josephine Wilson, 158. San Francisco: Security Publishing, 1922.

Kelley, Mary. *Learning to Stand and Speak: Women, Education, and Public Life in America's Republic.* Chapel Hill: University of North Carolina Press, 2006.

Kerber, Linda K. "Separate Spheres, Female Worlds, Woman's Place: The Rhetoric of Women's History." *Journal of American History* 75 (June 1988): 9–39.

Kerrison, Catherine. *Claiming the Pen: Women and Intellectual Life in the Early American South.* Ithaca: Cornell University Press, 2006.

Kessler-Harris, Alice. *Out to Work: A History of Wage-Earning Women in the United States.* New York: Oxford University Press, 1982.

Kidnie, Margaret Jane. *Shakespeare and the Problem of Adaptation.* London: Routledge, 2009.

Kiernan, Pauline. *Filthy Shakespeare: Shakespeare's Most Outrageous Sexual Puns.* New York: Gotham, 2007.

Kingsbury, George W. *History of Dakota Territory.* Vol. 3. Chicago: S. J. Clarke, 1915.

Kirschmann, Anne Taylor. *A Vital Force: Women in American Homeopathy.* New Brunswick, N.J.: Rutgers University Press, 2004.

Kleinberg, S. J. "Gendered Space: Housing, Privacy and Domesticity in the Nineteenth-Century United States." In *Domestic Space: Reading the Nineteenth-Century Interior,* edited by Inga Bryden and Janet Floyd, 142–61. Manchester, U.K.: Manchester University Press, 1999.

Knecht, Andrea. "'We Are from the City, and We Are Here to Educate You': The Georgia Federation of Women's Clubs and Tallulah Falls School." In *The Educational Work of Women's Organizations, 1890–1960,* edited by Anne Meis Knupfer and Christine Woyshner, 215–34. New York: Palgrave Macmillan, 2008.

Knupfer, Anne Meis. *The Chicago Black Renaissance and Women's Activism.* Urbana: University of Illinois Press, 2006.

———*Toward a Tenderer Humanity and a Nobler Womanhood: African American Women's Clubs in Turn-of-the-Century Chicago.* New York: New York University Press, 1996.

Knupfer, Anne Meis, and Christine Woyshner, eds. *The Educational Work of Women's Organizations, 1890–1960.* New York: Palgrave Macmillan, 2008.

Kolin, Philip C., ed. *Shakespeare in the South: Essays on Performance.* Jackson: University Press of Mississippi, 1983.

Koon, Helene Wickham. *How Shakespeare Won the West: Players and Performances in America's Gold Rush, 1849–1865.* Jefferson, N.C.: McFarland, 1989.

Kozusko, Matt. "The Shakspere Society of Philadelphia." *Borrowers and Lenders: The Journal of Shakespeare and Appropriation* 2.2 (2006). http://www.borrowers.uga.edu/cocoon/borrowers/request?id=781462.

Kraditor, Aileen S., ed. *Up from the Pedestal: Selected Writings in the History of American Feminism.* Chicago: Quadrangle Books, 1968.

Krug, Rebecca. *Reading Families: Women's Literate Practice in Late Medieval England.* Ithaca: Cornell University Press, 2002.

Kruger, Linda M. "Home Libraries: Special Spaces, Reading Places." In *American Home Life, 1880–1930: A Social History of Spaces and Services*, edited by Jessica H. Foy and Thomas J. Schlereth, 94–119. Knoxville: University of Tennessee Press, 1992.

Lancaster Veterans Memorial Library. "History of the Lancaster Veterans Memorial Library, Lancaster, Texas." http://www.lancastertxlib.org/history/index.htm.

Lanier, Douglas. *Shakespeare and Modern Popular Culture*. Oxford: Oxford University Press, 2002.

Larson, Katherine R. "Reading the Space of the Closet in Aemilia Lanyer's *Salve Deus Rex Judaeorum.*" *Early Modern Women* 2 (2007): 73–93.

Latimer, Elizabeth Wormeley. *Familiar Talks on Some of Shakespeare's Comedies*. Boston: Roberts Brothers, 1886.

Lerner, Gerda. *Black Women in White America: A Documentary History*. New York: Vintage Books, 1972.

———. "Early Community Work of Black Club Women." *Journal of Negro History* 59.2 (1974): 158–67.

Levine, Lawrence W. *Highbrow/Lowbrow: The Emergence of Cultural Hierarchy in America*. Cambridge, Mass.: Harvard University Press, 1988.

Lewis, Willie Newbury. *History of the Dallas Shakespeare Club, 1886–1970*. N.p., 197-?. Copy in the Dallas Public Library.

Lindell, Lisa. "Bringing Books to a 'Book-Hungry Land': Print Culture on the Dakota Prairie." *Book History* 7 (2004): 215–38.

Little, Arthur L., Jr. *Shakespeare Jungle Fever*. Stanford, Calif.: Stanford University Press, 2000.

Littlefield, Valinda W. "A Yearly Contract with Everybody and His Brother: Durham County, North Carolina, Black Female Public School Teachers, 1885–1927." *Journal of Negro History* 79.1 (1994): 37–53.

Long, Elizabeth. *Book Clubs: Women and the Uses of Reading in Everyday Life*. Chicago: University of Chicago Press, 2003.

———. "Textual Interpretation as Collective Action." In *The Ethnography of Reading*, edited by Jonathan Boyarin, 180–211. Berkeley: University of California Press, 1993.

L. R. C. Library: An Alphabetical List of the Books Belonging to the Ladies' Reading Club of Junction City, Kansas. Junction City, Kan.: Tribune Books and Job Printing House, 1886.

Lurie, Maxine N., and Marc Mappen, eds. *The Encyclopedia of New Jersey*. New Brunswick, N.J.: Rutgers University Press, 2004.

Lyford, James O., ed. *The History of Concord, New Hampshire*. Concord, N.H.: Rumford Press, 1903.

Lyons, Chandler, and Sharon Atteberry. *Women of Peoria, 1620 to 1920*. Peoria, Ill.: Wilde Press, 2003.

Machor, James L. *Readers in History*. Baltimore: Johns Hopkins University Press, 1993.

MacLeod, Anne Scott. "Reading Together: Children, Adults, and Literature at the Turn of the Century," in *The Arts and the American Home, 1890–1930*, edited by Jessica H. Foy and Karal Ann Marling, 111–23. Knoxville: University of Tennessee Press, 1994.

Marks, Patricia. *Bicycles, Bangs, and Bloomers: The New Woman in the Popular Press*. Lexington: University Press of Kentucky, 1990.

Marshall, Gail. *Shakespeare and Victorian Women*. Cambridge: Cambridge University Press, 2009.

Martin, Theodora Penny. *The Sound of Our Own Voices: Women's Study Clubs, 1860–1910*. Boston: Beacon Press, 1987.

Matthaei, Julie A. *An Economic History of Women in America: Women's Work, the Sexual Division of Labor, and the Development of Capitalism*. New York: Schocken, 1982.

Matthews, Glenna. *The Rise of Public Woman: Woman's Power and Woman's Place in the United States, 1630–1970*. New York: Oxford University Press, 1992.

McArthur, Judith N. *Creating the New Woman: The Rise of Southern Women's Progressive Culture in Texas, 1893–1918*. Urbana: University of Illinois Press, 1998.

McCrorey, Mary Jackson. "Lucy Laney." *The Crisis*, June 1934, 161.

McCulloch, David, ed. *Historical Encyclopedia of Illinois and History of Peoria County*. Vol. 2. Chicago: Munsell Publishing Co., 1902.

McElrath, Joseph R., Jr., Jesse C. Crisler, and Robert C. Leitz III, eds. *An Exemplary Citizen: Letters of Charles W. Chesnutt, 1906–1932*. Stanford, Calif.: Stanford University Press, 2002.

McHenry, Elizabeth. *Forgotten Readers: Recovering the Lost History of African American Literary Societies*. Durham, N.C.: Duke University Press, 2002.

McHenry, Robert, ed. *Famous American Women: A Biographical Dictionary from Colonial Times to the Present*. New York: Dover, 1980.

McKanna, Clare V., Jr. "Prostitutes, Progressives, and Police: The Viability of Vice in San Diego, 1900–1930." *Journal of San Diego History* 35.1 (1989): unpaginated.

McManaway, James G., ed. *Shakespeare 400: Essays by American Scholars on the Anniversary of the Poet's Birth*. New York: Holt, Rinehart and Winston, 1964.

McMullen, Haynes. "A Note on Early American Libraries for Women." *Journal of Library History* 13.4 (1978): 464–65.

McMurry, Linda O. *To Keep the Waters Troubled: The Life of Ida B. Wells*. New York: Oxford University Press, 1998.

McMurry, Sallie. *Families and Farmhouses in Nineteenth-Century America: Vernacular Design and Social Change*. New York: Oxford University Press, 1988.

Meyerowitz, Joanne, ed. *Not June Cleaver: Women and Gender in Postwar America, 1945–1960*. Philadelphia: Temple University Press, 1994.

Michaelis, Patricia A. "The Meeting Will Come to Order." *Kansas Heritage* 14.1 (2006): 17–21.

Millbrook, Minnie D. "The Highland Beef Club." In *The Clubs of Shawnee County from A to Z*, edited by John W. Ripley, 52–55. Topeka, Kan.: Shawnee County Historical Society, 1984.

Miller, Perry. *The Raven and the Whale: The War of Words and Wits in the Era of Poe and Melville*. New York: Harcourt, Brace, 1956.

Miner, Carl. *Kansas: The History of the Sunflower State, 1854–2000*. Lawrence: University Press of Kansas, 2005.

Mintz, Steven, and Susan Kellogg. *Domestic Revolutions: A Social History of American Family Life*. New York: Free Press, 1988.

Mjagkij, Nina, ed. *Organizing Black America: An Encyclopedia of African American Associations*. New York: Garland, 2001.

Moore, Jacqueline M. *Leading the Race: The Transformation of the Black Elite in the Nation's Capital, 1880–1920*. Charlottesville: University Press of Virginia, 1999.

Morrison, Theodore. *Chautauqua: A Center for Education, Religion, and the Arts in America.* Chicago: University of Chicago Press, 1974.

Morrissette, Kate Hutcheson. "Traveling Libraries in Alabama." *Sewanee Review* 6.3 (1898): 345–48.

Moschovakis, Nick. "Reading *Macbeth* in Texts By and About African Americans, 1903–1944: Race and the Problematics of Allusive Identification." In *Weyward Macbeth: Intersections of Race and Performance,* edited by Scott L. Newstok and Ayanna Thompson, 65–75. New York: Palgrave Macmillan, 2010.

Moses, Wilson Jeremiah. "Domestic Feminism, Conservatism, Sex Roles, and Black Women's Clubs, 1893–1896." *Journal of the Social and Behavioral Sciences* 24 (1987): 166–77.

Moynihan, Ruth B., Susan Armitage, and Christiane Fischer Dichamp, eds. *So Much to Be Done: Women Settlers on the Mining and Ranching Frontier.* Lincoln: University of Nebraska Press, 1990.

Murphy, Andrew. "Shakespeare among the Workers." *Shakespeare Survey* 58. (2005): 107–17.

———. *Shakespeare for the People: Working-Class Readers, 1800–1900.* Cambridge: Cambridge University Press, 2008.

———. *Shakespeare in Print: A History and Chronology of Shakespeare Publishing.* Cambridge: Cambridge University Press, 2003.

Murphy, Mary. *Mining Cultures: Men, Women, and Leisure in Butte, 1914–41.* Urbana: University of Illinois Press, 1997.

———. "Votes and Violets: Montana Women in the Twentieth Century." In *Montana Century: 100 Years in Pictures and Words,* edited by Michael P. Malone, 93–110. Helena, Mont.: Falcon Publishing, 1999.

Murray, Heather. *Come, Bright Improvement: The Literary Societies of Nineteenth-Century Ontario.* Toronto: University of Toronto Press, 2002.

Murray, Pauli. *Song in a Weary Throat: An American Pilgrimage.* New York: Harper and Row, 1987.

Myres, Sandra L. *Westering Women and the Frontier Experience, 1800–1915.* Albuquerque: University of New Mexico Press, 1982.

Nathans, Heather S. "'Blood Will Have Blood': Violence, Slavery, and Macbeth in the Antebellum American Imagination." In *Weyward Macbeth: Intersections of Race and Performance,* edited by Scott L. Newstok and Ayanna Thompson, 23–33. New York: Palgrave Macmillan, 2010.

National Association of Colored Women's Clubs, Inc.: A Legacy of Service. Washington, D.C.: Associated Publishers, 1984.

National Endowment for the Humanities. "We the People Fact Sheet." http://www.wethepeople.gov/about/We_the_People_Fact_Sheet.pdf.

The Negro in Chicago: A Study of Race Relations and a Race Riot. Chicago: University of Chicago Press, 1922.

Neverdon-Morton, Cynthia. *Afro-American Women of the South and the Advancement of the Race, 1895–1925.* Knoxville: University of Tennessee Press, 1989.

New Hampshire Women: A Collection of Portraits and Biographical Sketches. Concord, N.H.: New Hampshire Publishing Co., 1895.

Newstok, Scott L., and Ayanna Thompson, eds. *Weyward Macbeth: Intersections of Race and Performance.* New York: Palgrave Macmillan, 2010.

Novy, Marianne, ed. *Cross-Cultural Performances: Differences in Women's Re-visions of Shakespeare.* Chicago: University of Illinois Press, 1993.

———. *Engaging with Shakespeare: Responses of George Eliot and Other Women Novelists.* Athens: University of Georgia Press, 1998.

———, ed. *Transforming Shakespeare: Contemporary Women's Re-visions in Literature and Performance.* New York: St. Martin's Press, 1999.

———, ed. *Women's Re-visions of Shakespeare: On Responses of Dickinson, Woolf, Rich, H.D., George Eliot, and Others.* Chicago: University of Illinois Press, 1990.

Ogborn, Miles, and Charles W. J. Withers. *Geographies of the Book.* Farnham, U.K.: Ashgate, 2010.

O'Neil, William. *Everyone Was Brave: The Rise and Fall of Feminism in America.* Chicago: Quadrangle Books, 1969.

Ostendorf, Paul John. "The History of the Public Library Movement in Minnesota from 1849 to 1916." PhD diss., University of Minnesota, 1984.

Owen, Thomas McAdory. *History of Alabama and Dictionary of Alabama Biography,* vol. 4. Chicago: S. J. Clarke, 1921.

Palmer, Leigh Anne. "'A Thing of Shreds and Patches': Memorializing Shakespeare in American Scrapbooks." In *Shakespeare in American Life,* edited by Virginia Mason Vaughan and Alden T. Vaughan. Washington, D.C.: Folger Shakespeare Library, 2007.

Partridge, Eric. *Shakespeare's Bawdy.* 4th ed. London: Routledge, 2001.

Pascoe, Peggy. *Relations of Rescue: The Search for Female Moral Authority in the American West, 1874–1939.* New York: Oxford University Press, 1990.

Passet, Joanne E. "Reaching the Rural Reader: Traveling Libraries in America, 1892–1920." *Libraries and Culture* 26.1 (1991): 100–118.

Pawley, Christine. *Reading on the Middle Border: The Culture of Print in Late Nineteenth-Century Osage, Iowa.* Amherst: University of Massachusetts Press, 2001.

———. "Seeking 'Significance': Actual Readers, Specific Reading Communities." *Book History* 5 (2002): 143–60.

Pearson, Jacqueline. *Women's Reading in Britain, 1750–1835.* Cambridge: Cambridge University Press, 1999.

Perkins, David. *Is Literary History Possible?* Baltimore: Johns Hopkins University Press, 1992.

Peters, Julie Stone. *Theatre of the Book, 1480–1880.* Oxford: Oxford University Press, 2000.

Peterson, D. Thompson. "A Roster of 19th Century Clubs and Societies of North Topeka from *North Topeka Times.*" In *The Clubs of Shawnee County from A to Z,* edited by John W. Ripley. Topeka, Kan.: Shawnee County Historical Society, 1984.

Phegley, Jennifer, and Janet Badia, eds. *Reading Women: Literary Figures and Cultural Icons from the Victorian Age to the Present.* Toronto: University of Toronto Press, 2005.

Phelan, Mrs. Charles Tidwell. *Keys to Shakespeare's Treasure House: A Series of Questions Covering Certain of the Bard's Plays, Designed to Aid Students and to Point a Way for the Desultory Reader.* Dallas, 1906.

Phin, John. *The Shakespeare Cyclopaedia and New Glossary.* New York: Industrial Publication Co., 1902.

Pitts, M. F. "How Can the National Federation of Colored Women Be Made to Serve the Best Interests and Needs of Our Women?" In *A History of the Club Movement among the Colored Women of the United States of America*, 63–65. Washington, D.C.: National Association of Colored Women's Clubs, 1902.

Porter, Dorothy. "The Organized Educational Activities of Negro Literary Societies, 1828–1846." *Journal of Negro History* 5 (1936): 555–76.

Porter, Mary. *Place aux Dames, or The Ladies Speak at Last.* Chicago: Dramatic Publishing Co., 1910.

"Portia Club Restoration Begins." *Mountain Light: The Newsletter of the Idaho States Historical Society,* Spring 2005, 6.

Price, Florence. *Symphonies Nos. 1 and 3.* Edited by Rae Linda Brown and Wayne Shirley. Middleton, Wis.: A-R Editions, 2008.

Price, Leah. "From *The History of a Book* to a 'History of the Book.'" *Representations* 108 (2009): 120–38.

———. "Reading: The State of the Discipline." *Book History* 7 (2004): 303–20.

Putnam, Robert D. *Bowling Alone: The Collapse and Revival of American Community.* New York: Simon and Schuster, 2000.

Queens Library (New York). "Community and Library History." http://www.queenslibrary.org/index.aspx?page_nm=History.

Radway, Janice. *A Feeling for Books: The Book-of-the-Month Club, Literary Taste, and Middle-Class Desire.* Chapel Hill: University of North Carolina Press, 1999.

———. *Reading the Romance: Women, Patriarchy, and Popular Literature.* Chapel Hill: University of North Carolina Press, 1984.

Randall-Diehl, Anna. *Carleton's Popular Readings: Prose and Poetry.* New York: G. W. Carleton, 1879.

———. *Elocutionary Studies and New Recitations.* New York: E. S. Werner, 1887.

———. *Reading and Elocution: Theoretical and Practical.* New York: Ivison, Blakeman, Taylor, 1869.

———. *Two Thousand Words and Their Definitions, Not in Webster's Dictionary.* New York: J. S. Ogilvie, 1888.

Rawlings, Peter, ed. *Americans on Shakespeare, 1776–1914.* Aldershot, U.K.: Ashgate, 1999.

Richardson, Anna E. "The Woman Administrator in the Modern Home." *Annals of the American Academy of Political and Social Science* 143 (May 1929): 21–32.

Riley, Glenda. "American Daughters: Black Women in the West." *Montana: The Magazine of Western History* 38.2 (1988): 14–27.

Ring, Daniel F. "Women's Club Culture and the Failure of Library Development in Illinois, Michigan and Ohio." In *Carnegie Denied: Communities Rejecting Carnegie Library Construction Grants, 1898–1925,* edited by Robert Sidney Martin, 53–78. Westwood, Conn.: Greenwood Press, 1993.

Ripley, John W., ed. *The Clubs of Shawnee Country from A to Z.* Topeka, Kan.: Shawnee County Historical Society, 1984.

Robbins, Mary LaFayette. *Alabama Women in Literature.* Selma, Ala.: Selma Printing Co., 1895.

Roberts, Kim. "The Bethel Literary and Historical Society." *Beltway Poetry Quarterly* 11.2 (2010). http://washingtonart.com/beltway/bethel.html.

Roberts, Sasha. "Reading in Early Modern England: Contexts and Problems." *Critical Survey* 12.2 (2000): 1–16.

Robson, Catherine. "Standing on the Burning Deck: Poetry, Performance, History." *PMLA* 120.1 (2005): 148–62.

Rooney, Kathleen. *Reading with Oprah: The Book Club That Changed America.* Fayetteville: University of Arkansas Press, 2005.

Rose, Jonathan. *The Intellectual Life of the British Working Classes.* New Haven, Conn.: Yale University Press, 2001.

Roth, Darlene Rebecca. *Matronage: Patterns in Women's Organizations, Atlanta, Georgia, 1890–1940.* Brooklyn, N.Y.: Carlson Publishing, 1994.

Rouse, Jacqueline Anne. "Out of the Shadow of Tuskegee: Margaret Murray Washington, Social Activism, and Race Vindication." *Journal of Negro History* 81 (1996): 31–46.

Rowlands, Michael. "The Role of Memory in the Transmission of Culture." *World Archaeology* 25.3 (1993): 141–51.

Royster, Jacqueline Jones. *Traces of a Stream: Literacy and Social Change among African American Women.* Pittsburgh: University of Pittsburgh Press, 2000.

Rozett, Martha Tuck. *Talking Back to Shakespeare.* Newark: University of Delaware Press, 1994.

Rubin, Joan Shelley. *Songs of Ourselves: The Uses of Poetry in America.* Cambridge, Mass.: Belknap Press of Harvard University Press, 2007.

Rudolph, Frederick. *The American College and University: A History.* New York: Alfred A. Knopf, 1965.

Ryan, Barbara, and Amy M. Thomas, eds. *Reading Acts: U.S. Readers' Interactions with Literature, 1800–1950.* Knoxville: University of Tennessee Press, 2002.

Ryan, Mary P. *Womanhood in America: From Colonial Times to the Present.* New York: New Viewpoints, 1975.

———. *Women in Public: Between Banners and Ballots, 1825–1880.* Baltimore: Johns Hopkins University Press, 1990.

Saenger, Paul. *Space between Words: The Origins of Silent Reading.* Stanford, Calif.: Stanford University Press, 1997.

Salzman, Jack, David Lionel Smith, and Cornel West, eds. *The Encyclopedia of African-American Culture and History.* Vol. 1. New York: Simon and Schuster, 1996.

Sanders, Julie. *Novel Shakespeares: Twentieth-Century Women Novelists and Appropriation.* Manchester, U.K.: Manchester University Press, 2002.

Savage, Henry L. "The Shakespeare Society of Philadelphia." *Shakespeare Quarterly* 3.4 (1952): 341–52.

Sawaya, Francesca. *Modern Women, Modern Work: Domesticity, Professionalism, and American Writing, 1890–1950.* Philadelphia: University of Pennsylvania Press, 2004.

Schechter, Patricia Ann. *Ida B. Wells-Barnett and American Reform, 1880–1930.* Chapel Hill: University of North Carolina Press, 2001.

Schmid, Calvin F., and Stanton E. Schmid. *Growth of Cities and Towns: State of Washington.* Olympia: Washington State Planning and Community Affairs Agency, 1969.

Schwartz, Lynne Sharon. *Ruined by Reading: A Life in Books.* Boston: Beacon Press, 1996.

Schweickart, Patrocinio P., and Elizabeth A. Flynn, eds. *Reading Sites: Social Difference and Reader Response.* New York: Modern Language Association, 2004.

Scott, Anne Firor. *Making the Invisible Woman Visible.* Urbana: University of Illinois Press, 1984.

———. "The Most Invisible of All: Black Women's Voluntary Associations." *Journal of Southern History* 56.1 (1990): 3–22.

———. *Natural Allies: Women's Associations in American History.* Urbana: University of Illinois Press, 1991.

————. "Women and Libraries." In *Libraries, Books, and Culture*, edited by Donald G. Davis Jr. Austin: University of Texas Press, 1986.

Scott-Douglass, Amy. *Shakespeare Inside: The Bard behind Bars*. London: Continuum, 2007.

"Shakespeare Club Celebrates Bard's Creativity." *Palm Beach Post-Times*, 19 April 1969, 10.

Shakespeare Forget-Me-Nots: A Text Book of Shakespeare Quotation. New York: E. P. Dutton, 1880.

The Shakespeare Society of New York: Articles of Association. New York: Shakespeare Press, 1895.

Sharpless, Rebecca. *Fertile Ground, Narrow Choices: Women on Texas Cotton Farms, 1900–1940*. Chapel Hill: University of North Carolina Press, 1999.

Shattuck, Charles. *Shakespeare on the American Stage*. Washington, D.C.: Folger Press, 1976, 1987.

Shortridge, James R. *The Evolution of Urban Kansas*. Lawrence: University Press of Kansas, 2004.

Sicherman, Barbara. *Well-Read Lives: How Books Inspired a Generation of American Women*. Chapel Hill: University of North Carolina Press, 2010.

Simpson, Jeffrey. *Chautauqua: An American Utopia*. New York: Henry N. Abrams, 1999.

Sinfield, Alan. *Faultlines: Cultural Materialism and the Politics of Dissident Reading*. Berkeley: University of California Press, 1992.

Sklar, Kathryn Kish. *Catharine Beecher: A Study in American Domesticity*. New Haven, Conn.: Yale University Press, 1973.

Smith, Barbara Hernnstein. *Contingencies of Value: Alternative Perspectives for Critical Theory*. Cambridge, Mass.: Harvard University Press, 1988.

Smith, Catherine Parsons. *William Grant Still: A Study in Contradictions*. Berkeley: University of California Press, 2000.

Smith, Daniel Scott. "Family Limitation, Sexual Control, and Domestic Feminism." *Feminist Studies* 1.3/4 (1973): 40–57.

Smith, Gay. *Lady Macbeth in America: From the Stage to the White House*. Basingstoke, U.K.: Palgrave, 2010.

Smith, Katherine Louise. "Railroad Traveling Libraries." *New Outlook* 67 (1901): 961–63.

Solomon, Barbara Miller. *In the Company of Educated Women: A History of Women and Higher Education in America*. New Haven, Conn.: Yale University Press, 1985.

Span, Christopher M. "'Knowledge Is Light, Knowledge Is Power': African American Education in Antebellum America." In *Surmounting All Odds: Education, Opportunity, and Society in the New Millennium*, vol. 1, edited by Carol Camp Yeakey and Ronald D. Henderson, 3–29. Greenwich, Conn.: Information Age Publishing, 2003.

Sporn, Paul. *Against Itself: The Federal Theater and Writers' Projects in the Midwest*. Detroit: Wayne State University Press, 1995.

Sport, Kathryn, and Bert Hitchcock. *De Remnant Truth: The Tales of Jake Mitchell and Robert Wilton Burton*. Tuscaloosa: University of Alabama Press, 1991.

Springer, Marlene, and Haskell Springer, eds. *Plains Woman: The Diary of Martha Farnsworth, 1882–1922*. Bloomington: Indiana University Press, 1986.

St. Clair, William. *The Reading Nation in the Romantic Period*. Cambridge: Cambridge University Press, 2004.

Stansell, Christine, and Johnny Faragher. "Women and Their Families on the Overland Trail to California and Oregon, 1842–67." *Feminist Studies* 2.2/3 (1975): 150–66.

Stefanco, Carolyn, "Networking on the Frontier: The Colorado Women's Suffrage Movement, 1876–1893." In *The Women's West*, edited by Susan Armitage and Elizabeth Jameson, 265–76. Norman: University of Oklahoma Press, 1987.

Stewart, Ken. "Much Ado About Everything: The Melbourne Shakespeare Society, 1884–1904." *Australian Literary Studies* 19.3 (2000): 269–78.

Still, Judith Anne. "Carrie Still Shepperson: The Hollows of Her Footsteps." *Arkansas Historical Quarterly* 42.1 (1983): 37–46.

Still, William Grant. "My Arkansas Boyhood." *Arkansas Historical Quarterly* 26.3 (1967): 285–93.

Stock, Brian. *The Implications of Literacy: Written Language and the Models of Interpretation in the Eleventh and Twelfth Centuries.* Princeton, N.J.: Princeton University Press, 1983.

Sturgess, Kim C. *Shakespeare and the American Nation.* Cambridge: Cambridge University Press, 2004.

Sullivan, Dolores P. *William Holmes McGuffey: Schoolmaster to the Nation.* Rutherford, N.J.: Fairleigh Dickinson University Press, 1994.

Taber, Clarence W. *The Business of the Household.* Philadelphia: J. B. Lippincott, 1918.

Taliaferro, John. *Charles M. Russell: The Life and Legend of America's Cowboy Artist.* Boston: Little, Brown, 1996.

Tanner, Sarah E. "Reading." *Woman's Era*, June 1895.

Tarbell, Ida M. "The Cost of Living and Household Management." *Annals of the American Academy of Political and Social Science* 48 (July 1913): 127–30.

Tarbell, Mary Anna. *A Village Library in Massachusetts: The Story of Its Upbuilding.* Library Tract 8. Boston: American Library Association Publishing Board, 1905.

Tarbox, Gwen Athene. *The Clubwomen's Daughters: Collectivist Impulses in Progressive-Era Girls' Fiction.* New York: Garland, 2000.

Taylor, Quintard. *In Search of the Racial Frontier: African Americans in the American West, 1528–1990.* New York: W. W. Norton, 1998.

Teague, Frances. *Shakespeare and the American Popular Stage.* Cambridge: Cambridge University Press, 2006.

Terrell, Mary Church. *A Colored Woman in a White World.* Washington, D.C.: Randsell Publishers, 1940.

———. "Washington." *Woman's Era*, December 1894.

Thomas, Mary Martha. *The New Woman in Alabama: Social Reforms and Suffrage, 1890–1920.* Tuscaloosa: University of Alabama Press, 1992.

Thomas, William Taylor. "The Introduction of Shakespeare into the Schools." *Shakespeariana* 1 (1883): 10–11.

———. "Shakespeare Study for American Women." *Shakespeariana* 1 (1883): 97–102.

Thompson, Ann. "A Club of Our Own: Women's Play Readings in the Nineteenth Century." *Borrowers and Lenders: The Journal of Shakespeare and Appropriation* 2.2 (2006): 1–7. http://www.borrowers.uga.edu/cocoon/borrowers/request?id=781461.

Thompson, Ann, and Sasha Roberts, eds. *Women Reading Shakespeare, 1660–1900: An Anthology of Criticism.* Manchester, U.K.: Manchester University Press, 1997.

Thompson, Eleanor McD., ed. *The American Home: Material Culture, Domestic Space, and Family Life.* Hanover, N.H.: University Press of New England, 1998.

Ticknor, Anna E. *Society to Encourage Studies at Home.* Cambridge, Mass.: Riverside Press, 1897.

Tracy, Wegia Hope Hall. "Women's Clubs in Nebraska." *Midland Monthly* 5.3 (1896): 262–71.

Tucker, John Mark, ed. *Untold Stories: Civil Rights, Libraries, and Black Librarianship.* Urbana: University of Illinois Press, 1998.

Underwood, June. "Civilizing Kansas: Women's Organizations, 1880–1920." *Kansas History: A Journal of the Central Plains* 7.4 (1984/85): 291–306.

Uricchio, William, and Roberta E. Pearson. *Reframing Culture: The Case of the Vitagraph Quality Films.* Princeton, N.J.: Princeton University Press, 1993.

Van Orman, Richard A. "The Bard in the West." *Western Historical Quarterly* 5 (1974): 29–38.

Van Slyck, Abigail A. *Free to All: Carnegie Libraries and American Culture, 1890–1920.* Chicago: University of Chicago Press, 1995.

Vaughan, Virginia Mason, and Alden T. Vaughan, eds. *Shakespeare in American Life.* Washington, D.C.: Folger Shakespeare Library, 2007.

Velz, John W., and Frances N. Teague, eds. *One Touch of Shakespeare: Letters of Joseph Crosby to Joseph Parker Norris, 1875–1878.* Washington, D.C.: Folger Shakespeare Library, 1986.

Wall, Wendy. *Staging Domesticity: Household Work and English Identity in Early Modern Drama.* Cambridge: Cambridge University Press, 2002.

Warhol, Robyn. *Having a Good Cry: Effeminate Feelings and Pop-Culture Forms.* Columbus: Ohio State University Press, 2003.

Warner, William. "The Resistance to Popular Culture." *American Literary History* 2 (1990): 726–42.

Washington, Booker T., ed. *A New Negro for a New Century: An Accurate and Up-to-Date Record of the Upward Struggles of the Negro Race.* Chicago: American Publishing House, 1900.

———. "The Tuskegee Idea." *World To-Day* 6 (1904): 513.

Washington, Josephine T. "What the Club Does for the Club-Woman." *Colored American Magazine* 12 (February 1907): 122–25.

Waters, Kristin, and Carol B. Conaway, eds. *Black Women's Intellectual Traditions: Speaking Their Minds.* Hanover, N.H.: University Press of New England, 2007.

Watson, Carrie M., and Edith M. Clarke. *Handbook of Kansas Libraries.* Lawrence, Kan., 1903.

Watson, Paula D. "Founding Mothers: The Contribution of Women's Organizations to Public Library Development in the United States." *Library Quarterly* 64.3 (1994): 233–69.

Weare, Walter B. *Black Business in the New South: A Social History of the North Carolina Mutual Life Insurance Company.* Urbana: University of Illinois Press, 1973.

Weinrich, Harald. *Lethe: The Art and Critique of Forgetting.* Trans. Steven Rendall. Ithaca: Cornell University Press, 2004.

Welter, Barbara. *Dimity Convictions: The American Woman in the Nineteenth Century.* Athens: Ohio University Press, 1976.

Wenger, Mae. *Centennial History: GFWC Kansas Federation of Women's Clubs.* Shawnee Mission, Kan.: Kes-Print, 1988.

Wesley, Charles H. *The History of the National Association of Colored Women's Clubs: A Legacy of Service.* Washington, D.C.: Associated Publishers, 1984.

West, Elliott. "Beyond Baby Doe: Child Rearing on the Mining Frontier." In *The Women's West*, edited by Susan Armitage and Elizabeth Jameson, 179–92. Norman: University of Oklahoma Press, 1987.

———. "Heathens and Angels: Childhood in the Rocky Mountain Mining Towns." *Western Historical Quarterly* 14.2 (1983): 145–64.

Westfall, Alfred. *American Shakespearean Criticism, 1607–1865*. New York: H. W. Wilson, 1939.

Whayne, Jeannie M., and Willard B. Gatewood, eds. *The Arkansas Delta: Land of Paradox*. Fayetteville: University of Arkansas Press, 1993.

———. "Prosperity Eluded: Era of Transition, 1880–1900." In *Arkansas: A Narrative History*, edited by Jeannie M. Whayne, Thomas A. Deblack, George Sabo III, and Morris S. Arnold, 251–54. Fayetteville: University of Arkansas Press, 2002.

———. "Reasonable Progress: Limits of Progressive Reform." In *Arkansas: A Narrative History*, edited by Jeannie M. Whayne, Thomas A. Deblack, George Sabo III, and Morris S. Arnold, 272–302. Fayetteville: University of Arkansas Press, 2002.

White, Deborah Gray. "The Cost of Club Work, the Price of Black Feminism." In *Visible Women: New Essays on American Activism*, edited by Nancy Hewitt and Suzanne Lebsock, 247–69. Urbana: University of Illinois Press, 1993.

———. *Too Heavy a Load: Black Women in Defense of Themselves, 1894–1994*. New York: W. W. Norton, 1999.

White, Owen P. *A Frontier Mother*. New York: Minton, Balch, and Co., 1929.

Williams, Fannie Barrier. "The Club Movement among Colored Women of America." In *The New Negro: Readings on Race, Representation, and African American Culture, 1892–1938*, edited by Henry Louis Gates Jr. and Gene Andrew Jarrett, 54–65. Princeton, N.J.: Princeton University Press, 2007.

Wilson, Margaret Gibbons. *The American Woman in Transition: The Urban Influence, 1870–1920*. Westport, Conn.: Greenwood Press, 1979.

Winch, Julie. "'You Have Talents—Only Cultivate Them': Philadelphia's Black Female Literary Societies and the Abolitionist Crusade." In *The Abolitionist Sisterhood: Women's Political Culture in Antebellum America*, edited by Jean Fagan Yellin and John C. Van Horne, 101–18. Ithaca: Cornell University Press, 1994.

Winegarten, Ruthe. *Black Texas Women: A Sourcebook*. Austin: University of Texas Press, 1996.

———. *Black Texas Women: 150 Years of Trial and Triumph*. Austin: University of Texas Press, 1995.

Wiesepape, Betty Holland. *Lone Star Chapters: The Story of Texas Literary Clubs*. College Station: Texas A&M University Press, 2004.

Wintz, Cary D., and Paul Finkelman, eds. *Encyclopedia of the Harlem Renaissance*. New York: Routledge, 2004.

"Women's Clubs to Unite." *New York Times*, 20 November 1894.

Wood, J. W. *Pasadena, California: Historical and Personal*. Pasadena, Calif.: J. W. Wood, 1917.

Woodcock, Arthur. *The Shakespeare Club, a Sketch*. Chicago: privately printed, 1896.

Woodford, Frank. "Second Thoughts on Writing Library History." *Journal of Library History* 1.1 (1966): 34–42.

Woods, Randall Bennett. *A Black Odyssey: John Lewis Waller and the Promise of American Life, 1878–1900*. Lawrence: Regents Press of Kansas, 1981.

Wormser, Richard. *The Rise and Fall of Jim Crow.* New York: St. Martin's Press, 2003.

Wortman, Madeline Stein. "Domesticating the American City." *Prospects* 3 (1978): 531–72.

Wright, Louis B. *Culture on the Moving Frontier.* Bloomington: Indiana University Press, 1955.

———. "Shakespeare for Everyman." *Proceedings of the American Philosophical Society* 106.5 (1962): 393–400.

Yeakey, Carol Camp, and Ronald D. Henderson, eds. *Surmounting All Odds: Education, Opportunity, and Society in the New Millennium.* Vol. 1. Greenwich, Conn.: Information Age Publishing, 2003.

Yee, Shirley J. *Black Women Abolitionists: A Study in Activism, 1828–1860.* Knoxville: University of Tennessee Press, 1992.

Yellin, Jean Fagan, and John C. Van Horne, eds. *The Abolitionist Sisterhood: Women's Political Culture in Antebellum America.* Ithaca: Cornell University Press, 1994.

Zboray, Ronald J. *A Fictive People: Antebellum Economic Development and the American Reading Public.* New York: Oxford University Press, 1993.

Ziegler, Georgianna, Frances A. Dolan, and Jeanne Addison Roberts, eds. *Shakespeare's Unruly Women.* Washington, D.C.: Folger Shakespeare Library, 1997.

INDEX

Page numbers followed by letter *f* indicate figures.

Abbott, Frances M., 21, 51, 152n86, 168n120
Aberdeen, South Dakota, Shakespeare Club, 157n150, 157n158
Abraham, Spencer, 113
adaptations of Shakespeare, 47–50, 54
Addams, Jane, 178n58
African Americans: Chautauqua program and, 102, 104; co-ed clubs of, 105, 109–10; and communal reading, 164n48; and performances of Shakespeare, 98, 107, 108, 188n3; and racial uplift, 96–97, 98, 106–11; as readers of Shakespeare, 98–101, 115, 181n83, 192n40. *See also under* black women
Alabama: Shakespeare clubs in, 123; traveling libraries in, 186n63. *See also specific cities/towns*
Alpena, Michigan, Ladies' Shakespeare Class, 90
American culture, Shakespeare's place in, 121–22, 141n2; black readers and, 115; frontier experience and, 79–82, 94; Shakespeare clubs and, xii, 30, 157n165
American Shakespeare Magazine, 6, 14, 16, 49, 152n95
Anderson, Douglas, 174n5, 176n17
Anne Hathaway Shakespeare Club of Philadelphia, 5, 38, 55*f*
Anne Hudgins Shakespeare Class of Marietta, Georgia, xvi, 156n140, 200n7; origins of, 82; scrapbooks of, 75–76; Twelfth Night ceremony of, 77
archival materials, Shakespeare clubs and, xiv–xv, 26–27, 30
Arden Club of Topeka, Kansas, 105, 188n4
Arizona, Shakespeare clubs in, 80, 123–24
Arkansas: black women's clubs in, 106–7, 195n88; Shakespeare clubs in, 59, 124
Armstrong, Alice, 10, 23–24
Armstrong, Elizabeth, ix
Athenian Literary Society of Topeka, Kansas, 106

Atlanta, Georgia: Chautauqua Circle of, 102; Shakespeare Club of, 164n50
Auburn, Alabama, N. T. Lupton Conversation Club of, 6–7, 147n34
Avon, Illinois. *See under* Portia Club
Avon Bard Club, New Rochelle, New York, 27
Avon Club of Concord, New Hampshire, 37
Avon Club of Topeka, Kansas, 74
Ayers, Alice, 155n133
Azermendi, Candace, 156n140

Badia, Janet, 158n2
Balcam, Lucia C., 11
Bald Eagle, Minnesota, Shakespeare Club, 93
Banks, Emma Dunning, 11
Bankside Edition of Shakespeare, 4
Barber, J. Max, 102
Barnesville, Georgia, Woman's Shakespearean Club, 10, 43; civic work of, 59, 79, 121; intellectual work of, 13, 164n53; origins of, 23; reactions to Shakespeare's heroines, 52; records of, 77; town history and, 181n2
Baskin family, 69, 178n46
Bateman, Lillian, xvi
bawdy content, club women's response to, 50–52, 168n116
Baym, Nina, 199n4
Bay View Reading Circle program, 107, 150n71
Beecher, Catharine, 62
Bell, Charlotte J., 53
Bell, Philip A., 100
Belleville, Kansas, Shakespeare Club, 25
Benton Harbor, Michigan, Ossoli Club, 33
Besnier, Niko, 145n4, 158n2, 161n15, 165n71, 166n89, 174n5
Bethel Literary and Historical Association of Washington, D.C., 108–9
Birmingham, Alabama, Pieria Literary Society, 169n122

223